BEFORE REVELATION

M000295269

SUNY Series in Middle Eastern Studies
Shahrough Akhavi, Editor

Before Revelation

The Boundaries of Muslim Moral Thought

A. Kevin Reinhart

State University of New York Press

Sections of chapter 6, "Thanking the Benefactor," appeared in A. Kevin Reinhart, "Thanking the Benefactor," in *Spoken and Unspoken Thanks: Some Comparative Soundings*, ed. John B. Carman and Frederick J. Streng (Cambridge & Dallas: Harvard University Center for the Study of World Religions & Center for World Thanksgiving, 1989), pp. 115–133. I am grateful for permission to reprint portions of that work.

Published by
State University of New York Press, Albany

© 1995 State University of New York

All rights reserved

Printed in the United States of America

No part of this book may be used or reproduced
in any manner whatsoever without written permission
except in the case of brief quotations embodied in
critical articles and reviews.

For information, address State University of New York
Press, State University Plaza, Albany, N.Y., 12246

Production by E. Moore
Marketing by Theresa Abad Swierzowski

Library of Congress Cataloging-in-Publication Data

Reinhart, A. Kevin. 1952-
Before Revelation : the boundaries of Muslim moral thought / A. Kevin Reinhart.
p. cm. — (SUNY series in Middle Eastern Studies)
Includes bibliographical references and index.
ISBN 0-7914-2289-5 (alk. paper). — ISBN 0-7914-2290-9 (pbk. : alk. paper)
1. Islam—Doctrines—History. 2. Islamic law—Interpretation and construction. I. Title. II. Series.
BP166.1.R45 1995
297′.2—dc20 94-13372
CIP

10 9 8 7 6 5 4 3 2 1

For Anne Royal:
"Nun hast du mir den ersten Schmerz getan."

Contents

Preface ix

Conventions xi

Part I: Introduction and Overview 1

1. Introduction 3

2. Development and Doxography 10

Part II: The Three Positions 29

Introduction 29

3. Acts Are Proscribed (maḥẓūr) 31

4. The Permitted Position 38

5. "No Assessment" 62

Appendix: Two Translations of "Before Revelation" Texts 77

Translation of a Section from *al-Fuṣūl fī l-Uṣūl of al-Jaṣṣāṣ* 79

Translation of a Section from *Kitāb al-Mustaṣfá fī 'ilm al-uṣūl* Abū Ḥāmid al-Ghazālī 87

Part III: Thanking the Benefactor 105

6. God As Patron: Thanking the Benefactor 107

Appendix: An Early Debate on Thanking the Benefactor 121

Part IV: The Background 125

7. Conceptual Sources of the Problem 127

8. Abū l-Hudhayl and the Early Mu‘tazilah 138

9. The Basrans: Moral Ontology and Epistemology 146

10. The Critique of the Mu‘tazilah: Ignoring Ontology 161

Part V: Conclusions 177

Notes 185

Bibliography 231

Index 247

PREFACE

It is a pleasure to acknowledge some of those to whom I am indebted for their help over the years it has taken to bring this project to its conclusion. First, always, to my parents, for their support from the first days of my studies. Then to my teachers, particularly to my doctor fathers Wolfhart Henrichs, Wilfred Cantwell Smith, and John Carman; to Jane Smith my Dutch aunt and model, and to John Alden Williams, who bears heaviest responsibility for my entry into this field. Students owe debts to their teachers, and children to their parents, that can not only never be repaid, but can never sufficiently be acknowledged.

Here too is my chance to express gratitude, inadequately, for the intellectual fellowship of my colleagues in the Department of Religion, Dartmouth College, at the Center for the Study of World Religions, Harvard University, and particularly to James Laine, Carl Ernst and Aron Zysow. Carl Ernst with his generous reading of a manuscript of this work helped bring it out of the Slough of Despond. I acknowledge sadly the loss of Marie Bernand, who was an encouraging and stimulating senior colleague; I wish she could have seen the fruits of her generosity. Carol Bardenstein worked with me through a productive summer. Jessica Cormier helped with final production of the manuscript. And finally I must thank my wife, Marlene Heck, for her many kindnesses to me, not least of which was the patient reading of draft after draft of this work.

A work like this one, based on obscure manuscripts and printed works, is possible only with the help of devoted staff members in fine libraries. I am particularly indebted to the staff of Harvard's Widener library, and the library of the French Institute in Damascus. I profited from the generous assistance of the staffs of the Maktabah al-Gharbiyyah and Sharqiyyah in Yemen (where I was given permission to work by the director of the Manuscript and Museum Authority, Qāḍī, Ismā‘īl al-Akwa‘ and the Minister of Waqfs), Egypt's Dār al-Kutub, the Institute of Arabic Manusripts in Cairo, and the Maktabat al-Asad in Damascus. I am very grateful for the assistance of the kind staff of the Topkapı and Süleymaniye libraries in Istanbul, and for permission to work at the New Turkish Encyclopedia of Islam Research Institute in Bağlarbaşa. Above all I am indebted to the staff of my home library, the Baker Library of Dartmouth College, and most especially to Patricia Carter who makes it possible to study exotica at the College on the Hill.

I am grateful to the readers of this manuscript, particularly Reader A, for his thorough and helpful reading, and to my editor at SUNY Press, Clay Morgan, for his patience.

I gratefully acknowledge the financial support without which this study could never have been begun, much less completed: I was at various times supported by the Center for the Study of World Religions at Harvard University, by Dartmouth College, by the Foreign Language Area Scholarships of the Department of Education, by the Fulbright Fellowship program of the Department of Education, both at the pre- and post-doctoral level, by the American Research Center, Egypt, the American Institute of Yemeni Studies, and the American Research Institute, Turkey.

Finally, this work is dedicated to the memory of Anne Royal. This project, or a form of it, was conceived when under her influence and in her company, and her death remains an irretrievable and tragic loss to scholarship, as well as to her family and friends. Her family has also been generous and kind to me through the time of our mutual bereavement, and so to the memory of Anne, and to her family, I offer this work.

Conventions

Transliteration is according to the system of the Library of Congress; the *tā' marbuṭah* is indicated with an "h."

The patronymic (the *kunyah*) is transliterated with an ellipsed *alif*: for example, Abū l-Ḥusayn. Honorifics are generally transcribed in a single name, with any "sun letter" elided: "Shamsaddīn," rather than "Shamsaldīn" or "Shams al-dīn." Otherwise, Arabic words are transcribed as representations of the graphic, rather than the pronounced form. "Sun letters" are not written in elided form: "al-Shams," not "ash-Shams."

For plurals of Arabic words I have generally used the Arabic singular with the English plural suffix. Thus one *ḥadith,* three *ḥadiths,* so as not to afflict the non-specialist reader with "*aḥadīth,*" the actual Arabic plural.

Qur'ān is cited between curly brackets, with the *sūrah/ayah* cited between parentheses. Thus {Master of the Day of Doom (1:4)}. Numbering is to the Royal Egyptian version of the Qur'ān, translations are made referring to Arberry's *The Koran Interpreted,* and Pickthall's *The Glorious Qur'ān.*

Certain words with a semantic field broader than an English word have been retained throughout the text (e.g. *'aql*) with an appropriate translation often beside it.

Footnote citations are an abbreviated reference to author and title. The full citation can be found in the bibliography.

Certain frequently-cited books have been footnoted in abbreviated form:

Baḥr = al-Zarkashī, *al-Baḥr al-Muḥīt.*

GAL = Carl Brockelmann, *Geschichte der arabischen Litteratur.*

GAS = Fuad Sezgin, *Geschichte des arabischen Schrifttums.*

Kaḥḥālah = 'Umar Riḍā Kaḥḥālah, *Mu'jim al-Mu'allifin.*

Sharḥ- = [pseudo] 'Abdaljabbār, *Sharḥ al uṣūl al-khamsah* al-Subkī = al-Subkī, *al-Ṭabaqāt al Kabīr.*

Ta'rīkh Baghdād = al-Khaṭīb al-Baghdād, *Ta' rīkh Baghdād.*

ṬU = 'Abdal'azīz Muṣṭāfá al-Marāghī, *al-Fatḥ al-Mubīn fī Ṭabaqāt al-Uṣūliyīn.*

al-Ziriklī = Khayraddīn al-Ziriklī, *al-A'lām, qāmūs, tarājim li-ashhar al-rijāl wa-l-nisā' min al-'arab wa-l-musta'ribīn wa-l-mustashriqīn.*

Well-known dictionaries may be cited simply by the author's last name. Dozy, Lane, Wehr, etc.

Encyclopedia of Islam is cited according to its edition: e.g., *EI*2 = *Encyclopedia of Islam,* 2nd edition.

Part I

Introduction and Overview

Chapter 1

Introduction

This is a book about a controversy in Muslim religious thought. Muslim law assesses all acts against the norms of Revelation, and judges them to be Proscribed, Permitted, or Obligatory.[1] The problem that concerns us, because it so manifestly concerned Muslim jurists, is: What is the assessment (if any) for a useful and beneficial act before Revelation comes to assign it value? Are pre-Revelational useful acts Proscribed, Permitted, Obligatory, or something else? The problem is one that on the face of it would seem irrelevant precisely to those who argued most passionately about it, since Muslims live after the era with which they are here putatively concerned. Moreover, it is the sort of problem we moderns have been taught to disregard or at least not to take seriously; it is the sort of question we moderns do not find productive to pose.

Muslims argued heatedly about this question for 400 years, and they subsequently included discussions of it in their compendia for another 800 years. Evidently it was a useful question to discuss. The first question that strikes us is—why? Why would Muslims long after Revelation had come find it interesting and important to argue about acts that took place before Islam, in the usual sense of the term, existed? To answer this question fruitfully, it is useful to look at it in a way different from the way theological controversies have usually been studied.

Method of Approach

The study of Islam is littered with accounts of Islamic debates. These detail the minutiae of positions taken, catalog the disputants, and, usually, pigeonhole the controversialists—often as "rationalists" or "traditionalists" (sometimes traditionists). Nonetheless, the "why" of these arguments among sincere and piously motivated scholars seems usually to escape most monographs and articles. Islamicists seem often to forget that most topics debated were "things to think with," or *camerae obscurae* by means of which a delicate or a sensitive matter could be regarded indirectly, and without fear of injury. Muslim scholars cultivated these controversies like special strains of plants bred to study some anomaly or disease. Predestination, the createdness of the Qur'ān, and many other religious controversies must be understood in this way if they are to be *understood* at all, and it should be clear that a study of a controversy must ask what was truly being asked before it can be understood. What is needed is a work of interpretation.

Muslim scholars, it is obvious, did not care and were not arguing about "acts before Revelation" per se. Rather, when someone first posed this problem in debate it was eagerly seized upon and elaborated, we suppose, because through it Muslim intellectuals could examine notions too amorphous and sometimes too disturbing or unnerving to state baldly. Perhaps, also, through these "thought experiments" they could discuss issues too profound to think about directly. If a student of these controversies does nothing more than to state the argument and catalog its participants so as to press and mount it into the book of Muslim opinions, the point of these fierce discussions is missed, and students of Muslim thought become no more than taxonomists.

To begin: This debate was about "assessing acts," but the backdrop for the argument is the notion that assessing acts is the quintessential activity of the Islamic religious tradition.[2] Yet there is a tension in thinking about the assessment of acts: On the one hand, it is God alone who establishes assessments, and God alone who is Assessor (*ḥākim*). Yet God has nonetheless delegated a large domain of assessment to His bondsmen. By a vow, an act ordinarily assessed as Recommended can be made Obligatory, and a man may establish nearly anything to be the occasion for a divorce or manumission, thereby making divorce or manumission Obligatory when it is not otherwise so according to Revelation. Similarly, God has entrusted a group distinguished by their scholarship and probity with the assessment of acts in general—these are the judges and jurisconsultants who constitute the canonical Islamic religious elite, and they assess acts as Proscribed, Obligatory and so forth, just as God does.[3]

Furthermore, the process of assessing is fraught with uncertainty and tension. Humans are at once licensed to make assessments and guided only by an uncertain knowledge of what it is God commands in the circumstances. While mortals attempt to assess in parallel with God's assessments, it is recognized that they can do no more than *suppose* that the assessment arrived at conforms to the transcendent assessment of the act or thing under consideration.[4] Interpreting the texts of Revelation is at least sometimes a speculative enterprise, and the uncertainty of Islamic Revelational assessments led scholars to try to ground the valuations in something more certain than textual hermeneutic. However, they needed also to safeguard the unique position of the Qur'ān as the source of moral knowledge. To discuss these conflicting intentions, we believe, scholars elaborated the problem-complex that we study here. To concentrate only on this discussion is to watch only the foreground and ignore the background. By attending to more than just "who said what" we hope to demonstrate how the controversy was about much more than the question, Are useful acts forbidden until Revelation comes?

When Muslim scholars in the foreground were asking about acts before Revelation, I believe they were also reflecting upon important epistemological questions in the background. They were asking about the importance of Revelational knowledge over against other sources of knowledge; they were asking, What constitutes religious knowledge?; they were also asking questions about moral categorization and its relation to being itself: Does the goodness of gratitude or the badness of a lie come from some characteristic innate to the nature of gratitude and prevarication?; Can lies ever be good or gratitude wicked? They asked also, What is it that makes something good? Does its goodness reside in the structure of the created world or in the ungrounded determination of God?

What I believe was also being determined through reflection on such topics as these was the relation between morality and culture: Was morality to be understood as something innate within humans, and so, universal across denominational lines, or were humans so corrupted by individual and collective interest as to be incapable of dispassionate moral knowledge? Were the moral commands of Islam congruent with human capacity to know the good from the detestable, or were the commands of God utterly transcendent of human capacity, and therefore reliably true and objective?

It is clear that such questions are so grand as to be unanswerable on their face and almost so grand as to be unaskable. It was, initially at least, more productive to ask: Are useful acts good without Revelation to tell us so, and if so, how do we know?

The Problem Posed

By way of introduction, here is an example of how the problem was posed in a fifth-century juristic source:

> Scholars disagree concerning things from which it is possible to benefit, before the arrival of the *shar*ʿ. Among them there are those who say that [these acts] are Proscribed, so that it is not licit to benefit from them, nor to perform them. Among them are those who say that [these useful things] are Permitted, since whoever believes a thing allowed for him may use it and possess it. And among them are those who say that they are something In Suspension (*ʿalá l-waqf*): it may not be determined that they are either Permitted or Proscribed.[5]

The text is typical in its seeming plainness. The author states the problem and admits three possible answers. Nearly every textual discussion of this problem does the same. This text is typical also in what is unsaid but lies implicit in this simple formulation.

First, why should a Muslim living in a post-Revelational age care about acts before Revelation? The author does not say. Second, the author does not indicate whether the discussion is about the status of the acts, or the status of our knowledge about the acts. That is, is the question about the being of the act (an ontological question) or is it about our knowledge of the thing (an epistemological question)? The author does not specify. Third, the phrase used (*qabla wurūd ⁱl-shar'*) here translated as "before the arrival of the *shar'* "—can mean "before the *shar'* arrives," "before it is met with,"[6] or "before it takes effect."[7] Is it that useful acts are Proscribed before Muḥammad's Revelation?; or before someone living in North Africa, for example, knows of Revelation?; or before some Revelational command comes into effect, by a Muslim's attaining puberty, for example?; or are useful acts Proscribed when, indeed, there is effectively no Revelational command at all? Is the question "Are non-Muslim acts ever good?" or is it "Do acts of which Revelation has not spoken have religious assessments appropriate to them?" The author never clarifies.

The Answers

Fortunately, not all authors are so terse—other discussions are lengthier and easier to decode. It becomes clear that each of the answers proposed—that acts before revelation are Proscribed, Permitted, Un-assessable—has a series of ramifying implications. These can be summed up as follows:

1. Those who Proscribed the use of things before the coming of the *shar'* argue that "all created things are God's property because He created them and established them; it is not Permitted to use the property of another without His permission." Therefore, for the Proscribers it is God's permission that makes something Permitted, and God's command that makes something Obligatory. When there is no information as to God's command, it should be assumed that everything is Proscribed. The subtext here is that the world before, and outside of, Revelation is to be mistrusted on principle, and God's sovereign assessment alone makes acts and things licit. For the Proscribers, the pre-Revelational world is radically discontinuous from the post-Revelational world, in which useful acts are, by God's grace, Permitted.

2. Those who Permitted the use of things before Revelation said that "God created [these acts or things] and brought them into existence, obviously, either for some purpose, or without purpose. Creation cannot have been purposeless, for God cannot act futilely. It must be that He created them for a purpose, and that purpose must be either to cause harm or benefit. It is not possible to suppose that it is to cause harm; it must be that [He created them] for benefit." The Permitters believed acts to be of three sorts. Some acts such as grati-

tude were good and Obligatory before Revelation, and scripture merely confirmed their goodness. It could not have done otherwise. Some acts, such as lies, were similarly detestable[8] and Proscribed whether or not Revelation had come. Acts that appear useful comprise the third category. They are Permitted or Indifferent[9] before Revelation, but Revelation may reveal them to be Proscribed, as with pork, or Permitted, as with beef. It is their usefulness that, until Revelation comes to reveal hidden harm, justifies the Permittedness of these acts. Hence usefulness, and reasoning that recognizes usefulness, is a source of moral knowledge alongside Revelation. In this way, for the Permitters, there is a kind of continuity between the pre- and post-Revelational worlds since in both, usefulness is a ground for Permittedness.

3. Those who held the third position, that acts cannot be assessed at all without Revelation, justified their position by defining the Permitted as "that of which the Master of Stipulations (*ṣāhib al-shar'*) has informed [us]: there is no reward for doing it and no punishment for neglecting it. . . . Its assessment therefore awaits the arrival of Revelation, whereupon it is assessed according to what the *shar'* arrives with concerning it." On such an account, acts before Revelation simply can have no moral quality, No Assessment (*lā ḥukm[a] lahu*),[10] whatsoever. Morality does not exist outside of Revelation and neither the nature of the act, nor our own intellectual powers, can provide moral assessments to acts without Revelation's command. The world is amoral before Revelation and morally assessable only after it comes.

The Before Revelation Complex

As a final part of this introduction, we wish to explain the phrase *before revelation complex,* which we have used throughout this book. The problem of moral valuation is too complex to encompass with only a single single foreground question. Sometimes spread about, but more often juxtaposed, various set problems have as their ground bass the problem of moral epistemology. These stereotyped problems are united by their underlying theme, and often by textual propinquity but also, if one knows the position of a scholar on one of these issues, his position on the rest can be predicted fairly accurately. It would seem then that all of these discussions form a single complex of questions that can profitably be studied and referred to as a whole. These controversies include the following.

Acts before the Coming of Revelation (Al-Af'āl Qabl[a] Wurūd (sometimes Majī') al-Shar' (sometimes al-Sam')[11]

This problem is the most practical of the set. It poses the question of what can be said about acts before or more generally in the absence of Revelation.

Specifically this question asks if the categories of legal assessment, especially "Permitted/Indifferent (*mubāḥ*) can be used of acts outside of Revelation's writ.

Permitted/Indifferent (Mubāḥ)

Legists in particular worked to define the term "*mubāḥ*" used to assess an act: did it refer to a set of acts that were simply not considered by Revelation? If so, there must be an implicit moral continuity between the pre- and post-Revelational world, since silence after, and silence before, Revelation was proof of Permission. Alternatively, perhaps the term refers to acts *explicitly permitted* by Revelation but unconnected to transcendent reward or praise, punishment or condemnation. In this latter view no act could be said to be *mubāḥ* until Revelation could be applied to it.

Declaring "Good"/Declaring "Detestable" (Al-Taḥsīn wa-l-Taqbīḥ)

Metaphysicians in particular exercised themselves with the question of *al-taḥsīn wa-l-taqbīḥ*. At the first level, the problem is this: can humans use their natural faculties to determine the transcendent goodness or detestability of something, such as thanking the benefactor? The debate is therefore about the limitations of human moral-epistemological capacity. The problem is also about the nature of acts themselves—whether goodness or detestability are part of the acts' ontological natures. Was detestability a part of the being of a lie, the way redness or roundness were parts of the apple's nature? For the centuries in which theology was at the forefront of technical thought, *taḥsīn* and *taqbīḥ* were the most extensively discussed aspect of the before revelation complex.

Thanking the Benefactor (Shukr al-Mun'im)

Of the questions in this problem-complex, this sub-question of the metaphysical question is perhaps the most interesting, since it is most distinctively Arab, then Muslim. The question debated was whether we can know of the obligation to thank a benefactor (an Arab virtue par excellence) without Revelation to tell us of the obligation. This is clearly an early question and the answer to it changes as Muslim analogies between God and humankind evolve. What is ultimately at issue is the degree of similarity or difference between this world and the next, and the degree to which that apocalyptic world is immanent in this.

All of these discussions—and more besides—form what we are calling the before revelation complex. Of course Islamic legal thought connects everything to everything else and in hiving off this set of questions we do an injustice to the coherent whole. Nonetheless the value of the discussion that follows is, we hope, that it hints at the interrelatedness of all of Islamic thought, and explains something of its seriousness and subtlety.

Context

A final note. When these questions have been discussed previously, especially in George Hourani's lucid works, they have been considered as problems in practical philosophy. Here, however, they are seen as questions in the legal sciences, questions with practical implications for jurists. It is the practical concerns that give these questions their edge for practicing jurisprudents, we believe, and so we have preferred jurisprudential to theological sources whenever possible.[12]

This study is organized in three parts. It begins with a doxographic history that shows how these questions developed in the context of the formation of jurisprudential schools. In the process we attempt to re-describe how these *madhhab*s developed and what *madhhab* affiliation meant to adherents of the schools. The second section analyzes each of the three positions (Proscribed, Permitted, No Assessment) at length, along with their implications. In this lengthier chapter, we attempt to picture the kind of Islam that each of these positions assumes. This section includes extensive translations. A chapter on the special problem of *thanking the benefactor* follows. Here certain changes in the social background of Islamic thought are explored, and a hypothesis of the growing discontinuity of metaphysics from social practice is proposed. In the third part we discuss the technique of epistemology and ontology that affected this complex of questions. The purpose there is to show similar Islamic problems shaping a dialog that might seem far removed from any practical consideration. The concluding chapter attempts to gather what has been discovered in the previous chapters, so as to reinterpret some of Islam's formative intellectual history.

Throughout this book the method used is that of a historian of religion. Texts are read to reconstruct not only positions or concealed influences but to find the "unsaid" and the "assumed" that made up the worldview of these different kinds of Muslims. I take for granted that these scholars were not exercising themselves for lack of something better to do, but were engaged in what seemed the most serious of tasks—to determine what God required, so that they might be resurrected with those who had earned eternal reward.

ḥasbunā llāh, wa-naʿima l-wakīl (3:173)

CHAPTER 2

DEVELOPMENT AND DOXOGRAPHY

ORIGINS OF THE PROBLEM

It is usual in doxographic histories of Muslim ideas to consider the question of origins. Where did this notion come from? Is it "original"? In response to this time-hallowed approach to the study of Muslim thought, we might point out that the question of "What makes the good thing good," has been asked at least since the *Euthyphro,* where Socrates asks Euthyphro to explain the meaning of piety, where he asks, What is characteristic of piety that makes all pious actions pious?; where he asks, Do the gods love piety because it is pious, or is it pious because they love it? and so on.[1] Subsequently, no doubt many Christian and Jewish intellectuals pondered and discussed these and other notions, and later as some of them debated with Muslims, and as others of them converted to Islam, these questions passed into the storehouse of Islamic controversies.

We might then attempt to trace that process and show the presence of Christian, Jewish, or Greek elements in the Muslim discussions. Yet the value of asking the *urquellen* question is doubtful—first because it is ultimately unanswerable except by speculation: texts were never written or, if written, no texts survive, that allow us to trace the transmission of thought across religious boundaries. Consequently, attempts to portray transmission seem largely to be speculative and to reflect the author's view of the value and "originality" of Muslim thought.

More importantly, to the historian of religion, chasing origins is of doubtful value because locating a "source" tells us next to nothing about why Muslims bothered with it. Rather than asking Where did it come from? it is more fruitful to ask: What is it about this question that fascinated Muslim controversialists? And one might also ask: What aspects of Islam itself made this an interesting question?

If we set out to answer these two more productive questions, we are confronted at once by a fundamental obstacle. Most surviving sources write tendentiously and attempt from the perspective of the fifth and later Islamic centuries to reshape earlier dogmatic developments. As part of this process, the earlier sources were largely suppressed. Only edited fragments were excerpted and sanitized so as to suggest, for instance, on the question of acts before Revelation, that there was from the beginning a doctrinal school position on the question from which a few aberrant scholars deviated. This view is, in fairness, less argued than assumed, but it forces us to use biographical, heresiographical, and dogmatic sources suspiciously to control for this anachronistic rewriting of Muslim intellectual history. What we shall show in the rest of this chapter is that between the third and the late Islamic fifth century it is impossible to predict the position of a scholar on the before Revelation questions if we know only his *madhhab*. Rather, as with most religious traditions, in the early period of Islam's dogmatic life we have a community in search of an orthodoxy.[2]

In our case, the before revelation argument grows from an attempt to reconcile or hierarchize five different and sometimes conflicting pietist impulses located within Islam from its earliest history:

1. A belief in the historical uniqueness of the Qur'ānic Revelation, and a desire to exalt the significance of that transcendental moment;
2. A belief in the congruity of Islam with other Revelational religions;
3. An apologetic belief that Islam summons humankind to virtues and values not only reasonable, but indeed, upon reflection, commonsensical; in this lies part of its superiority;
4. A suspicion of any act or value not sanctioned by Revelation;
5. A commitment to the notion that Creation, as the act of a Merciful God, is beneficent and exists for the benefit of humankind.

All five impulses are authentically Qur'ānic, and all five can be found in early pietism: epistles, *ḥadīth*, apologetics.[3]

The Earliest Discussions

These impulses and sentiments are embodied in speculative thought as early as Abū Ḥanīfah (d. 150/767), who said, for instance, that when in doubt on some point of law, one can consult the Books of the other Scriptuary peoples,[4] and who is said to have held that the intellect is sufficient to bring one to knowledge of the Creator without Revelation. It would follow that one can truly be morally responsible in the absence of, or prior to, Islamic Revelation.[5] Though it is impossible to verify that these positions are genuinely Abū Ḥanīfah's, nevertheless there was clearly an early concern with questions of innate human moral knowledge and with the boundaries of Revelational signs.[6] The first subsequent Ḥanafī legist of whom an opinion on this topic is recorded is 'Īsá ibn Abān al-Ṭabarī (d. c. 220/835). Our sources tell us only that he held the position that the useful act before Revelation was "Proscribed".[7] It is not clear why this position is attributed to him. Certainly as a Ḥanafī he would have been expected to have held the position attributed to al-Shaybānī (d. 189/905) that the presumptive assessment of an act after Revelation is "Permitted." This was interpreted by al-Sarakhsī (d. 490/1097) as meaning that al-Shaybānī and all Ḥanafīs believed that before the dispatch of the Messenger, all things were in the condition of being Permitted.[8]

Among the early legists, it is not only Abū Ḥanīfah of whom we have a statement that seems to bear upon the later before revelation complex. Al-Shāfi'ī (d. 204/820) suggests that "justice is to act [only?] in obedience to God; thus [one] has the means to knowledge of justice and what is contrary to it." From this statement Hourani infers that al-Shāfi'ī held that God commanded the good, and that the good was understood to be nothing but what God commanded. If this reading is correct, then al-Shāfi'ī would be the earliest of those whom Hourani calls "theistic subjectivists." Yet it is typical of our sources that elsewhere it is recorded that al-Shāfi'ī took what seems to be the original Proscribed position by saying, "There is consensus that the one made-responsible (*mukallaf*) may not undertake to do a thing until he knows the assessment of God concerning it."[9]

Al-Shāfi'ī's follower, and eponym of another legal school, Aḥmad b. Hanbal (d. 241/855) was asked if one can use [for prayer] the Torah or Injīl "if he esteems it good,"[10] which suggests that a willingness to use other Scriptures was at least considered by one of his disciples. Further, some of his later disciples understood him as taking the Permitted position, since when asked about cutting down a palm tree he said: "There is no harm in it; we have heard nothing about cutting palm trees." Yet others understood him as taking the Proscribed position, since when asked about taking the fifth portion (*khums*) of the "hides, shanks and belly of a slaughtered animal," (*salab*) he said, "do not take the fifth-portion from *al-salab,* for we have not heard that the Prophet [did so]."[11] The Āl Taymiyyah[12] note that this is really a hermeneutical principle for post-Revelational times rather than a position on the question of the act before Revelation. Yet that this case was cited is indicative of some of the practical problems that may have led to the elaboration of the before revelation complex.

Another putative disciple of al-Shāfi'ī is reported in one source to have held the Proscribed position, namely Dā'ūd al-Ẓāhirī (d. 270/883). In general Dā'ūd believed in a limited scope for what was later called *sharī'ah.* For him, what was not explicitly covered by Revelation had no moral quality.[13] He is therefore unlikely to have held the Proscribed position. It is conceivable that some Ẓāhirīs held that liberty from Revelational command was itself a product of Revelation; in the absence of Revelation all might therefore be forbidden.[14] This attribution, if it does not necessarily tell us what Dā'ūd thought, may teach us to suspect that our sources want to father positions onto early figures to tell us what he probably held had we knowledge of all he said. Speculative attribution may also reflect a desire to show the antiquity of the problem and to show that positions later held to be deviant were held from the beginning only by scholars beyond the orthodox pale.

Among early theologians, the account of Abū Hudhayl al-'Allāf (d. c. 235/849) shows that, whether or not these words are his, Abū Hudhayl fretted about moral life before or in the absence of Revealed norms.[15] On the topic of

> *kufr*[16] before the arrival of Revelation (*al-sam'*) [he held] that it is incumbent upon one to know God by indicant (*al-dalīl*) without any interior prompting (*khāṭir*)[17] and [even] if cut off from knowledge [of God] eternal punishment [for infidelity] is requisite. Also, that one knows the goodness of the good and the detestability of the detestable so that it is incumbent upon one to undertake the good, such as veracity and justice, and to eschew the detestable such as falsehood and injustice.[18]

In this report we have at least a suggestion that early Muslims discussed the power of the individual to discern morality, unaided by Revelation. When the same source tells us of Thumāmah (d. 213/828) that

> his statements on the "esteeming good and detestable" by the '*aql* and the obligation to knowledge (*ma'rifah*) before the arrival of Revelation (*al-sam'*) were like that of his [Mu'tazilī] colleagues, save that he excelled them [in it],[19]

we still cannot be sure that the heresiographer is not paraphrasing whatever it was Thumāmah actually discussed. Certainly Thumāmah had a great deal to say about what a non-Muslim could know by the '*aql* and the consequences of a lack of that knowledge, but it seems unlikely that the particular phrases reported were current within his lifetime.[20] Al-Nāshī' al-Akbar (d. 293/906) discusses the question of whether someone who assents at the beginning of the [Islamic] summons is a *mu'min* "before the descent of specific obligations (*qabla nuzūl al-farā'iḍ*),"[21] which might have been a real question for Muslims in newly settled areas.[22] We are also told that the great Basran Mu'tazilī, Abū 'Alī al-Jubbā'ī; (d. 303/915) held the Permitted position, which certainly characterizes Basran thinking in the later period.[23] Yet from none of these formative figures do we have surviving texts that allow us to be utterly certain of their position on such questions. We do not have enough to contextualize these statements even if they are rightly attributed.

These scattered and uncertain references suggest only that in the late 100s and 200s questions adumbrating the before revelation complex were in circulation. What is the relation of Islamic norms to other Revelational norms? What is the moral status of the non-Muslim? How essential is Revelation to moral knowledge? What is the scope of Revelation's summons? These and other questions anticipated the controversy of the late 200s, the 300s and 400s. They are not proof of the existence of that controversy itself in the period before we have quotations and precise attributions.

Principles of Jurisprudence (uṣūl al-fiqh) As the Domain of this Controversy

We see this question as inchoate before the development of the science of principles of jurisprudence (*uṣūl al-fiqh*) in its classic form. Since the before revelation complex is about moral *action*, the complex must have been formed in a crucible in which are combined both legal thought and theoretical second-order reflection. This is a question of both real and theoretical praxis. It seems that the problem that concerns us here does not become fully articulated until the lifetime of Ibn Surayj (active roughly 270 to his death in 303/883–918). To suggest why this is so, it is necessary to digress slightly to discuss the development of the science of *uṣūl al-fiqh* (principles of jurisprudence) and the Shāfi'ī school of law.

One of the clichés of both Muslim and Western accounts of the history of law (*fiqh*) is that al-Shāfi'ī "founded" the science of principles of jurisprudence. It is generally asserted that *uṣūl al-fiqh* was born when al-Shāfi'ī introduced *hadīth* as a second source of law and subordinated analogy to the two scriptural sources, and to the consensus of the community. Yet so to argue is to ignore the *actual* content of this science. The *Risālah* does not resemble the classic works of *uṣūl al-fiqh* in form or, largely, in content. The received history of the science also ignores the doxographic question of who actually read al-Shāfi'ī's great work, and what they understood from it. It has been noted that in the century following his death there appear to be no commentaries on the *Risālah* mentioned in the sources.[24] Nothing that survives from two of his alleged followers, Aḥmad b. Ḥanbal and Dā'ūd al-Ẓāhirī, remotely resembles the *Risālah* in form or content.

The birth of *uṣūl al-fiqh* was probably a more gradual process than the received tradition recognizes. Al-Shāfi'ī was writing in Egypt—off the beaten track as far as legal scholarship was concerned—and the process of publication and transmission surely played a part in restricting al-Shāfi'ī's influences in the period immediately after his death. Moreover, both the Iraqī and Medinese schools, as well as other legal tendencies, had already considerable inertial motion. It would be surprising to learn that the Medinese or Iraqīs simply dropped their own methodologies and began to follow al-Shāfi'ī's.

A more appropriate picture of the development of principles of jurisprudence as a science is to see al-Shāfi'ī's ideas, if not necessarily his works, percolating through Islamic scholarly circles until these ideas were conjoined with the nascent science of dialectical theology, whereupon *uṣūl al-fiqh* exploded into efflorescence. Suddenly, around the end of the 200s, we have reliably attributed positions in arguments that are part of classical *uṣūl* discussions, we have quotations, we even have works that look like tentative attempts to define a literary genre in which to contain these arguments,[25] until finally in al-Jaṣṣāṣ's *Fuṣūl* we see a masterwork defining the form of later texts in this science.[26]

Ibn Surayj

It follows then that the crucial figure in this process is one who placed legal thought into the context of reflexive and speculative theology. It is, we believe, Abū l-'Abbās Aḥmad b. 'Umar b. Surayj who stimulated the creation of the classical science of principles of jurisprudence and, more particularly, whose reliably reported opinions on the before revelation complex help us to grasp what was at issue in this multifaceted discussion.

Ibn Surayj was heir to the tradition of al-Shāfi'ī as it had developed up to his time. He took his Shāfi'īsm from al-Anmāṭī (d. 288/900), who, the biographers say, was the cause of Shāfi'ian energy in Baghdad.[27] Al-Anmāṭī had studied in Egypt under both al-Rabī' (d. 270/884) and al-Muzanī (d. 264/877), thereby uniting in himself both the textual and the speculative lines of Shāfi'ism.[28] He seems to have been excelled by his students, however, and it is only as the teacher of the great Baghdādī Shāfi'īs that he is remembered; his most important student was Ibn Surayj.[29]

Abū l-'Abbās Aḥmad b. 'Umar b. Surayj (249–306/863–918)[30] wrote more than 400 books despite dying at the age of 57.[31] Among them, a reply to Ibn Dā'ūd on *qiyās*; a reply to him on questions contradicting al-Shāfi'ī; Principles and Derivations (or, Roots and Branches: *al-uṣūl wa-l-furū'*)—perhaps the first book in the Shāfi'ī school to use this title and imagery. He was brilliant at the rhetoric of debate, and his replies to Ibn Dā'ūd are proverbial.[32] He also taught many of the formative figures of Shāfi'ism, some of whom we will meet later.

Ibn Surayj seems to have been the font of a kind of speculative Shāfi'īsm that is characteristic of the late Islamic 200s and into the 300s. Praise for him pours from every account, and much of the praise is for introducing the techniques of speculative theology. Ibn Surayj is called "the one who opened the door of inquiry" and the "one who taught people the path of dialectics."[33] He was the first to open the door of speculation (*al-naẓar*), and teach the people the method of dialectic (*ṭarīq al-jadal*)." "Imām al-Ḍiyā' al-Khaṭīb, [father of al-Imām Fakhr al-Dīn] in his book *Ghāyat al-Marām* [said] Abū al-'Abbās was the foremost of al-Shāfi'ī's partisans in the science of *kalām*, just as he was the foremost of them in *fiqh*."[34] Shaykh Abū Isḥāq Ibn Surayj excelled over all of the partisans (*aṣḥāb*) of al-Shāfi'ī, even over al-Muzanī."[35] Quoting Abū Ḥafṣ al-Muṭawwi'ī:[36] "He was a great source (*al-ṣadr al-kabīr*); and al-Shāfi'ī was the lesser (*al-ṣaghīr* [!!]). . . ." Here then is a figure compared favorably to the very founder of the school.

Yet, despite this praise there is also real ambivalence about Ibn Surayj, not least because of the positions he defended on questions such as *before Revelation*. "Shaykh Abū Ḥāmid said: 'We go along with Ibn Surayj in the broad outlines (*ẓawāhir*) of *fiqh*, though not the details (*daqā'iqih*).' "[37] "He is *mujaddid* of the 300s in *fiqh*, not in *kalām*."[38] Al-Zarkashī reports

> from al-Qāḍī Abū Bakr [al-Baqillānī] in his *Taqrīb* and Ustādh Abū Isḥāq in his *Ta'līq fī uṣūl al-fiqh* and the explication of the *Kitāb al-tartīb:* among our colleagues Ibn Surayj excelled, but these had no firm footing in theology; they were acquainted with (*ṭāla'u*) the great books of the Mu'tazilah. They approved [Mu'tazilī] expressions without knowing to what bad things their categories would lead.[39]

This is the gist of many such comments. To later Shāfi'īs he was an opener of Pandora's box on theological, which means methodological, or *uṣūl al-fiqh* questions, though he remained always a great legist. A telling anecdote is related by al-Subkī, related in words alleged to be Ibn Surayj's:

> On the Day of Resurrection al-Shāfi'ī came to me, accompanied by al-Muzanī, saying: "Lord, This one [i.e. al-Muzanī] corrupted my learning (*afsada 'ulūmī*)." I said: "Go easy on Abū Ibrāhīm [al-Muzanī]! I have continued to correct what he corrupted."[40]

What was it that Ibn Surayj said and did that made him at one and the same time so important and so problematic? In general, it seems to have been his contribution to have applied the methodology of theology, already sophisticated by this time, to *fiqh*. In effect it is he who invented the science of *uṣūl al fiqh*, as any comparison between words attributed to him, and the works of al-Shāfi'ī and al-Muzanī, will show. Despite the relative disdain for his theological skills recorded in later generations, Ibn Surayj in fact esteemed the study of *kalām* more highly than the study of *fiqh*. "How seldom have I seen those who would be *fuqahā'* labor with *kalām* and succeed; *fiqh* overmasters them and they do not arrive at knowledge of *kalām*."[41] In other words, too few legists know enough about the second-order reflection to do it well.[42]

Perhaps the key to Ibn Surayj's use of speculative sources is to recognize the position of his debating partner, Ibn Dā'ūd al-Ẓāhirī. The latter in effect limited the scope of Revelation's application to praxis. For him, Revelation's writ ran to what it explicitly addressed and no more. This is the meaning of Ẓāhirī—it is the apparent meaning of a Scriptural text that applies, and *no more*. Revelation is applied strictly, but it applies to very little. By contrast, for Ibn Surayj it was an article of faith that Revelation spoke to all human activity; through the techniques of al-Shāfi'ī and those of the speculative sciences, Revelation became infinitely extensible. In one of the few fragments of Ibn Surayj's work to have survived, he affirms the limitlessness of Revelational law.

> I [al-Zarkashī?] saw in the *Book Affirming [the use of] Analogy* (*Kitāb ithbāt al-qiyās*) of Ibn Surayj: There is nothing but that God has a *ḥukm* for it because He says, {God is of everything accounting (*ḥasīb*[an]) and of

> everything the Nourisher (*muqīt*[an])} (Qur'ān 4:85–6). There is nothing in the world that lacks release (*iṭlāq*), or proscription, or obligation, since everything of food and drink or clothing or intercourse (*munkaḥ*) on the earth, or of judgment between two disputants or anything else whatsoever—[everything has] an assessment. Anything else is rationally impossible (*mustaḥīl fīl-'uqūl*). There is no disagreement about this that I know of; the disagreement is only in how [to come by] the indicants of its permissibility or forbiddenness.[43]

In other words, there is no limit to the scope of Revelation, when it is rightly applied using the intellectual techniques of speculation. Valuing the human capacity for moral knowledge as he does, it should be no surprise that Ibn Surayj asserted that useful things before Revelation are Permitted, that thanking the benefactor is Obligatory, that the unaided *'aql* can discern the good and detestability of some things.[44] I would suggest that there is every reason to suppose that it was Ibn Surayj who first posed the questions of the before revelation complex in their classical form. Speculatively, we might suggest that Ibn Surayj and other Permitters took the "wrong" position on the question of acts before Revelation because they wished to see the scope of divine supervision over human action extended as far as possible. To this end they used the term Permitted as both a legal and practical term. Perhaps to this end they applied the analytical techniques of *kalām* to the hermeneutic of al-Shāfi'ī, and in doing so extended moral responsibility back into the time before Qur'ānic Revelation. Yet as we shall see below, Ibn Surayj was not merely a radical, giving the *'aql* control over Revelation's domain due to infection by some Greek virus. He was the conservative heir to a long tradition, Qur'ānic in origin, which was an important part of early Islamic apologetic. In this tradition, Revelation had been vindicated by reference to things already known, including things known commonsensically (*bi-l-'aql*). It is only later that the *'aql* has to be defended by reference to Revelation; earlier the reverse had been true. So the position that the limits of what God can prescribe in Revelation are preset in the mind is not a new position, an innovation of the freethinking Ibn Surayj. It is only the means he uses to defend his argument that breaks new ground, and it is only from the perspective of settled orthodoxy that speculation itself seems heretical. Ibn Surayj's legacy was to pose a question that would sharpen and clarify Muslims' understanding of the nature of Revelation and of Islam itself. For a period, his answer too was influential.

In Search of Orthodoxy

Contrary to later doxographical assertion, nearly all of the prominent Shāfi'īs from the two generations after al-Anmāṭī, of whom an opinion is recorded, held that useful things before Revelation are Permitted, or that thanking the benefactor was Obligatory, or in general esteemed the *'aql* as a source of knowledge. Abū 'Alī b. Khayrān (d. 320/932), for instance, and al-Iṣṭakhrī (d. 328/940), both students of al-Anmāṭī, held positions on these questions with which later Shāfi'īs were uncomfortable.[45] Al-Iṣṭakhrī was a pietist who held that the acts of the Prophet indicated that that act was Obligatory, not Permitted, as later Shāfi'īs believed.[46] It may have been for him that acts without Prophetic approval or disapproval were by nature Permitted. In any case he was highly enough esteemed to be accounted one of only two Shāfi'īs (with Ibn Surayj) with whom it was worth studying.[47] One hundred and fifty years later he was still called a "head of the Shāfi'īs."[48]

In the next generation,[49] the Permitted position was widespread among the Shāfi'īs: Ibn al-Qāṣṣ (335/946) and Abū Isḥāq al-Marwazī (340/961), can be reliably believed to have held that the '*aql* enabled one to know that acts were Permitted before Revelation.[50] Abū Isḥāq was accounted also a head of the Shāfi'īs in Baghdad.[51] Likewise al-Qāḍī Abū Ḥāmid al-Marwazī (362/975), an often-mentioned Shāfi'ī founding figure, was said to hold that "useful acts are Permitted." Among all these, nevertheless, the most important of the Shāfi'ī scholars of the generation of students of Ibn Surayj was Abū Bakr Muḥammad b. 'Abdallāh al-Ṣayrafī (d. 330/942).[52]

Al-Ṣayrafī studied under Ibn Surayj and pioneered in the field of *uṣūl al-fiqh*. He was said to be the most learned in *uṣūl* after al-Shāfi'ī; his book in *uṣūl* is said to be one, "the like of which had never preceded him."[53] He was the first Shāfi'ī to write in "contracts" (*shurūṭ*), and he was perhaps the first to write a commentary on al-Shāfi'ī's *Risālah*. Nonetheless, he too held Surayjian opinions[54] and debated al-Ash'arī on the obligation to "thank the benefactor."[55] He is alleged thereafter to have been converted to the Ash'arian position, and from him we have particularly pungent encomia of al-Ash'arī himself.[56] From the point of view of the later tradition, al-Ṣayrafī seems to have ended his deviation with satisfactory repentance.

Although somewhat later, perhaps the most important figure after Ibn Surayj who held problematic views on the before revelation complex was al-Qaffāl al-Shāshī al-Kabīr (d. 365/976).[57] This well-traveled[58] scholar embodied the intellectual and methodological diversity of fourth century Shāfi'īsm, and wrote a commentary on al-Shāfi'ī's *Risālah*, and a work on *uṣūl al-fiqh*, as well as an interesting, almost Maimonidian, "justification of the ways of God to man," called *The Virtues of the Sharī'ah* (*Maḥāsin al-Sharī'ah*).[59] His successors count him as the first among the legists to write about the good kind of dialectic[60] and indeed al-Qaffāl is ranked as "the *imām* of his age among the Shāfi'īs in Transoxania, the most learned of them in *uṣūl* and the most traveled of them in searching for *ḥadīth*."[61] "Indeed he was the teacher ('*ālim*) of the people of Transoxania in this science."[62] According to some sources, he had been a student of Ibn Surayj, and although that seems to be historically unlikely, it is expressively significant, for al-Qaffāl was the heir to Ibn Surayj, in that he was decisive in the development of Shāfi'ism and revered by later tradition, though he defended positions eventually repudiated by the evolved orthodoxy.

On the question of acts before Revelation, the sources are unambivalent: He held that Revelation (*al-sam'*) is a confirmation of the knowledge of the '*aql*, and like Abū Ḥanīfah he held that knowledge of the Devisor (*al-Ṣāni'*) is Obligatory by the '*aql* alone, before the coming of Revelation.[63] He also held that two important Shāfi'ian principles—the obligation to act on "unique traditions" and to use analogical reasoning (*qiyās*) to extend the Revelational texts—are justified not by Scripture but by "common sense" (the '*aql*).[64] Most relevant for us, he is reported to have said that it is '*aql*s that indicate the obligation to thank the benefactor; that is, the '*aql* by itself constitutes an indicant of an obligation.[65] He seems never to have repented these elevated estimations of the power of the '*aql*.[66] Al-Zarkashī preserves a quote from al-Qaffāl's book on Principles of Jurisprudence, in which he presents an account of two kinds of Revelation, a natural one and a supplementary, supernatural one.

> Assessments (*aḥkām*) are of two kinds: intelligible-Obligatory ('*aqlī wājib*) and revelational-possible (*sam'ī mumkin*).
>
> The first [kind] is what we may not change; it is not even conceivable to permit what [the '*aql*] Proscribes, nor to Proscribe what it makes Obligatory to do, e.g., forbidding ingratitude and oppression and [making Obligatory] justice, and similar things. Revelation (*al-sam'*) may come with this kind [of command] so it *confirms* what is Obligatory [already] by the '*aql*.
>
> The second [kind; namely Revelational-possible] is [for example] the number of ritual worshippings, and these depend upon [*mawqūf 'alá*] the '*aql*'s sanction of it and its acceptance of it. What the '*aql* sanctions is acceptable; what it rejects is rejected.
>
> When Revelation (*al-sam'*) comes making [ritual worship, for instance] Obligatory, it then becomes Obligatory until something follows that abrogates it or substitutes for it. These are his words.[67]

Al-Qaffāl, like Ibn Surayj, defends the congruence of '*aqlī* and *shar'ī* judgments, but his emphasis differs. It would seem that during the two generations after the debates between Ibn Surayj and the literalist Ibn Dā'ūd, the battle for an extensive view of Revelation's scope had been won. Now, in the middle 300s al-Qaffāl seems to want to constrain the Shāfi'īan *fiqh* process somewhat by requiring that its assessments conform to assessments that reason produces on its own. He wants to read the Qur'ān through the '*aql*, not merely extend Qur'ān by means of the '*aql*. In this he did not succeed. There is no doubt that al-Qaffāl, however esteemed by later Shāfi'īan tradition, held a view on this question that was at variance with later orthodoxy. Is it best to use the language of later generations of Shāfi'īs and speak of "his infection by Mu'tazilism" or to recognize his importance to the development of Shāfi'ī thought even though his opinions were later rejected?

It is striking to read the distressed accounts of later biographers who try to understand the deviance of a revered later figure such as al-Qaffāl within their paradigm of a timeless truth transmitted from earliest Islamic times and crystallized forever in the eponymic founder. We can see both the distress and relief of the rather unimaginative al-Subkī, when he gratefully reports Ibn 'Asākir's [probably spurious] assertion that al-Qaffāl "was at first inclined [to Mu'tazilism—i.e., holding the 'wrong' opinion on such questions as the status of acts before Revelation], but later returned to the *madhhab* of al-Ash'arī." He takes us through all the stages of his distress.

> This was very useful and relieved me of a great worry . . . since the positions reported from this Imām in *uṣūl* are not sound except on the foundations of the Mu'tazilah. How often research in this led to supposing that he was [always] a Mu'tazilī! [I] had relied upon the report of Abū al-Ḥasan al-Ṣaffār who said, I heard Abū Sahl al-Ṣu'lūkī say—when asked about the *tafsīr* of Imam Abū Bakr al-Qaffāl—"in one respect he was sanctified; in another disgraced. That is, he was disgraced from the perspective of his support of *al-i'tizāl* (Mu'tazilism)."
>
> I say: This worry was relieved by what Ibn 'Asākir related, and it became clear for us that what was of this sort, such as his saying, "Acting on the basis of analogy (*qiyās*) is incumbent by the '*aql*, as is the unique *hadīth* and what is similar to that," we believe to [date from] when he was following this [Mu'tazilī] *madhhab*. When he returned, it must be that he repudiated [these views]. . . . I had [earlier] been delighted by the words I read of the Qāḍī Abū Bakr in the *Taqrīb*[68] and the *Irshād*, and of Ustādh Abū Isḥāq al-Isfarā'īnī in his *Ta'līq* in *uṣūl al-fiqh* on the matter of thanking the benefactor. It is that, when relating the opinion that [thanking the benefactor] is Obligatory by the '*aql* according to some of the Shāfi'ī legists among the Ash'arīs, they both said: "This group of our colleagues, Ibn Surayj and others, excelled in *fiqh*, but were not firmly grounded in *kalām*. They read the books of the Mu'tazilah in their old age and deemed their expressions good, as well as their saying 'thanking the benefactor' is Obligatory by the '*aql*' and they held to this, without knowing to what detestable (*qabīḥ*) positions this notion would lead."
>
> I used to listen to [my teacher] relate what I've just quoted about Abū Isḥāq, rejoicing in it. But I said to him: "Master: Abū Bakr [al-Baqillānī] also said this. But this can only be said of—Ibn Surayj and Abū 'Alī b. Khayrān and al-Iṣṭakhrī, and other legists who held that [position]—who had no firm footing in *kalām*. But someone like al-Qaffāl al-Kabīr, who was a master (*ustādh*) in the science of kalām and of whom

> al-Ḥākim said that he was the most learned of the Shāfiʿīs in Transoxania in *uṣūl*—how can one rightly excuse *him* by [this explanation], based on [the justification that excuses Ibn Surayj]?"
>
> When I happened upon what Ibn ʿAsākir reported, therefore, I was delighted: God had it happen that these matters were things that he held during his adherence to those [other] people's opinions. No blame attaches to him for that after he returned.[69]

This heartfelt description of an "orthodox" Shāfiʿī scholar's unhappy recognition that an honored predecessor was a heretic of sorts ought to alert us to the fact that other biographers must have felt similarly distressed and suppressed much of the deviant material from earlier periods in *madhhab*-history. So prominent were Ibn Surayj, al-Ṣayrafī, and Qaffāl al-Shāshī within the Shāfiʿī *madhhab* that their opinions could only be muted, not entirely effaced by later tradition. Their testimony bears witness to the rich ferment of Shāfiʿī possibilities in the Islamic 300s. In such a pluralist environment it makes no sense to call such positions or their defenders unorthodox or Muʿtazilī. Even a term like *rationalist* bludgeons the subtle differences of texture and emphasis among these scholars. In the 300s, the Shāfiʿī school's most prominent members supported the position that the *ʿaql* was an indicant of knowledge that correlated, at least, with *sharʿī* knowledge, once Revelation appeared. It would seem that this position arose from a desire to follow an aspect of al-Shāfiʿī's program and extend the scope of Revelation to cover all of human activity. In the late 300s, we suggest, the universal scope of Revelation was accepted by all. As part of the momentum of this movement, however, the aggrandizement of Revelation's scope came into conflict with the notion of the *ʿaql* as a sovereign source of knowledge which could itself be the measure of Revelation. The Shāfiʿīs were at the forefront of the movement to extend Revelation by the use of the *ʿaql*, and this pioneering effort later came to be something of an embarrassment to Shāfiʿīs who had arrived at a consensus at variance with the thought of their founding fathers.

Ḥanbalism and the Proscribed Position

It is not only the Shāfiʿīs who had, as it were, doctrinal skeletons in their closet; the hyper-orthodox Ḥanbalīs did as well. While the hallmark of the Ḥanbalīs was an affected primitivism in theology and law, they did toward the end of the fourth Islamic century begin gingerly to use speculative and technical thought.[83] When they did so, they began at first espousing the predictable range of opinions on such issues as are found in the before revelation complex. A number of important figures in the history of Ḥanbalī theology held the Permitted position, for instance—that is, they believed that the *ʿaql* could discern the value of acts in Revelation's absence and that useful acts were Permitted.

TABLE 2.1 The Shāfi'ī School in the 300s and 400s

Name	*Date*	*Position*
Ibn Surayj	306	Permitted[70]
Abu 'Abdallāh al-Zubayrī	317	Proscribed[71]
Abū 'Alī b. Khayrān	320	Permitted[72]
al-Iṣṭakhrī	328	Permitted[73]
Abū Bakr al-Ṣayrafī	330	Permitted[74]
Ibn al-Qāṣṣ	335	Permitted[75]
Ibn Abī Hurayrah, Abū 'Alī b.	340	Proscribed[76]
Abū Isḥāq al-Marwazī	340	Permitted[77]
Ibn Abī Hurayrah, Abū 'Alī	340	Permitted[78]
Abū Ḥāmid al-Marwazī	362	Permitted[79]
al-Qaffāl al-Shāshī al-Kabīr	365	Permitted[80]
Ibn al-Qaṭṭān, Abū l-Ḥusayn	369	Proscribed[81]
al-Daqqāq	405	Proscribed[82]

The most prominent Ḥanbalī defender of the permitted position was Abū l-Ḥasan al-Tamīmī (317–371/929–982), one of the founding figures in Ḥanbalī speculative thought.[84] As with Ibn Surayj, it is worth taking the measure of this distinguished scholar, who, despite the esteem in which he was held by subsequent generations, nonetheless held demonstrably heterodox positions from the perspective of later school discipline.

Abū l- Ḥasan al-Tamīmī appears to have been a figure of some controversy. He is highly respected in partisan Ḥanbalī circles—Ibn Abī Ya'lá praises him. Al-Khaṭīb al-Baghdādī, a partisan Shāfi'ī and Ash'arī, however, in his *Tā'rīkh Baghdād* attacks him as a forger of *ḥadīth.* Ibn al-Jawzī, Ḥanbalī partisan *par excellence*, defends al-Tamīmī, impeaches al-Khaṭīb's source, and accuses al-Khaṭīb of bigotry against this important Ḥanbalī thinker. At any rate, al-Tamīmī's positions in Ḥanbalī law and theology continued to be influential within the school, and 140 years later the Ḥanbalī, Abū l-Khaṭṭāb al-Kalwadhānī, is still quoting and supporting the Permitted position and referring approvingly to al-Tamīmī.[85] As for al-Kalwadhānī, he too was an important figure in Ḥanbalī *uṣūl* circles. He studied with Abū Ya'lá, the most important Ḥanbalī scholar in Baghdad, and was also treated in the prosopographical literature as a scholar of significance.[86] At the same time, he is an eloquent and expansive defender of the Permitted position.

More characteristic of the formative Ḥanbalī methodologians, however, was the position that the '*aql* might plausibly determine that useful acts not otherwise corrupt were Proscribed before Revelation. This position was reported to have been held by Dā'ūd al-Ẓāhirī (d. 270/883), but it seems inconsistent with what we know of al-Ẓāhirī from other sources.[87] The Proscribed position may have been held by later Ẓāhirīs, however, because it is characteristically associated with traditionists. The first reliable attribution of the Proscribed position is to Abū l-Qāsim al-Balkhī (319/931) who was leader of the Baghdādī school of the Mu'tazilah. To say he was a Mu'tazilī is not to say he was a "freethinker." Abū l-Qāsim was in fact distinguished from other traditionists and from Basran Mu'tazilīs by his hermeneutical suspicion of sources of knowledge other than the scriptural. From his sole surviving manuscript it is clear that al-Ka'bī's organizing principle in epistemology was a pious skepticism of every source of knowledge.[88] He preferred to exclude uncertain sources, however useful, because of their uncertainty, and was an acid critic of the too-lax standards of most ḥadīth-transmitters, no matter how uplifting their *hadīths* might be. His goal was clearly to err on the side of rigor if he was to err at all, and piety and asceticism—physical and methodological—characterize Baghdādī Mu'tazilism in general.[89] Clearly, for him the fear of falsely ascribing to God what was not His weighed heavily in al-Ka'bī's attempts to systematize the Muslim religious epistemology. He Proscribed useful acts unless Revelation proved their sanction, though it was through *'aqlī* knowledge that one comes to pietistic suspicion, according to him.[90]

It is rather difficult to trace the evolution of Proscription as an epistemology and praxis. It may be that its origin is speculation arising from Ibn Surayj's attempt to extend the scope of Revelation, but the Shāfi'ī school also produced a number of scholars who Proscribed rather than Permitted. The first of these is Abū 'Abdallāh al-Zubayrī (d. 317/929), a blind scholar of Basrah and Baghdad. His teachers are not recorded, only the fact that he held idiosyncratic views on various *fiqh* problems. He is described first and foremost as a reporter of *ḥadīth,* and was a rigorist of some sort.[91] As if to prove the unpredictable effects of the methodological explosion of the late 200s, Ibn Abī Hurayrah (d. 345/956) was a student of Ibn Surayj and Abū Isḥāq al-Marwazī, both, as we have seen, holders of the Permitted position, yet he was a Proscriber, as was his student Abū 'Alī al-Ṭabarī (d. 350/961), a distinguished Shāfi'ī.[92] The last of Ibn Surayj's students, Abū l-Ḥusayn Aḥmad ibn al-Qaṭṭān (d. 359/968),[93] also held the Proscribed position. Some Shāfi'īs continued to hold the Proscribed position into the late 300s, notably al-Ḥasan ibn 'Alī al-Daqqāq (d. 405/1015) who had studied with al-Qaffāl (a Permitter position) and himself taught the important Sufi, theologian and legist, Abū l-Qāsim al-Qushayrī, who came to hold the No Assessment position. Al-Daqqāq too is described as "the Imām of his age."[93]

In the mid-300s one very prominent Mālikī, Abū Bakr Muḥammad al-Abharī (d. 375/985–6) held the Proscribed position.[94] Al-Abharī seems to have been proficient at theology, and was in some way acquainted, it seems, with al-Ṣayrafī and perhaps al-Jaṣṣaṣ.[95] He was a very important figure—not only the head of Mālikīs in Iraq, but because, through his influence, Mālikism was briefly important there. Despite his own opinions, he taught and funded al-

Bāqillānī, the Mālikī Ash'arī so important in advancing Ash'arī thought and the No Assessment position.

Once again, we find the Ḥanbalīs belatedly arriving to the position already held by some Shāfi'īs, in this case the Proscribed position. The distrust of unsanctioned acts seems in some ways most consistent with their suspicion of *qiyās*-analogy and Greek logic. The eponym of the school, Aḥmad ibn Ḥanbal, was quoted to the effect that something unmentioned in scripture is unsanctioned, and this perhaps justified the Proscriptionism of later Ḥanbalīs. Yet it is not until the late 300s that we have a name from the Ḥanbalī school associated with Proscriptionism. From that time on until the 500s, technically adept Ḥanbalīs considered Proscriptionism their school position.

The first Ḥanbalī to espouse Proscriptionism, of whom we know, is Ibn Ḥāmid al-Warrāq (d. 403/1012).[96] Makdisi considers him one of the seven grand Ḥanbalīs of this period.[97] He wrote on theology and *uṣūl al-fiqh*.[98] Perhaps most notable to us, as to his biographer, is his astonishingly wide reading and, presumably, receptivity to debate. He lists the reading that went into one of his works and the list preserved goes on for some four pages.[99] This was no ignorant fundamentalist but a rigorous intellectual trying to bring his school's pietism into the world of advanced legal methodology and jurisprudence.

It may at first surprise that a Ḥanbalī holds a position associated with the Baghdādī Mu'tazilah, but it was not only Ibn Ḥāmid who held it. It appears as well that his student, al-Qāḍī Abū Ya'lá (d. 458/1066), the "organisateur de l'école ḥanbalite au Ve/XIe siècle" held this position as well.[100] He was designated head of the Ḥanbalī school by Ibn Ḥāmid, a title undisputed by any of his biographers. He published works in *fiqh* as well as all the speculative sciences—*uṣūl al-fiqh* and *uṣūl al-dīn*.[101] He was influenced in his conduct by the advice of al-Jaṣṣāṣ and was well regarded by Shāfi'īs; indeed, he was reproached for his Shāfi'ī leanings by at least one later Ḥanbalī.[102] For those who tend to suppose that Islam was at any point comprised of hermetically separate movements, it is worth noting that Abū Ya'lá's father was a Ḥanafī, and his brother died a professing Ḥanafī and Mu'tazilī.[103] It is somewhat difficult to tell from his account in the '*Uddah* where he stands on the before revelation question, especially since his theological work, *al-Mu'tamad* seems to take a No Assessment stance. But later tradition is universal in attributing to him the Proscribed position, which he alone preserves for us in extensive form. As late as 505/1112 a Ḥanbalī is espousing the Proscribed position—Abū l-Fatḥ Muḥammad al-Ḥulwānī who was among the last students of al-Qāḍī Abū Ya'lá.[104] What all of these Ḥanbalīs share is an ascetic life, a devotion to *ḥadīth*, and a constitutional resistance to what is recognized as blameworthy innovation (*bid'ah*). A perspective from which unsanctioned acts are Proscribed, before as after Revelation, makes perfect sense. Yet after Ḥulwānī, it appears that the Ḥanbalīs repudiated the Proscribed position, and No Assessment became for Ḥanbalīs, as for Shāfi'īs, "the orthodox position."

Table 2.2 The Ḥanbalī Positions on the before Revelation Question

Name	*Date*	*Position*
Aḥmad b. Ḥanbal;	241	Proscribed[105]
Aḥmad b. Ḥanbal	241	Permitted[106]
Abū Ṭayyib b. al-Khallāl; Aḥmad b. Muḥammad	324	Permitted[107]
Abū l-Ḥasan al-Tamīmī	371	Permitted[108]
Ibn Ḥāmid	403	Proscribed[109]
Abū Ya'lá, al-Qāḍī	458	Proscribed[110]
Abū Ya'lá, al-Shaykh	458	No Assessment[111]
al-Kalwadhānī, Abū l-Khaṭṭab Maḥfūẓ b. Aḥmad	510	Permitted[112]
Ibn 'Aqīl, Abū al-Wafā' (Sahib al-Wāḍiḥ min al-Mu'tazilah)	513	Permitted[113]
Ibn 'Aqīl, Abū al-Wafā' (Sahib al-Wāḍiḥ min al-Mu'tazilah)	513	No Assessment[114]

No Assessment

Who then supported the No Assessment position? As we have shown, the later scholiasts have an interest in homogenizing school positions on this issue and a certain amount of diversity is no doubt suppressed. Nonetheless, we are able to extract certain names from the later discussions with some confidence that they were formative figures in the development of this position. The first person to whom something like the No Assessment position can be reliably attributed is Abū l-Ḥasan al-Ash'arī (d. 324/935). It is not clear whether al-Ash'arī held that there was no assessment, or that the assessment was in abeyance (*'alá al-waqf*). Although it is speculation to suppose, it is likely that his position is a reactive one, that it is a reply to one who asserts that some useful act (before/in the absence of) Revelation is presumptively Permitted. Certainly the No Assessment position is consistent with al-Ash'arī's general epistemology.[115] When we look at the early figures to whom the No Assessment position is attributed, there is one, seemingly significant correlation.

The most prominent of these figures, and the ones from whom we actually have unambiguous attributions or quotations, are al-Ash'arī, al-Bāqillānī, Abū Naṣr al-Qushayrī, and then al-Juwaynī and al-Ghazālī. Al-Bāqillānī (d. 403/1013) was head of the Mālikī *madhhab* of his time, but he is also a noted Ash'arī polemicist. The bulk of Qāḍī 'Īyāḍ's biography is given over to his controversies, particularly with non-Ash'arīs.[118] If he is "head of the Mālikīs," he is also "Imām of the *Mutakallims*." He is "most knowledgeable of people in the science of *kalām*.[119] He is, even more than al-Ash'arī, cited in Ash'arī works as the definitive expressor of Ash'arī positions.[120] Of Imām al-Ḥaramayn and

TABLE 2.3 No-Assessors

Name	*Date*	*Madhhab*	*Position*	*Source for Attribution of Position*
Abū Ḥasan al-Ash'arī	324	Mālikī/ Ḥanafī/ Shāfi'ī[116]	No Assessment	al-Baḥr 18a; al-Baḥr 16a; Minhāj al-Sunnah 318
Abū Bakr al-Ṣayrafī	330	Shāfi'ī	No Assessment	al-'Uddah 186b; al-Baḥr 18a; al-Tabṣirah 532 (said to have changed position)
Abū 'Alī al-Ṭabarī	350	Shāfi'ī	No Assessment	al-Baḥr 18a; al-'Uddah 186b; al-Tabṣirah 532
al-Fārisī Abū Bakr	361	Shāfi'ī	No Assessment	al-Baḥr 18b (aside from a few mentions, very little is known).[117]
AbūḤasan al-Kharzī	391	Ḥanbalī	No Assessment	Rawḍah 22; al-'Uddah 186b; al-Musawwadah 473; Minhāj al-Sunnah 317; Musawwadah 474
al-Bāqillānī, al-Qāḍī	403	Mālikī	No Assessment	Juwaynī Burhān ms 3a
al-Khaṭīb al-Baghdādī	463	Shāfi'ī	No Assessment	al-Faqīh wa-l-mutafaqqih
al-Juwaynī	478	Shāfi'ī	No Assessment	al-Burhān
Abū Nasr b. al-Qushayrī	514	Shāfi'ī	No Assessment	al-Baḥr 16A:25
Abū Ṭayyib, al-Qāḍī			No Assessment	al-Baḥr 18b:20 (can't identify)

al-Ghazālī, little need be said. They are well-known Ash'arī partisans. Similarly Abū Naṣr al-Qushayrī (d. 514/1120) was an Ash'arī polemicist who caused a riot with his attacks from an Ash'arī perspective on certain Ḥanbalī doctrines.[121] All of these figures are scholars well known to sift their *fiqh* and *uṣūl al-fiqh* through Ash'arī sieves. It would seem that here we have a school position from theology that is gradually transformed into a legal school position during the 300s and 400s. By the 500s, No Assessment is the indisputable doctrine of Shāfi'īsm and Ḥanbalism. That it was so is a measure of the success of the Ash'arī polemicists. It must not be supposed that this consensus is anything other than a new development after a period of reflection and debate by these schools.

Conclusion

What then is the doxography of the before revelation controversy? Perhaps foremost it is clear what it is *not*. It is not the story of how Mu'tazilīs "infected" Islamic orthodoxy; the earliest Mu'tazilī to whom a position is reliably attributed is Abū 'Alī al-Jubbā'ī (d. 303/915), who was almost an exact contemporary of the Shāfi'ī Ibn Surayj and who worked in Basrah. It is also not a story of freethinkers struggling to liberate Islam from the shackles of traditionism (or traditionalism). As we have seen, many of the most important actors were authorities on *ḥadīth*, doctrinally committed to the superiority of Prophetic *sunnah* to any source of knowledge save the Qur'ān, as, for instance, the Mālikī al-Abharī, or the Ḥanbalī Ibn Ḥāmid. In short, during the Islamic 300s and 400s, one cannot, from knowledge of a scholar's legal school, predict his position on the Before Revelation complex.

A scholar's position on these meta-issues, issues of theory, was, in fact, indeterminate and this means that *madhhab* positions were more permeable than we might expect, as scholars of different schools studied with each other, changed affiliations, and appeared at first on one side of an issue and then on another.[122]

To those familiar with the development of orthodoxies in Christianity for instance, a field much better studied, the image of Islamic consensus emerging more from internal discussion than from confrontation between pre-existent scholastic entities does not surprise. Indeed, it is not surprising to find, as one does, self-identifying Shāfi'īs who are Ash'arīs, or Shāfi'īs who are Mu'tazilah in their *uṣūl al-fiqh*. As far as one can tell, it is only later scholars who are discomfited by the plurality of Muslim doctrine in its formative period.

In choosing this indeterminate image of Islamic scholarship, it should be clear that we are rejecting others. Among those incompatible with this image are these: (1) an authentically Muḥammadian Islam or traditional(ist) Islam, distorted then perhaps resurgent; (2) an orthodoxy founded by (one's choice of) al-Shāfi'ī, Aḥmad b. Ḥanbal, or al-Ash'arī that overcame adversities and eventually triumphed over its enemies; (3) an ongoing battle between "rationalists" and "traditionalists" for the soul of Islam, a battle eventually won by neither of them. A careful study suggests a less colorful but more plausible version of Islamic intellectual history.

There were, in reality, fewer schools and more tendencies, fewer leaders and heroes, but more explorers and experimenters. In the late 200s, 300s and 400s of Islam, we will view Islamic speculative thought as an organism moving slowly in many directions, extending itself first here and then there, advancing and retreating, surrounding ideas and ingesting them sometimes, but as often passing them out as indigestible. By the late 400s the Islamic intellectual corpus acquires a more definitive form, its bodily limits become firmly established—if never quite rigid—and its motion slows as it concentrates on internal elaboration and definition. The development of the before revelation complex results too from trial and error, positions advanced and later retracted (sometimes by the same person; sometimes by a single school of law or theology). Concord on this issue does not emerge quickly and when it does emerge, a limited plurality of perspectives remains acceptable, depending upon the legal/theological school to which one adheres. Only at this time is there anything that can usefully be called an orthodoxy.[123]

The problem unsolved by this demonstration of school indeterminacy is why the before revelation complex was useful in the formation of school thought and why indeed one chose the Proscribed, Permitted, or No Assessment position. For this we must examine each position conceptually and determine what characteristics attracted a particular scholar to a particular position.

Part II

The Three Positions

Introduction

Who won the argument about the assessment of acts before Revelation? By the 11th century C.E. and through the 19th century C.E., only two of the three, or four, or five positions—depending on how they are counted—are still being defended. Echoes of the other positions lived on only in dry doxographies imbedded in methodological handbooks. Since these texts themselves are committed to only one of the solutions, and since the passion had long since gone out of the argument, the "losing" positions, as presented, seem to the reader improbable or absurd.

In this section we wish to restore their probability by reconstructing each of these positions as it was at its high water mark, when the passion of their defenders flooded into otherwise pedantic technical works. Proscribers proscribed useful acts in Revelation's absence for good reasons; likewise Permitters; and No Assessors shrank from assessment in pious horror at usurping God's prerogative. To make these positions make sense, we must see their coherence.

Each one of these arguments followed from certain assumptions about the created world, human capacity, and divine dispensation. Once the initial assumptions were made, scholars followed the argument relentlessly to its outcome. The problem may be depicted so:

The initial problematic is approving (*taḥsīn*) and detesting (*taqbīḥ*)—can the '*aql* validly assess acts? If one believes this is *not* possible, then one is led inexorably to say that acts have No Assessment before Revelation. If one says it *is* possible to assess acts without Revelation, then either by external promptings of supernatural origin (*al-khāṭirayn*)[1] or by means of the '*aql*, one makes those assessments. If one trusts the world, one Permits useful acts; if one mistrusts, one Proscribes.

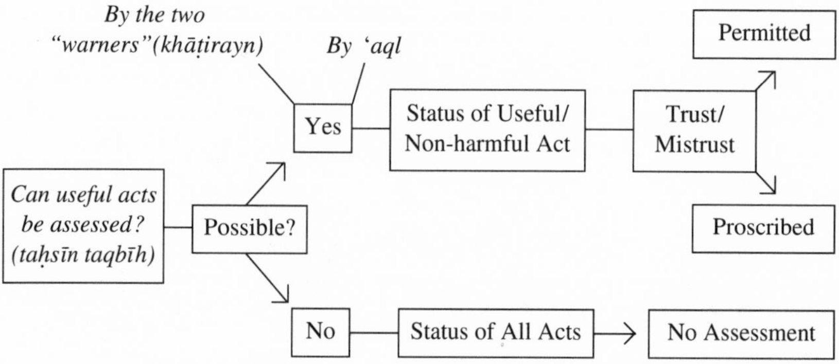

The debate, of course, was far from being so cut and dried. For these scholars the matter was of the utmost religious importance; on its balance hung questions of damnation and eternal felicity. In the chapters that follow, we hope to convey something of this question's urgency to those who debated the assessment of acts before Revelation.

Chapter 3

Acts Are Proscribed (mahẓūr)

Proscription As a Position

According to the Proscribers, most acts, even useful acts, must be considered blameworthy until explicitly Permitted by Revelation. According to some, even eating, breathing, and moving from place to place are Proscribed before Revelation.[1] Of the three or four positions taken on the problems of the before revelation complex, the least immediately plausible, at least to us, must surely be that useful acts are Proscribed (*maḥẓūr*) until Revelation permits them. From the three diverse schools that argued for this position only a single text—a Ḥanbalī one—has survived. Of the Shāfi'ī's, such as Abū 'Alī ibn Abī Hurayrah, not even quotations seem to remain. From the Mu'tazilīs we have quotations. From theḤanbalīs only the ambiguous '*Uddah* of Abū Ya'lá preserves extensive argumentation. Because the Proscribed position is so implausible, the most important task is to discover what larger purpose was served by a belief so counter-intuitive and at the same time so severe. What is being said when one says 'eating a pleasant food is Proscribed before Revelation's permission'?

Mu'tazilī Proscribers

The conceptual center of the Proscription argument during *uṣūl al-fiqh*'s formative period was the Baghdādī school of the Mu'tazilah, whose leader was Abū l-Qāsim al-Ka'bī (d. 319/931). The later Baghdādī school (after al-Khayyāṭ) seems not to have been much studied, but the Proscribed position seems to have been one of its hallmarks.[2] In common with other pietists, the Baghdādīs sought to emphasize the categorical differences between God and man, and the rigor of the Proscribed position accords with what we know of al-Ka'bī's moral stance.[3] Abū l-Ḥusayn al-Baṣrī, a late Basran Mu'tazilī who took the Permitted position, preserves an account of one version of the Proscribed position. It is regrettable to have to depend on an opponent, since his interest is usually a polemical rather than a historical one, but here he seems to fairly (if incompletely) transmit the Proscribed position. As for the identity of the opponent, it seems likely that Abū l-Ḥusayn al-Baṣrī would be arguing with a Baghdādī Mu'tazilī, since intramural argumentation seems more important to the Mu'tazilah than intermural.[4] While it is clear that there were others than Abū l-Qāsim al-Ka'bī who held the Proscribed position, for convenience, and lacking a more direct witness, we will ascribe the Proscribed arguments in the *Mu'tamad* to him.

Abū l-Qāsim asserts that the *probable* assessment of an act must be its Proscription. This rather odd position turns out to be a plausible extension of his moral-epistemology.

> The possibility [of an act's] being corrupt (*mafsadah*) suffices [to establish] its detestability, just as the possibility of a story (*khabar*) being a lie is sufficient [to establish] its detestability. Given that detestability [arises] with [mere] possibility, it is not necessary . . . to specify that [the act] is [in fact] corrupt.[5]

When we peel away the veneer of scholarly discourse, the core of Abū l-Qāsim's argument is a fear that an act of unknown value *might* be an occasion of sin. The '*aql* knows only enough to recognize the possibility of transgression and so, out of prudence, the *presumptive* assessment for all acts is Proscribed. Abū l-Qāsim's is the technical and theological expression of the pietist impulse seen among Sufis and jurisprudential conservatives such as Aḥmad ibn Ḥanbal. In pietist literature this suspicion of the uncertain action, deliberately cultivated as a religious virtue, is called *scrupulousness* (*war'*); in practice scrupulousness manifests itself as an aversion to the uncertainly licit.[6] For instance, the scrupulous person, having three dirhams, two of which he knows certainly to have been earned licitly, refrains from spending any until he determines which of them is uncertain and how it was acquired.[7] From the perspective of scrupulousness, acts are assessed only as the licit, the illicit, and the dubious (*ḥalāl, ḥarām, mashbūh*) and scrupulousness consists precisely in avoiding the dubious even though such avoidance is not, strictly speaking, Obligatory.[8] Abū l-Qāsim's view of useful acts as Proscribed is then plausible against a background of praxic rigor and suspicion. Hence he says: When the act's value is unknown, consider it Proscribed, because it could possibly be corrupt.

For the Mu'tazilah of the late 200s through the 300s, the "aspect" (*wajh*) of the thing was understood to be a portion of its existence, its being. It was believed to be that part of a thing that signified an innate quality—its moral quality, for instance.[9] For Abū l-Qāsim, one aspect of an otherwise useful thing is the perceptible possibility that it might be corrupt. For him, this outer sign indicated the inner fact of its detestability.[10] In perceiving the act's aspect of possible corruption, one perceives the ontological quality that makes its performance detestable and hence Proscribed.

Finally, he is reported repeatedly to have emphasized that "the *'aql* is not to be separated from the *shar'/sam'*."[11] This does not mean, as one might suppose, that the excesses of religion must be tempered by reason, but rather that the *'aql* by nature cannot decide between undertaking and refraining from the use of useful things. It can perceive aspects that might rightly be interpreted either way.

> If the *'aql* is isolated from the *shar'*, it cannot approve undertaking useful acts, nor forbearing to do them. It is conceivable that every one of them is corrupting. Nor can it detest undertaking or forbearing as a consequence of distinguishing between the two of them. . . . The separating of the *'aql* from the *sam'* leads to this mistake.[12]

What one can reconstruct is no doubt only a skeleton of his sophisticated and elaborate polemic. We do have enough, however, to recognize that the Baghdādī Mu'tazilī position grows from skepticism of the world and the means by which the world is known, a skepticism radical for the Mu'tazilah. It is only from the other world that knowledge of the virtues of acts and things can be obtained. Human capacities, including the *'aql*, are sufficient only to establish the likelihood that a particular deed is forbidden. Revelation is therefore not a burden, but is to be seen as a liberation, and in these patently absurd prohibitions we find the measure of Revelation's importance. The thrust of his argument, of course, is not pseudo-historical but practical. Al-Ka'bī is not suggesting that pre-Revelational humans trembled to breathe for lack of sanction, but that they lived every moment, at least potentially, in a state of moral transgression. Revelation provides certainty by giving Permission for some acts, and Prohibiting others. It is easy to see how this rigorist position could have attracted those seeking to harmonize scrupulous piety with the speculative language of the theologians. In the fifth Islamic century these included certain Ḥanbalīs, the last of the central Islamic legal schools to develop competence in theoretical speculation.

Ḥanbalī Proscribers

In the view of the most recent and prominent Western student of Ḥanbalism, the school of Aḥmad had almost as its raison d'être opposition to the Mu'tazilah, the so-called "rationalists."[13] Yet the position that acts done in default of Revelation were Proscribed was held by a number of esteemed Ḥanbalī figures, according to Ḥanbalī and other sources, and so on this question at least some Mu'tazilīs and more than a few Ḥanbalīs shared a position within a larger controversy. These Proscribing Ḥanbalīs include, obliquely, Aḥmad ibn

Ḥanbal himself, but more importantly Ibn Ḥāmid and probably the great Abū Ya'lá ibn al-Farrā' (d. 458/1064).[14] The discovery that a number of prominent Ḥanbalīs shared doctrine with the Baghdādī Mu'tazilīs—not just scandalous figures such as Ibn 'Aqīl but establishment figures such as Ibn Ḥāmid and Abū Ya'lá—ought to cause us to rethink the notion of a dichotomous Islamic intellectual history.

The '*Uddah* of Abū Ya'lá ibn al-Farrā' is a record of the time in which the Mu'tazilah, a few Shāfi'īs, and the most important Ḥanbalīs shared common ground.[15] Abū Ya'lá's position on the before revelation complex is actually a bit difficult to discern, but he records the arguments of the Proscribers in a fashion more vigorous than any other surviving source. Abū Ya'lá argues that since the world is God's property, His permission is necessary to use it. Unlike the Baghdādī Mu'tazilah, he denies that assessments apply to acts and things; only the *actor* (*fā'il*) can be judged (190b). Exceptions are made for those things which, if humans were deprived of them, would result in bodily harm. Yet the need to prevent damage to God's other property, namely ourselves, justifies these exceptions for necessities (187a, 188b). Therefore, what is not mentioned by Revelation is consequently forbidden; before Revelation, nothing has been Permitted, and so everything is Proscribed, prima facie.

His choice of the Proscribed position has two sources. The first is a partisan one. He asserts both that the school's eponymous founder Aḥmad b. Ḥanbal believed in some natural knowledge by the '*aql*[16] and that the governing principle for Aḥmad, in the absence of other knowledge, was Proscription.[17]

Second, He perceives that from one perspective at least there is only a trivial difference between the No Assessment and the Permitted positions. Though scholars like al-Ghazālī see this difference as crucial, Abū Ya'lá, rigorist that he is, points out that both positions imply *no harm* for acts performed without *shar'ī* sanction (186b). For Abū Ya'lá, this is morally unacceptable.

To know things as Proscribed before Revelation, the '*aql* must be granted a role in moral knowing, and Abū Ya'lá recognizes the epistemological implication of his position. He asserts that the '*aql can* know the reprehensibility of ingratitude, and the unicity of God (186b, 188b) and this knowledge is of course not Proscribed, since it has such an important role in Muslim theories of Prophetology. It is, however, irrelevant here. What matters is action, and so he wants to discuss only acts that *can* be Proscribed or Permitted, such as eating pork or mutton (186b).

Consider the case of a person created by God in the desert, knowing nothing of Revelation's stipulations. There are fruits and foods there: For this Robinson Crusoe, should these things be described as Proscribed or Permitted before the *shar'* comes to indicate their status? Abū Ya'lá's answer is these things are Proscribed. His argument is that all created things are the property of God because He created them, and one may not use the property of another without His permission. His proof is that one may not use the things of humankind without permission—this Proscription constitutes an indicant (*dalīl*) that one similarly may not use God's property without permission. Abū Ya'lá's underlying assumption is that one can use the practical knowledge of this world to understand the rules of the transcendent world. While God and man may be far apart, the transcendent and the immanent are, in some senses, analogous and parallel.

Like al-Ka'bī, Abū Ya'lá asserts that the '*aql* and the *shar*' cannot be separated from each other. One must use the '*aql* because without the '*aql* one can recognize neither the value of doing something useful nor the harm that comes from doing something without permission. Yet the '*aql*, left to itself, has no grounds to decide between Proscribing the thing and Proscribing the proscription of a thing's use.[18] In either case, however, inaction would itself lead to moral transgression. More specifically, though reason instructs that useful things are for use, God has in fact Proscribed some useful things as a test, such as pork and wine.[19] Reason might also assess fornication as good, or the slaughter of animals as detestable, for example (188b). Hence the '*aql* by itself is (rightly) paralyzed into non-action. The '*aql* must therefore be joined to a Revelational indicant (*sam*') and in this case, the *sam*' tips the balance away from utilization, since it Proscribes use of another's property without Permission. Hence Revelation is inseparable from the '*aql*.[20]

Abū Ya'lá's text is valuable particularly for his smooth rebuttal to a standard refutation of his position. Every anti-Proscription text from al-Jaṣṣāṣ onwards argues that the underlying *ratio* ('*illah*) for the prohibition of illegitimate usufruct is harm to the owner of the property. Since God is not harmed, say Abū Ya'lá's opponents, there is no question of forbidding use of the useful things in His world. This is taken, by those who use it, to be a crushing argument. Abū Ya'lá replies that it is not harm to the *owner* of the property that is the ground for its Proscription, but harm to the *illegitimate user*, since by transgressing a rule he ensures his own harm in the world to come. As an example, he points out that if a man had hundredweights of money, the theft of a *dirham* would not *harm* the victim; yet it is still forbidden to take that *dirham* without the owner's permission because of the harm to the thief in the hereafter.

In the absence of Revelation, the '*aql* is sovereign for Abū Ya'lá. The '*aql* dictates hesitation or Proscription to perform useful but unnecessary acts, as we have seen, while the '*aql* also justifies and impels necessary action. Abū Ya'lá's is not a rule-based argument that would hold *all* acts before the *shar*' to be Proscribed, but a commonsense-based argument which Permits some acts that are necessary. So to those who argue that by his logic necessary acts must also be Proscribed—either sincerely or a fortiori to absurdity—Abū Ya'lá replies:

> As for breathing air and moving [in different] directions, let [us] consider the occasion (*waqt*). If there is need, one may do it because the permission has been obtained for it from the '*aql* (*min jihat al-'aql*).[21]

> This is comparable to when one is forced [to eat] the food of another. It is Permitted to him since the *'aql* does not restrain one from it, just as the *shar'* does not restrain one from it in case of need; if there is no need, [the *shar'*] does restrain one from it (187b).[22]

Similarly, he easily dismisses the allegation that his Proscription would proscribe kindling a light from someone else's fire, or resting in the shade of someone's wall by pointing out that neither the fire nor shade are anyone's property per se.[23] To the objection that "before the *shar'* " has no meaning, since there is always Revelational knowledge available—Adam having been both first man and first Prophet—Abū Ya'lá cites Aḥmad b. Ḥanbal who said that such prophetic knowledge is interrupted from time to time;[24] from this Abū Ya'lá understands that there are times in which there is no perduring *shar'* but only people of knowledge who try and transmit the *shar'*.

So the basic argument—that Creation is God's property and it is His alone to loose or bind—stands. That is the moral axiom. Epistemologically Abū Ya'lá's position is more problematic. He not only argues that there is moral life before the *shar'*, but that it is the *'aql* that provides the moral knowledge that makes a moral choice possible. Subsequent to Revelation we come to know the limitation of the *'aql*, but since humans lack such knowledge so long as they lack Revelation, they are morally bound to act upon what they know.[25]

How to know to act in some cases and not to act in others is not clear. Indeed, as the argument proceeds (188b) he seems to move closer to the Permitted position. Nonetheless, the strength of his position for pietists is that unlike the Permitters, he does not assume the continuity of pre-Revelational and post-Revelational times. Illicit acts become licit and even obligatory when Revelation comes, and Muslim epistemology—in which *'aql* misleads without *shar'*—is upheld.

Abū Ya'lá's argument is in places elegant, but his lack of absolute conviction is perhaps reflected in his extensive quotation of al-Tamīmī's defense of the Permitted position, and his rather muddled conclusion (190a and following). In fact, Abū Ya'lá is trying to ride two horses—he wants to defend a notion of natural knowledge (i.e., that we are inherently capable of assessing something as evil for instance, a position that implicitly limits the sovereignty of Revelation)—and at the same time he wishes to place the *'aql* in a position of utter dependence on Revelation. He accepts al-Ka'bī's dictum that *shar'* and *'aql* are inseparable, but he goes on to urge that before the arrival of the *shar'*, humans know of punishment in the next world for the use of another's property. This clearly won't do. The Proscribers are ultimately caught between making the *'aql* a full-fledged source of moral knowledge and deriding its value altogether. The former leads naturally to Permitted, the latter to No Assessment. It should not surprise that after Abū Ya'lá there seem to be almost no defenders of the Proscribed position.

Yet the contradictions and seeming absurdities of this position must be seen as attempts to reconcile two conflicting strands of fifth-century Ḥanbalī pietism. Aḥmad b. Ḥanbal and his followers represent that strand of Islam most suspicious of the created world. For those of scrupulous (*war'ī*) sensibility, the implicit command of Revelation is to eschew anything of uncertain value, unless it passes the strictest test of legal knowledge. This heightened view of the Revelational event consequently estranges the Islamic present from the pre-Islamic or non-Islamic past. Abū Ya'lá was unable to follow this position to its logical extreme and completely sunder Islamic moral epistemology from the *'aql*. Hermeneutically he is consistent: the *'aql* contextualizes the *shar'*. Remove *shar'* and *'aql* remains. The *'aql* for Abū Ya'lá is untrustworthy, but to know the extent of its untrustworthiness requires a more certain measure—Revelation. Lacking that standard, the *'aql* must be followed.

Chapter 4

The Permitted Position

Introduction

If the Proscribed position reflects a suspicious and pessimistic view of the world—a world that deceives and ensnares—the Permitted position arises from trust and optimism. The world is essentially benign, and when it indicates goodness and utility those things are indeed good and useful. The Proscribed position despairs of human capacity correctly to discern the dangerous, and supposes our intuitions and appropriations of things to be intrinsically illicit. The Permitted position seems more respectful of human intellectual capacity and assumes its harmony with a world graciously created for our use. For the Proscribers, the cardinal sin is presumption, for the Permitters it is uselessness or futility. If the world has a point or purpose it is a mystery to the Proscribers. That the world should have no discernible purpose is blasphemy to the Permitters.

The source of the Permitted position is less some Greek rationalist virus than it is the Qur'ān itself, and it is no accident that the Permitters seem somewhat freer in their use of proof texts than either No Assessors or Proscribers. There is some evidence that the Qur'ān itself trusts the *'aql* as a source of knowledge. Indeed it appears that, in its own view, the purpose of Qur'ānic Revelation is to provoke reflection by the *'aql*.[1] Equally clearly, the Qur'ān presents the world as a benefaction filled with useful and pleasurable gifts.[2] Therefore to view the world as benign and useful and to believe that its benignity and usefulness are signs of value in accord with God's assessments is not only Qur'ānic, but surely an original position within the Muslim community. We view the Permitters, then, not as importers of an alien Greek perspective, but as conservative heirs to a long but, by the fourth Muslim century, archaic Muslim position. It is the Proscribers and No Assessors who introduce a new world view and proceed to transform inherited Islamic views of the world.

The Permitted position states that in the absence of Revelational knowledge to the contrary, useful acts are Permitted. Mu'tazilīs, Shāfi'īs, Ḥanbalīs and Ḥanafīs affirmed the Permitted position.[3] The Permitted position is usually imbedded in an argument that the *'aql*, unaided, can discern the detestability of *doing* some things—so that their Proscription is known—and the detestability of *not doing* other things—so that their Obligatory quality is known. Useful acts fall in between—they are otherwise good but not Obligatory, and so, are Permitted. This is in many ways an appealing argument, but there are at least two structural problems with it, when considered as an Islamic and religious argument.

1. The Permitted position seems to contradict the Revelational Proscription of things that seem good to the unaided intellect, such as the consumption of pork and wine, and to contradict also the imposition of irrational Obligations such as the duty to perform what seem to be useless acts in ritual worship, or to fast one day and not another.
2. More importantly, the Permitted view emphasizes the continuity and homogeneity of the pre- and post-Revelational world, and of the transcendent and immanent perspective on acts. A countervailing Islamic impulse, however, has been to distinguish a world before and without the Qur'ān and Prophet, and the world which has been given the Book through the Prophet. Similarly, Permitters assimilate the realm of the divine to the mundane. Yet the *shar'ī*-minded sought to heighten these contrasts in other discussions, such as the predestination or createdness of the Qur'ān arguments. There is a sense, then, in which the Permitted position minimizes the significance of Islam itself.

A final point: *Rationality* or the ability of the *'aql* to discern good from detestable is, for the most part, not at issue here. Advocates of all three positions agreed that the intellect could make these sorts of determinations for the ordinary world. The question debated was the continuity between the Hidden (*al-ghā'ib*) and the Manifest (*al-shāhid*) worlds. So it is an oversimplification, or even an error, to see this debate as Mu'tazilism versus orthodoxy or rationalism versus traditionism. It is rather a debate between an optimistic view of Providence and a pessimistic one, and between an archaic position and an innovative one.

THE PERMITTED POSITION: THE MU'TAZILAH

George Hourani and others have studied much of the Mu'tazilī *theological* literature connected with the Permitted position.[4] It is the Mu'tazilī *juristic* perspective on this question that most concerns us, however, and from it we have only one early Shī'ī text—the *Dharī'ah* of 'Ālamalhudá, Sharīf al-Murtaḍá (d. 436/1044)[5]—and one non-Shī'ī text—the *Mu'tamad* of Abū l-Ḥusayn al-Baṣrī (d. 436/1044).[6]

The Mu'tazilī Permitters know the obligatoriness and detestability of acts by evidence that triggers, as it were, an involuntary response in the *'aql*. If no response is provoked, then the absence of a response counts as evidence also—that the act is Permitted. Two exact contemporaries, al-Sharīf al-Murtaḍá and Abū l-Ḥusayn al-Baṣrī, wrote *uṣul al-fiqh* works in which "Proscription" and "Permittedness" are titles of chapters devoted to this problem. Though Sharīf al-Murtaḍá was an Imāmī Shī'ī, and Abū l-Ḥusayn al-Baṣrī was a Shāfi'ī or Ḥanafī Sunnī, both were Mu'tazilīs.[7]

Mu'tazilī assumptions about speculative thought pervade the discussions by al-Sharīf al-Murtaḍá and Abū l-Ḥusayn. Both argue that the ontology of the act is reflected in the *'aql*'s perception of the act's qualities. Both are more concerned with the qualitative terms *goodness* and *detestability* than with the moral-praxic terms Proscription and Obligation. Both are interested in what elicits praise and blame, rather than what provokes punishment and reward.

Abū l-Ḥusayn al-Baṣrī

The Mu'tazilīs were, as Richard Frank has shown, first and foremost students of "being," of ontology. The Mu'tazilī discussion of acts is predictably characterized by its assertion that there is some quality inherent in the act or thing, some part of its ontology, that accounts for its goodness or detestability. In other words, the perception of goodness or detestability in a thing arises from the nature of the thing itself.[8] The quality of acts is limited to good or detestable, but the assessment of acts, the characterization of them in terms of our response to them, is threefold: Obligatory, Proscribed, and Permitted. For the Mu'tazilah, the term *mubāḥ*, here translated as "Permitted," is a neutral term, meaning neither praiseworthy nor blameworthy. Good acts may be either Permitted or Obligatory, depending on whether the neglect of them is detestable and Proscribed, or a matter of indifference from these premises. Abū l-Ḥusayn's description of how to know the assessment of an act, such as eating something about which Revelation is silent, is straightforward:

> Our proof that the use of edibles is Permitted (*mubāḥ*) by the *'aql* is that the use of them is a usefulness in which there is no aspect (*wajh*) of detestability. Everything of this sort [i.e., that has no detestable aspect] is known to be good. The rationale (*'illah*) for saying such things are good is that the usefulness [of the act or thing] inclines one to do the deed and gives permission for it, since [usefulness] is an objective (*gharaḍ*) of a sort.
>
> If all aspects of detestability are eliminated, there remains only what would indicate goodness. . . . If there were something reprehensible (*mafsadah*) in it, God would give indication of it.[9]

The term translated here as "aspect" (*wajh*) is, as it turns out, an ontological term, that refers both to the nature and the actual context of the act.[10] Moral knowledge, then, is observing the act as it occurs and looking for detestable aspects, namely that the act seems oppressive, or a falsehood, or purposeless, etc. In the absence of perceptible detestability, the act is good. Then the observer asks if *neglecting* the act brings about oppression, falsehood, purposelessness, undeserved harm, etc.; if so, performing the act is Obligatory; if not, by default, its performance is Permitted. Often "usefulness" is the door through which purposefulness and therefore goodness is admitted. There is a sense of holding God responsible, in this position. "The rationale for the goodness [of edibles, etc.] . . . is that the usefulness [of it] *motivates* one to the act and justifies it."[11] If we are created such that we are motivated and if there is no sign to the contrary, either God is deceptive or eating these things is Permitted.

The machinery of moral knowing turns on the assumption of this *'aqlī* knowledge—that a falsehood is detestable, and so, Proscribed, or that rescuing a drowning person is good to do and detestable to neglect, and so, Obligatory. The linchpin of the Permitter theory of moral epistemology is that this knowledge is not in the first place deduced or inferred, but it is incontestable spontaneous (*ḍarūrī*) knowledge, common to all humans by virtue of being *compotes mentis*.[12]

Sharīf al-Murtaḍá

We can see the Mu'tazilī machinery running smoothly in Sharīf al-Murtaḍá's *Dharī'ah.* There he demonstrates the process of discovering the Permittedness of an act.

> What indicates [that a useful act is Permitted] is the knowledge that there is usefulness in [the act] and that [the act] is free from harm, either now or later. [All such things] have the characteristic/attribute of Permittedness[13] . . . This knowledge of which we speak is indubitable, like the knowledge that that which has the quality of oppression is detested. . . .

He goes on to add:

> [Indeed,] every kind of acts' assessments must have an indubitable basis in the *'aql*.[14]

For Sharīf al-Murtaḍá, the method is simply to avoid harm; whatever is not harmful is good. Harm may mean of course pain, and other corporeal harms, but for the religiously inclined, harm par excellence is damnation. Yet the Judgment at which damnation is imposed is neither here, nor now, and Sharīf al-Murtaḍá must solve the problem of how damage in the transcendent realm is known in this one. He begins with an analysis of harms.

> Damage is of two sorts: immediate and deferred. The absence of the immediate is known by the absence of means to knowledge or supposition of [harm, including indicants or signs]. If every aspect of knowledge or supposition [that harm will ensue] is absent, then one may determine the lack of immediate harm. . . . As for deferred [harm], namely punishment, the absence of that is known only from the absence of Revelation which has to have been sent down if [deferred] punishment is established [to requite performance of the act], because God most high must inform us of deferred harm imposed upon us, namely the punishment which implies the detestability of the act. If we have no such information, we establish thereby the absence of deferred harm as well.[15]

Note the "must" here, which refers to God's action in the world. The Arabic does not distinguish between "has to" and "must have done." Note too his trust in the human capacity to know the detestable at sight.

> *Objection:* How do you know the absence of aspects of detestability from your acts?
> *Reply:* The aspects of detestability are well known, so if the act is not a lie, nor oppression, nor desiring the detestable, nor charging with what is impossible, and so on from among the aspects of detestability, it is known that there is nothing reprehensible [in the act] because of the absence of information from God most high or an indicant to that effect. Thus we know of the absence of all aspects of detestability.[16]

The confidence of the Permitters and their trust in the ordered world emerges at every turn in their argument. For those whose religiosity was less sunny, this cheery account would not seem persuasive.

Toward the end of his discussion of the before revelation complex, Sharīf al-Murtaḍá makes two points, one that suggests the motivation behind the Permitted position, while the other will help us understand the objections to the Permitters.

As he is finishing an attack on the Proscribers—pointing out that if we follow their line to its logical end we end up harming ourselves—he asks what to make of the fact that humans need to eat and drink.

> Among the things that indicate [the Permitted position, contra the Proscribers] is that God, the most high, created bodies characterized by eat-

> ing and breathing, and this must have a purpose (*gharaḍ*), because pointless acts (*al-ʻabath*) do not occur from Him, because of their detestability. There is no aspect by which this [act of creating bodies so] can be accounted good by Him, except their being created thereby to benefit the bondsmen. Further, it is inconceivable that He created them as useful acts (*ʻalá wajh al-nafʻ*) except that they [are assessed] as Permitted.[17]

No better demonstration of the optimism that motivates the Permitted argument could be offered. For the Permitters, the world is a puzzle, but to solve it, it must be assumed that creation is purposive. Bodies are characterized by breathing and eating; breathing and eating are therefore useful and therefore good, otherwise they are pointless and detestable. It is a simple equation, and a satisfying one at this level.

Yet, their critics were somehow unconvinced. Not all of creation is so easily accounted for. More significantly, there is the problem of presumption, which is reflected in a line tossed off by al-Sharīf al-Murtaḍá as he closes his argument.

The Proscribers have argued that in the absence of assent one may not use the property of its owner. Revelation not yet having arrived, the world, God's property, cannot be used lawfully. To this Sharīf al-Murtaḍá replies:

> The *ʻaqlī* proof we have mentioned is a stronger indicant than Revelational assent and Permission (*al-idhn wa-l-ibāḥah min al-samʻ*). If undertaking [to do the act] with Revelational assent is good, all the more so with *ʻaqlī* proof. . . . If we bring food and seat the guest at the table, this is stronger than verbal assent; if one signals to take something, it is as if [one gave] verbal assent.[18]

The problematic side of the Permitter position shows here. The gesture is understood to be more powerful than the word, and the *ʻaql* is preferred to Revelation. If the *ʻaql* is superior to the Word, then that which every human has is more important than that which only Muslims have, namely, the source of Islam's very existence—Muslim Revelation.

The Permitted Position: The Ḥanafiyyah

It is among the most important arguments of this book that the Permitted position was held at one point or another by members of nearly every legal school. It seems generally to be believed that to hold the Permitted position or to value the moral knowledge provided by the *ʻaql* proves one to be a Muʻtazilī.[19] In fact, what was perhaps the most numerous and widespread school of law, the

Ḥanafī, generally held the Permitted position as its school position and believed the *'aql* yielded valid moral knowledge. Once this is recognized, the use of the term *Mu'tazilī* may be properly restricted to those who professed Mu'tazilism and adhered to it as a school of thought. Those who were not adherents of Mu'tazilism will be recognized as belonging at some point on the spectrum of opinion within the *madhhab* which they professed. In this way the dynamic and catholic nature of Islamic thought will more clearly be recognized.

Ḥanafī Sources

We have a range of Ḥanafī texts, from the *Fuṣūl* of al-Jaṣṣāṣ (d. 370/980) (which, because it is our earliest source for the entire discussion, is extensively analyzed and then translated below) to the *Sharḥ Musallam al-thubūt* of al-'Ayyāsh (d. 1235/1819), which together attest to a distinctive Ḥanafī discussion of these topics. The Mu'tazilah and the Ḥanafīs share not only the belief that useful acts are Permitted before Revelation, but they also share a belief that the assessment of an act is a reflection of its purpose, its teleology. They differ, however, in their ontological analysis, and in the emphasis they give to God's role in assigning assessments to acts, as well as in different views of the connection between behavior and requital: the Mu'tazilah believed that God *must* requite with punishment those who neglect what ought to be done and who do what ought to be shunned, and reward appropriately those who act rightly; the Ḥanafīs believe God may pardon transgressions if He wills.

It is usual to suppose that the before revelation complex of arguments took place between the "orthodox" on the one hand (Ash'arīs and Ḥanbalīs) and the "rationalists" (Mu'tazilīs) on the other. We have argued above that within the Shāfi'ī and Ḥanbalī schools there was a range of positions that included nearly every possibility. We have suggested that within the Mu'tazilah there were at least two positions that are identified with prominent types of Mu'tazilism. In this section the varieties of Ḥanafism will be addressed. It may be the case there was some *ur*-Permitted position, perhaps that of Ibn Surayj, from which Mu'tazilī and Ḥanafī Permittedism derived. It is clear, however, that Ḥanafīs and Mu'tazilīs went quite different ways in the fourth and subsequent Islamic centuries. Mu'tazilism, as we have seen, came to emphasize the natural order of the *'aql*'s recognition of moral ontology. "Detestability" is a constituent part of the act, and so, naturally, God and *compotes mentis* assess such acts as Proscribed.[20] Ḥanafīs, rather, emphasized the divine economy in which assessments remain God's prerogative, while the *'aql* by divine dispensation can recognize the assessments assigned to the act by the Assessor. The Ḥanafīs worked to keep God as the primary actor in the drama of morality, while for the Mu'tazilīs He became a stagehand who arranged the furniture and props before the play's first act.

Abū Ḥanīfah. The Ḥanafī position has its roots perhaps in earliest Ḥanafism when Abū Ḥanīfah and his eastern disciples articulated a doctrine appropriate to an expanding faith suddenly compelled to incorporate nominal and nominally informed Muslims. The Ḥanafīs suggested that inward disposition was more important than praxic detail, and that the non-Islamic, or imperfectly Islamic acts of the newly converted were licit until they knew better. On the other hand, ignorance of the Islamic summons did not excuse utter religious ignorance or indifference to the fundamentals of religion—especially the existence of a single god, his role as creator, and certain basics of moral conduct.[21] As the before revelation complex was elaborated, it became the device by which these sorts of issues were addressed and debated.

The legacy of early Ḥanafism and the rise of *madhhab*-chauvinsim in the fourth and fifth centuries meant that these early positions and their logical extension in the before revelation argument, which were ascribed to the eponymic founder of the school, could not easily be abandoned. Subsequent Ḥanafī discussions sometimes enthusiastically embrace the Ḥanafī doctrine and sometimes, with embarrassment, attempt to finesse it away. Nonetheless, this heritage guaranteed that any scholar who identified himself as a Ḥanafī would always differ from members of other schools in his approach to the before revelation complex. While we feel justified in discussing in general terms "a Ḥanafī position," it is true that Ḥanafism never fully consolidated around a Permitted orthodoxy the way that later Shāfi'īs and Ḥanbalīs unified around No Assessment.

For a detailed exposition of Ḥanafī Permittedism, we begin with what is in fact our earliest surviving discussion of the before revelation complex, the *Fuṣūl* of Abū Bakr al-Jaṣṣāṣ al-Rāzī.

al-Jaṣṣāṣ[22]

Biography. Abū Bakr Aḥmad ibn 'Alī al-Rāzī al-Jaṣṣāṣ was born in 305/917 and died in 370/980. His career took him from Rayy to Baghdad in 325/936, then to Ahwaz and Nishapur, then back to Baghdad in 344/955 where he was recognized as the head of the Ḥanafī school.[23]

He wrote a masterly *Aḥkām al-Qur'ān*,[24] a *Book of Stages* [of the Ḥajj?],[25] and a book of "replies" to questions put to him.[26] His work seems otherwise largely to have taken the form of commentaries: a gloss on the *Adab al-qāḍī* of al-Khaṣṣāf,[27] a commentary on al-Karkhī's *fiqh* work,[28] a gloss on the *Mukhtaṣar* of al-Ṭaḥāwī, a gloss on the *Jāmi'*[29] of al-Shaybānī, an epitome of Ṭaḥāwī's *Ikhtilāf* work,[30] and a gloss on the beautiful names [of God] (*al-asmā' al-ḥusná*).[31]

Despite these various works, his most substantial contribution to Islamic thought lies in the field of *uṣūl al-fiqh*. When we compare his work with that of his teacher Abū l-Ḥasan al-Karkhī, it seems probable that it was he who made the transition, at least for the Ḥanafīs, from a significance-of-the-case, or strictly "legal," understanding of *uṣūl*, to the analytical, theological version of the science with which we are familiar.[32] His *uṣūl* work, "*al-Fuṣūl*," is the first (to have survived, at any rate) that follows the form subsequently standard for such works. The work appears to have been extremely influential: it is, for instance, quoted at length (though without attribution) in the *'Uddah* of the Ḥanbalī Abū Ya'lá,[33] and, as we pointed out above, al-Jaṣṣāṣ himself was closely associated with, and respected by, Ḥanbalīs.[34]

al-Jaṣṣāṣ's Mu'tazilism. There are at least four published Western discussions of al-Jaṣṣāṣ,[35] two of which refer to al-Jaṣṣāṣ as a Mu'tazilī.[36] In the first of these, Shehaby's casually asserts that " . . . al-Jaṣṣāṣ belonged to the Mu'tazilī school of theology. . . . "[37] More recently, Professor Bernand, in her descriptive overview of the *Fuṣūl*, says that "his Mu'tazilī affinities are obvious," and she cites the biography of al-Jaṣṣāṣ in Ibn al-Murtaḍá, *Ṭabaqāt al-Mu'tazilah*, where al-Jaṣṣāṣ is listed as "a *faqīh* who spoke of justice," that is, identified himself with the Mu'tazilah doctrine of God's justice.[38] As far as I can tell, however, these are the only prosopographical sources to identify him in school terms as a Mu'tazilī. This vague ascription is not to be trusted: Ibn al-Murtaḍá's chronology is wrong (he puts al-Jaṣṣāṣ in the generation of al-Qāḍī 'Abdal-jabbār who died 45 years after al-Jaṣṣāṣ) and this Mu'tazilī biographer (and the later one as well—al-Ḥākim al-Jushamī) seems to have included important scholars almost at random and called them members of his school, including for instance Ibn Surayj and even al-Shāfi'ī![39]

It is true that al-Jaṣṣāṣ's *teacher* debated Abū 'Alī al-Jubbā'ī, the founder of the Baṣran Mu'tazilī school, and praised his son Abū Hāshim, but this does not make his teacher or al-Jaṣṣāṣ a Mu'tazilī any more than similar evidence proves Ibn Surayj a Ẓāhirī.[40] Another of his teachers, al-Barda'ī, is alleged to have had Mu'tazilī leanings,[41] but studying with someone did not mean allegiance to his school. In the construction of Mu'tazilī doxography these later Mu'tazilī biographers seem to have appropriated anyone at all whose thought was dubious from an Ash'arī point of view, and transformed him into a Mu'tazilī.[42] As far as can be seen, the sole reliable ground for calling al-Jaṣṣāṣ a Mu'tazilī seems to be that in his work he gave a more prominent place to *'aql* than was acceptable to later Ash'arī/Ḥanbalī orthodoxy. Yet the Ash'arīs and everyone else except the Ẓāhirīs had some place for the *'aql*, and many prominent Shāfi'īs and Ḥanbalīs, as well as Ḥanafīs, viewed it as a source of legal/moral knowledge. In the 300s, it was precisely the role and limits of the *'aql* that was in dispute within the legal schools. It begs the historical question to see the use of the *'aql* as proof of Mu'tazilism.

It is more likely that to write works disengaged from the assumptions and restrictions of later orthodoxy was to produce something that looks, from our perspective, to be Mu'tazilī. This was particularly true for the Ḥanafīs, as Massignon and Madelung have pointed out.[43] Yet aside from the prejudices of the fifth and later Islamic centuries, there is nothing to indicate that al-Jaṣṣāṣ had a *madhhab*-allegiance to the Mu'tazilīs. He associated with and was well regarded by Ḥanbalīs, he was a pietist, he was offered the judgeship by the caliph al-Muṭī' in the period after the separation of the caliphate from Mu'tazilism.[44]

There is certainly no good historical reason to label him a *Mu'tazilī*, and, tellingly, it is an accusation that *none* of the non-Mu'tazilī biographical dictionaries makes, not even Ibn al-Jawzī (who never, it seems, shrank from a defamatory statement).[45] There is also, I think, no ground in the *Fuṣūl* for calling him a Mu'tazilī. Careful attention to what al-Jaṣṣāṣ *says* and *does not say* allows us to see ways in which, on this question in particular, he differs markedly from the Mu'tazilah described above and below.

Overview of His Argument. Al-Jaṣṣāṣ's position assumes this: useful acts are good and good acts are useful—either now or in the hereafter. Consequently the usefulness of something is an indicant (*dalīl*) that it is good. Because acts are equally useful before and after Revelation, moral epistemology is the same before and after Revelation. Revelation augments other sources of knowledge and brings knowledge of goods (of fasting the last day of Ramadan, for instance) and harms (of drinking wine, for example) of which we would not otherwise be aware; but most acts retain their usefulness, goodness and so, indexicality, across the fissure between the Islamic and the pre- or non-Islamic.

Al-Jaṣṣāṣ defines the good and the useful negatively: Harmful things are necessarily useless and consequently detestable and Proscribed. Necessary things are Obligatory as well as good. What remains is neither Proscribed nor Obligatory; it is useful and consequently good and so, of course, Permitted.

Just as the quality of acts and of moral knowledge is fundamentally unchanged by Revelation, the moral capacity of human beings is similarly not changed by Revelation. Humans, for al-Jaṣṣāṣ, are made-responsible (*mukallaf*) before Revelation as they are after Revelation (i.a., para. 32).[46] The ability to differentiate the good from the detestable by use of common sense (*'aql*) is held by both the post-Revelational Muslim and the pre-Revelational non-Muslim, and so for al-Jaṣṣāṣ the demarcation between Muslims and non-Muslims is as blurred as that between non-Islamic and Islamic.

Commentary

Al-Jaṣṣāṣ deserves attention not merely for his priority in the history of *uṣūl al-fiqh* but for his perspicacity as well. The first section of his before revelation treatment is subtle and agile. He portrays this controversy as taking place on two levels (4–7). The first level is of scope. Are there signs other than the Revelational ones (such as usefulness, for instance) that signify the assessment appropriate to the act? At this level the Permitters and Proscribers stand together in regarding Revelation as an informational event—one among others (7, 28ff). The second level is what might be called the optimism/pessimism level, where the problem is what to say about the world when Revelation is not (yet) heard from. Here the Permitters and No Assessors are optimists, believing that acts not obviously designated as harmful are likely to be harmless. The

Proscribers are pessimistic, mistrusting all acts until Revelation Permits them (5,7,15).

In what we have called the first two sections of this discussion (A and B), al-Jaṣṣāṣ argues the benignity of the world (9,10) and its indicativity as well (11,12). The two are connected because a benign God wishes humans, including Muslims, to learn from the world so as to avoid harm.

In (12) he argues that the existence of God—which must be accepted prior to acceptance of Revelation—is known by reference to indicants *in creation*. "We find the heavens and earth and ourselves to be indicants of God most high. . . . Indeed, if there were an indicant of [some aspect of the world's] Proscription, then the arrival of Revelation with Permission could not be, because what the indications of God most high require is not overturned."[12] Thus Muslims already harmonize the knowledge derived from creation and that derived from supernatural Revelation. For al-Jaṣṣāṣ there are, in effect, two kinds of Revelation—natural (creation) and extra-natural (Qur'ān and *sunnah*)—and both impart moral knowledge. If this is so, it follows that neither of these two Revelations can be in contradiction with the other, since both ultimately have the same origin, and so, the same authority. This is why the moral imperatives that obtain before Revelation are unchanged with the coming of Revelation. With this argument al-Jaṣṣāṣ not only establishes the consistency of *natural* and *extra-natural* Revelation, but also the Revelational significance of silence, i.e., non-indication. God would have indicated if acts were harmful; therefore the absence of '*aqlī* or Revelational indicants is a positive sign of its harmlessness and Permittedness.

In al-Jaṣṣāṣ's last three sections (C, D, E) he attacks other possible assessments of the pre-Revelational act. Against the Proscribers he argues first the absurdity of his opponents' position: It is incredible that essential aspects to life itself should be Proscribed (15 and all of D). For al-Jaṣṣāṣ the Proscribers' assertion that the world is God's property, not to be used without Revelational permission, is invalid because it is not mere use, but *using up,* or consumption of another's property that is impermissible (21–27). As a counter to the analogy of using another's property without permission, he offers the analogy of our permissible use of something whose use does not harm the owner (e.g., resting in the shade of his wall). God is similarly unharmed by our using "His" food and water. In later terminology, al-Jaṣṣāṣ makes harmlessness the *ratio*[47] that links the analogy between the use of the wall for shade, and use of God's food and drink for sustenance (26).[48] The Proscribers also urge that the absence of sign indicates lack of permission, that silence effectively amounts to that thing's Proscription (6,20,24), and in response to them (section B) al-Jaṣṣāṣ deploys his most refined arguments.

He suggests that since there is no sign to indicate the moral status of breathing, and since breathing must be permissible, we know that as a rule the absence of a sign of goodness or detestability is a sign that the act is to be further evaluated. In this it differs from those acts that immediately display their detestability, for instance. Once acts are placed on the heap of things not immediately detestable or Obligatory, they are to be investigated for usefulness or harm. When the balance between these two elements is totted up, the result constitutes a sign of its status: either *useful*, in which case it is good and therefore Permitted, or on balance *harmful*, in which case it is detestable and therefore Proscribed. Both al-Jaṣṣāṣ and the Proscribers believe in innate abilities to "read" creation, but while the world is a hostile and treacherous place for the Proscribers, it is a beneficent and straightforward place, ours to use unless otherwise informed, for the Permitters.

In his brief fifth section (E), al-Jaṣṣāṣ takes on those who deny that creation is readable in moral terms. His argument against them is simple—really too simple in fact to convince. He dismisses their point by saying that "they agree with [our] principle when they say 'there is no consequence for the doer of it' "(28). They too are optimists. What he has failed to grasp, however, is that when his opponents say "the Proscriber of ingratitude is God most high Who established indications of these [rules]" (29), they are pleading that there is a radical discontinuity between the time before and the time after Revelation. These No Assessors say that the significance of the *Qur'ān* lies not in the fact that it is *a* form of Revelation (extra-natural) among others, but that it is *the* prior condition for communication between the transcendent and the mundane realms. Since in Islamic *heilsgeschichte* it was the *Qur'ānic* moment that created the Muslim community ex nihilo, an argument heightening and highlighting the significance of the *Qur'ān* is sufficiently attractive to require a more substantial refutation than the one al-Jaṣṣāṣ deigns to give. It would seem that he has not quite grasped the religious force of the No Assessment argument.[49]

He closes with proof texts from *ḥadīth* and *Qur'ān* that establish that *after* Revelation, good things are permitted because of their usefulness and that things about which there is no indication are allowable. The implication is that Revelational silence has always meant permission (see especially 34c).

Is this a Mu'tazilī text? Al-Jaṣṣāṣ certainly shares certain notions with the Mu'tazilah. He uses the calculus of harm to infer the relative goodness or detestability of an act. And he uses the term *wajh*, which for the Mu'tazilah is a technical term having to do with the ontology of the act.[50] Yet, the most striking fact about the *Fuṣūl*'s discussion is that al-Jaṣṣāṣ is not concerned with the issues of *being* (ontology) that characterize the Mu'tazilah argument.[51] He has no section on "esteeming and detesting *(al-taḥsīn wa-l-taqbīḥ)*, in the technical sense, nor does he discuss attributes, accidents, or essences. All that concerns him is knowing. Indeed, al-Jaṣṣāṣ avoids *goodness* and *detestability* but rather prefers to discuss "*Obligatory*" and *forbidden,* terms of Permission and Proscription.[52] In this he is closer to the Shāfi'ī al-Qaffāl than to the Mu'tazilī al-Ka'bī or Abū l-Ḥusayn al-Baṣrī. Finally we note that al-Jaṣṣāṣ defines Obligatory and Proscribed not in terms of the blame (*dhamm*) or praise (*madḥ*) deserved by the doer, but by reference to punishment and reward. His definitions therefore more closely resemble those of Ibn Qudāmah the Ḥanbalī, than those of any Mu'tazilī whose works survive.[53]

General Themes

Al-Jaṣṣāṣ's essay at resolving the problems of the before revelation complex should be seen as creative and not responsive; this dispute is less about dogma than it is about competing visions of the world. For the Permitters, moral knowledge can always be attained from the world, and those who deny it, deny the foundation of religious knowledge itself, for we know of God from the world's signs. Recognition of Revelation depends upon this prior apprehension of a Creator who may send messengers. For al-Jaṣṣāṣ, the world is rich with meaning. It is filled with signs. Muslims differ from non-Muslims only in that they alone may read the world's signs against another set of signs which are of guaranteed veracity—Revelation. That the world is full of signs is certainly a Qur'ānic position, but it is a notion that his opponents explicitly repudiated.[54] A specific instance of the use of signs is the calculation of harm that allows one to consider the relative balance of good and detestability, benefit and harm from the use of a thing (8,10,17,19). The usefulness of a thing, in al-Jaṣṣāṣ's view, is as much a sign as a Qur'ānic verse, and to ignore these signs is like ignoring Revelation. It leads one to harm in the next world, for even those living without Revelation are made responsible to act virtuously.

The indicativity of the world is only comprehensible if one assumes, with al-Jaṣṣāṣ, the analogous quality of the pre- and post-Revelational, and the transcendent and immanent worlds. One of the most prominent aspects of al-Jaṣṣāṣ's argument is the high degree of *consistency* he assumes between moral life before and after Revelation. Acts that the *'aql* knows as Obligatory before Revelation must be Obligatory after Revelation (8). The very definitions of Obligatory, Proscribed, and Permitted seem for al-Jaṣṣāṣ to be primordial and independent of Revelation. Thus before and after the Revelation, "*wājib*" means that "for the doing of which one deserves reward and for its shunning, punishment" (2).

Most startling, perhaps, is al-Jaṣṣāṣ's assignment of the same status to persons before and after Revelation: before Islam has come, persons are "made-responsible" (*mukallaf*), just as they are after it (2,9,11,17,18,32). So sure is he of the obvious similarity between the pre- and post-Revelational worlds that he considers it prima facie absurd to suppose that thanking the benefactor, for example, might ever be other than Obligatory (28). There are, therefore, limits to Revelation's power to confer moral value, and these amount to limits on God. Obligatory things *cannot* be declared harmful by Revelation, because that would mean God had provided either a false or a futile sign. Al-Jaṣṣāṣ indeed argues that God is *constrained* to provide a sign of the harmfulness of the act (para. 12). While the scope of morality is enlarged by seeing the world as always significant, at the same time the contrast is flattened between the stipulations of Revelation and the dictates of self-interest.

If, for al-Jaṣṣāṣ, there is so little difference between moral knowledge and moral culpability before and after Revelation, what is Revelation? It seems clear that for this particular fourth century Ḥanafī scholar, Revelation is a source of *knowledge*, as 34c (quoting *Qur'ān* 5:101) suggests: the information Revelation brings, while it may be privileged in content, is not privileged in type. For al-Jaṣṣāṣ Revelation augments knowledge by providing information about those things that seem neutral but which turn out to have some other assessment (8); this Revelational data *confirms* knowledge otherwise derived, through the *'aql*, from the world (13,33).[55]

In sum then, al-Jaṣṣāṣ has a minimal or "low" view of Revelation in relation to moral acts. Revelation is one source of knowledge among others, and it is not categorically different from these other sources in either scope or authority. One who seeks moral knowledge has to examine all the sources: not only *Qur'ān* and *sunnah* but likewise the created world and the resources of the *'aql*.[56]

Later Ḥanafīs

Samarqandīs and Iraqīs. According to Madelung, there were two varieties of speculative thought (often called Māturīdism) vying for Ḥanafī allegiance.[57] In *uṣūl al-fiqh* the sources speak of at least three regional schools, Irāqī, Samarqandī, and Bukhāran, and two methodologies, ancient and modern.[58] In epitome, Madelung tells us the Samarqandīs were closer to Mu'tazilīs, the Bukhārans, closer to Ash'arīs and Ḥanbalīs in doctrine.[59] It would seem that the Iraqīs occupy a space to the "left," that is, the Mu'tazilī side of the spectrum of the Samarqandīs, particularly if we take al-Jaṣṣāṣ as a representative Iraqī. Supposing al-'Ayyāsh's commentary on *Musallam al-Thubūt* to be an example of the "modernist" position, it seems that the modernists, using the technical language of late theology, backed still further away from the Iraqīs, particularly on questions of innate moral knowledge.[60]

Because of accidents of publication, there are fewer Ḥanafī sources than Shāfi'ī or Ḥanbalī available to us, so this reconstruction can only be tentative, but on the before revelation problem it appears that the Iraqīs took a Permitted line closest to the Basrans, the Samarqandīs hedged somewhat more but were still Permitters. The Bukhārans were rather uncomfortable with Permittedness, but could not deny it altogether, and the "moderns" tended to move further in a Bukhāran direction.[61] Nonetheless, all of these varieties of Ḥanafīs were methodologically committed to understanding the positions of the Imām of their school, whose position on what were seen as proto-Before Revelation questions was well-known and (sometimes reluctantly) transmitted. This means that the Ḥanafī position, even of the most reluctant modernist discussing the Bukhāran position, will always differ from the Shāfi'ī/Ḥanbalī position.

Ḥanafī Assumptions

Of course it is not merely Ḥanafī dogmas that are distinct; the entire Ḥanafī legal methodology is distinct from that of other schools.

A helpful way into the debate between Ḥanafī Permitters and (particularly) Shāfi'ī No Assessors is the discussion in al-Zanjānī's (d. 656/1258) *Takhrīj* of the difference between the Ḥanafī and Shāfi'ī theory of assessments. Al-Zanjānī, who belonged to the Shāfi'ī school, points out that for the Shāfi'īs, most of the *shar'ī* assessments and *shar'ī* concepts have nothing to do with the things to which they are attached, but are ultimately arbitrary (*taḥakkum*^{an}) and ritualistic (*ta'abbud*^{an}).[62] For the Ḥanafīs however, the assessments of an act are attributes of the act's substrate and essence, which are established for the acts by God, and which He stipulated, motivated by nothing but the welfare of His bondsmen.[63]

Indeed, al-Zanjānī says that for the Ḥanafīs, the Obligation and Proscription, goodness and detestability, Recommendation and Discouragement attributed to an act in assessing it are actual attributes of the acts so described. Hence the major division of acts is into those whose values are recognized by the *'aql* and those whose true assessment awaits Revelation.[64] The Ḥanafīs, al-Zanjānī says, believe that if the stipulations of Revelation were not for the bondsmen's welfare, they would be pointless and therefore blameworthy, like a sensible person carrying water from one ocean to another.[65] The Ḥanafīs, then, (at least in seventh-century Baghdad) believed that all acts have a purpose and that there is a moral quality which is part of the acts' ontologies. Assessments are recognitions of those qualities, which on the one hand God has assigned to acts for reasons having to do with the welfare of the bondsmen, and which on the other He has allowed the *'aql* to recognize, in many cases, spontaneously. It would follow that the time before and the time after Revelation are homologous since the ontology of the act is the same at both times. It is at least possible therefore that some acts' values can be known as the act itself is known, by the *'aql* both before and after Revelation.

Ḥanafī Epistemology. Later Ḥanafīs remained rationalists but they drew a sharp line between themselves and the Mu'tazilah.

> As for the Mu'tazilah, for them the *'aql* is assessor (*ḥākim*) of goodness and detestability and it leads necessarily to knowledge of [the assessments of acts], but among us, [the Ḥanafīs] the Assessor of [acts] is God and the *'aql* is the instrument (*ālah*) of knowledge about them. God created knowledge to result from the *'aql*'s inquiry, when one inquires soundly. . . .

> For [the Mu'tazilah] the *'aql* makes acts Obligatory, Permits them and Proscribes them, without God assessing them whatsoever, but as for us, the Assessor of good and detestable is God and He is ever higher than to have anyone other than He assessing.[66]

The Ḥanafīs believed themselves to differ from the Mu'tazilah in that for them God retained His sovereignty as assessor, but arranged things so that humans could know assessments by means other than Revelation. For most Ḥanafīs, the quality of the act was not in abeyance (*mawqūf*) until Revelation. Rather, because humans can know goodness and detestability, these two are the ground (*manāṭ*) of the connection between [good acts/detestable acts] and the assessment.

> So if one grasps [the assessment] of some things like faith and thanking and infidelity, it is God most high who links the assessment of [ingratitude and infidelity] with blaming the bondsman. This is the approach of [the classical period Ḥanafīs] and the Mu'tazilah. However, among us [moderns], punishment is not Obligatory on account of *'aqlī* detestability [before the *shar'*], as it is not after the arrival of the *shar'*, because of the possibility of forgiveness. This is by contrast to [the Mu'tazilah and the classical period Ḥanafīs] who based themselves upon the Obligatoriness of justice which for them meant conveying the reward to those who do the good deeds and conveying punishment to the ones who act detestably.
>
> [Other Ḥanafīs believe, however that] the good and detestable are indeed *'aqlī* but [these judgments do] not compel [the *shar'ī* assessments] and do not reveal the connection to blaming the bondsman. This is the preferred position for Shaykh ibn Humām, the author of the *Taḥrīr*. Also the author of this work, [*Musallam al-Thubūt*] follows it. I've also seen in some books, [Ḥanafī] scholars who propound statements like the statement of the Ash'arīs.[67]

Ḥanafīs agreed that the *'aql* could recognize moral assessments. They differed among themselves and with the Mu'tazilah only on the question of consequentiality. What does Proscription mean for the fate of someone who does the Proscribed act? The Mu'tazilah say that the indicants of its Proscription have been futile and God is unjust if He does not always punish the doer of the Proscribed act. The Ḥanafīs to varying degrees acknowledge the divine dispensation to do as He desires.

We have seen that for the circle of Abū Ḥanīfah the human, unaided by Revelation, can and must come to certain elementary forms of religious knowledge. It is this unambiguous but slightly difficult dogma that exercises Ḥanafī ingenuity throughout the following centuries. A clear instance of reconciliation between school-heritage and *zeitgeist* is the acrobatic argument of the Indian scholar al-Bihārī, author of *Musallam al-thubūt*, who was also something of a religious politician, who tried to denature the Ḥanafī position on non-Revelational knowledge of the Creator [al-Bihārī's portion in boldface, commentary in roman]:

> **Among the Ḥanafīs are those who say that the *'aql* has independently attained some of the assessments of God most high, and so this group regarded as Obligatory faith and forbade infidelity and everything unsuitable to Him** for everyone whatsoever, whether the summons had reached them or not, *even a compos mentis youth*—this is the statement of most Ḥanafīs like shaykh al-Imām 'Alamalhudá Abū Manṣūr al-Māturīdī and Imām Fakhralislām, and the master of the Mīzān [al-Samarqandī], and Ṣadralsharī'ah chose it as well as others. From Imām al-Humām it is related of **Abu Ḥanīfah** that he **would not excuse anyone for ignorance of his Creator because of the manifest indicants that** establish [God's] unity. . . . [68]

This would seem to be a fairly inflexible dogma from which to work, but author and commentator labor hard to whittle away its significance.

> **I say: Perhaps he means:** by "there is no excuse" **'after a period of contemplation has passed,'** for contemplation (*al-tā'mmul*) **[which] can take the place of the summons of the messenger in alerting the heart; this period differs,** and cannot be determined **because '*aql*s differ** in comprehension.

> The commentator adds:

> And this is what Fakhralislām [al-Bazdawī] means when he says: The meaning of our saying that he is not made-responsible by the '*aql* is that if God assists him with experience and grants him aid to grasp the consequences [of his acts], he is not excused even though the [Prophetic] summons has not reached him, based upon what Abū Ḥanīfah said, namely, if he reaches 15 years, his property cannot be withheld from him because he has passed the period of experience.[69]

In the 900 years or so that separates Abū Ḥanīfah from his Indian disciples, the world has changed. The kerygma of Abū Ḥanīfah, demanding of the non-Muslim majority that they acknowledge their "anonymous Islam" has been transmuted into a milder epistemological claim that sometimes some persons can replicate the knowledge that Muslims inherit by being Muslim. Unlike Shāfi'īs and Ḥanbalīs, these Ḥanafīs must come to terms with an earlier period in their history and they remain Permitters, albeit of a sort al-Jaṣṣāṣ would hardly recognize.

The Ḥanafīs trusted the independent *ʿaql*, but they perceived themselves to differ in many crucial respects from the Muʿtazilah, particularly in their ontological theory. As they understood it, the Muʿtazilah regarded assessments as acts of categorization performed by the *ʿaql* in response to the thing assessed. The Ḥanafīs seem to have seen Muʿtazilī epistemology as cognition involving only the assessor (the *ʿaql*) and the assessed (the act or thing). They, by contrast, envisioned a tripartite epistemology in which the *ʿaql* and thing are linked by God's assigning value to the act and then lodging knowledge of that value in the *ʿaql*. "God created knowledge [such that it is consequent] to the inquiry of the *ʿaql* when one inquires soundly."[70] In this sense, it is God, not the *ʿaql* that is the assessor. For the Ḥanafīs, the *ʿaql* is nothing more than an instrument devised to recognize the qualities of acts.[71] The Ḥanafīs sum up the difference between themselves and the Muʿtazilah thus:

> The Muʿtazilah say that the *ʿaql* is an ultimate cause (*ʿillah*)[72] for esteeming and detesting . . . and finally it is superior to the *rationes* of the *sharʿ*, for they do not accept that one can affirm by an indicant of the *sharʿ* what *ʿaql*s cannot grasp. . . .[73] However, the correct statement about this topic is our statement that the *ʿaql* discloses the competence [of the person to be made-responsible because he is *compos mentis*].[74]

The congruence between *ʿaqlī* assessment and *sharʿī* assessment establishes the competence of the individual and hence his responsibility to live morally. Where the Muʿtazilah saw the assessing process telling us about the thing assessed, the Ḥanafīs saw the assessing process as telling us about humankind.

What did the Ḥanafīs say about the thing? Like the Muʿtazilah, they believed that things had qualities that conformed to their assessments.

The fundamental difference between the No Assessors and the Permitters is that for the No Assessors, as we shall see,

> the goodness of an act . . . comes from its being commanded, and for [the Ḥanafī Permitters] not so, but rather it is commanded because it is good. God Most High said {God has commanded the just and the beneficent} implying its justness and beneficence before the command. However its [being good] is hidden from the *ʿaql*, then God manifests [its goodness] by the command . . . indicating its goodness because of a quality (*maʿná*) [resident in the act] itself."[75]

We should see the Ḥanafīs as they saw themselves: They occupied the middle space between the theistic subjectivism of the Ashʿarī/Ḥanbalīs and the objectivist phenomenalism of the Muʿtazilah.[76] They want to affirm that the act is good for a reason, and that reason cannot simply be because it is commanded. They are unwilling to abandon teleology.[77] Therefore the goodness of an act must be either part of the thing itself, or something to facilitate a thing that is good in itself: e.g., hastening (*sa'ī*) is not good in itself (*li-dhātīh*) as worship is, but hastening to worship is good.[78]

It should be clear that the Ḥanafīs differed from the Mu'tazilah. Mere rationalism does not establish that a scholar is one of the "freethinkers of Islam" as the Mu'tazilah have been called. The Ḥanafī position, seen structurally, lies in various places between the Ash'arī and Mu'tazilī position. Seen historically it preserves a kerygma in which a dynamic but minoritarian Islam summons—on the basis of moral universals—the non-Muslim or nominally Muslim to conform to the dictates of Revelation. Revelation's content is not new, though it is sometimes different. It does not divide Muslims from non-Muslims but affirms what binds them. It confirms its extra-natural message by reference to naturally obtained certainties. Revelation's knowledge, for the Ḥanafīs, is unique in content but not in category.

The Permitters versus their Opponents

Although the Permitters most probably came to their position not in critique of their opponents but asserting a positive position, all Permitters were adept in its defense, and in their attacks on alternatives.

The Ḥanafīs seem to spend the bulk of their effort attacking Ash'arī No Assessors. For example, the Ḥanafīs reported the Ash'arīs saying that because human acts in general cannot be said to be "unconstrained," the terms *Permitted* and *Proscribed* apply only as technical terms, as it were, for acts so assessed by the *shar'*.

> The act of the bondsman is not by his own choice, according to [al-Ash'arī], and so is not characterized as good or detestable. Nonetheless, despite this, he permits [the act's] connection with reward and punishment through the *shar'*, based upon [his argument] that it is not detestable for God to reward[79] the bondsman or punish him for what was not his to choose.[80]

Although I am unable to locate the argument in any Ash'arī text, it is a credible assertion, since the Ash'arīs deny that humans bring acts into being, and in law acts compelled or randomly occurring are not said to be "good" or "detestable."[81] The corollary is that Ḥanafīs believed that for Ash'arīs, acts are good for no reason other than that they are commanded by God, or detestable because forbidden by Him. God could, if He so desired, damn one for honesty and reward one for lying.[82] Predictably, the Ḥanafīs defend the value of the *'aql* and the justice of God, though their style of argumentation seems more to provide a counter-assertion than an argument.[83]

Another tack used against the No Assessors is Sharīf al-Murtaḍá's in the *Dharī'ah*. He argues that there is, in effect, no difference between what he calls the *Refraining* position (*waqf*) and the *Proscribed* position,

> with regard to the Obligation to refrain from undertaking [the act]. They differ only in rationale: the Proscribers do not act because they believe that [in undertaking the act] they are undertaking something recognizably detestable; those who Refrain do not act because they cannot be guaranteed that they are not, thereby, undertaking something Proscribed and detestable.[84]

Yet we have argued all along that members of every school participated in every position, and so the critical voice we shall present at greatest length is the Ḥanbalī, al-Kalwadhānī (d. 510/1117), who was a Permitter and faithful transmitter of the work of Abū l-Ḥasan al-Tamīmī (d. 371/982).[85] Al-Kalwadhānī has by far the most extensive list of arguments against both Proscribers and No Assessors, and we may suppose that in his time, the late four hundreds and early five hundreds, both were prominent in argument against the Permitted position.

Al-Kalwadhānī against the Proscribers

Against the suspicions of the Proscribers, al-Kalwadhānī offers the optimism of the Permitters. Proscribers suggest that one should avoid the inclinations of the *'aql* as one avoids information that might conceivably be a lie. Al-Kalwadhānī replies that a witness is presumptively truthful unless there is proof to the contrary.[86] The Proscribers urge Muslims to shun what might be potentially reprehensible; al-Kalwadhānī replies that avoiding the thing might also be reprehensible, which would logically oblige one both to do and avoid the same act; indeed there may be more harm in refraining than in doing.[87] Moreover, the much-contested Qur'ānic dictate, {We do not chastise until We send a Messenger}[88] is offered as proof that humans had been immune to reproach for the use of useful acts until the arrival of Revelation.[89] The cheerful Permitter is to reflect thus: "I have a wise deity and He would not forbid both usefulness and harm." Therefore, on the basis of the *'aql*'s knowledge alone, one is to act, because the absence of a sign that something is detestable is a sign that it is good.[90]

Al-Kalwadhānī dismisses the Proscriber's claim that the world is God's property, and use without His permission is a transgression. Indeed, he argues, that, as property of God, we have an obligation to preserve ourselves by eating and drinking what is useful to us.[91] Otherwise, we could not breathe or move about from place to place.[92] It is a greater harm to refrain from useful acts, than to perform them.[93] Or we might say that on this basis no one has the right to use anything, which is absurd, so that the analogy to ownership of property is invalid from the start.[94] If the Proscribed argument is accepted, moreover, one would have to perform every possible ingratiating, or worshipful act, since there is at least a chance that it too may have been imposed, and neglect of that duty would be Proscribed.[95]

For al-Kalwadhānī, as for all Permitters, the world is a conundrum that, for a priori reasons, must have purpose; without purpose it is incomprehensible. Al-Kalwadhānī's data is the usefulness of acts, the inclination of the *'aql* to use these acts, and the benefit that accrues from their use.[96] It is impossible that these things are for someone else, (as the pleasures of Paradise are for the virtuous after Resurrection, not for the angels), or that they are a test, unless there is something to indicate this less likely explanation.[97] It could not be merely that He wishes to display His creative power, since He needn't conjoin accidents to bodies and make food.[98] Creation does not exist for God's benefit, since He is above benefit and harm. The only sensible explanation that remains is the Permitted position: that He created useful things to use, and that these things are Permitted—even wine—until Revelation arrives with more precise and informative guidelines.[99]

Al-Kalwadhānī against the No Assessors

Al-Kalwadhānī next attacks the agnostic position, which maintains either that there is no assessment of acts apart from those that the *shar'* provides (hence, before the *shar'* there can be by definition no assessments) or that, if there are assessments already assigned to acts, they are unknowable before Revelation. He refers to this position which we have generally called *No Assessment,* by its alternate name, *Refraining* (*waqf*).

Here the bulk of his argument is a prosecutorial insistence that either there is, or is not, punishment for doing useful acts, and that saying 'there is no punishment' is indistinguishable from saying "it is Permitted." Further, he insists on epistemological fair play: If the world is as inscrutable as the No Assessors believe, how is it they know that Refraining (in one of its meanings) is the appropriate human response to acts?

As we shall see and have seen, the definition of *mubāḥ*, which we consistently translate as "Permitted," is the crux here. For Permitters the term as used means "neutral," that is, uncharacterized by preference, blame, praise, reward, or punishment. Consequently al-Kalwadhānī hits again and again at his opponents.

> If the *'aql* is separated from the *shar'*, is it good for us to undertake these useful acts or not? If you say 'it is not good,' you have taken the

> Proscribed position [and all that we have said above against it, applies to you]. If you say 'it is good' then you have taken the Permitted position. . . . If you say 'the *'aql* cannot declare good or detestable,' we say, 'a *compos mentis* must either act or refrain. Do you blame one for both [acting and refraining]?' If they say, 'there is no blame,' then they have taken the Permitted position.[100]

The Refrainers want to argue that there is a *tertium quid*, that Proscription and Permission do not exhaust the analysis of pre-Revelational acts. Al-Kalwadhānī is determined to deny any such third possibility, asking what the epistemological ground of such a third assessment might be.[101]

> "If [when asked what the assessment of useful acts might be] they say, 'We don't know,' they have admitted the possibility of blame for that from which one cannot refrain. . . . Then [we say] 'By what do you know that the *'aql* has no standing in Permitting and Proscribing? If it is from the *shar'*, then [the absurdity] is clear. . . . 'Or [we] say 'You know by the *'aql* and so you have established that the *'aql* is capable of assessments and of indicating them.'
>
> It is said to them, 'Do you know the Permittedness of Refraining or not?' If they say, 'We don't know,' we ask why they undertake to Refrain; 'Can you not undertake other useful acts as you undertake to Refrain?' Or if they say 'We know of its Permittedness' we ask, 'How do you know?'. . .
>
> "Things must be either Permitted or Proscribed—for something to combine the two [assessments] is impossible because they are mutually contradictory, and denying them to things is not possible because that makes the things pointless (*'abath[an]*). . . . We cannot conceive of an act neither Permitted nor Proscribed."[102]

In sum, al-Kalwadhānī's strategy is to expose a foundation underlying the agnosticism of the Refrainers. That foundation is either Revelation, in which case it is irrelevant, or the *'aql*, in which case the battle becomes Proscribers versus Permitters.

Like other Permitters, al-Kalwadhānī and al-Tamīmī demand a morally stable world in which at least some things are immutably Obligatory or Proscribed. Thanking the benefactor is Obligatory and it is impossible for the *shar'* to Proscribe what in this case the *'aql* knows to be Obligatory.[103] To assert that moral knowledge might be impossible would be devastating to the Permitters because then, in their view, there would be no credible way by which to know the existence and moral perfection of God. In their view, one reflects upon the existence of a Creator, on the likelihood of His dispatching messengers, and when presented with Revelation, one infers from its miraculous character that it is of supernatural origin. Together with the knowledge that a good God does not deceive, one apprehends that the demands that this Revelation makes require fulfillment. If truth-telling is not fixed immutably in the moral firmament, then there is no solid basis on which to come to accept any of Revelation's claims.[104]

In the view of al-Kalwadhānī, logically, one has to assess acts. If it is denied that acts can be assessed, the religious consequences are troubling. How is it, however, that al-Kalwadhānī is certain of the assessment that the *'aql* makes? The answer is, essentially, an appeal to a benevolent nature. These judgments are elemental components of the *'aql*.[105] Wherever the *'aql* is found, there too we find praise for good deeds—such as thanking a benefactor—and blame for the detestable.[106] This is so with all people, whether they are people of "religion" or fatalists, or natural philosophers.[107] God, in this way, has a case against the heedless (*ḥujjah 'alayh*). To the objection that this view minimizes the significance of Messengers, making them merely conveyances of the details (*furū'*) of morality, al-Kalwadhānī replies that on the contrary, they have the greatest significance because they are the warning to the heedless, and they facilitate comprehension of the warnings, as a teacher facilitates reading a book by explaining the written forms.[108]

Unlike some critics of a position that we have seen and will see, it is clear that al-Kalwadhānī understands the positions he critiques. It is clear, however, that he does not agree that constraint upon God's freedom of action, and reliance upon a natural source of knowledge diminish the supernatural source. For many Muslims, these two principles—God's utter power and the categorical otherness of Revelation—were Islamically true and compelling and had to be affirmed even at the cost of paradox. It is arguable that the alternative position, the No Assessment position, drew its strength precisely from its illogicality and paradox which could symbolically express the ineffable importance of Islam in history and of God in the cosmos.

Conclusions

Three implications of the Permitted position seem clear:

1. That a consequence of arguing that the *'aql* is a source of moral knowledge is that Revelation is devalued, since there are other "signs" that supplement the *sam'* and allow one to make valid inferences about the moral qualities of acts.
2. That the world itself is evaluated most positively by those holding the Permitted position, since the mundane world is declared morally licit, with the presumption being that an act has been affirmed as good and acceptable in the absence of evidence to the contrary.

3. That in the Mu'tazilī view, God has tipped His hand at creation. Lies, for instance, have been made detestable and cannot be changed to "good" by Revelation or even perhaps by circumstance.[109] Mu'tazilīs and Ḥanafīs differ on the extent, but both see God as constrained to act in certain ways once the order of the world has been established.

The optimism of Permittedness fits well with the earlier centuries of Islam; perhaps a less certain, more ambivalent perspective however was best suited to the fifth and subsequent centuries in the central lands of Islamdom.

Chapter 5

"No Assessment"

Introduction and History

If the Proscribers are pessimistic, and the Permitters optimistic, the No Assessors are, characteristically, neither this nor that. They are agnostic, and believe that term well fits every human being in the absence of Revelation. The No Assessor position says that before Revelation there is No Assessment of an act, because Revelation is the source of assessments. This position is associated with the Ash'arīs, who tended to be Shāfi'īs in their jurisprudence;[1] it became the school position of the Ḥanbalīs as well, and as we saw in the last chapter, over time even the Ḥanafīs began to move in the Ash'arī direction.

The No Assessors dismiss the evidence of the "consensus of the gentiles" as insignificant. The No Assessors are unimpressed by the alleged congruence between the dictates of Revelation and those of the '*aql*. They are certainly unmoved by the assertion that God would have to tell humankind something of the moral axioms or He would be unjust. Theirs is a religiously grounded position. These scholars are unfazed by paradox because they hold a maximalist position on God's unfathomable sovereignty. Consequently moral life before or without Revelation is for them simply non-existent. To speak of the moral life of humans without the *shar'* is tantamount to speaking of the moral life of animals or madmen or children.

God and Islam could be viewed as a particularly sound and reliable part of the natural order or as distinctly removed from this world. Positions like the No Assessment position are found earliest among those who distinguish most severely between this world's rules and those of the other world.[2] Hourani, in his search for the roots of "theistic subjectivism," has found the following in al-Shāfi'ī's *Risālah*:

> Justice is to act in obedience to God; thus [humans] have a way to knowledge of justice and what is contrary to it.[3]

From this statement Hourani infers that al-Shāfi'ī held not only that God commanded the good, but that the good was understood to be what-God-commanded. It seems, then, the position that holds that there is no moral knowledge before Revelation has its roots deep in Islamic intellectual history, going back at least to the late second/early ninth century. Certainly by the early fourth Islamic century, the argument that there is No Assessment of an act without supernatural knowledge, together with its supporting constellation of counterarguments and proofs, was well formulated and defended. What happened between these two moments in Islamic intellectual history?

There seems to be no surviving textual evidence of continuity between al-Shāfi'ī and later, Ash'arī *kalām*. Yet given the rapid transmission of al-Shāfi'ī's (d. 204/820) thought to Baghdād, where figures like Aḥmad b. Ḥanbal (d. 241/855) and Dā'ūd al-Ẓāhirī (d. 270/882–3) identified themselves with al-Shāfi'ī and his positions, it is likely that some nascent form of "good-is-what-God-commands" was in currency among pietists in the middle to late third century. The position would have a natural appeal to those mistrustful of speculative thought. Yet its most persuasive exposition was by speculativists, defending pietists' slogans such as that al-Ash'arī with whom the No Assessment position is usually identified. The role of al-Ash'arī himself in the development of this argument is far from clear. His position on thanking the benefactor is known (he believed it not to be incumbent without Revelation).[4] We understand the No Assessor position best, I believe, if we understand its relation to the famous passage in his *Kitāb al-Luma'* where he argues that a lie is detestable only because God made it detestable "and if He had esteemed it good, it would be good, and if He had ordered [us] to it, there would be no gainsaying him."[5]

The No Assessor position has two prerequisites. One must first link assessment solely to Revelation, and one must be able to conceive of acts being assessed other than they are: one must be able to imagine thanking the benefactor as a condemned activity. Otherwise, the assessments of the '*aql* will always be present somewhere in the process of assessment, and as '*aql*s exist before and after Revelation, so too will assessments. The radical theistic subjectivism of al-Ash'arī is the intellectual prerequisite for No Assessment. It is ungrounded in anything outside the sphere of the transcendent—which for the convinced makes its claim stronger; for the unconvinced, of course, it removes the possibility of discussion. No matter; the No Assessment position was held, and could only have been held, in the central Islamic lands where there was no need to demonstrate the truth of Islam—there was only the recurring need to assert its sovereignty over other norms and kinds of knowledge.

As a school position, No Assessment subsumes another early position on this question. In early references to a third position besides Permitted and Proscribed, the sources speak of "the people of Refraining" (*ahl al-waqf*). The term can refer both to refraining from an act—assessment, in this case—or to suspension of effect: One can either not rule on a case because one cannot come to a decision, or one can have come to a decision but decline for some reason immediately to pronounce it and have it come into effect. Some of the people of Restraint said that while there might be an assessment for acts, without Revelation it is not known what it might be. Others said simply that before Revelation, God refrained from assessing.[6]

The indeterminacy between the two Refraining positions appears in the earliest surviving *waqf*-position text, al-Khaṭīb al-Baghdādī's (d. 436/1044) *Kitāb al-Faqīh*, where he discusses the "assessment of things before the *shar*'."

> Scholars disagree concerning [acts] from which it is possible to benefit before the arrival of the *shar*'. Among them there are those who say that [these acts] are [recognizable by humans as] Proscribed, [by God] so that it is not Permitted to benefit from them, nor to perform them. Among them are those who say that [these useful acts] are Permitted, since whoever believes a thing Permitted for him may use it and possess it. And among them are those who say that it is something "in abeyance"(*'alá l-waqf*): it may not be determined that it is either Permitted or Proscribed.[7]

Though he uses the standard phrases of the No Assessment position—that the *shar*' is the sole source for Permission or Proscription—he seems to believe that an assessment for acts existed from the beginning; it was just not yet in force. Its assessment is in abeyance until the arrival of the *shar*'.[8]

Al-Khaṭīb's criticism emphasizes that the *'aql* does not judge—not even on the immorality of usufruct without Permission: "the taking of possession [of a thing not owned] by mankind: it is forbidden to make use of that thing without the Permission of its owner by the *shar*' (*bi-l-shar*'), not by the *'aql* (*dūna l-'aql*)." Al-Khaṭīb al-Baghdādī objects to the idea that utility might be a sign that indicates its assessment. Utility does not establish Permission, he says, because a useful thing, even if forbidden, is not necessarily futile (*'abath*); it could, rather, be a test, or its purpose could be to indicate God's creation of it. What the purpose of that thing might be cannot be said, since we cannot assign ultimate causes to God's actions.[9] The last point is the nub of the matter for al-Khaṭīb. To assign causes to God's action is to confuse the realm of the transcendent and the immanent and suppose God to be subject to rules at the level of human understanding. God cannot, he believes, be in any way constrained.

No other Refrainer text survives, but from the criticisms preserved in al-Kalwadhānī's *Tamhīd* we can reconstruct somewhat more of the Refrainer position. It appears that, like some Proscribers, the Refrainers argued that the *'aql* by itself will imagine the value both of doing and not doing an act. Accordingly, it is paralyzed and refrains from assessing until Revelation comes to tip the balance in one direction or the other. Humans simply lack the knowledge to make a meaningful assessment, and so ought to Refrain.[10] Another approach is to point to the Qur'ānic statement, {We do not chastise until we send a Messenger} and {The People have no case [against God] after the Messengers} and argue that without punishment, there are no significant assessments. It is not merely that the Refrainers point to the decisive quality of Revelation, but they argue that it is in fact Obligatory to say nothing, as with a jurisconsult who is asked for an opinion on something for which he can find neither Revelational information for or against.[11] The Refrainers are quoted as saying explicitly that the opposing, Permitted position minimizes the significance of the messengers and makes their dispatch nothing more than the conveying of details.[12] The Refraining position, as Sharīf al-Murtaḍá pointed out, meant refraining from action, and may be considered part of the scrupulousness movement of various ascetics.[13] The Refraining position in its agnostic mode did not enter into the thought experiment of the before revelation complex sufficiently to make its point. Scrupulous restraint is correct but not persuasive. Another interpretation of the Refraining position was more assertive. For these Refrainers, for all intents and purposes there was No Assessment until Revelation because there could be No Assessment. God is the Assessor and until Revelation comes with the deontic command there are no grounds on which to make transcendentally significant assessments.

The No Assessors of the Classical Period

At some point the Refraining position crystallized into the No Assessor position. Given the importance of al-Bāqillānī in the development of classical Ash'arism, and given that many of the distinctive arguments of later No Assessors are attributed to him, it seems reasonable to suppose that No Assessment was articulated first by this talented Mālikī Ash'arī.[14] The other major source for No Assessor argumentation appears to be Ustādh Abū Isḥāq al-Isfarā'īnī (d. 418/1027), whom al-Juwaynī—like Abū Isḥāq, a Nishapurī—also quotes extensively.[15] These two scholars most probably articulated the core of the No Assessment position as we know it from later Shāfi'īs and Ḥanbalīs.

For those who hold this position, possible sources of knowledge such as the *'aql* do not belong beside the discussion of "real" sources of signs—the Qur'an and *ḥadīth*. As part of the process of describing the nature of the assessment, these scholastics generally spend time deriding other definitions of the *ḥukm*; how better to catalog alternatives than to discuss the term *ḥukm* abstracted from time and history? This discussion in No Assessor sources is characteristically found in the definitional, prolegomena section of the *uṣūl* work. There the transcendent assessment (*ḥukm shar'ī*) is distinguished from other sorts of assessments.

The possibility of knowing depends on knowing where to look, and for the No Assessors, knowledge of "where to look" for the assessment is provided by first defining what the assessment is: a locution (*khiṭāb*) of the *shar'*.[16] Accordingly, the Ẓāhirī and No Assessor Ibn Ḥazm (d. 456/1064) denies that the judgments of the *shar*ʿ—Permitted, Obligatory, and Proscribed—can be found elsewhere: specifically they cannot be found in the ʿ*aql*.[17]

> We do not say that the Permitting of a thing (*ibāḥatu l-shay*ʾ) or its Proscription, is in the ʿ*aql*; in it is only the distinguishing of existents according to how they are (*alá mā hiya* ʿ*alayh*) and [the ability] to understand the locution (*khiṭāb*).

Though he denies that the ʿ*aql* makes transcendent assessments, it is clear that this is not, like Ibn Ḥazm's putative leader Dāʾūd, a denial of any value to the ʿ*aql* whatsoever.[18] Ibn Ḥazm, rather, denies the epistemology of the Permitters and says assessments are to be understood as statements linked to reward and punishment. Without Revelation there can be no knowledge of reward and punishment, hence no evaluation of acts.[19] Further, he denies "continuity of status" between the times before and after Revelation, arguing that God has indeed created things (passions, for instance) that He has (subsequently) Proscribed:

> [God] has created in us passions that incite wickedness from every beautiful woman we see and every handsome youth, and drinking wine in gardens, and taking everything the lower soul deems good, and rest, and ceasing to oppose the heathen by the sword, and sleeping through the prayers on hot noondays, and cool luncheons: then He forbade all of these to us.[20]

Ibn Ḥazm's belief in the decisive nature of Revelation is seen most clearly in his account of a virtuous hermit who is a moral paragon in every respect but that he never hears of Muḥammad except in the context of lies and the attribution of evil characteristics to him. When he dies uncertain of, or in denial of Muḥammad's mission, "is not his fate everlasting, eternal, permanent Fire, without end?" By contrast, a corrupt Jew or Christian, innocent of no sin and who has fought against Muslims: if he should become convinced of the mission of Muḥammad, and cleanse himself of all religion (*dīn*) save Islam, and then die, "is he not of the people of Paradise? . . ." Many indubitable Islamic truths—e.g., the special status of Muḥammad and of the other prophets—are not found in the ʿ*aql*; how then can one expect to find the Permission and Proscription, esteeming good and detesting? "All of these things await what God has sent down in His Revelation, period."[21]

Moreover, in what would seem to have been an obvious point, Ibn Ḥazm argues that since Adam, the first man, was a prophet, the entire argument for the need of ʿ*aqlī* judgments in the absence of the *shar*ʿ is pointless.[22] Ibn Ḥazm also discusses maturity: If it were Permissible to remain without *shar*ʿ (Adam's prophecy and others ignored), our judgment would be like our judgment before we attain puberty—of no moral significance. "The condition of [one whom the *shar*' has not reached] is as the condition of one who has not reached the threshold of being made-responsible until he reaches maturity."[23] Those to whom the *shar*' has not yet been transmitted, though it has arrived in the world, are morally incapacitated, morally minor, or morally incompetent.

For the Shāfi'ī Abū Isḥāq al-Shīrāzī (d. 476/1083), the before revelation complex provides an opportunity to discuss various matters of interest.[24] After sketching the various positions, he supports the "no judgment" position: "else, for what did the *shar*' come?" He adds, "and why is it possible that the *shar*' comes with Permission one time and Proscription another?"[25]

THE NISHAPURĪS: AL-JUWAYNĪ AND AL-GHAZĀLĪ

In the work of the great Ash'arī theologians and Shāfi'ī legalists al-Juwaynī and al-Ghazālī, the No Assessment position reaches its classical form. The position defended is still that of *lā ḥukma lahu* (No Assessment), but now the defense is more formal, more philosophic, more technical in its critique.

With these grand masters of Ash'arī *uṣūl*, a subtler criticism of the Mu'tazilī position begins to take shape. The fault of the Mu'tazilah, say al-Juwaynī and his pupil al-Ghazālī, lies not in asserting that the '*aql* makes assessments, but in suggesting that those assessments are what we would call *moral* assessments. The '*aql* is reconceptualized by the Ash'arīs and is understood to be not a collection of knowledge, but an instrument for discrimination and recognition of possibility. Thus for them it cannot be itself an *aṣl*, a source of knowledge as the Qur'ān is a source, but it is a tool used to manipulate the data of the world and Revelation. Nonetheless, it does evaluate and in that sense makes "judgments." Yet these assessments made by the '*aql* are not linked to reward and punishment in the hereafter, or obedience and rebellion here on earth. They are rather, as al-Ghazālī makes clear,[26] mere prudential evaluations of situations, and so cannot be the equivalent of *shar'ī* assessments: Self-interest cannot be synonymous with morality.[27]

Al-Juwaynī and the Burhān

Al-Juwaynī's *Burhān fī uṣūl al-fiqh* is a difficult work,[28] and in the very obscurity of his syntax and vocabulary we can see him groping toward a new exposition of the before revelation complex. The *Burhān* is a synthesis of the new Ash'arī school's pondering this problem, and in it he quotes liberally from his predecessors, especially Ustādh Abū Isḥāq al-Isfarā'īnī (d. 418/1037) and Qāḍī Abū Bakr al-Bāqillānī (d. 403/1013). Yet al-Juwaynī is trying, not always successfully, to push beyond his masters, and while he attributes to them many of his arguments, he also extends and supplements their positions.[29] It is rather difficult to represent al-Juwaynī's argument, since it is so unpolished, so inarticulate at times. It is most helpful to begin with his agendum throughout this work.

As an Ash'arī, he must emphasize the gulf between God and humankind. To this end he established that human assessments are not objective responses to the situation as it presents itself. Our ascription of good to some things and detestable to others is not a necessary (*ḍarūrī*) recognition of the moral nature of those things, because, as al-Bāqillānī had pointed out, these ascriptions are disputable.[30] What is advanced as knowledge, is instead ignorance.[31] His opponents assert that "the '*aql* comprehends veracity and falsehood, and demands veracity."[32] To the contrary, says al-Juwaynī, "what *they* think good or detestable, they ascribe to us all."[33] His opponents want to argue that the '*aql* merely recognizes the moral quality of the act, because that quality is an attribute of its being. This is not so, because the assessment is grounded in command and prohibition.[34] The implication here, developed by his student al-Ghazālī, is that human assessments are not to be trusted because they are shaped by human prejudice and desire.

The assessments of the '*aql* are also demonstrably not correct because they deviate from the assessments of Revelation. To drink wine is not Proscribed in all cases; if one is perishing of thirst, one is Obliged to drink wine.[35] Likewise causing pain to beasts and infants without compensation would seem to be detestable, but is in fact a good.[36] Telling a falsehood to rescue a people from destruction is also good, despite the '*aql*'s indication that falsehood is detestable.[37] To the Proscribers al-Juwaynī points out how counter-intuitive Prohibition is to the '*aql*:

[quoting al-Bāqillānī]

> [Consider the case of] One who owns an inexhaustible lake, and who is characterized by liberality, and is in no need of improvement of his property, [while at that moment] his slave is panting with thirst; a mouthful will quench his thirst, and even the froth of water will suffice him. The owner is aware of the thirst of [his slave], and there is no intellectually perceptible prohibition of [the use of] the amount set aside from the lake, which [in any case] will not be depleted an appreciable amount by what is taken from it.[38]

In other words, in such a situation it would be absurd to expect the owner to Proscribe use of the lake to his slave.

When it comes to the Permitters, al-Juwaynī takes a conciliatory position:

> As for the people of Permission, there is no difference, essentially, with them: they do not mean by Permission the arrival of information about [the assessments], they mean by it the equivalence of the matter, as far as

> doing it and refraining [are concerned]; the matter is [for them also] as we mentioned [above].[39]

This is not to say that he takes the Permitted position; it is only that he agrees that there is nothing to suggest that doing or not doing the act will have any consequence.

Al-Juwaynī's opponents are, he believes, in general, guilty of blurring the distinction between the immanent realm (*al-shāhid*) and the transcendent realm (*al-ghā'ib*), as with thanking the benefactor. "[Those holding the position contrary to al-Juwaynī's] allege that thanking is Obligatory immanently, then they adjudge that to apply [also] to the transcendent. This obviously fails. What they mention—if it were accepted—would [be the case] with respect to [thanking's] usefulness, but the Lord Most High is above attribution of usefulness and harm."[40]

Al-Juwaynī's summary statement is far-reaching in its consequences—more so, one suspects, than he realizes, for in it he grants the power of the *'aql* to make assessments, but denies their relevance to the transcendent moral assessments, connected as they are with command and prohibition, eternal punishment and reward.

> The right course as we see it in this, unites the good parts of the contradictory schools so as to smooth them out. [And so] we say: We do not deny that rationality (*al-'uqūl*) requires [people] to avoid destructive things, and to utilize possibly-useful things, according to their particularities. Rejection of this is to go beyond the rational, but this is with respect to humans. Yet discussion of our topic is oriented toward what is declared detestable or good in the assessment of God most High. [From that perspective], even if [the act] brings us no damage, [and by doing it there is] a utility that the *'aql* does not permit us to neglect,[41] or what is similar to this, [nonetheless] the perception of its [transcendent] detestability and goodness [arises solely] from the [its association with consequences [directed] towards us by God most High, or His favoring us when we do [these things]. This is a transcendent [matter]. For God is praiseworthy and elevated above being affected by our harm or benefit. [Given that] the matter is thus, it is impossible [for us to determine] the detestability of a thing, or its goodness, in the assessment of God most high. It is not, however, forbidden to apply these two attributes [namely good and detestable],[42] [meaning that] a harm is [thereby] eliminated or it is possible to benefit, so long as [nothing] is ascribed to God, and it is not [implied that it is] required of God to punish or reward [on this basis].

Haltingly, al-Juwaynī's *Burhān* leads Shāfi'īs to what becomes the classic position of the school: Certainly the *'aql* motivates one to make use of useful things in Revelation's absence, and it is sensible to call these assessments *good* and *detestable* or even *Permitted*; or if the *'aql* suggests that the thing must be avoided, it may be called *Proscribed.* There is to be no confusion, however, of these mundane assessments with the Revelational, transcendent assessments brought by Revelation. It is only Revelation that informs us as to the eternal felicity or pain awaiting one who is obedient or rebellious. It remained for al-Juwaynī's star pupil, al-Ghazālī, to state this position in its definitive form.

Al-Ghazālī

Overview. Al-Ghazālī takes up the argument from al-Juwaynī, and in the early work of his, the *Mankhūl*, he clarifies and simplifies his teacher's position. The beauty of his argument comes from his addition of human psychology to the argument, an element never again employed with such subtlety. He suggests that "the *'aqlī* assessment is somehow connected to an "interest" (*gharaḍ*) on the part of the agent.[43] In the *Mustaṣfá* this psychologistic element (perhaps strengthened by al-Ghazālī's espousal of experiential Sufism) is stronger, and his brilliant exposition of what he takes to be Mu'tazilī thought is devastating.

Al-Ghazālī criticizes the rigidity of Mu'tazilī ontology by pointing to the variability of a given act's status, citing the Obligation to lie in order to protect a Prophet. He criticizes the Mu'tazilī attribution of knowledge to the *'aql* by explicitly characterizing the *'aql* as an instrument, and not a body of knowledge. Further, what seem to be universal perceptions of good and detestability are, in fact, rooted in interest or association with interest in a quasi-Pavlovian way. In sum, al-Ghazālī subjectivizes the Mu'tazilī position and attacks their ontology as insufficiently fluid to account for indisputable moral facts. In doing so he makes very few positive assertions about how the assessment is in fact determined, except to repeat the slogan, first found in Abū Isḥāq al-Shīrāzī, "the assessment is the dictum of the *shar'* (*al-ḥukm khiṭāb al-shar'*)."

Al-Ghazālī on Moral Epistemology and Ontology

Introduction. The three centuries between the probable origin of the before revelation complex and the flourishing of Abū Ḥāmid al-Ghazālī saw increasing refinement of argument and counterargument, and the evolution of school positions. By al-Ghazālī's time, it is hard to imagine a Shāfi'ī or Ḥanbalī defending the positions of the honored Ibn Surayj or Ibn Ḥāmid, and it is hard to imagine a Mu'tazilī defending al-Ka'bī's ontological rigidity. Yet within the established dogmatic boundaries of the middle fifth century, there is still room for innovation; this is still a good problem to think with. Even within the lifetime of al-Ghazālī himself we can see a development in his thought from his first work, the *Mankhūl*, to his penultimate work, the *Mustaṣfá*. The earlier *Mankhūl* is remarkably original and discontinuous from the argument and organization of its predecessors, particularly including the work of his teacher Imām al-Ḥaramayn al-Juwaynī. So original is this part of the *Mankhūl*, particularly in its epistemology, that one suspects that the matter was personally important to the young Ghazālī.[44]

For al-Ghazālī, the "graduate student," the question is whether the terms *good* and *detestable* have any objective meaning. For the Mu'tazilah, this assumption is prior: something is Proscribed because it is detestable. Al-Ghazālī comes to the conclusion that *good* and *detestable* are meaningless terms, morally speaking. It follows predictably then that any discussion of how one can know the good or detestable without Revelation is futile.

In both the *Mankhūl* and the *Mustaṣfá,* al-Ghazālī takes the polemically bold step of granting his opponents' assertions about the '*aql*—particularly that the '*aql* does indeed make judgments—in the *Mankhūl* he attacks the validity of '*aqlī* judgments with only a glancing reference to "interests" (*aghrāḍ*) that (he says) move the '*aql* to assess an act as good or detestable. By the end of his life al-Ghazālī has taken this latter point, developed it fully, and made it the centerpiece of his rebuttal. In the *Mustaṣfá* the number of al-Ghazālī's arguments has been trimmed. He is no longer picking at his opponents but is mounting a cutting attack from a position that seems deeply felt. Most importantly, his distrust of human motives has come to the fore and to occupy the most prominent place in his epistemology. Darkly, almost nihilistically, al-Ghazālī urges that human interest determines even the most altruistic acts. Now, it is not merely school allegiance that brings him to attack the '*aqlī* epistemology, but a profound, almost misanthropic, distrust of human nature. If there is a single consistent difference between the two works, and indeed between the *Mustaṣfá* and anything preceding it, it is that the older Sufi aspirant now writes with richer and deeper psychological insight. Alone among the Ash'arī discussants, he probes the motivations and sensitivities of humans in moral action. By the time of the *Mustaṣfá*, al-Ghazālī has arrived at a theory of knowing which, if it does not engage with that of, say, 'Abdaljabbār, is its match for subtlety and insight.

Content. Al-Ghazālī has one overriding purpose in this section of the *Mustaṣfá*, and that is to justify the slogan, "the assessment (*ḥukm*) is the dictum (*khiṭāb*) of God, connected to the acts of humankind" (3).[45] But the sophisticated rhetorician of the Niẓāmiyyah college does not baldly argue so; instead he takes as his two themes for this section

1. that there is no analogy from the mundane to the transcendent realm (with the two corollaries)—
   a. that Revelational knowledge is therefore unique and
   b. that the other sources of knowledge are too fallible to be the basis for moral knowledge, and

2. that there are alternative explanations that better account for the "facts" cited by the Mu'tazilah in defense of their positions.

The disjuncture between this world and the next, between the mundane and the transcendental is perhaps *the* issue between the No Assessors and their opponents.[46] Once this "otherness" of the other world is accepted, the uniqueness of Revelation as a source of knowledge follows, as does the fallibility and confusion of this world including knowledge of good and detestable whose ground is mundane knowledge.

Al-Ghazālī's definitions do most of his work, but these are definitions so blunt-edged as to be more slogans than nuanced conceptual descriptions.[47] The first of these slogans is, "an assessment is the dictum of *shar*'," or, in his formulation, "the assessment (for us) is tantamount to the dictum of the *shar*' when [the dictum] is applied to the acts of those made-responsible (9)." In effect, "assessment" (in the context of *uṣūl al-fiqh*) has no meaning other than "a statement about an act" applying the Revelational imperative.

From this controversial and dogmatic definition all else follows, for if the assessment is a *statement by someone* determining the status of the act or actor (rather than a *description of the act*) then the epistemological question becomes How do we find these statements? rather than What kind of act is this, so we can evaluate our response to it? To restrict moral knowledge about an act to knowledge of statements about the act is the whole of al-Ghazālī's enterprise, and that of his contemporary Ash'arī *uṣūlī*s.

Thus, "Obligatory is the declaration about [an act] 'do it and do not shun it (3),' " and more significantly "Permitted is the declaration about [an act] 'if you wish, do it; if you wish, shun it. (3).' " Contrast this definition with that of al-Jaṣṣāṣ who declares, *Permitted* means "that for which there is neither reward nor punishment." (2) For al-Jaṣṣāṣ, the assessment describes the consequences of the act: all acts which are inconsequential are called *Permitted.* For al-Ghazālī the assessment is a relational statement stipulating the character of an act and the actor who performs it. For al-Jaṣṣāṣ the assessment is descriptive, for al-Ghazālī it is an imperative.

Al-Ghazālī follows the same question-begging procedure when he defines the term *good* (*ḥasan*). In paragraphs (12) and (13), al-Ghazālī asserts that good is a hopelessly subjective term, and as such is shaped only by individual preference; it in no way describes an objective aspect of the act. This is so because goodness is not a part of the act itself (17) but is rather a term to describe individual preference or benefit from the act in question. It is this definitional part of al-Ghazālī's argument that is most readily accepted into later *uṣūlī* scholarship, because it is a sufficient argument, and persuasive, as far as it goes. Yet what makes the Ghazālian demonstration brilliant is not his tactics nor his insight into those who oppose him, but rather his shrewd examination of the implications of this entire debate. The result is nothing less than a complete moral psychology containing a persuasive account of spontaneous moral judgment and a plausible explanation of how mundane knowledge differs from transcendent knowledge.

In their debate with the Ash'arīs and others, the strongest argument in the Mu'tazilite arsenal was their appeal to experience. Human beings *do* make commonsense assessments of acts without the aid of parochial religious information. Some of these assessments are held so widely—across cultural and denominational lines—that they appear to be universal, and part and parcel of the human intellectual apparatus. How then can it be denied that the '*aql* can make moral assessments? Al-Ghazālī's task is to account for these universals in such a way as to distinguish them categorically from *real* moral assessments, namely, those obtained through Revelation. To do so he first questions the *reliability* of '*aqlī* assessments, then their *ontology*. By attacking the Mu'tazilī account of an act's ontology, he is able to attack both the means by which the '*aqlī* assessments are known, and their universality.

In order to question the reliability of '*aqlī* assessments, al-Ghazālī severs the commonsense link between assessments of quality (good/bad) and prescriptive assessments (Obligatory/Proscribed). Goodness has no meaning apart from the perspective of the assessor. What seems to be our spontaneous assessment of a thing as good, for instance, arises in fact from associating the thing judged with something else that we like (44f), or from imagining ourselves in a similar situation (50f), or it reflects no more than what we have been taught (42f). But most generally, these assessments of ours are produced by a subtle, often unconscious estimation of the extent to which an act or thing serves our objectives (12ff, 36ff, 41ff, 51ff, etc.). When the interests of many peoples are served by an act, it seems most emphatically and objectively good.

The most powerful part of Ghazālī's argument comes from his ability to pinpoint the ways in which human interests and objectives affect the assessment of acts far beyond what is obvious. The assessment of acts independently of Revelation is grounded either in egocentricity or unacknowledged dependence upon Revelational norms (36, 39). The ways in which egocentric interests affect moral assessment are various. The interest served may be conformity to habitual generalization, e.g., that a lie is always detestable (42). It may be aversion to what harms one's self, or is associated with harm (45f). It may be that one imagines the gratification of praise (51, 55), or one imagines oneself in a similar situation and seeks a kind of vicarious satisfaction of interests: Ghazālī gives as example a drowning man. When we see that man in danger, we imagine ourselves in a similar condition and by rescuing the man endangered, we obtain vicariously the satisfaction of being rescued. Proof of this is that one would risk life to save another human, but not an animal (50f).

If interests affect even what seem to be the most disinterested acts, then the claim of the Permitters and Proscribers that one can spontaneously discern the moral quality of the act is dissolved. Interest interferes and interposes itself between the *'aql* and the act in a way that makes the *'aql* entirely unreliable as a source of knowledge. This unreliability is proved not only by the demonstration that interest warps the *'aql*'s assessment, but also by showing that the *'aql* is often simply wrong. Its assessment of specific acts or things is too often due to the actions of the capricious faculty translated here as "fancy" (*wahm*). The fancy mediates between the deliberative *'aql* and the merely reactive sensual faculties. Its task is immediately to depict and react to the information of the senses. It is flighty, often misled, and undependable. And yet it is the fancy that conditions the post hoc assessments of the *'aql* (41ff). It accepts conditioned responses to stimuli that may or not be associated with a painful memory, or a pleasurable one (45, 46). Habit too leads the fancy into error by discouraging inquiry into the particularity of acts (42). One fails to recognize exceptions to general rules because of the deception of the fancy.

For all these reasons, the spontaneous judgments of the *'aql* are not trustworthy, and what seems to be universality is either coincidence or no more than the transient correspondence of interests. Such judgments as the *'aql* makes are certainly nothing to compare with the certainty and objectivity of assessments brought by Revelation. Al-Ghazālī argues that his opponents have too simple, one might say in the context of the fifth Islamic century, too much an out-dated notion of the nature of the *'aql* and its place in the process of knowing.

In two places (67ff, 87) al-Ghazālī directly confronts the question of the *'aql* and its place in the process of Revelation. Al-Ghazālī's opponents say the *'aql* Obliges humans to inquire into claims to be a Messenger, and then the compulsive force of Revelational miracles moves one to accept true Revelation as Truth. Al-Ghazālī, mistrusting human capacity as he does, is loath to have moral obligation rest upon frail human nature. Instead the claim of Revelation is for him independent of any faculty of humankind. God sends His command to inquire in Revelation, and the miracles compel one to attend to the Message. There is no innate urge to inquire. There is simply the prudential recognition that a Message, accompanied by miracles threatening everlasting punishment for disregarding it, ought to be taken seriously. The *'aql* merely recognizes or discloses, but properly speaking the esteeming good, detesting, Obliging, or Proscribing is done only by God. The only human participation in the process is the recognition of Revelation's claim to obedience and the innate inclination to avoid pain and seek pleasure. Moral categorization is not a human capacity.

With the role of the *'aql* redefined and limited to its proper position in the epistemological process, al-Ghazālī need say little about ontology. Since he accords no place to ontology in moral epistemology, he offers no alternative ontology, he simply shows that the evidence from which his opponents inferred ontological characteristics of goodness and detestability is misinterpreted.

When he shows that the possible agreement of *compotes mentis* is due to sources other than the spontaneous recognition of the *'aql*—to interest, socialization, habit—he is not only subverting the notion that the *'aql* is an epistemological faculty, he is also attacking his opponents' ontology as well. It is in the nature of essential ontological attributes that they are stable. A good act will always be good—categorically—regardless of accidents of circumstance. That killing can in a certain case be Permitted, even be Obligatory and commendable, or that lying can be Obligatory, when ordinarily both acts are Proscribed, makes it impossible that these acts or any others should have their moral quality as constituents of their being. It follows then that goodness and detestability are not part of an act's essential nature.

Al-Ghazālī's argument now trails off into repetitious assertions of the gulf between the phenomenal and the transcendent. He wends his way through thanking the benefactor and the assessment of acts before Revelation asserting that there is no Permission if there is no information from the Permitter. His counterarguments to Proscribers and Permitters are not as subtle as those in the *Mankhūl*, and he has clearly exhausted his interest after the brilliant section on psychology.

The *Mustaṣfá* was regarded by *uṣūlī*s as one of the classic works in the field, and its organization and in many cases its arguments were copied by the likes of Ibn Qudāmah the Ḥanbalī, and al-Rāzī, and al-Āmidī who were Shāfi'īs. Though the section on "interests" is transmitted by these later writers in condensed form, never again is the argument presented with this kind of passion and subtlety. Subsequent arguments seem increasingly to be assertions of dogma, that *this* not *that* is the definition of Assessment. While Ḥanafīs and Mālikīs develop new arguments and approaches, the Shāfi'īs, perhaps because of the decline of the central Islamic lands, are content with restatements of earlier successful arguments. The innate appeal of the No Assessment argument seems enough to carry it through the next 700 years.

Some Conclusions

The persuasive power of this No Assessment position comes in part from the limited nature of the claim it makes. In denying any moral status to the world before or outside Revelation, the No Assessors neither have to defend reasonable matters contradicted by Revelation nor have they to justify the Proscription of matters essential or useful to life itself: walking, breathing, etc.

Secondly, as we argue below in the chapter on thanking the benefactor, this medial position is in harmony with the historical situation of the Islamic fourth century and later times, a time of Muslim majority and power. At this time, as was not the case before, it is possible to ignore the moral claims of the smaller and intellectually irrelevant Christian, Persian, and Jewish communities. Moral life before the definitive Revelation is, in this view, non-existent or at least irrelevant.

The major challenge to this position comes from the experiential fact that human beings do tend to assess acts whether there is Revelation or no, and many of those assessments happen to be in accord with those of the *shar'*. It seems that until al-Juwaynī and al-Ghazālī satisfactorily disposed of this issue by their systematic analysis of the role of interest in moral judgment and the illusory independence of the *'aql*, the resolution of the debate is in doubt. After them, it is increasingly difficult to defend any position other than theirs. This combination of limited claims and brilliant analysis, in a context of Muslim triumphalism, made the No Assessment position the strongest available description of human moral life, and the one subscribed to by the majority of Muslim intellectuals in the central Islamic lands after the fifth Islamic century.

Not the least of its appeal, finally, is this position's embrace of paradox. Yes, humans make moral assessments, but no, they are not significant. Yes, the *'aql* is important, but no, it is not parallel to Revelation. Yes, acts in default of Revelational assessment are Permitted, but no, not before Revelation. The claims of the opposition are granted, yet at the end, the uniqueness and significance of Revelation are safeguarded.

Appendix

Two Translations of "Before Revelation" Texts: Al-Jaṣṣāṣ (Permitted) and Al-Ghazālī (No Assessment)

Translation of a Section from *al-Fuṣūl fī l-Uṣūl* of al-Jaṣṣāṣ[1]

[Chapter on] what is said concerning the assessments (aḥkām) of things before the coming of the Revelation (qabla majī'[2] al-sam') concerning Proscribing (ḥaẓr) and Permitting (ibāḥah). [3:247]

A. Introduction

1. Abū Bakr [al-Jaṣṣāṣ], upon whom be God's mercy said: The assessments[3] of the acts of those made-responsible,[4] which take place deliberately, are of three sorts in the *'aql*: Permitted[5] (*mubāḥ*), Obligatory (*wājib*), and Proscribed (*maḥẓūr*)."
2. 'Permitted' is that for doing which the person made-responsible does not deserve[6] reward, nor punishment for shunning it. 'Obligatory' is that for the doing of which one deserves reward, and for its neglect, punishment. 'Proscribed' is that for the doing of which one deserves punishment, and for the neglect of which there is reward."
3. Thereupon, people disagree concerning the assessment of those things by which it is possible to benefit,[7] before the coming (*majī'*) of Revelation (*al-sam'*).
4. Some say: All [useful acts] are Permitted, except those whose detestability or obligatoriness the *'aql* indicates.[8] Those [acts] whose detestability the *'aql* indicates are ingratitude, oppression, falsehood, and similar things. These things are Proscribed in the *'aql*. Those [acts] whose obligatoriness the *'aql* indicates are affirming God's unicity, thanking the benefactor, and what is similar to these [things]. What is other than these is Permitted.[9]
5. They say [further], When we say 'Permitted' we mean that there is no consequence for the actor; he [also] deserves no reward for doing [the act], as we have explained.

6. Others say: Other than that whose obligatoriness the ‘*aql* indicates, such as faith in God most high and thanking the benefactor and what is similar to these things, is Proscribed.
7. And others say: It is not said concerning things before the arrival (*wurūd*) of the Revelation (*al-sam*‘) that they are Permitted, and it is not said that they are Proscribed, because Permitted implies a permitter and Proscribed implies a proscriber.

In addition, they say There is no consequence for doing [248] one of those things whose detestability the ‘*aql* indicates, such as oppression and ingratitude.

1. That Acts can be Assessed into Three Categories

8. Abū Bakr [al-Jaṣṣāṣ] says: We say that the assessment of things in the ‘*aql* before the coming of the Revelation is of three sorts.
   a. Among them are the Obligatory: [There may be] no change or replacement [of their assessment]; e.g., faith in God most high and thanking the benefactor and the necessity of equitable action.
   b. Among [the acts] are those which are detestable in themselves, [and therefore] Proscribed: there is no exchange or change from their condition, such as ingratitude and oppression. Their assessment does not differ for the ones made-responsible.
   c. Among them there is that which is in the ‘*aql* such that[10] Permitting it is possible sometimes, Proscribing it at other times, and making it Obligatory at still others, according to whether its context is beneficial and harmful.[11]

2. That Silence means Permittedness

That which is not of the first two divisions [a and b] is Permitted before the coming of the Revelation, so long as in [doing it] there is less harm than the benefit that inclines one to do it. It may be that Revelation comes sometimes with these acts' Proscription, at other times with their Permittedness and at others with their Obligatoriness, according to "what is best."[12]

9. That which indicates the Permittedness, as we have described it [above 8c] for an agent who is made-responsible: It is known that [these things] are created for the beneficial use of those who are made-responsible: This is because [these acts'] creation obviously cannot be other than one of four things:
   a. Either that God, the Mighty, the Sublime, created them for the benefit of *no one*, and this is futility (‘*abath*)[13] and foolish—God most high is far removed from [such things]; or

b. it is that He created them in order by means of them to effect harm, without any benefit; and this is more disgraceful and more detestable [than (a)]: one may not [attribute] this to God; or
c. His creation of [these useful acts] was for His own benefit: but this is impossible because neither benefit nor harm can accrue to Him, the Most High.

Thus it is established that He created them for the beneficial use of those made-responsible.

10. Therefore it must be that they are to benefit from them, in any circumstance in which they are manifested,[14] so long as they do not bring about a harm greater than the benefit by which one is drawn to it.
11. [249] An indication of this: When He created [these things] by which the ones made-responsible might infer [assessments], they [then were able] to infer from them. This is [itself] a type of use.[15] So too with the rest of the aspects (*wujūh*) of usefulness which have been placed [in this world] for them: It must be possible for them to utilize them.
12. Another indication: We find the heavens and earth and ourselves to be indicants of God Most High, and in [the heavens, the earth, ourselves] nothing indicates the prohibition of benefiting from these things. Indeed if there were an indicant of its Proscription, then the arrival of Revelation[16] with Permission could not be[17] because what the indications of God most high require is not overturned. Therefore we know that nothing about [the act indicates] its prohibition. If [useful acts] were Proscribed, He would not have left them without an indicant to require their Proscription and [signify that] their occurrence is detestable. This proves that [useful acts] are Permitted, and that there is no consequence, for the doer of them: If there is a consequence, it may not be that God leave him without establishing an indication [to the effect] that for [doing the act], there is a consequence, [thereby] to deter [him] from it. This is the assessment of the *'aql*.[18]
13. [Revelation confirms] this notion, with God Most High's saying It was never God's part to send astray a folk after He had guided them until He had made it clear to them . . . . [what they should avoid.] [9:115] [Here] He informs us that so long as nothing indicates [a thing's] forbiddenness, there is no consequence for doing it.

B. Contra the Proscribed Position

14. Another proof: It is obvious that the things [such as] we have described can only be [either] Permitted, according to what we have said,[19] or Proscribed; or some of them are Proscribed and some of them are Permitted.

15. One may not say that *all* of them are Proscribed, because that would require that movement and rest, and getting up, sitting, and lying down would be Proscribed for human beings. One would be commanded to leave off all acts. When it is realized that this is impossible, we know that *some* [necessary acts] are Permitted.
16. Now, for the other group [of acts]: It is obvious that [these acts too] are either Permitted or Proscribed. Were [all of the rest] Proscribed, there would have to be an indicant by which to distinguish [the Proscribed] from the Permitted [in the first group]. Finding no indication of this, we come to know that this group [too] is equivalent to the Permitted, in this respect, and so, is Permitted. It is therefore established that every one [of those things] for which there is no [explicit] indicant of its being Proscribed, is Permitted.
17. [250] Also: In imposing (*taklīf*) the Proscription of these things a hardship is introduced [with regard to] one's self. But human beings may not bring harm and distress upon themselves without deriving benefit, and there is no proof in the '*aql* of [a benefit being produced by refraining from the use of useful things]. In addition, to require [self-harm] would bring about detestable consequences.
18. Furthermore: Imposition of a duty (*taklīf*) is a gracious act by God Most High to hold firm to what '*aql*s require. For this reason, their being Obligatory is good. God could not conceivably fail to establish a sign of the necessity (*luzūm*) of avoiding what is of this sort, if it were Proscribed.[20] This indicates that whatever is like this, [namely, seeming useful to the '*aql*, without an indication that it is Proscribed], as long as no Revelation has been sent down making it Obligatory, or Proscribed, is Permitted.[21]
19. Also, in shunning the undertaking to eat and drink, one's self is damaged, and this is detestable since it does not lead to a benefit greater than the damage which is attached to it. When we do not know that there is utility in relinquishing something, the relinquishing of it is not Permitted.

C. No One is Harmed by Use of the Useful Act

20. Objection: [Surely] you do not deny that in the '*aql* there is an indication of the Proscription of these things before the coming of Revelation, namely that these things are the property of God, the Mighty, the Sublime, and in the '*aql* of every *compos mentis* person one may not dispose of the property of someone else except by his permission.
21. Reply: It is not the usage per se of another's property without his permission that is Proscribed, because one may make use of someone else's property without his permission if there is no damage to him in it—e.g., seeking

shade in the shadow of a wall, or sitting in the light of his lamp (*sirāj*) or kindling a lamp for oneself from [the owner's lamp]. Since that is a kind of use of another's property, and it is not detestable [merely] because it takes place without the owner's permission, we know that the use of the property of another *is* possible without his permission. One who infers the Proscription of [the useful thing] from its being the property of another,—i.e. that it is making use of it without his permission—is in error. This aspect of the problem is disposed of.

22. And we say further that the assessment of these things, with regard to the permissibility of benefiting from it before the coming of Revelation, is [exactly equivalent to] the assessment of the use by one of us of the shade of someone's wall, or the light of a lamp, and kindling [of a light for ourselves] from it: This is because God Most High is the Owner of these things and He incurs no harm in the use of them by the user. [Likewise] there is no harm incurred by us [in the use of these things] that is greater than [the benefit] we expect from the use [of it] because, if there were [251] harm to us "in religion" (*fī l-dīn*), God, the Mighty and the Sublime, would not have kept us ignorant of [this fact]. It is necessary, therefore, that undertaking to use another's property is permissible, just as one may benefit from the property of another when there is no harm to [the owner] by [this usage].
23. As for the use of another's property among ourselves, it is forbidden only because of the damage which is connected to [its use] and because [the owner] is in need of it, just as we [would] need it. We may not benefit ourselves [by] harm to someone else without thereby bringing him a greater benefit, unless the owner gives permission to me [to use it] in return for compensation. Here [the owner] is God Most High.[22]
24. Objection: The difference between what you have mentioned and the things that we have mentioned is that in the undertaking to eat and drink there is consumption of the property of someone else, and there is no consumption of anything in seeking the shade of a wall by a person, or by sitting in the light of [a person's] lamp.
25. Reply: The consumption [of the food and drink] does not deprive the owner of it, since God Most High possesses them, [both] before their consumption and afterwards; for He is capable of returning them to what they were before. Their consumption does not deprive Him of them, just as the shade and the lamp are not taken from possession of the owner by someone else's use of it, in the manner we have described.
26. Moreover, there is no difference between the [two cases] in the aspect we discussed, because the underlying notion (*ma'ná*) in the permissibility of benefiting from the shade of his wall or sitting in the light of his lamp is that there is no harm to the owner by [the use], and there is a benefit in it. This principle is [likewise] present in what we have just mentioned [that

God is not harmed by our consumption of "His" food and drink while we benefit].

27. With regard to these instances, inasmuch as they constitute benefit, without harm to the owner, it must follow that [these acts] are assessed as what we have described [in the case of shade and light]. Their differences in a certain respect—namely that in one of these examples [food and drink] there is consumption and not in the others—does not prevent their equivalence in all that they have in common, of the aspect we have described.

D. Contra "Neither Permitted nor Proscribed"

28. [252] As for those who say: I do not say that it is Permitted, nor that it is Proscribed, because Permitted implies a permitter and Proscription implies a proscriber. [Before Revelation, there is neither.] Yet, they deny only the application of the *word* that is, "*al-ibāḥah*" (Permission) and "*al-ḥaẓr*" (Proscription), but they agree with the underlying notion (*ma'ná*) when they say, "there is no consequence for the doer of it." This is the notion [behind] the Permitted—namely that one does not deserve reward for the doing of it. Otherwise, they must deny saying anything is *Obligatory* before the coming of Revelation, such as faith in God Most High, and thanking the benefactor, and the necessity of equitable action. Moreover, one could not say that ingratitude to God and oppression and falsehood are *Proscribed* before the coming of the Revelation, because Obligation implies an obligator and Proscription implies a proscriber.
29. Objection: The One who "makes Obligatory" holding fast to faith, and the Proscriber of holding fast to infidelity (*kufr*) is God Most High who established the indication of these [rules].
30. Reply: Why not say the same for those things [Permitted] in the [time before] the coming of the Revelation? The Permitter is God, the Mighty, the Sublime, who created [these things] for [the purpose of our] obtaining benefit by them. Thereafter, He did not establish the indicant of their being [Proscribed.]
31. Objection: If Permitted [referred merely to] that for the doer of which there is no consequence, it would be necessary that things be [called] Permitted for beasts, the insane, and the absent-minded.
32. Reply: This does not follow since we have said that the definition of the Permitted is that there is no consequence to the doer who is among those made-responsible, //and that [the act] takes place intentionally, deserving no reward for the doing of it, and no penalty for its neglect. These [conditions] are not met //[23] in what you mentioned, because [neither the beasts nor the insane] are made-responsible, and the absent-minded one does not act deliberately.

E. Proof texts

33. Abū Bakr [al-Jaṣṣāṣ] says: Everything we have presented [above] is speculative discourse (*kalām*) about the assessment of these things in the '*aql* only before the coming of Revelation. Then Revelation came with confirmation of what was in the '*aql* with respect to Permittedness.

a. E.g. God Most High's saying: {And He has made of service to you whatsoever is in the heavens and on the earth; it is all from him.(45:13)}
b. And God Most High said {Eat and drink and be not prodigal. (7:31)}
c. God Most High said {Say: Who hath forbidden the adornment of God which He hath brought forth for His bondsmen and the good things of His providing? (7:32).}
d. God Most High said {Hast thou not seen how God has made what is on the earth of service to thee, and ships go upon the sea by His command? (22:65)}
e. He, the Mighty and the Sublime said {..And lofty date palms with ranged clusters provision [made] for men.(50:10)}

God Most High said {Licit for you are good things(5:4; 5:96)}[24]

f. He said {[O People]: Eat of that which is lawful and wholesome in the earth. (2:168)}
g. He, the Most High, said {[Say]: My Lord forbids only indecencies, what are apparent of them and what are hidden, and transgressions. (7:33)}[25]
h. And He, the Mighty and the Sublime, said {So walk on the [earth's] paths and eat of His providence. (67:15)}
i. And He said {And the fruits and fodder; provision for you and your cattle.(80:3l) }
j. He said: {Therewith He causes crops to grow for you, olives, the date palm, grapes and all kinds of fruit. Lo! Herein is indeed a portent for people who reflect. (16:11)}
k. He said {And He has created cattle that you might thereby have warm clothing and benefits and thereby eat. (16:5)}

Other verses [also] imply the Permissibility of these things.

With Regard to the Sunnah

a. There is the *ḥadīth* of Abū Tha'labah al-Khushanī, from the Prophet, "God, the Mighty and Sublime, imposed duties; do not be heedless of them. He defined (*ḥadda*) boundaries (*ḥudūd*); do not transgress them. He forbade [some] things; do not violate them. He was silent on [some] things without forgetting them as a mercy to you, so do not go seeking after them.[26]

b. There is a *ḥadīth* of al-Zuhrī from 'Āmir ibn Sa'd, from his father from the Prophet. He said, "The most criminal of Muslims toward Muslims is the one who asks about a thing which had not been forbidden, and it is therefore forbidden to the Muslims because of his asking about it." He tells [us] that if it was not forbidden, it must be Permitted, fundamentally (*fī al-aṣl*).[27]

c. A *ḥadīth* of Abū Hurayrah: He said "The Messenger of God preached to us (*khaṭabanā*) saying, 'O People: Verily God has written for you[28] the pilgrimage.' 'Ukāshah ibn Muḥṣan said, 'O Messenger of God, is it [required] every year?' And [Muḥammad] said, 'As for me, if I said yes, I would have [then] made it Obligatory; if I made it Obligatory [to do] it, you would neglect it and thus be led astray. [Therefore] be silent to me concerning that [about which] which I have been silent to you. Those before you were destroyed solely from the multitude of their questionings, and their disagreement about their prophets.' God most high sent down {O You who are faithful: Ask not of the things which if they were known to you would trouble you; but if you ask of things when the *Qur'ān* is being revealed, they will be made known unto you. God pardons for this. (5:101)}

d. From Salmān. He said, "The Messenger of God was asked about clarified butter, cheese, and wild asses[29] and he said, 'The licit (*ḥalāl*) is what God most high permits, and the forbidden is what God the Mighty, the Sublime, forbids in His Book. What He is silent about is what is forgiven you.' "[30]

Translation of a Section from *Kitāb al-Mustaṣfá fī 'ilm al-uṣūl* Abū Ḥāmid al-Ghazālī[1]

[55] The First Axis: the Harvest—namely, the assessment[2]

1. Discussion of [the Assessment] is divided into four components (*funūn*): a component about the real nature (*ḥaqīqah*) of the assessment, a component concerning [the assessment's] divisions, a component for its constituent elements (*arkān*), and a component for that which brings [the assessment] to light.[3]
2. *First component*: [The assessment's] "real nature," comprising a preface [section A] and three controversies [sections B–D].

A. The Preface:

1. Definitions

3. [The word] assessment (*ḥukm*) (for us) represents the dictum (*khiṭāb*) of the *shar'* when [the dictum] is linked to the acts of those-under-obligation.

   Thus, Forbidden (*ḥarām*) is the declaration concerning [an act]: 'Shun [imperative plural] it and do not do it.' Obligatory (*wājib*) is the declaration about [an act]: 'Do it and do not shun it.' Permitted (*mubāḥ*) is the declaration about [an act]: 'If you wish, do it; if you wish, shun it.' If there be no such dictum by the Legislator, there *is no assessment*.
4. Therefore we say:
   1. The '*aql* neither commends nor detests[4]
   2. nor does it make thanking the benefactor Obligatory,
   3. nor is there a *ḥukm* for acts before the arrival (*wurūd*) of the *shar'*.[5]

But let us sketch each controversy under its heading.

B. Controversy [1 Moral Epistemology]

1. The Mu'tazilī Position

5. The Mu'tazilah hold that [56] acts are divided into good (*ḥasanah*) and detestable (*qabīḥah*). Some acts are such that they may be perceived immediately[6] in the *'aql*, such as the goodness of rescuing drowning persons or persons perishing; and [the goodness of] thanking the benefactor; or knowledge of the good of veracity (*ṣidq*); or as [one knows immediately] the detestability of ingratitude (*kufr*); or of inflicting pain on an innocent; and of a purposeless falsehood.
6. [They also allege that there is a class of acts such that] they are perceived through rational inquiry (*naẓar al-'aql*), such as the goodness of veracity [even when] harmful, and the detestability of falsehood [even when] useful.
7. In addition [they say there are] those [goods and detestables] perceived through Revelation (*al-sam'*), such as the goodness of worship (*ṣalāh*), the pilgrimage to Mecca (*ḥajj*), and the rest of the cultus.[7]
8. [The Mu'tazilah] allege that [these Revelational goods] are distinguished from [other goods] by an attribute of their essence, that is, gracious assistance (*luṭf*), which prevents corrupt acts[8] and motivates one to obedience.
9. So the *'aql* is not [utterly] self-sufficient in its apprehension [of the quality of these cultic acts].

2. Al-Ghazālī's Rebuttal

10. However, *we* say: One who says, "this is good, this is detestable," has not fully grasped the meaning [of his statement] so long as he has not [yet] understood the meaning of good and detestable.

3. Definitions of Good and Detestable

11. The conventional senses for the application of the words goodness or detestability vary. We must, therefore, summarize them. There are three conventional senses:

a. Subjective Evaluation

12. [1st usage] The widely known, general sense: Acts are divided into what accords with the objective (*gharaḍ*) of the actor, into what is contrary to that [objective], and to what neither accords with nor is contrary [to his objective].
13. [According to this usage,] that which is in accord [with the objective] is called good and what is contrary is called detestable; the third is called pointless (*'abathan*). According to this usage, if the act is agreeable to an individual [while] contrary to [the goal of] another, it is good with respect

to him [to whom] it is agreeable, and detestable with respect to him to whose [objective] it is contrary.

14. Thus, were a great king killed, [that killing] would be good with respect to his enemies, and detestable with respect to his protégés (*awliyā'ihi*). Those [using the word in this sense] will not shrink from [describing as] detestable [even] an act of God's, if it be contrary to their objective. Therefore they curse[9] Fate (*al-dahr*) or the celestial spheres (*al-falak*), saying, "The celestial spheres destroy" and "fate makes wretched," while they know that the celestial spheres are subservient [to God];" nothing is at all due to [them].[10] Thus [Muḥammad] said, "Do not curse Fate; for God is Fate."[11]
15. So, the application of [the terms] good and detestable to acts is like applying them to forms (*al-ṣuwar*): One whose nature is favorably disposed to a form or to an individual's voice judges him to be good (*qaḍá bi-ḥusnih*); one whose nature is averse to a person deems it detestable. Many a person is loathed by one nature and attracted to another: He is therefore good for one nature and detestable for the other. For example, one group may approve (*yastaḥsin*) of [things] brown and another detest them.
16. Therefore as far as these [people] are concerned, good or detestable represents acceptance or aversion.
17. [Good and detestable] are relational [predicates], not objective [predicates] like blackness or whiteness, it being inconceivable that a given thing be black as far as Zayd is concerned and white as far as 'Amr is concerned.

b. Shar'i Evaluations

18. (2nd usage). The application of good is to what the *shar'* commends by praising its doer: [In this sense] the act of God will be good in every circumstance whether contrary to [a person's] objective or in accord with it; the thing commanded in the *shar'* (whether as Recommended or as Obligatory) will be good. The Permitted will not be [called] good.

c. Evaluation by Permissibility

19. (3rd usage). The application of good to everything that a doer ought to do. [In this sense] the Permitted will be [called] good, together with things commanded; [in this usage, also,] the act of God will in every circumstance be good.

d. Summary and Conclusion

20. All three of these usages [of good and detestable] are relational predicates. [57] They are [all three] intelligible (*ma'qūlah*) and there is nothing to hin-

der one who uses the word good as an expression of any of [these three] things. Thus, there is no problem with the words [themselves].

21. On this account, if the *shar*ʻ had not come down (*yarid*ᵘ) no act would have been distinguished from another other than by accord [with one's objectives] or contrariness [to them], while differing in [what is] predicated. But these usages [do not refer to] an attribute of essence.

4. Muʻtazilī Moral Epistemology and a Rebuttal

22. Objection:[12] We do not dispute with you about these ascriptive predicates, nor concerning these usages as you have posited them. However, we claim that goodness or detestability *is* a predicate of essence for the good and the detestable that the *ʻaql immediately perceives* in some things, such as oppression (*ẓulm*), falsehood, ingratitude, and uncouth ignorance. Therefore, we do not deem it possible that any of these things [viz. falsehood etc.] be attributed to God because of their [essential] detestability. Furthermore, we regard [these essentially detestable acts] as forbidden to any *compos mentis* before the coming of the *shar*ʻ, because [these acts] are detestable in themselves.[13] How can this be denied, when *compotes mentis*[14] as a whole agree upon this judgment (*qaḍā*ʼ) without specifying any particular circumstance?[15]

23. Reply: In what you have mentioned, you are alleging three matters:

    (One) That detestability is an essential predicate.

    (Two) That it is something *compotes mentis* know necessarily.

    (Three) Your supposition that if *compotes mentis* agree upon it, this [agreement constitutes] decisive proof and is an indicant of its being necessary [knowledge].

24. (One) The allegation that [detestability] is an essential predicate: This is an arbitrary judgment based upon something unreasonable.[16]

    Two examples of acts that vary in quality, but not in essence: a. For [the Muʻtazilah], killing, in its essence, is detestable, so long as[17] it is not preceded by a crime, or [so long as] there is no subsequent compensation; yet it is Permitted to cause pain to beasts and slaughter them. It is not detestable to God, since He rewards [the beast?] for it in the Next World.[18] Yet killing, in its essence, has a single real nature (*ḥaqīqah*) which is invariant, whether preceded by a crime, or followed by something pleasurable: [Killing does not differ] except with respect to advantages and objectives connected to it.

25. b. Such is the case also with falsehood: How could its detestability be essential when, if [a falsehood] were to preserve [thereby] the blood of a prophet by concealing his location from a tyrant whose aim was to kill [the prophet, the falsehood] would be good, indeed Obligatory. One disobeys God by neglecting [to do so].

26. How could an essential attribute be exchanged [for its opposite] through the connection [of the act] to variant circumstances?

5. Moral Epistemology

27. (Two) The immediate (*ḍarūrī)* perception [that something is good or detestable]: How is this possible when we dispute with you about it? The immediately [perceived] is by definition that about which] there is no dispute by a large group of *compotes mentis*.[19]
28. Objection: You *are* indeed compelled to knowledge and you do agree [that this act is detestable for instance]. However, you *suppose* that the ultimate source of your knowledge is Revelation, just as al-Ka'bī supposed that the ultimate source of his knowledge by plurally-transmitted-information was speculative inquiry *(naẓar)*.[20] [If we Mu'tazilah are correct,] it is likely that there might be confusion about what *perceives* the knowledge; it is unlikely only that there would be disagreement about *the information itself.* There is no dispute about [this knowledge that the infliction of pain, for instance, is detestable].[21]
29. Reply: This is ineffectual argument (*kalām fāsid*) since we assert that it is commended by God that animals be caused pain; we do not believe there is a [prior] crime nor is there compensation for them. This proves that we dispute about *the knowledge itself.*

6. Accord in Moral Judgments Does not Constitute Proof

30. (Three) Even if we conceded the accord of [*compotes mentis*] upon this, [this accord] would still not constitute proof, for it [still] would not be conceded that [*compotes mentis*] are forced to [this knowledge]. Rather, it is possible that they might agree upon what is not [known] *necessarily*:
31. People have agreed on the demonstrability (*ithbāt*) of the Devisor (*al-Ṣāni*') and the possibility of sending Messengers, so that no one disagrees, except the odd person (*shawādhdh*). But even if these persons agreed to support [the majority in their argument, knowledge of the existence of the Devisor and His sending of Messengers] would [still] not be *immediate.*
32. Similarly, the accord of people upon this belief might possibly be [because] some of them [would be basing their judgment] upon an indicant (*dalīl*) of Revelation indicating the detestability of these things. Some of them [might judge] through indirect knowledge (*taqlīd*) [relying upon] the understanding [of those who derive their knowledge] [58] from Revelation. Some of them [might judge] from specious knowledge which occurred to people of error (*ahl al-ḍalāl*). Thus the fact that the agreement is patched together from these various causes does not establish that it is necessary [knowledge].

33. So, such [agreement] does not indicate that [the point on which they are in agreement] is [known] *necessarily*. Therefore [common agreement by *compotes mentis*] would not [ordinarily] indicate [that the agreement itself constitutes] a proof, were it not [for the fact] that Revelation (*al-sam*‘) specifically declares the impossibility of error by the whole of this community [acting] collectively. For the agreement of the whole upon an error grounded in imitation, or in specious knowledge, is not [by itself] unlikely.

    How so in any case, when, among atheists (*al-mulḥidah*) there are those who do not believe the detestability of these things, nor their opposites: How then can one invoke "the agreement of reasonable people"?

7. Mu‘tazilī Assertion of Innate Inclination to Good

34. Objection: [The Mu‘tazilah] argue that we know *absolutely* that one to whom veracity and falsehood are equally [possible] prefers veracity and inclines to it if he is *compos mentis*. This [preference, they say] must be on account of [the act's innate] goodness.
35. [Even] a mighty king who rules climes: When he sees someone weak [who is] on the verge of destruction, he is moved to rescue him, even if he has no religious basis, thereby [not] anticipating reward, thanks or requital. Further, this [rescue may] not accord with his objective—indeed perhaps he will be wearied by it. Moreover, *compotes mentis* affirm the goodness of enduring the sword, should one be compelled to a declaration of infidelity, to reveal a secret, or to infringe upon an agreement—though this is contrary to the objectives of the one compelled. On the whole, the approval of [acts of] good character and liberality is among the things no *compos mentis* person would deny, except from sheer obstinacy.
36. Reply: We do not deny the widespread [affirmation] of these judgments among humankind and that they are generally thought praise-worthy. Yet the basis [of these judgments] is either (a) religious commitment to revelational stipulations (*tadayyun bi-sharā'i*‘) or (b) [conformity of the act to one's] objectives .
37. However, we deny this [latter] with regard to God so as to reject [the attribution of] objectives to Him.[22] As for people's application of these phrases to what takes place among them there remain [still other] objectives, but objectives may be subtle or hidden and none may be aware of them but those who know the truth (*al-muḥaqqiqūn*).

8. Errors of the Mu‘tazilī Position

38. [Now], let us call attention to what gives rise to error in [their argument]. There are three causes to which their fancy (*wahm*) has led them.[23]

a. First Error: Evaluations are Subjective

39. Humans apply the word detestable to what is contrary to their objectives (*gharaḍ*), even though it may accord with the interests of another, due to the fact that they do not take others into consideration. Every nature is enamored of itself and disdains the other. Thus it determines detestability unrestrictedly.
40. One may predicate detestability of the essence of the thing and say [the thing] is, in itself, detestable. [In saying] this one has stated three things: they hit the mark in [only] one of them, and that is *basic fact* of disapproval. They err in the other two matters:
    a. the predication (*iḍāfat*) of detestability to [a thing's] essence (*dhāt*) (for they ignore [the fact that] its being detested is [really] because of its contradiction of their objectives).
    b. [They err also in] their assessment that [an act] is detestable unrestrictedly. The origin [of this error] is disregard of anyone else, and even their inattention to their own [various] circumstances. Thus they may *approve* in some circumstances the very same thing of which they *disapprove* when it contradicts their objective.

b. Second Error: Over-generalization

41. The second error. Their fancy may not draw attention to [the knowledge that an act may] contradict their objective in all but a single rare circumstance; indeed, [the exception] may not occur to them at all. Such a one considers [the act or thing] to be contrary [to his objectives] in all situations, so that he judges it to be detestable *unrestrictedly* due to the domination in his mind (*qalb*) of the circumstances of its detestability, and the recession of the rare circumstance from his recollection.
42. For example, his judgment that a falsehood is detestable unrestrictedly, and his heedlessness to the falsehood that provides protection of a prophet's life, or a saint's. If he adjudges [it] to be detestable unrestrictedly, and persists in this for a while, and it is repeated in his [59] ear and on his tongue, then disapproval is implanted in his soul (*nafs*), which makes him recoil [from the act]. Yet if that rare circumstance did occur [in which the falsehood were actually good], then he would find in his soul the antipathy to [falsehood that was there] because of an entire upbringing in disapproval [of falsehood]. For it has been put to him since his youth, in the course of training and guidance, that falsehood is detestable and no one ought to do it. But his attention has not been called to its goodness in some circumstances, for fear that his antipathy to falsehood might not be ingrained, (so that he might [tell a falsehood]), since [falsehood] *is* detestable in most circumstances.

43. What he has heard as a youth is as it were engraved on stone, so it is implanted in the soul, and because of this he longs to consider it true without qualification; and it *is* true, but not unrestrictedly; rather, [it is true only] in the majority of circumstances. If he does not recall except [what is the case] in *most* circumstances, then from his perspective [this judgment applies] to *every* circumstance. Thus, he believes it [to be good or detestable] without restriction.

c. The Third Error [Resulting from Associative Conditioning]

44. The immediate cause [of their third error] is the haste of their fancy [to suppose] the entailment (*al-'aks*) [of something associated with it]. When what [is seen] is associated with [another] thing, one supposes that the [second] thing is always, without exception, associated with [the first]. One does not recognize that the more restricted is always associated with the more general, while the more general is not necessarily associated with the more restricted.
45. For example, the aversion of the soul (*nafs*) of the "sound one" (*al-salīm*)[24]—that is, the one bitten by a snake—to a speckled rope, because he has found unpleasantness associated with this [particular] form, and he fancies that this form is [always] associated with unpleasantness. Similarly the aversion of the soul from honey when it is compared to feces, because there is unpleasantness and [a feeling] of disgust associated with brown liquids. So one fancies that brown liquid is associated with [feelings of] disgust: The fancy so dominates that eating [honey becomes] difficult, even though the '*aql* determines the [objective] falsity of the fancy. The faculties of the soul, however, have been created compliant to fancies, even if they are false.
46. Thus one's nature is averse to a beautiful woman who is labeled jewess, for one finds the name [generally] associated with detestable [people], and one supposes therefore that detestability is a necessary consequent of the name.
47. For this reason, if some of the laity (*al-'awāmm*) are presented with a controversial position, and they approve of it—when [subsequently] you say, "This is an Ash'arī or a Ḥanbalī or Mu'tazilī doctrine" (*madhhab*), they become averse to it, if they dislike the belief of him to whom it is attributed. This is a natural characteristic particular not only to the laity; but also, it is characteristic of the nature of most *compotes-mentis* imbued with learning, save the well-grounded scholars whom God truly guides to the truth (*al-ḥaqq*), and whom He strengthens to follow Him.
48. The faculties of most creatures' appetitive souls are obedient to their fancy, though they know its falseness. Most of the undertakings and refrainings of creatures are caused by these fancies. For the fancy is powerfully sovereign over the soul.

49. Thus human nature is averse to spending the night in a house in which there is a dead person, even though one is certain that [the dead person] will not move; still, one fancies [the corpse's] movement or his voice, every moment.

If you have attended to these causes, let us return [to the topic].

d. Summary and Elaboration

50. We say: One prefers rescuing [a drowning man] to indifference—[supposing him to be] one who does not hold to the *sharā'i'*—only so as to defend against the injury which afflicts a man from creaturely sensibility. [Such empathy] is a natural characteristic inseparable from him. Its cause is that man foresees himself in this distress and imagines someone else abandoning him and his rescue; he detests [that neglect] as contrary to his objectives. Thereupon he re-assesses that disapproval as one witnessing [his own] destruction, from his own point of view, and [60] fends off from himself this fancied detestableness.
51. But, posit a beast, or person with whom he has no [creaturely] sensibility and it is unlikely he will conceive [this empathy and obligation to act]. If he conceives it, there remains another matter [that may be motivating him to act], namely the seeking of esteem for his good deed. If it is posited that it is not [certain to be] known that he is the rescuer, he may [still] anticipate that it *might* be known. This anticipation, therefore, is a motivation. If we posit a situation in which it is impossible [that his good deed] be known, there remains the inclination of the soul (*nafs*), and a preference which resembles the natural aversion of the snake-bitten person to "the speckled rope." That is, he visualizes this image [sc. rescue] associated with esteem and supposes that praise is connected to it in every case, just as, when he visualizes pain connected to the shape of the rope, his nature being averse to pain, he is then averse to what is connected with pain: circumstances of pleasure are pleasurable, the circumstances of the unpleasant are unpleasant.
52. Indeed if a person has sat with someone whom he loves in a certain place, and if he [later] comes to it, he will feel in his soul a distinction between that place and any other. Thus, the poet says:

> I pass by the dwellings, the dwellings of Layla.
> I kiss that wall: that wall;
> It is not those dwellings that fill my heart with passion,
> But love for the one who dwells in the dwellings.

And Ibn al-Rūmī draws attention to the cause of love of [one's] homeland:

Men's homelands have been made dear to them,
By desires that youth has carried out there.
If they make mention of their homeland,
[It is because the homeland] reminds them of the vows of love,
so that they yearn for it.

These are but a few of the many proofs [that might be instanced]. All this belongs to the category of "fancy."

53. As for enduring the sword with tranquillity of the soul when being compelled to a statement of infidelity, not all *compotes mentis* approve of it. Indeed, were it not for the *shar'*, they would possibly disapprove of it; but only those approve of [such endurance] who anticipate the reward for endurance, who anticipate praise for courage and perseverance in religion. How many of the courageous plunge steadfastly into danger and rush blindly upon a number larger than their own while knowing they cannot best them! [Still, they] disdain their suffering for what is offered in exchange, namely fancied acclaim and praise—even after their death.

54. Similarly, keeping a secret and keeping a vow: People commend [these acts] for the benefit from them, and they are copious in their acclaim for [these acts]. Who thereby endures harm endures it for the sake of acclaim.

55. If we postulate that there be no acclaim, there is [nonetheless] still an association [of the act] with acclaim: there remains an inclination of the fancy to what is associated with pleasure, though it be [itself in fact] devoid of it. If it is postulated that this fancy does not control him and that he does not anticipate reward and acclaim, then [surely in such a case] he would disapprove of hastening self-destruction for no benefit, and would consider someone who did that an absolute fool. Who would admit that someone like that would prefer perishing over life? [In just this fashion] would run [61] the answer to the [problem of the disapproval of a] lie and the rest of what they posit.

e. Irrelevance of Analogies to Human Conduct

56. Then we say: We do not deny that among themselves, some people customarily disapprove of oppression and falsehood. But the [present] discussion concerns only the attribution of [the assessments] detestable and good to God. Those who do so base [their opinion] upon analogy to the transcendent from the mundane [realm]. Yet how can one so analogize when [for example] a master would be scorned if he left his male and female slaves [together] and some of them incited the others, and they acted immorally while [the master] was aware of it and able to prevent it. But God has done [just] that with his bondsmen, and this is not detested on his part.

57. Their assertion that He may have left [his slaves alone] so that they might restrain themselves and [thereby] deserve reward is folly, because He

knows that they *will not* restrain themselves: Let Him hold them back forcibly! How many are kept from immorality [only] by impotence and inability! That is better than enabling them [to commit immorality], since he knows *they will not* restrain themselves.

C. Controversy [2 Thanking the Benefactor]:

58. Thanking the benefactor is not Obligatory according to the *'aql*, contrary to the [assertion of] the Mu'tazilah. An indication of this is that there is no meaning to Obligatory (*wājib*) except "what God makes Obligatory and commands and threatens punishment for neglecting." If no dictum (*khiṭāb*) has come, what does Obligatory mean?
59. Then: the substantiation of [our] assertion is: The *'aql* must "make [thanking the benefactor] Obligatory" [either]
    (A) for an advantage (*fā'idah*) or,
    (B) not for an advantage.
        (B.1) It is impossible that it make it Obligatory for no advantage for that is futility (*'abath*) and foolishness.
    (A) If it is for an advantage it must be either
        (A.1) connected to one [whose] bondsman we are; this is impossible since He is too sublime and too sanctified for objectives—or [it must be]
        (A.2) [connected] to the bondsman. And, [in that case] it must either be
        (A.2.a) [an advantage] in the material world (*al-dunyā*) or
        (A.2.b) in the next life (*al-ākhirah*).
        (A.2.a) There is no advantage to it in this world, rather, one is wearied by inquiry, reflection, recognition, and thanking; by it one is barred from passions and pleasures.
        (A.2.b) There is no advantage to him in the Next World [either, as far as he knows], for the reward is gratuitous preferment from God and is known [only] by His promise and His informing. If one is not informed of it, whence does he know that he is rewarded for it?

1. Moral Psychology

60. Objection: It may occur to [the bondsman] that if he is ungrateful and disclaims [the benefaction], *perhaps* he will be punished: The *'aql* summons one to travel the more secure path.
61. Reply: No. Rather, the *'aql* makes known the more secure path, and thereupon a natural characteristic (*al-ṭab'*) impels him to travel it. For every person is created with a disposition to love himself and dislike unpleasantness. You have erred in saying that the *'aql* is a summoner; rather the *'aql* is a

guide; inducements and motivations proceed from the lower soul consequent to the assessment (*ḥukm*) by the *'aql*.

62. You err also in saying that one is rewarded for thanking and knowing God in particular. This notion rests upon fancying the existence of some purpose [in preferring] thanks by which [thanks] is distinguished from ingratitude. Yet they are equivalent [to each other] in relation to the majesty of God most high.
63. Indeed, if one opens the door of fancies, it may occur to him that God will *punish* him if he thanks Him, and inquires into [the moral qualities of acts]—since He supported [humankind] with the means to the good life; perhaps He created him to live at ease and enjoy [himself].[25] [The bondsman's] tiring himself [by inquiry and thanking] is "usage of His property without His permission."
64. [To support this position, the Permitters] have two specious arguments:
65. Their assertion that the agreement of *compotes mentis* on the good of thanks-giving and the detestability of ingratitude leaves no way to deny [their position]. The merit of thanksgiving is agreed to, [but only] with respect to themselves, because they are affected and gratified by thanking and grieved by ingratitude. But for the Lord the two matters are equivalent: disobedience and obedience for Him are equal.
66. As evidence, two examples:
    1. The one who would seek to ingratiate [himself] with the sultan [62] by the movement of his fingertips from the corner of a room in his house is despicable: [God's] bondsmen's acts of worship, in relation to the Majesty of God, are even less significant.

a. First Specious Argument [The Objective Futility of Thanks]

    2. One given a morsel of bread for his hunger as alms from the Sultan: If he were to take it around the city and call to the chiefs of the notaries [to witness] his thanks: This, with regard to the king, would be detestable and a disgrace. Yet the whole of God's benefactions to His bondsman, in relation to His capabilities, is far less than the relation [of the morsel of bread] to the treasuries of the king. For the treasuries of king [could eventually be] exhausted by the like [of this gift] of a morsel, because of their finitude. But the capabilities of God would not be exhausted by double what He has conferred upon [His] bondsman.

b. Second Specious Argument: Innate Moral Knowledge Is Not Necessary to Validate Revelation[26]

67. Objection: Making the *shar'* the sole means of perceiving obligation to the *shar'* leads to a silencing of the Messengers: If [the Messengers] manifest miracles, the ones summoned [to Islam] may say to them:

Inquiry into your miracles is not Obligatory except by the *shar*'. The *shar*' is not confirmed except by our inquiry into your miracle. [The Messengers] confirm our obligation to inquire so that we might inquire. But we are not able [to know to inquire] so long as we do not inquire. This leads to a vicious circle.

68. Reply: from two aspects:
    1. With respect to verification [of the Prophetic Message]: You err supposing that we say the confirmation of the *shar*' waits upon the inquiry of the inquirers. On the contrary, when the Messenger is sent and [his message is] confirmed by his miracle in such a way that, through it, the possibility of knowledge materializes, if a *compos mentis* should inquire into it, then [by that time the obligation to follow] the Revelation is already established. The arrival of the dictum has settled [the question of] the obligation to inquire. For there is no meaning to Obligatory other than "that the doing of which is preferable to its being shunned, so as to prevent a known harm or one [merely] fancied." For the meaning of the Obligatory is [only] the preference of doing over shunning.
69. The Obliger is the one expressing the preference. God is the One expressing the preference, and He it is who informed His Messenger, commanding him to inform the people that ingratitude is fatal poison and disobedience is a malady, while obedience is healing.
70. Thus, the one expressing the preference is God, the Messenger is the informant, and the miracle is the proximate cause (*sabab*) enabling the *compos mentis* to come to knowledge of [God's] expression-of-preference. The '*aql* is the instrument that makes known the veracity of the informer [who conveys God's] expression-of-preference. Natural disposition (*al-ṭab*')—which is inclined against suffering [resulting] from chastisement [and inclined] toward the pleasure of reward—is the instigator which motivates to wariness against harm.
71. After the arrival[27] of the dictum, the making-Obligatory—that is, the expression of preference—obtains; by the confirmation through miracles comes the possibility [of knowledge] with respect to the *compos mentis* inquirer; by [this knowledge] he is able to know the preferred.
72. One's saying "I shall not inquire so long as I do not know, and I shall not know so long as I do not inquire," is similar to [the case] of a father saying to his child "Turn around! Behind you is a lion attacking! It is likely that it will attack you if you are heedless of it." Whereupon the child says to him "I shall not turn around so long as I do not know the obligation to turn around. To turn around is not Obligatory so long as I am not aware of the lion, and I do not know of the lion so long as I do not turn around." Then [the father] would say to him, "surely you shall perish by neglecting to turn around. You are not exempt, since you are capable of turning around and ceasing to be obstinate; neglecting [to do so] is obstinacy."

73. Just so the Prophet says: "Death is behind you, and further, there are agonizing worms[28] and painful chastisement if you shun faith and obedience. You know this by the merest glance at my miracle. If you inquire and obey, you are rescued; if you are heedless and turn away, God has no need of you and your deeds—you have harmed only yourself."
74. This [63] matter can be grasped by the *'aql* and there is nothing internally contradictory in it.

c. Second Answer: [Moral Ontology]

75. Using their own arguments against them: They determine that the *'aql* is the obliger. It does not oblige by its essence (*jawhar*) immediately. Everyone has an *'aql*, yet were [it the case that the *'aql is* obliged by the act's essence], no *compos mentis*'s *'aql* would be without [immediate] knowledge of the obligation; but in fact one must contemplate and inquire. If one did not inquire, he would not know the obligation of inquiry; if he did not know the obligation to inquire, he would not inquire. That also leads to a circle as above.

2. [Innate Knowledge: the Warners]

76. Objection: No *compos mentis* is without the two Warners (*khāṭirān*), one of which warns him that if he inquires and thanks, he will be rewarded, and the second, that if he shuns inquiry he will be punished. They signal to him of the impending obligation to travel the more secure path.
77. Reply: How many *compotes mentis* has time (*al-dahr*) claimed without the warning having occurred to them! Rather it [may] have occurred to him that, from God's perspective, the one cannot be distinguished from the other [i.e. the good from the detestable]. "Why should I chastise myself for no advantage to myself or to the one worshipped?"
78. Moreover: If having the two Warners is sufficient knowledge to enable one [to know the good and detestable], when a Prophet is sent, and summons one [to Islam], and manifests miracles, then the presence of the Warners becomes all the more likely. Indeed after the Prophet's admonishing and his cautioning one cannot be separated from this Warner.[29] We do not deny that when humankind perceives something fearful, their natural disposition motivates them to shun the fearful thing. But perception [takes place] only by [means of] reflective thought produced by the *'aql*. If someone should call that which *discloses* the obligation, "the obligater," he is using figurative speech. However, the actual fact which is not figurative is that God is the Obliger; that is to say, [God] is the one expressing preference for the doing [of a particular] act rather than its avoidance: The Prophet is the in-

formant, the ‘*aql* discloses, natural disposition is the motivator and the miracle is what enables the disclosure. But God knows best.

D. Controversy: [3. The Status of Acts before the Shar‘]

79. A group of the Mu‘tazilah holds that acts before the coming of the *shar*‘ are Permitted (‘*alá l-ibāḥah*). Some of them say they are Proscribed (‘*alá l-ḥaẓar*). Some of them say, In Abeyance (‘*alá l-waqf*).
80. Perhaps [the Permitters] mean by this, "concerning those [acts] regarding which the ‘*aql* does not determine goodness or detestability immediately or through inquiry," as we have analyzed their doctrine.[30]
81. All of these schools are invalid (*bāṭilah*).

1. Contra Permitted

82. The invalidation of the Permitted school is that we say: Permitted implies a Permitter, as knowledge or recollection implies a recollector and knower. The Permitter is God, for He gives the choice between doing and shunning in His dictum. Thus, if there is no dictum, there is no "being-given-the-choice," so there is no Permission.
83. If they mean by being Permitted that there is no harm either in doing it or in shunning it, they have hit the meaning, though they have erred in its formulation. For the act of a beast, a minor, or a madman is not described as being Permitted, though there is no harm in their doing or shunning [that particular act].
84. Acts, with regard to God—I mean, what is done by God—are [also] not described as Permitted, though there is [similarly] no harm in [His doing it] or in [His] shunning it. But if one denies choice-giving by a choice-giver, one has negated [the applicability of the term] permission. If one dares to apply the word Permitted in an unqualified sense to the acts of God, and one means by this nothing but the negation of harm, he has hit the meaning, though his formulation is repulsive.
85. Objection: The ‘*aql* is the permitter because it chooses between doing [the act] and shunning it, for [the ‘*aql*] forbids the detestable, obliges the good, and chooses [freely?] among what [64] is neither good nor detestable.
86. Reply: We have falsified [the idea of] "making good by the ‘*aql*" (*taḥsīn al-‘aql*) and making detestable; this [argument of theirs] is based upon that [prior assertion]. Thus it [too] is falsified.
87. Further, their naming the ‘*aql* Permitter is figurative, as is naming it Obligor. For the ‘*aql* [only] discloses the expression-of-preference and the non-preference; the meaning of being Obligatory is "the preference of his doing it over shunning it"; the ‘*aql* discloses this. The meaning of its be-

ing Permitted is *non*-preference. The *'aql* is the discloser, not the permitter. It is not the expressor-of-preference nor is it what [deems two possibilities] equal; it [merely] discloses preference and equivocation.

88. Then we say [to those who hold the Permitted position]: By what do you refute the Refrainers (*aṣḥāb al-waqf*), if they dispute the equivalence of doing and shunning, saying,

> [Knowledge of the assessment of the act awaits Revelation.] Any act that the *'aql* neither commends nor detests can be made Obligatory by the *shar'*. This therefore indicates [in retrospect] that [the act] was distinguished by an essential attribute because of which [we are] graciously, and by way of being prevented from vile deeds, summoned to bondsmanship. Thus, for this [reason] God obliges it. The *'aql* cannot independently perceive this. It is [also] conceivable that the *shar'* come prohibiting [that act] which would indicate that it was distinguished by an essential attribute because of which [the act] motivates us to vileness that [likewise] the *'aql* cannot apprehend. God has reserved for Himself this knowledge. This is their teaching.

89. Then *they* say: By what do you [Ash'arī's] refute the Proscribers—people who hold that prior to Revelation all acts are forbidden, for they say "We do not accept the equivalence of doing and shunning; for truly, usage of the property of another without His permission is detestable. God is owner and He has not [yet] given consent."
90. Objection: If it were detestable He would prohibit it, and Revelation would arrive with [that prohibition]; therefore the non-arrival of the *shar'* indicates negation of [the act's] detestability.
91. Reply: If it were good He would permit it, and the Revelation would arrive with [that permission]; therefore the non-arrival of Revelation [would be] proof of negation of its goodness.
92. Objection: If God informed us that it is useful, and there is no harm in it, He has given permission for it.
93. Reply: Then being told by the owner that his food is useful and there is no harm in it, ought also therefore to be [considered] permission [to eat it].
94. Objection: The owner among us can be harmed, but God cannot be harmed, so use of His creation in relation to Him has the same status as a person's use of someone's mirror by glancing into it, [use of] his wall by seeking the shade of it, or a lamp by seeking its light.

a. [Irrelevance of Human Analogy]

95. Reply: If the detestability of the use of another's property were for the damage done to him, and not for the absence of his permission, then [usage]

would [still] be detestable though [the owner] had given him permission, so long as [the owner] had been harmed [by the use of his property]. How so when an owner's preventing [use] of the mirror and the shade and seeking light from a lamp is detestable?

96. Yet God has prevented His bondsmen from [use of] a group of edible things, and that is not detestable. If [He forbade these foods] for some harm [that eating them causes] the bondsman, what act is there of which it cannot be conceived that there is a concealed harm in it which the *'aql* cannot perceive, so that [Revelation] then [might] come forbidding [usage of the thing].
97. Then we say: As for your saying that since there is no harm to the Creator by our use of it, it is Permitted: Why do you say this when, if one moves the mirror of someone else from one place to another—though its owner is not harmed by it—it is [still] forbidden? It is only looking [into the mirror] which is Permitted, because looking is not usufruct of the mirror, as looking toward God or toward the sky is not usufruct of the thing beheld. Nor is seeking shade usufruct of the wall, nor in seeking a light is there usufruct of the lamp. If one were to use these things themselves, it might be that they would be judged forbidden, except when Revelation indicates their permissibility.
98. Objection: God's creation of taste in [food] and the faculty of taste is indication that He wants us to use them [65]. He is capable of having created [food] without taste.
99. Reply: We Ash'ariyyah and most of the Mu'tazilah are in absolute agreement on the impossibility of separating [edibles or anything else] from the accidents which they can receive.[31] Therefore [that argument] does not stand. Yet even if we granted it, it might be that He created [edibles] not for anyone to use; perhaps He created the whole world for no cause whatsoever. Or perhaps He created [edibles] so that the reward of avoiding them be received, despite one's craving [for it], just as He rewards the shunning of [other] reprehensible cravings.

2. *[Contra Proscribed]*

100. As for Proscribers: [Their argument] is even more obviously invalid: We do not know [of an act's] being Proscribed by the *'aql* immediately, nor by an indicator [of the *'aql*]. The meaning of Proscribing is "expressing-a-preference for the portion of shunning over the portion of doing," because of some connection between harm and doing. But whence does one know this, when Revelation has not come, and the *'aql* [cannot] determine it? Perhaps he will be *harmed* in this world by shunning the pleasurable: How then does shunning [a thing] come to be preferred to doing it?
101. Their saying that this is the usufruct of the property of another without His permission, which is detestable, is invalid for us: We would not ac-

cept the detestability of it if the *shar'* did not forbid and prohibit it, whatever the custom. [Further, use of property] is detestable [only] with respect to one who is harmed by use of his property. Indeed, what *is* detestable is preventing [the use] of that in which there is no harm.

102. We have already made it clear that the reality of the perception of detestability is grounded in its contradiction of objectives, and that that [supposed detestability] has no reality [in fact].

3. [Contra Refraining]

103. As for the school of refraining *(waqf)*: If they intend by [the term] that the determination of assessment is in abeyance (*mawqūf*) until the arrival of Revelation and there is no [effective] assessment in this circumstance, then [they] are correct. For the meaning of assessment is the dictum, and there is no dictum before the arrival of Revelation. If they intend by it that *we* refrain and do not know [what is in fact the case]—that [the act] is [in fact] Proscribed or Permitted—they are wrong. This is because we *do* know that there is no Proscription, for the meaning of Proscription is the statement by God, "Do not do this," and there is no Permitting, for the meaning of Permitting is His saying, "If you wish do it; if you wish, neglect it," and no such thing has come.

Part III

Thanking the Benefactor

CHAPTER 6

GOD AS PATRON: THANKING THE BENEFACTOR

As we have argued, Thanking the Benefactor was part of the problem-complex with which this study is concerned. We have chosen to study Thanking the Benefactor separately because in this question we most clearly see the continuity of an idea from pre-Islamic times, and most clearly see the conservatism of the Mu'tazilah, the so-called rationalists who were supposedly the product of the interaction of the Greek with the Islamic.[1]

What we hope to show here is that the Mu'tazilah were, on this question (as well as on the questions discussed above), defending the old Islamic and pre-Islamic position, against the novel position of the so-called traditionalists. The traditionists "won" because their position accorded with the changed circumstances of fifth and sixth century Islam and Islamdom. We hope also to show the limited significance of theology when attempting to understand Muslim piety.

THE PROBLEM

Thanking the Benefactor is one of a list of virtues which a human might be expected to know or be able to discern before or in the absence of revelation. Most of these seem familiar and predictable: justice (*'adl*), equity (*inṣāf*), the existence of God, truthfulness.[2] Among these ethical commonplaces thanking the benefactor seems to stand out as particular to Islamic and Islamicate culture.

As it turns out, inquiry into this example of a virtue leads to sociological and psychological questions far more complex than might be anticipated. There is a characteristic shift in Islamic thought in the period between the era preceding the rise of Islam and the 600th year of the hijrah. Change is to be expected, of course, but the change we find is not simply a growing sophistication in analysis and conceptual terminology; it is a change from manifest social behavior as the realm of moral reference, to the interior and affective as the domain of ethical experience. Less surprisingly, the change in the understanding of "*shukr al-mun'im*," Thanking the Benefactor, represents a change in the understanding of the nature of moral knowledge itself: In the early period, moral knowledge tests and validates Revelation. In the later period, Revelation validates all moral knowledge and all duties owed God come to belong to the same class of prescribed and required obligations.

The earliest discussion of Thanking the Benefactor as a controversial issue seems to be the debates that oppose al-Ash'arī to Ibn Abī Hurayrah and al-Ṣayrafī.[3] In these debates there is an air of precaution: If one does not know what to do, one ought/ought not to do it as a hedge against divine disfavor.

Abū Bakr al-Jaṣṣāṣ's elaborate discussion in the *Fuṣūl,* reflects something of the intense debate that must have taken place around this issue. Al-Jaṣṣāṣ's formulation is typical of later discussions and surely preserves earlier discussions of which we have no surviving record.

> We say that the evaluation (*ḥukm*) of things in the '*aql* before the coming of Revelation (*al-sam'*) is of three sorts: (a) the Obligatory (*al-wājib*): [These acts do not permit of] change or exchange, for example, faith in God Most High, thanking the benefactor, and the necessity of equitable action (*al-inṣāf*). (b) Those which are detestable (*qabīḥ*) in themselves [and therefore] Proscribed: there is no exchange nor change from their condition (*ḥālih*). [These would include] ingratitude (*kufr*) and oppression (*ẓulm*). . . .[4]

What is at issue for al-Jaṣṣāṣ is not the appropriateness or necessity of thanking the benefactor, but whether one can know of this obligation before or in the absence of Revelation. From al-Jaṣṣāṣ's time on, in both theology and jurisprudential works, this problematic example of '*aqlī* knowledge appears again and again. Thanking the Benefactor as a translation of *shukr al-mun'im* is imprecise. It is the culturally specific meaning of thanking the benefactor that forms the substance of this chapter.

Pre-Islamic Usage

The concept of thanking the benefactor for a benefaction is Qur'ānic, but it is useful to begin by considering the meaning of the terms *shukr* (thanking) and *mun'im* (benefactor) in the Qur'ān's milieu: the Arabia of pre-Islamic times.

Bravmann has tried to describe some of the underlying social and religious norms preceding Islam, drawing his information from the only documents surviving, the poetry and sagas (*ayyām al-'arab* literature) of the pre-Islamic and early Islamic period.[5] In a discussion of the concept of *jizyah ʻan yad*, Bravmann suggests that in pre-Islamic times a person who spared another person's life had a claim to reward for that deed. Sparing a person's life was called *niʻmah* (benefaction, kindness);[6] the refusal to recognize that obligation was called *kufr*, the term used above in al-Jaṣṣāṣ.[7]

In the interaction of clemency and gift, to be truly recognized as benefactor the person with the claim to reward must have acted not from need but from choice.[8] One was *obligated* to give a reward for this *niʻmah*, but not *compelled*, as in ransom; it was not given under duress. In any case, custom required the one benefacted (*al-munʻam ʻalayh*) publicly to acknowledge the benefaction.

As an example Bravmann cites al-Ḥuṭay'ah as quoted in the *Book of Songs* (*Kitāb al-Aghānī*):

> "He spared my blood and released me without ransom and
> I shall never forget this benefaction."[9]

Also:

> We spared the blood of the Muslims and this was
> accounted for us a benefaction which was praised at
> the fairs (of the festival seasons).[10]

Sparing life then is, in this context, the benefaction par excellence. The person conferring the *niʻmah* has a right to reward from the beneficiary and by this act of benefaction a relationship is established between two otherwise unrelated, even antagonistic persons. After the conferral of the benefaction—the sparing of life in this case—the most important element in the creation of this relationship is the *acknowledgment* of the new relationship. Bravmann shows that controversy could arise over whether a person had in fact performed a *niʻmah*, but so important was it not to seem to renege on this obligation that it was preferable to over-reward rather than be seen to be shortchanging a *munʻim*. Thus, in one story, ʻAmr b. ʻAmr is freed by Qays b. al-Muntafiq. Al-Ḥārith b. al-Abraṣ says he has a claim on ʻAmr as well, which ʻAmr at first denies. Subsequently ʻAmr gives al-Ḥārith 100 camels "fearing blame from him."[11]

The beneficiary's hope is to satisfy, or content, the benefactor. In another story mentioned by Bravmann [in somewhat confused form, here corrected],[12] one ʻĀmir waives his right to reward by Laqīṭ after freeing a prisoner, saying,

> But satisfy my brother and my confederate who participated in the matter. . . . So Laqīṭ gave to each of [the others] a hundred camels and [these two] were contented.[13]

In sum, then, a kindness done supererogatorily obligates the person receiving the kindness to acknowledge that relationship, and gives the benefactor a claim on the benefacted one.

What role does *shukr* play in the complex of benefaction-obligation-requital? From the *Aghānī*:

> When al-Ḥuṭay'ah *returned to his people* he began praising Zayd, proclaiming (*shākir^{an}*) his benefaction. . . . [14]

Shākir^{an} li would ordinarily be translated "thanking for" or, literally, "a thanker for"; note here that the "thanking" is done not to Zayd, but when the poet has returned to his people. *Shākir*, "thanker," and its verbal noun *shukr*, "thanks," must mean something more public: "proclaiming" as above, or, in the context of the obligation established between Zayd and al-Ḥuṭay'ah, "acknowledging his benefaction" and the claim that Zayd has on him. *Shukr*, then, is a public act performed in response to a benefaction. It is not a statement of *gratitude* to the benefactor, but it seems to be *an acknowledgment of the claim* that the benefactor has on the beneficiary. In this historical context the Qur'ānic invocation of these two concepts can best be understood.

Qur'ānic Usage

Shukr, *ni'mah* and their derivatives appear abundantly in the Qur'ān.[15] There are, however, a few passages where the meaning of these terms and their relation to each other emerge most clearly.

Perhaps the clearest sense of the meaning of *ni'mah* comes from Sūrah 8:52–59.

> { . . . The way of Pharaoh's folk and those before them: they repudiated (*kafarū*) the signs of God. God took them for their faults: God is strong, severe in punishment. (53) That is because God does not alter a benefaction bestowed upon a folk until they alter their part of it. . . . (55) The worst of beasts from God's point of view are those who repudiate, for they will not be faithful. (56) Those of them with whom you have made a contract: they deny the contract at every chance. . . . (57) If you come upon them anywhere in the war, deal with them so as to scatter the ones behind them; perhaps they will be reminded. (58) And if you fear from a people treachery, dissolve it with them equally: God loves not the treacherous. (59) Let those who repudiate not think they will win: They are unable. . . .}

The usual translations of this passage seem unclear here and present the Qur'ān discussing God's "changing of grace" or some other such term,[16] without any clear sense of why "blessings" are being discussed in the context of war and treaties. Such discontinuity is common enough in the Qur'ān of course, but if we follow Bravmann and suggest that the phrase refers to humankind refusing to acknowledge the claims God has on them for the benefactions He has provided, then the passage becomes not only clear, but unified and coherent. "God does not alter a contract made by Him as a result of their acceptance of an unearned benefaction, until they alter what is [due] on their part. . . ." In the context of the passage God is a model for the behavior He enjoins upon the Islamic community in wartime, saying in effect: "He does not alter until betrayed, but then He is stern. Similarly, if you (Muḥammad) have made a contract, when it is transgressed, you may repudiate it. . . ." Here is a passage where not only the context (the discussion of treaties and their observance) but the formulation points not to blessings metamorphosed by God because of what a folk have in their souls but to transactions between benefactor and beneficiary.

If *ni'mah* in this context implies transactions, what then of *shukr*? What is a thanker (*shākir*) doing in thanking (*shukr*)? Qur'ān 5:6–7 is, I believe, a locus where *shukr* as a response to *ni'mah* is clarified.

> {God does not desire to make a burden upon you but He desires to purify you and that He may complete His blessing upon you; perhaps you will give thanks. . . . And remember (or make mention of) God's blessing (*ni'mah*) upon you and His covenant (*mīthāq*) He made with you when you said "We hear and obey."}

Ibn 'Abbās summarized this passage in these words:[17]

> God reminds them of His covenant which they had confirmed (or consented to) [making it binding] upon themselves, and He orders them to carry it out.

In this passage too, *ni'mah* occurs in the context of a discussion of contractual obligation (*mīthāq*—covenant). I would suggest this passage is best paraphrased as

> God desires to purify you; He appointed for you His gratuitous good deed in hopes you will acknowledge it. [Therefore] mention the gratuitous and obligating benefaction of God [by which you are obligated], and His covenant by which you are [also] covenanted. . . .

Shukr in this passage [and plausibly elsewhere] seems to be parallel to *dhikr*, "recollection," "recalling," "mentioning," and is the response to the *ni'mah*. Obedience is also at issue, but it is, I think, subsequent to the thanksgiving by the benefacted.

An Early Post-Qur'ānic Discussion

For confirmation of the interpretation proposed for this term's Qur'ānic usage, an early theological source, a treatise or letter on Free-will and Predestination by the first century Baṣran rigorist, al-Ḥasan al-Baṣrī (d. 110/728) offers additional evidence.[18] In this letter to the Umayyid caliph, 'Abdalmalik, al-Ḥasan wants among other things to argue that the cycle of retribution for wrongdoing begins with the human, God's bondsman. It is the human act of transgression that leads to punishment and not a divine act of predisposition or predestination. Along the way, he discusses how it is that humans err. Al-Ḥasan begins with the Qur'ānic quote:

> {God does not alter a benefaction (*ni'mah*) bestowed upon a folk until they alter their part in it.}

and then says as a paraphrase:

> The benefaction (*ni'mah*) was from God Most High and the changing from the bondsmen, by their turning their backs upon that to which he had commanded them.[19]

This argument he follows with another Qur'ānic quote:

> {Do you not see those who exchanged the *ni'mah* of God, repudiating it?}

Again his gloss:

> "The *ni'mah* was from God Most High and the exchange from the bondsmen."

Al-Ḥasan's understanding of Qur'ān in this passage confirms the contractual understanding of *ni'mah*. Those who are at fault, in al-Ḥasan's eyes, are those who try to change the terms of the patron/client relationship established by the act of bestowing a *ni'mah*. This reprehensible change is an adjuration of the obligation to obey, which must be understood to come about *under the terms of the benefaction.* Obeying therefore follows the recognition and acknowledgment of the benefaction contract. This order of obligation is clarified in another passage in al-Ḥasan's treatise.

Arguing that God could not have foreordained humankind's wicked actions because He would not command what does not please Him, he quotes:

> {If they repudiate, then God has no need of you;[20] He is not content with repudiation for his bondsmen, but if you acknowledge (?),[21] He is content (*raḍiy*[a]) with you} (Qur'ān, 39:7)[22]

Change and repudiation lead to God's disapproval. What then, according to al-Ḥasan, leads to His contentment (*riḍā'*)? It is *shukr*. Bearing in mind the story of 'Āmir and Laqīṭ above, it would seem that here *shukr* must refer to the response by the beneficiary to the claim of the benefactor, just as, in response to the claim upon Laqīṭ, he offers 'Āmir's confederates one hundred camels, with which they are contented. For al-Ḥasan and early Muslim pietists, thanks or thanksgiving is performative: it is an acknowledgment and statement of intention. In the Qur'ānic (and in al-Ḥasan's) view, *shukr* is the recognition of God's claim to obedience resulting from the numerous benefactions enumerated throughout the Qur'ān.

After the thanks by the beneficiary, to which God as Benefactor is entitled, He demands not a hundred camels, but fealty: obedience to His command. Envisaged here is a transaction of sorts in which the first element is a gift that obligates the receiver and the second is the receiver's acknowledgment of that relationship and its obligations. Thus, thanking is not saying "thank you" to God, but recognizing a sort of moral claim to sovereignty.

Here is an instance of a Qur'ānic norm which indubitably reflects a social norm. Indeed, the concept of a duty owed a benefactor becomes one of the organizing social principles of Islamicate society, at least up to Būyid times. According to Mottahedeh, *Shukr al-mun'im* is used as a formulaic method for expressing the claim of a ruler upon his subjects, especially the military (who more than other subjects were creatures of royal bounty). Functionally, the bestowing of benefaction, and the reciprocal bond that resulted was an important method of tying together individuals who had no kinship relationship; the concept of *shukr al-mun'im* was a way to distinguish oneself with individuals to whom one was otherwise an undifferentiated stranger.[23]

In sum, in the early period of Islamic thought it seems clear that a benefaction received meant an obligation incurred. Thanksgiving was a medium for acknowledging this obligation; subsequently, the satisfaction of the claim depended upon the terms set by the claimant, the *mun'im*. The goal was the satisfaction (*riḍā'*) of the benefactor. Mu'tazilīs and others who insisted on the ability of human beings to know the obligation to thank the benefactor, without Revelation, are defending the notion we describe here: the acknowledgment that makes obligation reasonable.

SHUKR AL-MUN'IM, 400–600 A.H.

Al-Juwaynī

In order to understand the change that takes place between al-Ḥasan's time and later periods, it is important to realize that one possible meaning of al-Jaṣṣāṣ's doxographical passage quoted above is that "by virtue of being human one knows that a benefaction lays one under an obligation that must be acknowledged. Not to do so is unthinkable (*ghayr 'aqlī*)." It follows for al-Jaṣṣāṣ that moral knowledge comes in part from human nature, and that Revelation is another sort of knowledge parallel to the knowledge of the *'aql*. In this dispute no one denies that thanking is Obligatory; what is in dispute is how we know it is so. At issue for the Mu'tazilah is obedience itself; not so for their opponents.

Thus, later Shāfi'ī/Ash'arī *uṣūl* texts differ from al-Jaṣṣāṣ and the Mu'tazilah in two ways: they differ in their opinion on the matter under discussion (the obligation to thank a benefactor before Revelation) but they also reflect a different set of intellectual assumptions. The earlier and the later texts differ, and the later author does not argue, but rather assumes the difference. In those changed assumptions there is evidence of developments that are not differences of doctrine, but of worldview.

In his *uṣūl al-fiqh* masterpiece, the *Burhān*, Imam al-Ḥaramayn al-Juwaynī does not deny that *shukr al-mun'im* is Obligatory, but asserts that its Obligatory character cannot be known without Revelation, and in fact does not exist until Revelation.[24]

> The certain proof of the invalidity of what [the Mu'tazilah, al-Jaṣṣāṣ etc.] hold is that thanking is wearisome effort (*ta'b*) for the thanker to effect, and it is of no benefit to the One thanked. How then should the *'aql* determine its Obligatory [character]?
>
> If it is said, "The thanker will benefit from the reward which is his recompense in the afterlife; the *'aql* deems the enduring of wearisome effort in the immediate term [to be less] than the anticipated benefit in the hereafter [which consideration] is sovereign [in comparison]." We say, "How is that apprehended by the *'aql*?" From what should a *compos mentis* person (*'āqil*) know that? The One thanked [might] say, "Your benefit is not incumbent upon Me as a principle; and [being thanked] does not benefit Me so that I should recompense you [for it]. [Therefore, why should I reward you?]" . . . Ingratitude and thanks are equal as far as the thanked One is concerned.
>
> Abū Isḥāq [al-Isfarā'īnī] said, "The thanker wearies himself; he is the property of his Creator. There could come about [through the effort required to give thanks] a depreciation of the property of its Owner without His permission, by which loss the Owner does not benefit. . . . "
>
> They allege that *shukr* is Obligatory in the visible world (*al-shāhid*), then they determine this to be so in the hidden world (*al-ghā'ib*). This is manifestly inapplicable, for what they have mentioned, if we accepted it, pertains to the benefit of the One thanked; and the Lord most high is far above being able to benefit or be harmed. . . .

It is quite clear here that the Ash'arīs held that moral knowledge could be known only through Revelation. Yet careful scrutiny shows that a shift has taken place in the formulation of the problem. It is difficult to know whether the shift is the self-conscious result of a general Islamization/de-Arabization of Islamic culture, or whether it is the result of a carefully thought-out polemical construction. Al-Juwaynī does not dispute that obedience to God is a desideratum, nor that thanks are owed to a benefactor. He argues instead that while thanksgiving is an Obligation, Obligation is understood within the phraseology of the *fiqh* sciences. By so doing, he implicitly describes *shukr al-mun'im* as *an instance* of obedience to the divine command, rather than an *acknowledgment* of the legitimacy of such a command. Al-Juwaynī lives in an Islamic society, and the issue of God's moral claim is no longer a subject of debate—it is assumed. Thus he is here discussing the second-order problem of how to know this obligation *among others*.[25]

By contrast, for al-Ḥasan al-Baṣrī and for al-Jaṣṣāṣ, there seem to be two moral domains: that of Arab tribal humanism,[26] which according to al-Jaṣṣāṣ has its roots in human nature itself; and another kind of moral knowledge, the Islamic or Qur'ānic, understood *by reference* to Arab humanism. It is from the domain of Arab humanism that we know that God as a benefactor has the right to require obedience to His commands. The first claim legitimates the second. For al-Juwaynī, this order is reversed, and no appeal to human nature has any epistemological status since Revelation is itself the information of what in human nature is virtuous and what is not. Note too that for al-Ḥasan, a claim resulting from a benefaction is to be honored for its own sake. For al-Juwaynī, it is the fact of consequences (reward, for instance) attached to an act (such as thanking) that makes that act worthy of our attention.[27]

And what of the *ni'mah*? The complete absence of discussion of the term in these texts itself suggests a change in the concept: In the early texts *ni'mah* is at the heart of the discussion. For al-Juwaynī, gratitude is not connected structurally, as it were, to *ni'mah*, but *mun'im* (benefactor) seems to have become merely one more synonym for the acts of the Creator, equivalent to *iḥsān* (kindness), *faḍl* (generous act), and so on. The idea of a particular kind of gift mandating reciprocal obedience has been lost, at least in the relations between God and His creation. In the first work of al-Juwaynī's pupil, al-Ghazālī, we can see that some changes occur in the argumentation of this problem even within the span of a generation.

Al-Ghazālī

More clearly than his master, al-Ghazālī explains that there must be an interest (*gharaḍ*) for someone in order for the *'aql* to deem something necessary. One thanks because it is in someone's interest to do so. Such a personal interest on the part of God is impossible since God is above such things, and the putative thanker has no reason to think it is in his own interest to do so either.[28] Moreover, were one to thank, one would be tiring oneself for no discernible reason. Al-Ghazālī makes concrete the implication of previous arguments: God did not *have* to make thanking Him an obligation. It does not stand to reason.

> Then also it may occur to the bondsman that if he speculates and thanks, he may be punished, for he is a bondsman leading an easy life whom God has granted ease as a benefaction; perhaps He created him for well-being. So wearying himself [by thanking] is an infringement on his part on His sovereignty, without His permission.[29]

What is particularly interesting about the Ash'arīs is that they are willing to discuss the possibility that *shukr al-mun'im* is not Obligatory in order to show that it is not the *'aql* that legitimizes our knowledge of this moral principle. Since the Mu'tazilah allege that, on the model of a beneficent King, one should express one's gratitude to the greatest of benefactors (namely God), al-Ghazālī suggests that, on the contrary

> One who would seek intimacy with a Sulṭān merely by wiggling his fingertips from the corner of the room, seems a fool in [the judgment of] his *'aql*. Yet the bondsmen's acts of worship, when measured against the Majesty of God, are less in stature [than the wiggling of the fingers to the Sulṭan]. . . . One who is given as alms by the Sulṭān a morsel of bread in his hunger—[30]when he takes to going about the countryside, summoning the chiefs of the notaries [to record] his thanks—this is ignominious and disgraceful. But measured against His capacity, all of the benefactions given by God most high to His bondsmen are less than this [giving of a morsel of bread by] the Sulṭān.[31]

Here, the young al-Ghazālī points out that, given God's infinite capacity and power, such thanking as might be offered to God is so disproportionate as to make any analogy to human affairs irrelevant.

In his later work the *Mustaṣfá* al-Ghazālī follows his teacher, al-Juwaynī, in more boldly arguing that as far as *'aqlī* knowledge is concerned, thanking the benefactor is not Obligatory, and it may be an impertinence.[32]

> Thanking the benefactor is not Obligatory by the *'aql*, contrary to [the position of] the Mu'tazilah. . . . It is obvious that the *'aql* would either make something Obligatory because of a gain (*fā'idah*) or for no gain. It is impossible that it would make something Obligatory for no gain, for that would be pointless and foolish. If it were because of a gain, it is obvious that [the benefit] must either be something connected to the One worshipped, (and this is impossible because He is far too sublime and too holy to have [earthly] purposes), or [for a gain of] the bondsman.

> Here it is obvious that the gain must be in this world or in the next. There is, however, no gain in this world—rather [the thanker] wearies himself by speculation, thought, knowledge, thanks[giving], and forbidding himself passions and pleasures. There is [likewise] no benefit to him in the next world, for the Reward is a gracious act from God, which one knows by His promise and His informing [us]. . . . But if He has not informed [us] of [the reward that follows virtuous conduct or obedience], how should one know that one is rewarded for it? . . .
>
> One might [even] imagine that God would punish [the thanker] if he thanked Him and speculated about Him, because He supplied him with the means for a pleasurable life; perhaps He created him to live at ease and enjoy [himself]. [The bondsman's] tiring himself is "usage of His property without His permission. . . ."

Here at the edges of theistic subjectivism[33] virtuous moral action is grounded solely in Divine command. Hence the obligation to thank a benefactor, which the Qur'ān and al-Ḥasan al-Baṣrī assume to be known by all humans, is for al-Ghazālī, unknowable. In fact, al-Ghazālī cannot conceive of an act of thanks directed toward God the Benefactor except in the forms prescribed in Revelation. As a result, he assumes that *'ibādāt* (ritual acts of worship) are the equivalent of the *shukr* discussed by his opponents. Put this way, their argument becomes absurd since there is no way to know the details of ritual acts before the Qur'ān is sent down. Al-Ghazālī seems simply unfamiliar with the possibility that the obligation to perform *ṣalāh* (ritual worship) might be conceptually dependent upon knowing of the obligation to thank and gratify a benefactor. From the minimal value that al-Ghazālī assigns to giving thanks per se, and because of the link he assumes between thanks and ritual worship, it seems likely that for him Thanking the Benefactor means the mere saying, "I am grateful," and even that obligation is necessary only because of a Revelational injunction.

It is clear that al-Ghazālī writes as a Muslim, living in a Muslim world, inhabited by a Muslim populace. The obligation to perform *'ibādāt* is so thoroughly woven into his view of the world that to conceive of some other, prior form of thanks is impossible. This marks a significant change from the Qur'ānic world and that of al-Ḥasan al-Baṣrī, in which the obligation to thank a benefactor is less controversial than the obligation to obey God's revelational dicta. That the obligation to worship is conceptually dependent upon the obligation to thank would seem to al-Ghazālī absurd.

Al-Shahrastānī

For confirmation of this supposed change in understanding of the meaning of *shukr* let us turn briefly to the discussion of *shukr al-mun'im* in *Nihāyat al-Iqdām*, the sixth century dogmatic work written by the Shāfi'ī-Ash'arī, al-Shahrastānī. In the discussion of *shukr al-mun'im* he provides a highly suggestive definition of both *ni'mah* and *shukr*.

> Broadly speaking a *ni'mah* is everything by which a person is benefacted in state or property. . . . A *ni'mah* (using the word in its proper sense) is what is of praiseworthy effect. It is restricted to religious matters. . . . Thanks for the benefaction is Obligatory . . . and for sustenance [received]; that is, that you perceive in your mind that it is a gracious act from the Benefactor, and you praise Him in speech, and you do not use [the benefactions and sustenance] in disobedient action. . . . [34]

Not only is the proper sense of the word *ni'mah* now restricted to the realm of religion, but it seems that the affective has totally replaced the effective. Thanking is intellectual (or emotional, depending on where one understands the mind to be).[35] Thanks is no longer a response implying action. Thanks is a realization of one's dependency and a declaration of one's gratitude. But there is no partnership established, no client/patron. The inner domain has become the realm of (especially religious) experience and knowledge, and the social model of human/divine relations has disappeared. Like al-Ghazālī and al-Juwaynī, for al-Shahrastānī, thanking God is an act different from thanking one's fellow human beings. There is nothing known from human relations that is relevant to human relations with God. The human polity is no longer a source of theological knowledge. Only sources of knowledge which are explicitly connected to that realm can provide information about it.

The Irrelevance of Scholarship

Despite the extensive discussion of possible reasons why thanking God might be an impertinence, thanking—particularly the cognitive/affective understanding of the term—remained a central concept of Islamic piety. In the very period in which al-Ash'arī and others were arguing that thanking might be understood to be offensive, books were being written by pietists to prove the merit of thanking. A brief look at this genre of literature might round out the more theological/legal and scholastic picture presented thus far.

There are at least two early works on thanking itself: the *Kitāb al-Shukr* of Ibn Abī Dunyā (d. 281/894), and the *Kitāb Faḍīlat al-shukr li-llāh 'alá ni'matih wa-mā yajib min al-shukr li-l-mun'am 'alayh* of al-Kharā'iṭī (d. 328/939–40). These two works have in common with other pietistic works, (for instance the *Tanbīh al-Ghāfilīn* of al-Samarqandī)[36] the form of a collection of *ḥadīth* strung together around the theme of thanking. Since, as the editor of *Faḍīlat al-Shukr* establishes in his notes,[37] there are few differences between Ibn Abī Dunya's work and that of al-Kharā'iṭī, the two may be here discussed as a single work.

These collected *ḥadīth* reflect a general understanding of *shukr* as praise (*ḥamd*).

> No. 1: "God . . . has not bestowed upon a bondsman a benefaction whereupon he then has said Praise is God's—except that the praise was more than the benefaction."[38]

Note that while there may be a public aspect to praise, what is required by the *ḥadīth* is not praise but the saying of the phrase *praise is God's* (*al-ḥamdu li-llāh*) for benefactions. In this context the phrase is not a public declaration of responsibility and fealty, but a pious ejaculation that both reminds the beneficiary of the source of benefactions, and is somehow pleasing to God.

Parallel to this understanding is the emphasis in the *ḥadīth* on recalling or mentioning (*dhikr*):

> No. 25: It has reached us that Moses asked his Lord, "Who among your bondsmen is most beloved to You?" He said, "Those who most recall Me."[39]

The *ḥadīths* collected in the *Tanbīh* of al-Samarqandī have much the same content, though in his selection he seems (characteristically) to have stressed the apocalyptic so that the requital for thanks or ingratitude is more prominent than in the other two works.[40] As with al-Kharā'iṭī, al-Samarqandī also stresses that obedience (*ṭā'ah*) is a kind of thanks, and rebellion (*'iṣyān*) is a kind of ingratitude. However, it is still the interiorist aspect of thanking with which al-Kharā'iṭī is here concerned.

If it is somewhat surprising to find that scholars of more or less the same persuasion as al-Ash'arī are collecting *ḥadīth*s to show the obligation to thank while he himself is arguing that thanks is an innately valueless act, it is still more instructive to see the same al-Ghazālī who argues so persuasively that thanking is not an absolute good writing an entire chapter in his monumental *Iḥyā'* on thanks.[41]

Al-Ghazālī begins this section with the phrase "You should know that God Most High has associated thanks with recollection (*dhikr*) in His book."[42] He then lists various Qur'ānic and *ḥadīth* usages with the odd bit of commentary interspersed.[43] Al-Ghazālī begins his discussion proper of this concept with the proposition that

> [Thanking] is composed of knowledge (*'ilm*), interior disposition (*ḥāl*), and action (*'amal*). Knowledge is the basis (*aṣl*); knowledge effects interior disposition, and interior disposition effects action.[44]

Actually, for al-Ghazālī thanking has a particularly important status: He quotes approvingly the *ḥadīth* to the effect that "*shukr* is half of faith,"[45] and to be ignorant of it is to be ignorant not only of one of the two portions (*shaṭr*) of faith, but of an attribute of God Himself.[46]

Thanking then is an important aspect of Islamic piety. Seemingly no one denies this, and it is often praised and encouraged. Yet even this most elemental value is, for the Ash'arī scholars, dependent upon Revelation. Revelation is the sine qua non of religiosity and morality, and al-Juwaynī, al-Ghazālī, and al-Shahrastānī are perfectly willing to imagine a world in which thanking is a vice, in preference to imagining a world in which Obligations arise from some source other than divine fiat.

Conclusion

What conclusions can be drawn from this evidence? As far as the history of Islamic thought and religion is concerned, it seems clear that in the period *450–550* A.H. the transactional nature of the human-divine relationship is lost, and as Muslims become more and more intellectually sophisticated and ponder more and more the general thrust of the Qur'ān, they come to see God increasingly as Someone or Something other, and apart. Thanking God becomes something categorically different from thanking another human being. Given the separation between the immanent (*al-shāhid*) and the transcendent (*al-ghā'ib*) these scholars argue no analogy between the two is informative.

In this shift from thanks as an acknowledgment of social obligation to thanks as an interior experience, it is the Mu'tazilah who argue the archaic position. For scholars of the fifth and sixth Islamic centuries, in the central Islamic lands, it no longer seems "reasonable" to link thanking a king and thanking God, since the entire view of the cosmos as a society in which God is one among many generous benefactors has disappeared.

Yet at the same time, as we consider the argument about the importance of Revelation over against innate knowledge, it must not be lost sight of that thanking the benefactor and the other topics retain for all Muslims their Obligatory nature. The *shar'* can be seen to gain significance as its content is seen increasingly to be incomprehensible by innate human capabilities.

APPENDIX

An Early Debate on Thanking the Benefactor

It is noteworthy that the earliest reliable accounts we have of debates on any issue in the before Revelation complex are on Thanking the Benefactor. It seems worthwhile to append two accounts of al-Ash‘arī's debates on this topic. There are two accounts surviving, one in the *Baḥr al-Muḥīṭ*, the other in al-Subkī's *Ṭabaqāt*.

FROM THE BAḤR:

Al-Zarkashī transmits his account of the debate on Thanking the Benefactor as recorded by a contemporary of al-Ash‘arī, Abū Sahl al-Ṣu‘lūkī via a contemporary of Ibn Abī Hurayrah:[47]

> [Abū Isḥāq al-Isfarā'īnī][48] said, "Abū ‘Alī al-Ṣaqaṭī, that is, al-Ṭabarī—and he is known as Ibn al-Qaṭṭān—was a companion of Ibn Abī Hurayrah and followed him jot and tittle in this matter [of thanking the benefactor]."[49]
>
> And *he* said:

1. Abū Sahl al-Ṣu‘lūkī narrated that Abū ‘Alī Ibn Abī Hurayrah happened by (*waqa‘a ilá*) Abū l-Ḥasan (that is, al-Ash‘arī) and Abū l-Ḥasan debated (*kallamahu*) with him [the obligation to thank the benefactor], and [the debate] did not have any effect on him.[50] So Abū l-Ḥasan said to Abū ‘Alī "You are hateful (that is, odious) to me." [Al-Ṣaqatī] said "There arose [bad feelings] between them."[51] (Abū Sahl continued): We were fierce partisans of Shaykh Abū l-Ḥasan.
2. [The two of them] went and sat at the head of the bridge which was on Ibn Abī Hurayrah's way, the bridge to Baghdad called *al-Ṣarāh*. We used to wait for him in order to benefit from him.[52]

3. As for Abū Bakr al-Ṣayrafī, he passed by Shaykh Abū al-Ḥasan and [al-Ṣayrafī] reproached[53] [Abū l-Ḥasan] on this question.
4. Abū l-Ḥasan asked him, "Do you seriously maintain that all created existents (*kā'ināt*) [exist] by the will (*irādah*) of God most high, the good of them and the detestable of them?" [Abū Bakr] said, "Indeed."
5. Abū l-Ḥasan said " If the cause (*'illah*) of the [supposed] obligation to thank the benefactor is that one is not sure [but] that there [might be] a benefactor who has created him, who has willed of him thanks, it is [also] possible that He willed of him *not* to thank Him, because He is in no need of his thanks.
6. But either one believes that He wants only what is good, as the Mu'tazilah say[54], or he is not sure but that He [might] will of you shunning thanking [Him]: if you thanked Him He would punish you.
7. Then it follows that it is not Obligatory upon you to thank the benefactor, because of this possibility.
8. Thereupon Abū Bakr al-Ṣayrafī departed from this school of thought [to which he had formerly belonged] and repudiated it. But as for Abū 'Alī [Ibn Abī Hurayrah] and Abū Bakr al-Qaffāl, no repudiation is established for them on this topic.

From Subkī

Another, obviously sanitized version of the debate is preserved in the *Ṭabaqāt* work of al-Subkī on the authority of Abū Muḥammad al-Juwaynī, whose authority is not specified.[55]

1. Abū Muḥammad al-Juwaynī related in his gloss on [al-Shāfi'ī's] *Risālah* that Shaykh Abū Bakr al-Ṣayrafī met with Shaykh Abū l- Ḥasan [al-Ash'arī]. Abū l-Ḥasan said to him:
2. You hold that the Obligation to thank the benefactor is based upon what you have mentioned: It is probable that He wishes (*irādah*) thanks. Then if one does not thank Him, He will punish him for it.
3. Yet this statement [is held] together with the belief that God created the ingratitude of the ingrate (*kufr al-kāfir*) and wills it (*irādahu*). These are mutually contradictory. Either you say, "Our acts are created for us," or you say, "thanking the benefactor is not Obligatory whatsoever, of itself."
4. [Al-Ṣayrafī] asked: "Why?"
5. [Al-Ash'arī] said: Your doctrine is that God wills the ingratitude of the ingrate. His willing his ingratitude does not make ingratitude Obligatory; suppose that He—the Most High—wills thanks from us. His willing it does not make thanking Obligatory, just as it does not make ingratitude Obligatory. Either you deny God's willing of ingratitude and follow the doctrine of the Mu'tazilah, and your principle (*aṣl*) goes along with you, or you leave this doctrine.

6. Al-Ṣayrafī said: "Departing from the statement of the Obligatory nature of thanking is the lesser [evil]. I will hold fast to that [namely that God creates the ingratitude of the ingrate and that thanking the benefactor is not Obligatory of itself]."
7. Then he was wont to write on the margins of his books where he argued the obligation to thank the benefactor: "While we stated its obligatoriness, we state it [to be so] in association with the *shar'* and its *sam'*."[56]
8. I [al-Subkī] say: "In [this] disputation is evidence for what al-Qāḍī Abū Bakr [al-Bāqillānī] said in *Kitāb al-Taqrīb*, and what Ustādh Abū Isḥāq [al-Isfarā'īnī] said in *al-Ta'līqah*, namely that certain circles of legists followed the doctrine of the Mu'tazilah on some questions, unaware of their invalid deviation (*tasha''ub*) from their principles (*uṣūlihim*), as we shall relate, God willing, in the biography of al-Qaffāl al-Kabīr of this generation."
9. Furthermore I [al-Subkī] say: "The answer of al-Ṣayrafī [should be] that the obligation to thank is because of the possibility that it has been said [by God], 'it is Obligatory;' not that it has been said, 'He wills it.' Such as this has not come regarding ingratitude. We are certain that it is said, 'It is not Obligatory, it is forbidden'—even though He will it. It does not follow necessarily from His willing it for him that it is Obligatory for him. In making Obligatory thanking the benefactor, there is no mutual contradiction with the statement that He wills existents in their totality, both the good of them and the evil of them."

Part IV

The Background

In Islamic legal thought everything seems connected to everything else: the urge to coherence was perhaps the single most important motivation in the literature of "principles of jurisprudence."[1] In this section we hope to lay out the background to the before revelation complex. The term *background* may mislead, because in many cases it is background issues that are overtly debated in before revelation texts: the nature of the '*aql*, the relation of a moral assessment (good, detestable, Proscribed, Permitted, Obligatory) to the ontology of the act (the essences and accidents of which it is composed), and other matters of this sort. *Backdrop* might be a more appropriate term perhaps, since we visualize these scholars on stage before a depiction of some particular metaphysic, declaiming their positions on the before revelation controversy. With each actor, the scenery changes, and it is this particular backdrop that is assumed to "set the scene" for the actor's speech.

So it is the assumptions of these scholars that we will discuss below. We show first how certain legal problems led inevitably to the questions and methodologies defended in the before revelation complex. We then show the intramural debate among Mu'tazilīs to find a metaphysic that best expressed the flux of moral life as it is actually lived. We close with the critique by the non-Mu'tazilah of *any* moral ontology, and we contrast the "high" revelation theory of the non-Mu'tazilah with the "low" Revelation theory of the so-called "rationalists of Islam." We hope to show that the Mu'tazilah were not crypto-philosophers infiltrating an authentically traditionalist Islam, but rather, they were every bit as much religious thinkers as the non-Mu'tazilah. The goal here is to demonstrate how high were the stakes in the debate over acts before Revelation: at issue were the nature of being, the nature of knowing, and the definition and significance of Islam itself.

Chapter 7

Conceptual Sources of the Problem

Setting the Stage—Adequacy and Boundary Problems

"Before Revelation" was for Muslims, and ought to be for students of Islam, a *camera obscura,* as we said above, a means rather than merely an end. The problem was posed not to ask about the obligations of proto-Muslims, but the duties of contemporary Muslims.

In this chapter the goal is to bring the background to the fore and show some of the matters implicit in the before revelation complex. It seems clear that the setting for this debate is what might be called adequacy problems: Revelation once closed is limited in the subjects it addresses. Is that limitation to be accepted or is Revelation to be extended, augmented somehow? In this setting the conflict comes from two distinct and competing visions of the moral world, one ontological and subjectivist, the other deontic and objectivist. The former is associated with the Permitted and Proscribed positions, and the other with No Assessors.

To show how this is so, however, it must first be understood that the before Revelation question, at its most fundamental, asks questions about boundaries: What is inside and what is outside? Where are boundaries to be drawn in time, in space, between Islam and not Islam? Where are the lines drawn between inside and outside the community, between what Revelation includes and what it does not, and between acts that Revelation categorizes and those it does not? What determines the lines between things denominated by a particular word, and things not included in its meaning?

Islamics scholarship has for the most part offered the polemical hypothesis to explain the origin of Muslim controversies: These debates came to be as a result of controversies between conservatives and liberals, traditionists and rationalists, Muslims and non-Muslims. The argument of this chapter is that the source of these debates was a constructive one: While elaborating the heritage of successive generations of Muslim thought, scholars found certain structural divides. If reflected upon, a choice made in one domain was seen to ramify in another. Decisions taken on legal terminology, as this chapter will demonstrate, had consequences for ontological theory, and positions held on how language worked had important consequences for Islamic praxis.

IGNORED OR PERMITTED?: THE MEANING OF *MUBĀḤ* (PERMITTED)

Mubāḥ denotes the medial category in the fivefold Muslim assessment of acts, and may either be translated as Neutral, or Permitted. Like the other four, the assessment *mubāḥ* is defined by its relation to antitheses: praise or blame, reward or punishment, doing or refraining from doing[1]. Yet which of these antipodes *mubāḥ* lies between is a matter of utmost significance because each pair defines an ethical epistemology sharply at odds with the other alternatives. Fundamentally, however, the question at issue is whether acts classified as *mubāḥ*—Neutral or Permitted—lie within or outside the shadow of the *shar*ʿ. Are these acts towards which Revelation is indifferent, or are they acts without consequence which are nevertheless permitted by the Legislator?[2] It was partly to help define the scope of the *shar*ʿ that the before revelation complex was discussed.

The problem arises from the indeterminacy of the concept "medial act." These medial acts are of two sorts—acts which Revelation explicitly permits and stipulates that doing it and non-doing it are equivalent—and acts about which Revelation seems to say nothing.[3] It is the second category, the problem of Revelational lacunae, that was most controversial. "What the *shar*ʿ is silent about: It is said: 'It continues as it was,' and it is described as Permitted, in one sense."[4]

With the dichotomy good/detestable, the *mubāḥ* act rests with the good side; and with the dichotomy Obligatory/forbidden, it is a third category, outside the scale. On this all agreed. Further definitions, however, led to controversy. Some defined *mubāḥ* as that for which there is neither reward nor punishment. These are the consequentialists. For others, it is "something about which there is no assessment"; something legitimate (*ḥalāl*) and unrestricted (*ṭilq*), since things for which there is no assessment are implicitly Permitted and good.[5]

These who might be called *subjectivists* rested their definition on innate responses to the quality of the act. *Mubāḥ* is "that for the doing of which there is neither praise nor blame,[6] and as something having no attribute other than 'goodness' that causes it to deserve praise or reward";[7] in the fancier language of the theologians "*mubāḥ* is something the existence of which is not preferred to its non-existence in terms of deserving reward and blame."[8]

The third group, the deontologists, argued simply that Permitted meant "that which was Permitted by a Permitter," namely the Legislator, God. Al-

Zarkashī shows quite clearly the link between definitions of *mubāḥ* and consequences for the before revelation argument when he defines the term:

> [*Mubāḥ*] is what one is allowed to do or not do . . . without specifying either of the two of them. [Any definition involving praise and blame] would go beyond allowance (*idhn*) [since] these things remain assessments before the coming of Revelation (*al-shar'*); hence [the act] could not be called Permitted.[9]

Consequentialists

Perhaps the earliest perspective is the consequentialist school: For them, acts are categorized according to whether the doer is promised reward or threatened with punishment.[10] This understanding of the value of acts is clearly consistent with the Qur'ān, which is entirely consequentialist throughout. For the consequentialists, *mubāḥ* meant "inconsequential." Al-Jaṣṣāṣ, for instance, defines *al-mubāḥ* as "that for the doing of which the one made-responsible (*mukallaf*) does not deserve reward, nor [does he deserve] punishment for the avoidance of it. . . ." A conceptually synonymous definition of *mubāḥ* is "harmlessness" (*lā ḥaraj*).[11]

Yet this straightforward, and scripturally based definition was not adequate. The standard critique was that it was too broad to be of use, since included within its pale were the inconsequential acts of God, madmen, minors, and animals, whose actions were—particularly in the case of the Almighty—certainly not stipulated (*shara'a*) by anything or anybody.[12] Some thought that the absence of harm implied a continuity between pre- and post-Revelational acts, since an act may be harmless both before and after Revelation if it does not manifestly damage its doer in this world or the next. More importantly, this definition might let a whole class of acts remain outside the purview of the *shar'*.[13] In addition, focus on consequence in the definition of assessments may restrict the scope of God's mercy. Moreover it also allowed a kind of continuity between pre- and post-Revelational acts that diminished the significance of Revelation itself as a community-forming, epochal event.[14] Though later scholars often cited the consequentialist definition they generally used other, more sophisticated ones as well.

Subjectivists

Another understanding of the meaning of *mubāḥ*, one that clearly defined the term to mean "neutral," "indifferent," or "unmarked," arose from a subjectivist epistemology, typical of the Jubbā'ī Mu'tazilah, but shared by some Shāfi'īs and Ḥanafīs as well.[15] For these scholars, *mubāḥ* acts are those which arouse neither approval nor disgust (*istiḥsān/istiqbāḥ*), for which one neither praises nor blames (*madḥ/dhamm*). These acts are insignificant because there is no instinctive attraction or repulsion to signify their value. For the subjectivists, moral knowledge is precisely the attention to these inner promptings, and so the *mubāḥ* act is effectively outside the scope of morality, and outside the scope of the *shar'*.

Abū l-Ḥusayn al-Baṣrī, for instance, says that the *mubāḥ* act is something about which "*there is no assessment*."[16] He defines Permittedness as "something the existence of which is not preferred to its non-existence in terms of deserving (*yastaḥiqqu*) reward and blame,"[17] as something "having no attribute other than goodness that causes it to be deserving of praise or reward," or, as being something that "God has permitted and indicated to us its goodness (*ḥusnih*). . . ." The *mubāḥ*-thing is described as "legitimate (*ḥalāl*)" and "unrestricted (*ṭilq*)."[18]

All of these definitions point to the outsideness, and the unmarked character of the *mubāḥ* act. To say that an act is good means simply that the act belongs to the largest category of acts, since the presumptive assessment of all acts is goodness. The absence of any aesthetic response to an act (detesting, or approving it), the absence of any response to the one who performed the act (praise or blame), and the absence of any threat or promise which would attract one to or repel one from the act, all indicate that the act lacks any moral quality whatsoever, and so it is pushed to the side: Doing it or not is a matter of indifference to God and humankind both.

The "et cetera" quality of *mubāḥ* is particularly clear in the definition provided by the Mu'tazilī Imāmī scholar, al-Sharīf al-Murtaḍá. Here he points out by analysis all the things that *mubāḥ* acts are not.

> By being good, [the *mubāḥ* act] is distinguished from the detestable, and from what is neither good nor detestable. Inasmuch as there is no harm in [doing] it, and neither praise nor blame, it is distinguished from "the Recommended" (*al-nadb*) and the Obligatory (*al-wājib*). By correlating [the actor's awareness to the act's] status, it is distinguished from the good that takes place [solely by the action of] God Most High.[19] [For, God's acts] have no attribute other than being good, such as consequentiality (*istīfā'al-'iqāb*), because it is inconceivable that God Most High be informed or indicated to [by anyone else, of their moral status]. [And by its correlation, *al-mubāḥ* is similarly differentiated from] the acts of animals [who cannot discern the status of acts from the act's circumstances]. . . .[20]

For these subjectivists, who tend also to be Permitters, the term *mubāḥ* signifies acts to which humans have no affective response. They are "so what" acts. Because human response to them is So what? they infer that God and Revelation respond similarly. Acts about which Revelation is silent, and to which there is no reaction, lack any quality except the general one of being good. In a sense then, Revelation remains silent about a whole class of acts, and these acts are outside the moral concern of Muslims and their Revelation.

Deontologists

It is the third group, the deontologists, who were most successful at integrating a triumphalist *heilsgeschichte* with a more-or-less logically coherent account of neutral acts. They were able successfully to combine an awareness of the significance of Islamic Revelation with the recognition that not all acts have moral significance.

The deontologists understood the term *mubāḥ*, with philological justification, as meaning Permitted. For them, Permitted acts were part of the imperative of Revelation; Revelation—and through Revelation, the Legislator—explicitly *Permitted* these acts. To know the value of these acts required knowledge of the will of the Permitter. Revelation, for them, is indifferent to nothing; even acts that have no value nonetheless remain within the awareness of Revelation. As such, they are medial but not marginal; they fall fully within the scope of Revelation's dictates.[21]

On this account any assessment (*ḥukm*) relates information about how the actor ought to act vis-à-vis the act, but that information is provided solely through Revelation. Consequently the status quo ante is irrelevant to the act's assessment afterwards, even if before and after Revelation the act seems to be neither good nor detestable. In this view, moreover, Revelational silence is not neglect or indifference but a positive sign, positively provided by the Legislator that this act is Permitted, but without consequences for doing or not doing it.[22] The term *mubāḥ* differs from the other four assessments only in that it is not a charging-with-duty (*taklīf*).[23] Every act, therefore, is qualified by Revelation's dictates. No act is marginal, no act is assessed by any assessor other than God, through His speech.

Each of these understandings of the medial category, that it is inconsequential, that it triggers no attraction or aversion, that it is explicitly Permitted, has its attractions. For the consequentialists, there is a clear correspondence between their language and that of Revelation itself: acts have consequences, for good or ill. Those acts that do not, have no value. They are *mubāḥ*. For the subjectivists, an entire epistemological and ontological edifice, as we shall see below, is constructed on human response to acts and things. The bond linking acts' moral value to their ontology is preserved, as is the role of human intellectuality. The deontologists, for their part, preserved God's sovereignty and maximized the scope of His Revelation. They insured that no act lay outside the *shar*ʿ, and they kept human reason firmly in its proper, subordinate place.

Stepping back from the argument, it is clear that what is at issue is the significance of Revelational silence. Does it signify a moral lacuna, or is it a positive sign of Permission? In the absence of explicit Revelational information, can one augment moral knowledge from other sources, or must one rest content with the datum of the Legislator's silence? It is surely this larger issue that gave rise to the discussion of the value of acts before revelation.

Revelational Silence

Necessarily, a historical Revelation is limited in its scope; it may be seen to be inadequate when pressed to measure every event in a world different from that in which it first appeared. In the face of this inadequacy, Muslims proposed three possible solutions. 1. Revelation's application may be limited to those matters explicitly discussed within it.[24] The solution is not without difficulties: a literalist hermeneutic is as difficult to define as any other. More importantly, by limiting Revelation to its most manifest meaning some sectors of life are hived off from the rest as religious—in this case, Islamic—and the remainder is left an amoral void. 2. Revelation may be extended in scope, beyond its obvious Revelational boundaries, so as to be all-encompassing and never silent.

> There is nothing but that God has an assessment for it. . . . There is nothing in the world that lacks exemption, or Proscription, or Obligation, since every food, drink, clothing or intercourse on the earth, or judgment between two disputants, or anything else whatsoever—[everything has] an assessment.[25]

This extension may take place in two ways. 2a. Either Revelation may be extended in its scope by a hermeneutic that augments its address, so that in prescribing A, it is also seen to address B, C, and D. Or 2b, Revelation may be augmented by referring to other sources of moral knowledge. This latter method has a certain intrinsic appeal since the Qur'ān itself is far from narrow in the sources to which it appeals for confirmation: it invokes the *'aql*,[26] indicants and signs from nature, the Revelations of other Peoples of the Book—all are cited to confirm the message of the Qur'ān. Those confronted by the limitations of Islamic Revelation might very well be inclined then to turn to those extra-Qur'ānic sources which, conversely, are then legitimated by Qur'ānic reference to them.

The sources used by those who took this last approach would include the *'aql* which can calculate the relative harm and benefit accruing from an act. Extra-Scriptural sources might include pre-Islamic custom or assessments.[27] Revelation might also be extended by referring to other Revelations, outside the boundaries of Islam.[28]

Revelational silence, or questions of Revelational adequacy, lead inexorably to boundary problems. What are the boundaries of Revelation?; is anything *not* covered by Revelation?; how permeable are the boundaries of Islamic knowledge to other sources of moral information?[29]

A Particular Instance of Revelational Silence

In his *Kitāb al-Ashribah*, Ibn Qutaybah has preserved an early controversy over the permissibility of *nabīdh*, the alcoholic drink produced from steeped fruit or grain, and therefore of uncertain relation to *khamr*—a fermented product of grape juice, a drink more or less clearly forbidden in the Qur'ān.[30] *Nabīdh*, however, is not mentioned in the Qur'ān.

It is well known that Muslims forbid the drinking of wine. Yet in an early period the scope of this prohibition was a matter of some controversy. No less a personage than the great Syrian jurist Sufyān al-Thawrī (d. 161/778), drank burned *nabīdh* (*nabīdh ṣalb*), "from which his two cheeks would redden."[31] Ḥanafīs regularly permitted *nabīdh* and pointed to the Prophet's consumption of something of the same name as a precedent.[32] While Ibn Qutaybah's school abhorred the drinking of wine, in his book he presents a rather lengthy account of his opponents' position which helps us to see what is at issue in such questions as the before revelation complex. As he sees it, his opponents, the defenders of *nabīdh*-drinking, when confronted with Revelational silence chose to augment the text of Revelation with knowledge drawn from elsewhere—generally accepted maxims, consensus, and the practice of other Revelational communities—rather than supplementing Revelation from within.

Extra-Revelational Signs

To augment Revelation, *nabīdh* drinkers invoked first a general legal maxim against those who would ban the drink: "All things," they said, "are licit (*ḥalāl*) except those that God has (explicitly) forbidden."[33] In other words, if there is no sign of a thing's prohibition, that silence amounts to a sign of its permissibility. Revelational silence means that the act is Permitted.

The *nabīdh* drinkers use general principles through which the detailed stipulations of Qur'ānic legislation are to be read. For instance, God's restrictions of things are themselves limited: "He never forbids a thing but that he provides a compensation; the compensation for the loss of *khamr* being the licitness of *nabīdh*(!)."[34] In addition, "God created provisions and fruits as an enablement (*qādir*[an]) for some need of humankind." Therefore its *usefulness* is a sign of its licitness.[35] Further, the *nabīdh* drinkers pointed to communal practice: "All of the Kufans save Ibn Idrīs [al-Shāfi'ī] are agreed that such is the case." Moreover, Ibn Idrīs himself is said to confess that the best among the Kūfans are precisely those who drink wine.[36] Here Revelation is supplemented with local custom.

The *nabīdh* faction also argued for a restrictive hermeneutic that limited Revelation's scope. Given that silence meant Permission, a restrictive hermeneutic in fact means a more permissive Revelation. The tool for this argument was philology, which they invoked to defend a literalist hermeneutic. In a prohibition, they said, it is the *restricted* sense of a word that defines a word's juristic field. The name (*ism*) describes a thing, and in the process limits its extension and scope; it is not the implication of the word (*ma'ná*) that is operative:[37]

> As for the statement [of the ones who would forbid *nabīdh*] that *khamr* is what ferments;[38] and intoxicants are fermented; so that [*nabīdh*] is a *khamr* like [*khamr* itself]: [We say]: "things may resemble each other in some respects (*ma'ānī*) and thus be so described (*yusammá*) for a [certain] reason (*bi-'illat*[in] *fīhi*); [that aspect may also] be found in another [object]; but that description is not [necessarily] applied to the other [thing]."[39]

All resemblances are not legally efficacious and it is not the fullest but most restricted, most precise, understanding of the word that applies. As examples, the *nabīdh* drinkers offer something called by nearly the same name as *khamr*, namely *khamīr*, leaven.

> Do you not see that milk ferments in the curds you find when you leave it till it curdles, but milk is not called *khamr*. The leaven of dough (*khamīr al-'ajīn*) is called leaven (*khamīr*) but it is not, nor is dough that is fermented with it, called *khamr*.[40] [Do you not also see that] infusion of dates [is called] "intoxicating spirits (*sukār*) because of its power to intoxicate (*iskār*), but nothing other than it is called intoxicant (*sākir*[an]), though it [too] may intoxicate."
>
> It is the more normal practice in the speech of the Arabs [to restrict the meaning of a word] rather than to use it in the widest possible sense (*nuḥīṭ*[u] *bih*)[41]

Perhaps most disturbingly, the Kufans who drank *nabīdh* also appealed directly to sources outside the Islamic community for vindication.

> Were the forbiddenness of wine on account of intoxication, why did He not apply [the prohibition] to the Prophets and nations before us? Noah drank [*nabīdh*] when he went out of the ark . . . until he became intoxicated from it; . . . Lot drank it; and Jesus drank it on the night of the Ascension (*laylat al-raf'*),[42] and Muslims drank [*nabīdh*] at the inception of Islam.[43]

This is unequivocally a turn toward outside sources: Neither in Qur'ān nor in Islamic tradition is wine associated with these prophets,[44] yet Biblical accounts all associate these figures with wine, albeit not always in the most positive way. Noah gets drunk on wine and his son Ham sees him in that condition and is subsequently cursed.[45] Lot gets drunk and sleeps with his daughters.[46] And Jesus of course consecrates wine at the Last Supper.[47]

So the *nabīdh* drinkers argue from the Hebrew Bible and the New Testament that because these other communities drank wine, the Qur'ānic dictum is restricted. In other words, the Qur'ān is limited in its meanings by the praxic norms of other religious communities. These legists sought to amalgamate a moral epistemology from sources inside and outside the boundaries of Revelation. They used maxims—both Muslim revelation and not—, social custom, and the norms and practices of those before and outside historical Islam. The test for this synthetic method was a literalist hermeneutic that minimized the compass of Revelational dictates.

This perspective is not illogical, nor is it impossible to defend from within Revelation itself; at the same time the threat to the integrity and hegemony of the (still young) tradition is obvious. The conflict here is between those who cast the net of moral epistemology broadly and those who cast it closer to Revelation's shore and this is surely part of the backdrop of the before revelation debate.

A sketch of Ibn Qutaybah's method will clarify the alternative and the critique of the more integrist Islamic moral epistemology.

Ibn Qutaybah offered an alternative theory of Revelational scope. He argues that intoxication *in potentia* is the measure of whether something falls under the scope of *khamr*'s prohibition. Thus, he says, in choosing the word *khamr*, the Qur'ān provides a sign indicating that all intoxicants, including *nabīdh*, are enjoined. But what is his proof? It is entirely revelational. "Khamr is forbidden by the Book; and intoxicants by the *sunnah* [of the Prophet]." "The Messenger of God . . . said Every intoxicant is wine; every intoxicant is forbidden . . . Every intoxicant is forbidden and what intoxicates in a *faraq*, a sip of it is forbidden. . . . "[48]

He refers to etymology only secondarily: to quote the maxim "*khamr* is what beclouds (*khāmara*) the '*aql*, and to define intoxication as the loss of the '*aql*.[49] The logic of his argument extending the Scriptural sources to *nabīdh* is this:

1. Words refer by suggesting an underlying, essential concept.
2. When the Qur'ān bans *khamr*, and the *sunnah* bans intoxicants, they metonymously ban the class of intoxicants of which *khamr* is an *exemplum*.
3. *Nabīdh* belongs also to the class, "intoxicants."
4. Therefore *nabīdh* is forbidden as *khamr* is.[50]

Two points require mention here: The first is that Ibn Qutaybah argues exclusively from Revelational sources. The second is that to make this epistemology work every Revelational dictate must be understood to have the widest possible scope unless explicitly restricted. Consequently Revelation is able, in effect, to supplement and amplify itself. The result is an epistemology that is very flexible, very extensive, but one capable in most cases of remaining solely within the boundaries of Revelation.[51]

The coherence of supplementing Revelation from within, rather than from without, was, as it turned out, persuasive. In the process of clarifying the theory behind Ibn Qutaybah's (and al-Shāfi'ī's) juridico-linguistic thought, other problems arose, however.

For instance, al-Muzanī (d. 264/878), one of al-Shāfi'ī's students (and roughly a contemporary of Ibn Qutaybah), demonstrates quite clearly how legal and linguistic issues can easily lead to other, ontological questions.

> If God or his Prophet orders something and names it [by way of specification], then to anything to which the name applies, to it applies also the assessment without restriction and definitively.[52]

Al-Muzanī's point is that the assessment is unrestricted and obligatory unless God or His Prophet indicate otherwise. This is Ibn Qutaybah's point also—that a ban on *khamr* is a ban on everything to which that term could reasonably be applied. In the process, however, al-Muzanī affirms an identity between the thing named and the assessment. An equation is established between *being a certain thing* and *having a certain moral quality* (*ḥukm*).

When acts are praised or damned in the Qur'ān they are seldom qualified; commands seem seldom to reflect situation ethics. Humans are commanded to do this, abjure that, for the most part without specification of situation, and the rare instance of a circumstantial modification would seem to confirm al-Shā fi'ī's hermeneutic rule that the most obvious (*ẓahir*) and least restricted (*'āmmī*) meaning of a of a Qur'ānic locution is to be preferred.[53] Something is good because it is "a truth-telling," detestable because it is a "falsehood"; a useful act, being good, is Permitted because good things are Permitted: all of these seem to follow in a comprehensible way from the identity of a thing (red fruit, for example) and its name (apple), from the link between its qualities (good, useful) and its name (apple).[54] It is taken for granted that a divine command refers to an act as an instance of a category of acts. When this principle is combined with the hermeneutic rule that al-Muzanī assumes—that a phrase or command is unrestricted unless there is an explicit textual restriction—it becomes a natural inference that good acts are good without restriction, and are always and everywhere good; and that the moral quality of a thing (good, commanded) may be as much a part of its being as its other intrinsic qualities—redness, roundness, sweetness, etc. This categorical identity is reinforced by the quasi-identity between a thing and its name found in both Revelation and early Arab linguistic scholarship.[55]

Debate on the sources of moral knowledge led to debates on the nature of language. Assertions about the nature of Revelational language led in turn to controversy over distinguishing the thing from its moral quality. Is there something in the nature of the lie that "makes" it detestable/forbidden? Can a lie exist that is *not* detestable, *not* forbidden? And if the lie, for instance, is forbidden, is it forbidden because it is detestable, or is it detestable because it is forbidden?

The before Revelation debate, it should be clear, was found profitable as a "thing to think with" because of structural ambiguities in nascent Islamic legal thought. It will not do simply to see this debate as rationalists versus traditionalists, not least because there are rationalists and traditionalists on both sides of the argument. All Islamic legists faced the problems of what to do in the face of a limited body of Revelation, and all legists were forced to choose some theory of the relation between the linguistic term and that to which it referred, when determining the scope of a Revelational imperative.

Chapter 8

Abū l-Hudhayl and the Early Mu'tazilah

At roughly the same time that al-Muzanī was affirming the identity of the thing and its assessment, a metaphysician, Abū l-Hudhayl b. 'Allāf (135/752–3 40 226/840–1), was making similar claims.

At this point we must veer from legal thought to metaphysics since some of the positions attacked in *uṣūl al-fiqh* literature, as in al-Ghazālī's section translated above, survive only in theological works and heresiographies, and we know them only in their theological guise. Moreover, to arrive at an understanding of Revelation's role in moral knowledge, one path taken was a metaphysical one. The problem of acts before Revelation is a theological one as well, and attempts to ground the moral quality of the act in the act's nature cannot but lead to epistemological and ontological discussions of considerable abstraction and technicality.

The problems that shape the next two sections are these:

1. It seems that there is a consensus among human beings that certain acts—lying, unjustified killing, for example—are reprehensible. How can these common moral assessments be accounted for in a way that maintains a place for the imperatives of the specifically Islamic Revelation not shared by Christians, Jews, Brahmins, and the like? If Muslims rejected the notion that all humans can intuitively recognize some acts as good, others as repellent, then a whole part of human experience was cut off and denied, and the *urgency*, the emotional force of even the Islamic kerygma was lost. Yet if they accepted moral intuition as a source of moral knowledge, they derogated Revelation as the ground of moral knowledge and action.
2. The second, and subsidiary problem was this: If one identifies the moral assessment of an act with the act itself, as al-Muzanī does, how can one avoid saying, "lies are bad," which as al-Ghazālī points out, does not take account of the lie that is good or even Obligatory. More broadly, the problem is how

to reconcile the generic prohibitions and commands of Revelation with the complexity and ambiguity of lived moral experience.[1]

This section and the next describe first some early Mu'tazilī attempts to link tightly the act and its moral quality, and then the refutation of that early attempt by another group of Mu'tazilīs. Criticism of the Baghdādī Mu'tazilah by 'Abdaljabbār and his school arises from a discontent with the static quality of the early attempts at moral ontology. We argue here that the Basran moral system—elsewhere extensively discussed by Peters, Frank, Bernard and Hourani[2]—must be seen as an attempt to loosen the bonds of ontology by moving the locus of an act's value from its *being* qua being, to a more transient aspect of the act—that part of its ontology that arose from its being a specific act occurring in specific circumstances of time and place.

Moral Knowing

As the first formulator of many of the problems that were subsequently to occupy Mu'tazilī thinkers, Abū l-Hudhayl (d. 226/840) set the agenda for the discussion of epistemology in the moral realm.[3] For Abū l-Hudhayl, and even more for his opponents, it was the definition of the '*aql* that differentiated his epistemology from that of other scholars.[4] Knowledge is conveyed by God's lodgment of knowledge and perception in the knower or perceiver, not simply by hearing or being informed (*ta'līm*).[5] "Mind" (*al-'aql*) is both the underlying *capacity* for acquired knowledge, and the innate or acquired possession of certain obvious and indisputable facts, such as that the sky is different from the ground, or that the person himself is not a donkey.[6] This notion that the '*aql* as knowledge is pivotal in Mu'tazilī moral ontology, and is much misunderstood. Al-Ash'arī reports that Abū l-Hudhayl held the '*aql* to be

> the indubitable knowledge by which a person differentiates between himself and a donkey, between the sky and earth, and things similar to that. [It is also] the faculty (*al-quwwah*) by which one acquires knowledge. They allege also that the '*aql* is knowing (*ḥiss*),[7] that we call "the '*aql*," meaning, "what is known as reasonable [through the '*aql*] (*al-ma'qūl*)."[8]

If this account is to be trusted, Abū l-Hudhayl and his circle defined the '*aql* as *both* the means of knowing, and the knowledge thus acquired. The hazy boundaries between action and thing in Arabic verbal nouns means further that '*aql* may be understood as the process of knowing certain things as well. Thus all knowledge had its locus in human capacity; there could be little significant knowledge arriving from elsewhere.

What is not generally understood is that the problematic of the *'aql* arises in part from the universal recognition of its place in legal responsibility.[9] In the *Maqālāt*, al-Ash'arī's section on *'aql* begins, "people differ concerning the attainment of [legal] majority (*al-bulūgh*)."[10] And while a group called "the ones-who-do-*fiqh* (*al-mutafaqqihūn*)" (probably anti-speculativists) tried to argue that it was mere age (attaining 15, or 17 years) that made one subject to the obligations of the *shar'*, the majority held that it was soundness of the *'aql* (*salāmat al-'aql*) together with the physical changes of puberty that brought one under the scope of the *shar'*. Those whom al-Ash'arī calls "theologians" saw majority coming solely from the *perfection* of the *'aql* (*kamāl al-'aql*).[11] For some, at any rate, to have the *'aql* was to be responsible; to lack it or have it imperfectly was to be released from responsibility. Hence, for all but the least speculative of legists and theologians, the mere presence of the *'aql* made one morally, legally responsible.

What was it about the *'aql*, whether knowledge or faculty for obtaining knowledge, that brought one to moral obligation? One answer was Abū l-Hudhayl's. He evidently had a schema of moral development by stages—now lost to us—that accounted for human recognition of God and our obligations towards God. In it are three important aspects of Abū l-Hudhayl's moral epistemology: First, he says, moral knowledge is innate in all human beings. This knowledge arrives merely as part of human development. Second, moral *knowledge* is part of self-awareness. One is necessarily informed by one's self-knowledge, of God, his unity and his justice. (There remain, however, some sorts of knowledge—of secondary importance one cannot help but feel—that can be known only by Revelation.) Third, and consequently, moral *duty* and knowledge of its obligations depends not upon Revelation but upon human nature and capacity independent of Revelation.

> "[Abū l-Hudhayl] based his statement concerning the progression of experiential knowledge (*ma'rifah*) [upon his notion of two sorts of knowledge of God: indisputable and acquired]. [In this] he contradicted the rest of the Muslim community. He said, concerning an infant that is in the second stage of its self-consciousness,[12] all must necessarily come to the experiential knowledge of the unity [of God] and [His] justice without any lacunae.[13] Similarly it is incumbent upon him to come—given his knowledge of the unity of God, Glory be to Him!, and His justice—to experiential knowledge (*ma'rifah*) of all that God has charged him to do. If he does not come to all of this knowledge in the "second stage of self-consciousness," and he dies in the "third stage," he is an ingrate (*kāfir*) and an enemy of God, and he deserves eternity in the Fire. But as for his knowledge of that which is known only by report of Revelation (*al-sam'*), he must come to know this in "the second stage" upon hearing information which constitutes a proof, and precludes excuses.[14]

In other words, a human being can discern God's characteristics, and from those draw conclusions about moral life. Not to discern God's preeminent characteristics, and not to draw the implications from His justice and unity for moral action, justifies punishment of one who has been in effect summoned to moral life but has rejected that summons—whether or not one is acquainted with any Revelation whatsoever.[15] Consequently,

> [Abū l-Hudhayl] alleged that there is no holder of fanciful opinions (*ṣāḥib hawá*) nor any *zindiq*, but that he is obedient to God Most High in many things, even if he disobeys Him as far as his infidelity (*kufr*) is concerned.[16]

Of what significance is Revelation if one can be said to be obedient to God while at the same time rejecting (*kafara*) Revelation? For Abū l-Hudhayl and others, Revelation was no more than cultic detail. This understanding of Revelation proved ultimately unacceptable to Muslims as a whole.

Moral Essentialism: Abū l-Hudhayl and al-Ka'bī

Abū l-Hudhayl's moral ontology can fairly be characterized as an attempt to recognize an inextricable unity tying the qualities that make a thing what it is, definitionally or in the abstract (apple), to those qualities that qualify the being (red). There was, for Abū l-Hudhayl, no "Apple" to be qualified by "Redness." Rather, the apple is red inseparably. For him, an accident inheres in all the atoms of the substrate and so, the substrate that makes something "an apple," and the accidents that make it "this apple" are indissolubly connected.[17]

Of course Abū l-Hudhayl distinguished between the substrate—the atoms that are the locus for the accidents, and the accidents themselves.[18] At the same time, he argued that the substrate is nonexistent apart from the accidents that qualify it. There is no essence without its accidents; there are no accidents apart from the atoms in which they inhere.

The implications of this theory for moral thought are these: in the case of the good act, there is no "act" qualified by "good." There is only "this good act, now." The good pertains to the act just as the other elements that might define it—color, size, shape, duration, are part of it and indissoluble from it;[19] its goodness is inseparable from its existence. Consequently, Thanking the Benefactor is good, because it is an instance of Thanking the Benefactor, which is made up from, inter alia, "goodness."

From the notion that accidents and substrates commingle, two important ideas follow:

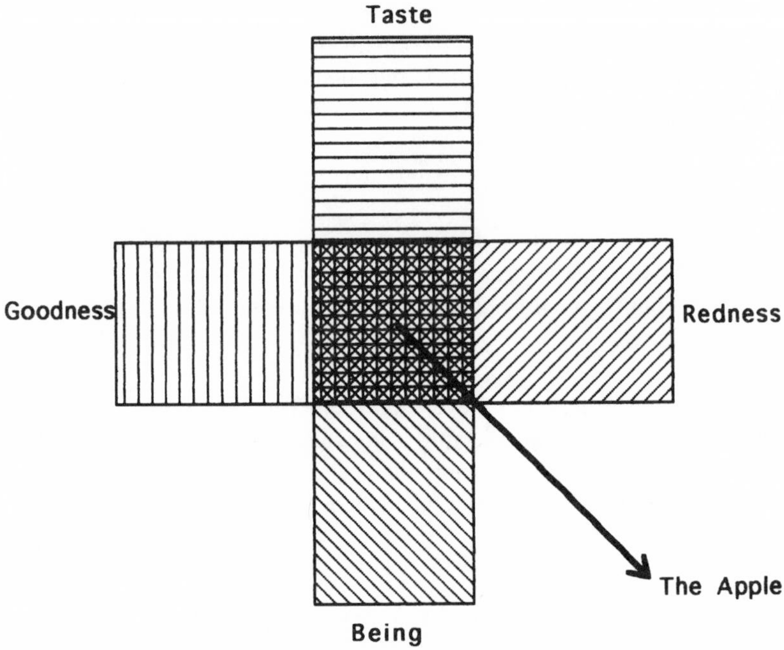

1. We *know* whether or not an act is good the way we know other features of the thing or act: its duration, its color, etc. This doctrine is consistent with the identity of the name of a thing and its assessment, asserted by al-Muzanī and others, as we saw above.
2. It also follows, however, that a "good" *being* is "good" ontologically in the same way that it is what it is, definitionally. It may follow that to imagine a "good lie" is as impossible to imagine as a five-legged horse.

This rigid view of ethical ontology was transmitted to—or at least shared by—the later catalytic figure, the Baghdādī Mu'tazilī Abū l-Qāsim al-Ka'bī (d. 319/931).[20] Al-Ka'bī shared Abū l-Hudhayl's views on the inseparability of accident and substrate, or the commingling of the two, and he did identify the evaluation of an act and its nature.[21] A detestable act is detestable, he said, "by what this specific thing is, as itself and as a genus."[22]

For al-Ka'bī, and presumably for the pious Abū l-Hudhayl as well, the consequence was an uncompromising moral system, as we learn from a critic:

> [Chapter heading]: That no willed [act] that is detestable could conceivably exist being good.
>
> Abū l-Qāsim [al-Ka'bī] held that this [shift from good to detestable] was not possible. Thus he says, concerning every accident, "If

it exists and is detestable, it is inconceivable that it should come to exist and then be good."[23]

The rigor of this perspective is clear. There is no situational ethics. All lies are detestable; this particular lie, no matter its situation, is consequently detestable.

Al-Ka'bī, as we saw above in the discussion of the Proscribed position, occupies a unique position: a rigorist who trusted the uncomplicated judgment of the *'aql*, while being at the same time suspicious of *hadīth;*[24] indeed, he believed that the *'aql* was the criterion to judge the *sunnah*, not the other way around, as other rigorists believed.[25] He was both a pietist and a speculativist, and we may suppose that here he is preserving the plain meaning of Qur'ānic commands ("Do not drink wine,") by building the assessment of the act into its nature. Thus good wine, good lies, detestable gratitude, detestably veracity, are all incoherent and impossible. He preserves, as does Abū l-Hudhayl, the powerful, intuitively appealing notion that some acts are good per se, and are immediately perceived as such. This rigor comes at a cost, however. The whole structure is vulnerable to reasonable counter-examples of the kind al-Ghazālī gives.[26] With one plausible instance of an act both good and detestable according to circumstance, the whole ontological edifice comes tumbling down. And there are, in fact, many such acts.

On just such grounds his most persuasive critics attacked him. These were first and foremost not "traditionists" or traditionalists, but Mu'tazilīs as well, not schooled in Baghdad, but in Basra.

Critics

Indeed, even within al-Ka'bī's own school of Baghdādī Mu'tazilīs, some retreated from his too rigid moral theory.

> Some of the more recent among [the school of al-Ka'bī] hold, concerning something detestable, that there is that which is detestable in itself (*li-nafsih*) and there is that which is detestable because of detestability (*qubḥ*); and similarly [with] the good: [Therefore] they say that a body is good because of the existence of a causal determinant (*ma'ná*) and this is "the good." [Thus,] it is possible that it exist [as good] and then become detestable by a detestability arising in it. And they say 'good' is one of the accidents and is good in itself. What is detestable is detestable of itself. (This is not permissible according to Abū l-Qāsim.)[27]

The critics of al-Ka'bī attacked all those who identified the assessment of a thing with knowledge of the thing itself. Al-Muzanī and other rigorists had wanted to assert the identity of the "name" and the assessment, but for the Basran Mu'tazilah, this meant imbedding the assessment of the act too deeply within the act's ontology. Instead, the Basrans preferred to locate moral qualities of the act as far from its essence as possible. The Basrans' general rule was that the more transient aspects of ontology must first be tried as possible links to an act's quality. Assessments reflect qualities more fleeting than, for instance, the redness of an apple. Since the transient-causation (which they called the *wajh*) *can* account for an act's value, it must be allowed to do so.

> If it is possible to account for the "good" of a body by [reference to] its coming-to-be in a certain way (*'alá wajh*) then it is not permissible to [account for its goodness by reference to] the existence of a causal determinant (*ma'ná*)
>
> In other words: The manifestation in-a-certain-way (*wajh*) is what brings about the attribute (*ṣifah*) [goodness], if it acquires sufficient effect. Therefore it is not permissible to locate [the attribute goodness] in a compelling causal determinant. If you [did so] then the assigning of a cause would not be defined with sufficient precision.[28]

According to the Basrans, if one does otherwise, one is led to the absurdity of saying that something detestable is always and everywhere detestable, which is clearly not the case.

> Anyone's desire to move when they are [for some reason] unable to do so is detestable;[29] if one were enabled, by this capacity it would be possible [to move]. Then, if we [moved], it would be good provided all aspects (*wajh*s) of detestability were excluded.[30]

Al-Ka'bī is clearly unable to account for certain moral "facts," particularly including the variability of moral assessments according to circumstance. Knowing what a thing is, does not tell you *how* it is, morally. The thing would otherwise have to have a moral quality assigned to it before it actually occurred, among other absurdities.[31]

While the ontology of the Mu'tazilah is no longer sympathetic to us—accidents, essences, substrates and the like—the Mu'tazilah did disagree over questions whose implications at least still move us to debate. Is killing, for example, categorically wrong? The Basrans, in effect, broke this problem into three separate technical questions:

1. If we know of an act, merely by knowing what it is, do we know what its moral assessment should be? (Is *this* act of killing—slaughtering a sheep, in this particular circumstance—reprehensible because "killing is always bad?"[32])

2. Can an act, considered in the abstract, have any moral quality at all, prior to its actualization, its becoming embedded in existence and reality? ("Does killing, in the abstract, have any moral quality whatsoever?")
3. Given the notion that the assessment of a particular act is part of its ontology, if the quality of acts of the same type (killing) varies, how can we account for and describe the effect of circumstance on "being"? In other words, what is the effect, ontologically speaking, of particular and various reality on genres of action (killing, lying, being grateful etc.)?

It was with these questions in mind that the Basrans criticized the rigid moral ontologies of al-Ka'bī and his followers. Of course, these questions also determined the form of their own moral theory, as we shall see below. Basran moral theory cannot be understood except as an attack upon and substitute for another more rigid description of the relation of moral assessment to reality, one they took pains to criticize as prolegomena to their own more constructive work. Their account was largely not pitched against the "traditionalists," or even the Ash'arīs, and then, only casually and perfunctorily. It was a dispute within their own ranks that shaped the theory that has from one perspective been most elaborately preserved for us.

Chapter 9

The Basrans: Moral Ontology and Epistemology[1]

Basran Mu'tazilī moral theory arose as a critique of the static essentialism of Abū l-Hudhayl and others. The whole thrust of its arguments cannot be understood unless this point is grasped firmly. Though scholars have written the story as the battle between traditionists and rationalists, such a perspective makes sense only because our (traditionist) sources present it so.[2] The Basrans attacked instead the rigid ethical ontologies of the Baghdādīs.

For the Basrans, like the Baghdādīs, acts are things, and for them, things have essences, attributes, and aspects. The question that 'Abdaljabbār and the other Basrans faced was: where in the act does the its moral status (good/detestable) reside? Abūl-Hudhayl and the Baghdādīs wished to lodge its moral quality within its very being, to make the moral quality part of what made it what it was. For the Basrans, such a theory entailed too rigid a view of the act's moral qualities—since, consequently, similar acts could not differ in value though they differed in context. Yet the Basrans were unwilling to divorce the acts' qualities from the act's being entirely, for this might entail the inability of the mind to perceive its qualities. Instead the Basrans took a commonplace notion, the "*wajh*" (aspect of a thing), and reified it. The *wajh*, they believed, was part of the ontological composite that constituted the nature of a thing or act; yet the *wajh* was only tenuously a part of the act's existence. Precisely because of this tenuosness *it* was the locus of moral quality. In sum, they sought to correct the too-rigid moral theory of the Baghdādīs in three ways.

First, while affirming a connection between the being of a thing and its moral quality, 'Abdaljabbār and the Basrans focused upon the act in situ and the role of moral perception. They refused to assess acts per se but instead judged the act as it manifested itself in practice. Consequently, they recognized that some acts may be both good and detestable at the same time and devised a calculus for determining the dominant moral quality in these acts; nonetheless, some acts could only be, for example, detestable, whatever their context. Second, the Basrans affirmed the significance of the affective aspect of moral assessment. Fear, inner proddings, "tranquillity of the soul," "dispositions of the heart"—in their view all these rightly informed the process of moral judgment. Not only could the qualities of the act be many but the sources of moral knowledge were diverse as well. Finally, to justify this plural epistemology, the Basrans took a pluralistic view of Revelation itself, allowing for knowledge lodged by God in every person, as a form of direct speech, additional to Revelation.

Being and knowing are bound together in what has been called a *phenomenal* moral theory.[3] Since the Basrans imagined themselves to be moral realists—merely perceiving the moral qualities of the act as they existed—the act's nature must be the beginning point in a study of their ethical theory.

Particle Metaphysics: The Ontology of the Act

Conditioning Accidents

For the Basrans, every being is composed of atoms (*jawhar*)[4] and these form a substraté (*maḥall*) in which accidents (*'araḍ*) inhere. The various accidents give a thing its distinctive qualities and its transient qualities as well. Accidents *condition* the composite being of the thing, and make it red, or tall, or heavy, or salty, or moist, or moving, or good.[5]

The problem for the readers of Mu'tazilī texts is that terms used to specify different kinds of accidents seem sometimes to be used as technical terms and sometimes not; worse, the terms used for a given accident vary. A particular accident is named differently depending on the perspective from which it is described, as the same object might be a "paperweight" if used to keep notes from blowing away, a "blunt instrument," if used in an assault, a "nutcracker" if used to open a walnut, and a "hammer" if used to drive a nail.[6]

For accidents, terminology varies according to whether the subject is ontology, or what causes us to perceive ontology. The four terms used are *ma'ná*, *'illah*, *ṣifah*, and *ḥukm*. *Ma'ná* is used to describe the ontological nature of a quality, insofar as it can be imagined to be apart from the thing in which it resides.[7] Thus, "redness" is the "redness" of the apple's being red, and is said to be, as "redness," its *ma'ná*; but when the redness is considered as causative (of the apple's being red) it is called *'illah*.[8] The quality that it causes, namely the apple's *redness*, is called *ṣifah*;[9] the *ṣifah* is the attribute, or adjective in the phrase "the *red* apple." Declaring the apple to be red, or assessing it to be red, or predicating redness of the apple, is an "assessment," (*ḥukm*).[10] In the phrase "this apple is *red*," "red" is the *ḥukm* of the apple.[11]

The temptation is immediately to put goodness or detestability among those qualities that define the thing; one might then say, as al-Ka'bī evidently did, that the detestability of a lie arises because of the attribute detestable (*qubḥ*) inherent in its substrate; detestability for him was a *ma'ná* resident in the category of acts called "lying." Attributes that constitute the act per se are always part of it, no matter the circumstances of the act's existence. There is no circumstance in which the apple becomes less red due to the circumstance in which it comes to be or be used. A red apple is no less red if eaten in a park as opposed to a house; its redness remains if eaten by someone hungry or full, and by a man or a child. Yet an act of informing (*ikhbār*) may be a falsehood or not a falsehood depending on its circumstances (see below), and as al-Ghazālī points out (above) a falsehood can be not merely "not detestable" but even "obligatory" if told to protect a prophet's life. Similarly, an act performed by one unconscious, insane, or asleep, has no value.

For the Basrans, knowing an act's value is a little like judging the taste of an apple. Knowing the characteristic features of an apple—its redness, its roundness—is not sufficient to assess the taste of a particular fruit. For that one must bite the apple, for it is only in the circumstances connected to the occurrence of the particular thing that its otherwise hidden qualities may be found.

The Wajh.[12] According to the Basrans, acts contain attributes that always and everywhere are connected with them, and *wajh*s, "faces" that arise (*waqa'a*) only with the occurrence (*ḥudūth*) of the act. Sometimes these faces present themselves to the observer immediately (*ḍarūratan*). Sometimes in order to discern the relevant *wajh*s he must wonder about it (*naẓar*) and then contemplate it (*tā'ammul*).[13] The *wajh* reveals the value of the act, and when he perceives the *wajh* correctly he has perceived the moral quality of the act he contemplates.[14] If *wajh*s of detestability are found, one considers the effect of the detestability upon the act, considered as a whole.[15] If, on the other hand, one determines that the act is free of these detestable aspects and has a purpose (*gharaḍ*), it is good.[16]

> One knows of an entity (*dhāt*), that if it has a certain attribute, clearly it has another attribute. Subsequently it is known that a specific entity has the [first] attribute. We must then decide that it has the second attribute. This is like the knowledge that wrong-doing (*ẓulm*) is detestable, while we know that this specific thing is [a form of] wrongdoing. At this point we must decide that [the act] is detestable.[17]

Wajh is an elusive, perhaps vague concept, and its difficulty is due partly to the ordinariness of the word. *Wajh,* meaning face, aspect, perspective,[18] is used constantly in legal and speculative literature.[19] To understand its technical meaning, the literal meaning must be kept in mind: Just as a face is the aspect of the person that reflects the inner life and informs us of it, the *wajh* is that part of an act that presents itself towards us and reflects its real nature, including its *ma'nás* or *'illah*s or *ṣifah*s of good and detestability. The *wajh*, or perhaps the supposition or knowledge that follows from perceiving it, is the conveyer (*mu'tabir*) of the act's moral quality.[20] It is not the act itself that gives rise to an assessment about the act, but the *wajh* of the act that comes into existence with it.[21]

The *wajh* is variable, sometimes good and sometimes bad, and the *wajh*s cannot be predicted merely from knowledge of the act's genus.[22] Presumptively any act is good, and even if it has *wajh*s of detestability, these may be counter-balanced by *wajh*s of utility, repelling harm, or appropriateness (*istiḥqāq*).[23] Yet while the act can have aspects of good and be detestable at the same time, or vice versa, there is only one appropriate assessment for the act as it occurs.[24] The *wajh* points to the reality of the act's nature[25] but it is the reality of the *wajh* that causes the assessment good, for example, to be appropriate for the act.[26] The *wajh* arises along with the act, and with it, the assessment.[27] This process negates all other possible *ḥukm*s for the act.[28] The most important point here is the ephemerality and hence the variability of the *wajh*s attached to a particular act. The *wajh* arises only when the act is produced, hence the act in the abstract[29] cannot truly be assessed since its *wajh* of good or detestability cannot yet have manifested itself.[30]

In effect Abū l-Qāsim and the Baghdādīs had made the actual *existence* of an act subordinate to its moral classification. For them, good lies were theoretically inconceivable, regardless of circumstance. Yet the Baghdādīs' opponents, we suppose, had no difficulty imagining at least the potential dilemma of causing beneficial harm—not least because God appeared to do just that. Moral theory had to recognize the reality of acts' variability according to their purpose and environment. The Basrans faced the problem of wanting to assert that acts have values in and of themselves, while at the same time recognizing that an inflexible moral ontology simply could not account for the complexity of the moral world. Sometimes falsehood might be better than telling the truth, but telling falsehoods itself is detestable, as is harm—even when harm to achieve some good is better than no harm.[31] *Wajh* solves the problem of rigidity because the *wajh* is not perduring; it is with the act but not part of what makes it what it is.[32]

Consider first 'the making of a statement,' or, 'an act of informing.' This act by itself is presumptively good. But if it is oppression, futility, a falsehood, ingratitude, an act of ignorance, willing or commanding the detestable, or charging one to do what cannot be done, then any of these aspects are *wajh*s that signify the detestability of the act.[33] It is not that circumstances *condition* the act; rather, the same act in different circumstances has a different nature which is manifested when we discover it occurring (*waqa'a*) as falsehood, futility, etc.

Another example: Harm, which al-Ka'bī evidently considered detestable per se, is not always so, says 'Abdaljabbār. When harm has a *wajh* of usefulness that leads to the supposition that the harmful act is good, its proper assessment is good, even though there is no certain knowledge to that effect.[34] The calculus of value is particularly important where harm is concerned. "The *wajh*s of detestability do not [lead us to] reject the harmful act if it is known that its usefulness is greater—which takes the place of certain knowledge [about the status of the act.]"[35]

Thus an act's aspects may be plural—in that case the *wajh*s of goodness are weighed against the *wajh*s of detestability in a particular circumstance and a valid judgment for the act results. This allows for the recognition of acts whose value is complex. Because the *wajh* is occasional it can also explain subtle qualities in acts that can significantly affect their assessment.[36] Authentic knowledge (*'ilm*) and pseudo-knowledge (*taqlīd*)[37] both assert the same thing and are of the same genus—they have the same essence (*dhāt*). Nothing added and nothing subtracted from the essence of the stating makes it knowledge, as opposed to rote. It is rather that authentic knowledge has *wajh*s arising from the authentic knower's inquiry into it and consequent psychic tranquillity that supposition does not.[38] The conditions in which knowledge arises are reflected in the act's being, and so, in its assessment. Genuine knowledge is good. Imitative knowledge is not.

It was to solve a problem, namely the rigid ontology of those who sought to keep names and things inflexibly bound together that the elusive notion of the *wajh* was developed. The *wajh* concept must be understood as an argument, one that comes to terms in a sophisticated way with such facts as that "prostration to Satan is detestable and prostration to God is desirable."[39] For the Basrans, assessments and things are still linked but the bond is attenuated. What is

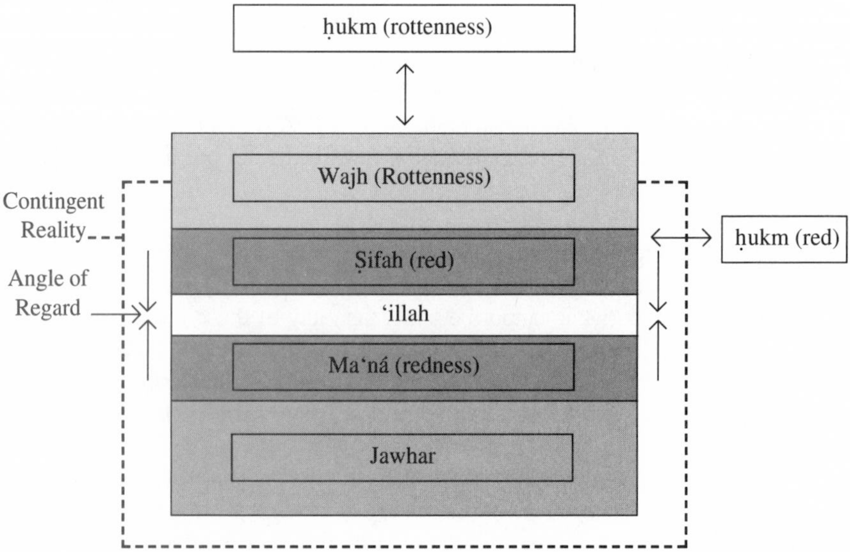

gained in flexibility, of course, is in part due to the vagueness of the concept of *wajh*. What does it *mean* to say, An act occurs in some *wajh*s of oppression which we know to be detestable? No answer from the Basrans survives. At the same time it is refuting an inflexible ontology, the concept of *wajh* is shifting attention from acts in the abstract to acts in particular. By their use of the term 'aspect', the Basrans also shift attention from the being of the act to its perception. Hence the concept of *wajh* directs the focus away from the object of moral perception to its subject, from the ontology of ethics to ethical epistemology, as we shall see below.

The Epistemology of the Act: Perception from Within

The moral epistemology of the Basrans, unlike their ontology, is relatively static. Though there is a place for inquiry and contemplation, 'Abdaljabbār and his group based their theory of moral knowing on a set of relations and perspectives programmed into the *compotes mentis* as part of their human nature. Properly understood, Basran epistemology is the response of a reliable and *stable* human nature to a fluid and dynamic world.

The 'Aql

Since the nineteenth century the Mu'tazilah have been described as free thinkers and rationalists, and it is only recently with the publication of Mu'tazilī texts that more nuanced descriptions have emerged.[40] Yet the term rationalist continues to be used as a shorthand for their views, echoing the heresiographers catchphrase *qāla bi-l-'aql*. Both Western and Eastern scholars, as well as heresiographers, agree that what separated the Mu'tazilah from other Muslims was the prominence and reliance they placed on *'aql*. Yet what is not sufficiently grasped is that the *'aql* represents less humankind's presence in the epistemological process than God's.

The *'aql* according to Abū 'Alī[41] is knowing (*'ilm*).[42]

> It is called *'aql* because by it a person restrains himself[43] from that from which an insane person (*al-majnūn*) does not restrain himself. . . . He alleges that these knowledges (*'ulūm*) are many, and among them is indubitable knowledge (*iḍtirār*) . . . . [One may attain perfection of the *'aql*] by testing things and experiencing them, and by inquiry into them. In some of what is contained in the totality of the *'aql*—such as reflection [*tafakkur*] by a person, if he sees an elephant, that it cannot enter through the eye of a needle in his presence—one inquires into it and reflects upon it until he knows that it is [also] impossible for it to enter through the eye of a needle even if he is not present. . . . [Abū 'Alī] denied that the fac-

ulty of acquiring knowledge was [equivalent to] '*aql*, although . . . with the perfection of his '*aql* one becomes capable of (*qawīan* '*alá*) acquiring knowledge of God. . . . [44]

Or as 'Abdaljabbār says more concisely,

'*Aql* is a term referring to a collection of particular knowledges. When one-made-responsible has them, his inquiry and inference are consequently sound, as is his undertaking to do that with which he is charged.[45]

The '*aql*, he says also, is a means by which one acquires knowledge.[46] It is the basis (*aṣl*) of things known.[47] The conception of the '*aql* as things known was a characteristic feature of Mu'tazilī epistemology, over against the philosophers.[48] It is quite clear that, for the Basrans, the '*aql* is neither a body (*jawhar*) nor an instrument (*ālah*), neither a sensing organ (*ḥāssah*) nor a faculty (*quwwah*). It does not perceive; it does not act.[49]

'*Aql* is therefore a set of knowings or knowledges, so it is well briefly to define knowing before we precede. '*Ilm* (pl. '*ulūm*) usually translated as knowledge is a kind of conviction that has a correspondential quality—one knows the thing as it is, but it has also an affective quality—it is conviction accompanied by tranquillity of the soul.[50] The term '*ilm*, given the indeterminacy of Arabic substantives, means both knowledge and knowing.[51] To say that the '*aql* is knowledge(s) suggests that it is a storehouse of various *stuff*. The formulations of Abū 'Alī and 'Abdaljabbār above, however, imply something more dynamic: *When* one sees an elephant *then* one *knows* that it cannot enter the eye of a needle. He cannot help but know this.[52] The '*aql* is not a mental faculty or capacity, as reason is understood to be.[53] Rather it is knowing; and though this knowing matures by exposure to the world, it cannot be said to come from the world. It is innate.[54] The '*aql* then is not a file drawer full of things known, but a poised, alert, correctly conditioned responsiveness to situations as they arise. It balances (restrains) the person's apprehension and interpretation. It is a kind of perceptiveness, both to things that confront the *compos mentis* and compel indubitable and immediate recognition ('*ilm ḍarūrī*), and to those things that require reflection, inquiry, and effort ('*ilm iktisābī*). The set of knowings that collectively are referred to as '*aql* are circumscribed. Not all knowing belongs to the '*aql*. Rather, it is the small set that humans have by virtue of their humanity, regardless of culture, religion, etc. In this sense, what the Mu'tazilah understood by '*aql* was something akin to 'common sense' in both our workaday understanding of the term, and in the Stoic sense of the 'common notions.'[55] These are knowings that all normal persons know and by virtue of which human beings are fully human (neither insane, retarded, nor under-aged). They can, therefore, rightly be charged by God with certain duties and obligations.

The *'aql* is the sine qua non of being made-responsible. It is appropriate apprehension in some particular context.[56] What then does it apprehend?

What the 'aql knows. The *'aql* is knowing—simple or common sense sort of knowing—that a human is not a donkey, that elephants can not pass through needles' eyes, whether one is present or not, and the like. Some of its knowing is more complex. A rational person knows what he perceives and he knows from his own situation that another person seeing the same thing will similarly know it.[57] Upon perceiving a body, he knows whether it is compound or simple and of the impossibility that it be in two places at once,[58] or be simultaneously pre-existent and created, or existent and non-existent.[59] He will know whether an attribute is or is not present.[60] He will know to seek the useful and avoid the harmful.[61] Moral knowledge too is part of what the *'aql* knows.[62] A rational person will know some things as detestable, some things as good, and some things as obligatory.[63] He will also know the detestability of wrongdoing (*ẓulm*) or of ingratitude for a benefaction, or of the lie that is neither useful nor repels harm. He will know the goodness of the good deed and the magnanimous act, and of the obligation to thank the benefactor, the obligation to return a pledge upon demand, and the obligation to be equitable (*al-inṣāf*).[64] Indeed, knowing the detestability of oppression, for instance, is simply derivative of knowing it to be oppression, which in turn is only a branch of the knowledge that it exists.[65] This innate knowing is necessary for humans to be made-responsible and for God to be exempted from detestable acts.[66]

Simply by virtue of being *compos mentis*, then, and independently of Revelation, any human will have considerable pragmatic moral knowledge. There is still more that he will know. A rational person will also know the goodness of blaming for detestability (if there is nothing to prevent that), and the appropriateness of blaming someone for impeding [performance of] an obligation so long as there are no preventative circumstances.[67] He will know too the goodness of praising someone for performing an obligatory act. Praise for good acts and blame for detestable acts stand in relation in a way that helps to clarify the *phenomenal* character of Mu'tazilī moral epistemology.[68]

Deserving (*istiḥqāq*). Condemnation (*dhamm*) and detestability, praise (*madḥ*) and good are linked for 'Abdaljabbār.[69] Likewise, appropriate harm follows condemnation.[70] The tie between these is deserving (*istiḥqāq*). According to the Basrans, instinctively one is offended, filled with pain, and one's mind is affected by the detestable thing in such a way that harm is seen as deserved for the blameworthy and detestable act.[71] Therefore,

> It is good for one of us to blame one who does something detestable to him or undertakes a serious wrong . . . it is good because of the deserving (*al-istiḥqāq*) for what he has done; this [deserving] becomes the

basis for the goodness of the pain that is the punishments resulting from the deserving.[72]

It may seem that there is a circularity here—that it is good to blame and punish because it is good to do so.[73] A careful reading of 'Abdaljabbār, however, clarifies both his use of this crucial term and his underlying theory of the phenomenon of detestable acts. Deserved, says 'Abdaljabbār,

> includes as part of its meaning "it is good to do it." It is not that ["it is good to do it"] is useful as an explanation [of the full scope of the term.]
>
> It is determined in the *'aql* that it is right that blame requite detestability[74] and abuse (*al-isā'ah*) in such a manner as it be a recompense for it . . . . When this is established, we convey this sense [by saying] "it is deserved." We make [deserving] to be, as it were, both the *ratio* (*'illah*)—inasmuch as it is good [to blame] if [blame] comes about [as a result of] the thing done—and also the co-extensive sign (*sabab*) inasmuch as it is it is proper to this act (*min ḥaqq hādhā 'l-fi'l*) to attach to it, as a consequence, recompense.[75]

Willing or not, it seems, the mind and *'aql* are distressed by the detestable. Deserving is simply another way of saying "this blame arises instinctively in the mind of one who perceives it." Similarly, punishment instinctively seems to be the proper requital for a detestable act. It is in this sense that 'Abdaljabbār uses the legal terminology (*sabab*). The relationship between punishment and detestability is the cause for the punishment, and also a sign that the punishment ought appropriately to take place when the detestability is perceived.

Some confusion may arise from the use of the term 'deserve' to translate *istiḥqāq*. Two points will clarify: first, the context of the discussion, and second an understanding of the precise meaning of the term, *istiḥqāq* as it is used.

We must ask why 'Abdaljabbār rests punishment upon deserving, rather than on some more pragmatic ground. Might it not be that one punishes in order to allay harm either real or supposed, or for some benefit? 'Abdaljabbār rejects these possibilities, and for good reason.[76] God punishes for detestable acts, but He cannot be doing so for pragmatic reasons, since He is beyond either utility or harm. It must be that He punishes because of something intrinsic to the detestable act, something that instinctively connects blame and punishment.

When considering this problem, we must not be misled by the English term 'deserves', which has implications of valuation.[77] The Arabic terms *ḥaqq* and *istiḥqāq* are not valuative but are expressions of ownership and correctness. *Istiḥqāq* means "having a claim on," "owning," "belonging to," as is shown here:

> Q: Did you not make the basis [of your extrapolation] the "claiming as right" (*istiḥqāq*) the return of a deposit and payment of a debt ?

> R: It is established . . . that it is good [to return a deposit] only because it is [the depositor's] claim (*li-annahu mustaḥaqq*); it is not permissible [to say] that it is obligatory, or recommended, as in the case of acts of worship. It has been established in [the matter of] repayment of a debt [also] . . . .[78]

In other words, the thing owed, and the deposit, are the property of the creditor, and the debtor, respectively. They belong to them. Similarly, Ibn Mattawayh says, "This atom has as its property (*istaḥaqqa*) this attribute."[79] It is not that this attribute is entitled to, or deserves, the atom but that this attribute belongs to the atom.[80] Just so blame belongs to detestability; detestability is such as to appropriately or necessarily call forth blame. It is part of the innate human moral apparatus symbolized in the word *'aql* that the detestable act evokes, by virtue of what it is, the blame of all *compotes mentis*. The *'aql* is knowledge, but is also a set of predetermined responses to, and recognitions of relations between, phenomena.

Motivations to Action. The *'aql* is the in-built knowing and assessment of situations in the world, but knowing is not enough; one must act. The act that most concerned the Mu'tazilah as epistemologists was the act of inquiring (*naẓar*) that led to the occasion in which the *'aql* could assess an act. To understand the root of moral inquiry we must once more consider the Mu'tazilī theory of knowledge. For the Basrans, conviction is the product of inquiry, which is the basis of Mu'tazilah epistemology.[81] Supposition (*ẓann*) is a conviction that may be true, but it is not accompanied by the affective confidence that knowing engenders. Knowledge is a species of conviction as well.[82] Knowing (*'ilm*) is both correspondence of the knowledge with the object of knowledge, and the tranquillity of the soul produced which arises from knowing the means through which the conviction (*i'tiqād*) was produced, with confidence in its correspondence to reality. Inquiry, in sum, is the movement of the mind from a sign

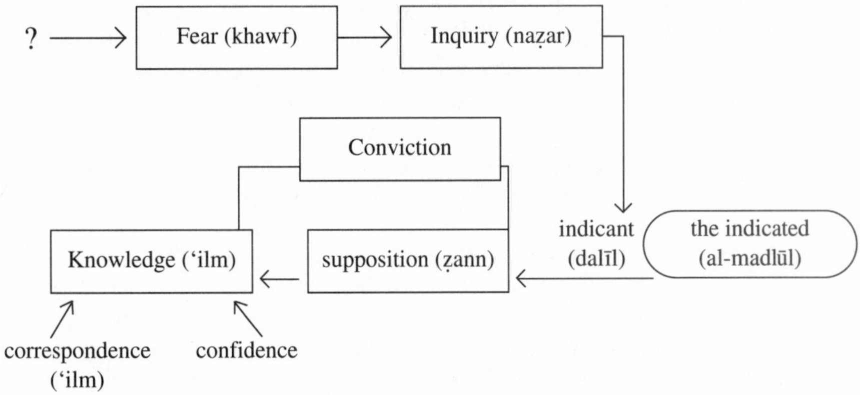

(*dalīl*) to knowledge of that which the sign indicates (*al-madlūl*). Since it is the obligation of the moral agent to know what is incumbent upon him, inquiry is in fact the first duty of the moral agent.[83] However, in this scheme, there is something still prior to inquiry and that is the sign (*dalīl*, *amārah*). Why is it that we inquire into the value of acts, or of a specific act, or into the existence of a Creator, or anything else? The Basrans' epistemology assumed that humans inquired, wondered, and thought, but they were not certain whether, left to themselves, humans would do so. Through introspection, the Basrans came to believe that there is only one motivation reliably to induce speculation—fear.[84]

What then is the sign that moves us to inquire? It is, generically, fear,[85] which temporally is the beginning of being made responsible.[86] Anxiety about one's ignorance drives one to inquire, and to come to supposition.[87] While the experience is of a void in the agent,[88] this fear is not some kind of existential angst, it is fear for one's self. Fear may be excited by reading a book, by a habit, by being told of something fearful, or something else.[89] Without fear induced by something or someone, the Mu'tazilah believed humans could not reliably be expected to inquire, and their entire epistemology, including moral epistemology, was liable to collapse. Fear of judgment, anxiety at one's imperfection, all these are notions deeply-rooted in Islamic piety. To recognize the centrality of psychology in Mu'tazilī thought is important if the *religious* quality of their intellectual schema is to be appreciated. An epistemology usually characterized as rationalist turns out to be grounded in feeling.

Fear, rightly understood however, is not nameless, featureless dread, but it is, itself, a response. Fear leads to inquiry, but there must be a sign that inclines us to fearfulness.[90] That sign is a Warner from God.

The Warner (khāṭir).[91]

> The Mu'tazilah and the Barāhimah disagree among themselves concerning the manner of the connection of obliging and the proscription to the '*uqūl* . . . . [They claim that] no rational person's mind is devoid of two Warners (*khāṭirayn*): One of them is from God; by means of it [the rational person] is alerted to what his '*aql* obliges him to do: namely to know God, that it is obligatory to thank Him; it [also] summons him to reflection and inferential thought about [God] by its signs and indicators.
>
> And the second Warner is from Satan and by means of it he dissuades [humans] from obeying the Warner from God.[92]

Originally *khāṭir* means 'passing thought', and refers to those notions that arise unbidden in the conscious mind. The term also takes its force from the other meaning of the Arabic root, danger. The *khāṭir*'s role is to serve like lions' tracks in the snow—to make one prudently fearful.[93] It is also causes the pain that leads to condemnation of the detestable act.[94] For the Mu'tazilah the psyche is a kind of forum in which, unbidden, two impulses debate. Both, it seems, provoke fear, the one by reminding the agent of the consequences of doing something, the other by alerting him to the advantages of not doing it. The Warner is the means by which knowledge that a certain act is detestable is translated into fear of doing it and so, avoidance of it. It is also the cause, of inquiry into morally complex or ambiguous acts so as to discern their assessment. The warning is what conjoins knowledge which is lodged in the *'aql*, and the mental movement that is moral discernment.[95] So the spring of moral life is *affect*, particularly fear.

Humans, it would seem, are passive knowers or recognizers until the warning comes, which is an alert (*tanbīh*) and a motivation to act.[96] In the Mu'tazilī system, the Warner is the *primum mobile* which sets the entire machinery of moral epistemology in motion.[97] So before inquiring, the inquirer first feels a lack, an anxiety, whereupon one Warner urges him to inquire so as to know, the other urges him to desist, not to make the effort. In this case, the first Warner is God, the second Satan, and it is here, in a sense, that the cosmic struggle really takes place. 'Abdaljabbār calls the Warner of disobedience *waswās*, the "whisperer" which scripturally is the one against whom one takes refuge,[98] and the Warner of obedience is none other than God.

The form of the warning is a source of controversy, even among the later Basrans. While all agree that it is a species of conviction, 'Abdaljabbār wants to emphasize that it is information from someone else (or Someone else) that reliably incites the fear that leads to inquiry, probably because he suspects merely human nature is insufficient and requires reinforcement from the outside,[99] and because his image is of one man on a path warned by another.[100] It is important that the *khāṭir* confirm what the *'aql* knows, and if, as Abū 'Alī al-Jubbā'ī wanted, the Warner were a form of interior conviction, then its plausibility as a Warner would be diminished.[101] This suspicion of human frailty leads 'Abdaljabbār and his teacher Abū Hāshim to hold that the Warner is a form of speech, an "act of the limbs," that is, a physical, not noetic act. Understanding language is therefore a precondition of being made responsible.[102]

It is not just the insufficiency of human nature that produces the theory of the *khāṭirayn*. All of the Basrans use this notion to explain how one can be made-responsible independently of acquaintance with Qur'ān or Prophetic message,[103] for there are more motives to the fear that produces inquiry than can be counted, even before Prophecy.[104] In effect the Basrans, denying Revelation as the sole motive of moral knowledge, introduce divine speech through the back door, giving each individual a private Revelation that moves him to act.

Mu'tazilah Revelation

If each person is endowed with revelation, what then of the Revelation-event (*al-sam'*) and the Revealed stipulations (*al-sharā'i'*)? The Mu'tazilah assume that the *'aql* knows the assessments of things. This is part of its very nature. It knows that unjustified pain is detestable; it knows that futile acts are likewise detestable. Knowledge, moreover, is stable because it corresponds to how things are. As such, it cannot be contradicted; it cannot later change.[105] What then is Revelation?—it is not merely repetition of what is in the *'aql*, nor confirmation of it, nor an alert *(tanbīh)* and warning of what is already known.[106] That would be pointless on God's part, and so, detestable. For 'Abdaljabbār and the Basrans, Revelation brought knowledge, but knowledge of a kind different from that which the *'aql* possessed.

> One knows of some pains that they constitute oppression and the detestability of oppression has been established in the *'aql*. One knows then that [the pains] are detestable; this knowledge is in accord with what is established in the *'aql* but the *'aql* does not exhaust all knowings—they cannot be comprised; rather, what is established is only general knowledge and fundamentals (*bi-l-jumal wa-bi-l-uṣūl*). Then one individually finds the detailed and derivative knowledge by indicants.[107]

The stipulates of Revelation (*sharā'i'*) then are details or further specification (*tafṣīl*) of what the *'aql* already knows.[108] Indeed the *shar'* is constructed upon the *'aql*.[109] Further, the detestability of the detestable act as determined by the *'aql* differs from the detestability of the detestable act as determined by the *shar'*, for

> the *'aql*'s detestable act (*qabīḥ al-'aql*) is detestable because of being qualified by an attribute that is traceable to it [itself]. However, the *shar'ī* detestable act is detestable inasmuch as it leads to the detestable or to the prevention of what is Obligatory.[110]. . . . The Revelation-event discloses something about the state of this act which, if we knew it by the *'aql*, we would [also] know its detestability or its goodness.[111]

There is no contradiction between the two, because "the one who set up the indicant of Revelation set up the indicant of the *'aql*; thus it is not possible for the two to contradict each other."[112]

This is not to say that the unaided *'aql* will by itself assess as it will in light of Revelation. The relation of Revelation's perspective to that of the *'aql* is analyzed by 'Abdaljabbār thus:

- There is that which is Obligat3ory or desirable by Revelation and detestable to the *'aql*, such as canonical worship or supererogatory worship [because, in the absence of Revelation they seem futile acts];[113]
- that which is Obligatory by Revelation, but is merely good in the *'aql*, such as alms and compensatory payments (*al-kaffārāt*);
- that which is detestable in Revelation but Permitted by the *'aql*, such as adultery and eating on the days of fasting;

- that which Revelation detests but which is desirable to the *'aql*, such as the poor eating on the days of fast;
- and that which is Permitted by Revelation and Proscribed by the *'aql* such as the slaughter of beasts.[114]

"But there is no means for the *'aql* to know that something is corrupt except by the dispatch [of Messengers]."[115] Revelation is thus information (*khabr*) and an indicant (*dalīl*). Still it only supplements what was otherwise known. Had the *'aql* other means of obtaining this information, Revelation's judgment and that of the *'aql* would conform.

> If we knew by the *'aql* that ritual worship brought us a mighty benefit and that it would incline us to choose to do what is Obligatory and that by it we would have a reward, we would know of its obligation by the *'aql* . . . . Thus we say that the *sam'* does not *cause* the detestability or goodness of a thing to exist; it *reveals* the [actual] condition of the act by means of indicants as does the *'aql*.[116]

The *shar'*, then, is essential to moral knowing, but only as information about "the hidden." Moreover, it is relevant to a moral assessment, but only at a particular time and place.

'Abdaljabbār's discussion of Revelation comes in the context of how it is that Muḥammad's Revelation abrogates that of Moses. Revelation is particular to time, place, and occasion, he says. To know one Revelation does not obviate a subsequent one. Therefore Revelation does not contradict the *'aql*, and moreover it also does not contradict another *shar'*, even if it differs from the other revelation in its stipulations.

> [It is as] if you said: "Your knowing the day in which you are, negates knowing the arrival of night, and your knowing winter negates knowing the arrival of summer . . . because one's knowing that it is not night, in daytime, is particular to a time; if the second time comes, knowledge that it is night and not day is Obligatory."[117]

Revelation supplements; it does not determine. That in short is the Mu'tazilī understanding of Revelation. Without Revelation moral life is not only possible, it is required; with Revelation a perfected understanding of human obligation leads to a perfect understanding of what is incumbent upon humans as humans. In this view, Revelation is superimposed on a prior structure of morality and of course Qur'ān and sunnah become appendages to the more substantial and more perduring sources of moral knowledge. This perspective may be described as very much a 'low' view of the Revelation event.

The subtlety and capaciousness of the Basran moral theory compels admiration. ‘Abdaljabbār’s vision is of a world less stable than that of Abū l-Hudhayl or al-Ka‘bī—one in which acts come into being and pass away, with essential natures predictable but moral natures in flux. A statement this time may be informative and at another time may be a falsehood; both share essential characteristics but each differs from the other in its most crucial aspect. Even further—this statement may be a falsehood and that statement may be a falsehood but it may be that the second is good, despite the prima facie detestability of falsehoods, by the moral calculus of the system, because the *wajh*s of good outweigh those of detestability—when the falsehood is told to protect a prophet, we may suppose.

If the Mu‘tazilah are ‘low church’ on Revelation, they are ‘high church’ on humanity. When the world is unknowable in advance of its becoming, when acts surge between good and detestable in their contexts, humans stand aloof, removed, timelessly capable of knowing most actions’ moral status. Revelation provides information previously unavailable but its application is through the same capacities previously and fruitfully used to discern the good. In the flux of the world, the stable, unchanging and reliable fact was the human capability to respond rightly to moral uncertainty. Yet this is not an Enlightenment or Existentialist autonomous will, responding in the cool light of Reason to choice. It is, rather, a fearful and anxious agent sensing a gap and fearing its consequences for his or her own prosperity. Human autonomy is not compromised only by fear, but also, upon a closer examination, by other-worldly intervention at crucial points in the chain of knowing. It is, after all, God who structures the ‘*aql* such that it perceives the act’s “faces” and weights their value correctly. Equally crucially, it is God who implants the fear, through the Warner, that moves the human to inquire so that the knowing that is the ‘*aql’s capacity* is brought to bear on acts. Particularly, for ‘Abdaljabbār and the Baṣrans it is, in the end, revelation that provides sure ground for moral knowledge, but it is the a-historical and particular revelation of the individual ‘*aql* that proves more fundamental than the communal and temporally bound Revelation of prophets.

CHAPTER 10

THE CRITIQUE OF THE MU'TAZILAH: IGNORING ONTOLOGY

> The description of the school [of the Mu'tazilah] became mixed up on the tongues of the legists and others to the point that they used vague and imaginary expressions such as their saying, 'the '*aql* approves and detests,' or 'the '*aql* requires and forbids' or 'Proscribes and Permits' until some of them understand that the '*aql* is a Legislator (*shāri'*) above Revelation (*al-shar'*). . . . The reason [for this confusion] is that some of them accept these expressions from others without inquiry or care.[1]

After the fifth century fewer and fewer Muslims identified themselves as Mu'tazilīs, though in Eastern Islamdom there may have been Mu'tazilīs as late as the early ninth/fifteenth century.[2] Those who were not Mu'tazilīs defined themselves over against the Mu'tazilah on many issues, including the issues of the before revelation complex, and particularly on the goodness and detestability of acts (*al-taḥsīn wa-l-taqbīḥ*).[3] Yet one looks in vain for a precise and detailed refutation of the subtleties of 'Abdaljabbār or Abū Rashīd. Looking at critiques of the Mu'tazilah, it is not clear that their opponents read them carefully—even Abū l-Ḥusayn al-Baṣrī, whose work clearly influenced many later scholars, seems to have argued more subtly than his opponents gave him credit for or understood.[4] It is frustrating to realize that the Mu'tazilism critiqued is often a straw man; it is no real Mu'tazilī whose position is savaged but a creature of the critics' own making. Al-Ṭūfī (d. 716/1316), whose account begins this chapter, understood the situation well.

It is too simple to say, as Islamicists have usually done, that this discussion can be summed up as Reason versus Revelation. Very few Muslims denied the efficacy of the '*aql*,[5] and no one denied the power of the '*aql* to apprehend reality. The critics of the Mu'tazilah simply denied that the transcendental goodness of prayer or thanksgiving had anything to do with the being of those acts. Most critics in fact believed the '*aql* to be essential to recognize authentic Revelation, but the critics refused to accept any identity between the act and its assessments; they believed any act could occur with any assessment. In addition, they refused to recognize that humans could themselves independently apprehend the moral assessment appropriate to a particular act. With these two objections, as we shall see, the critics of the Mu'tazilah safeguarded God's sovereignty and elevated Revelation to a unique and all-encompassing role in human moral knowing.

Errors in Ontology

It is not that the critics of the Mu'tazilah rejected what we have called their particle metaphysics. With some qualification, the ontological structure of bodies, substances, and accidents was held commonly among almost all speculative religious thinkers.[6] Instead, critics attacked the assertion that the moral status of an act was part of its nature. For them, morality was not a part of reality. It is not its nature that leads to the valuation of an act, but God's command; the act's status was made known not by reflection, but by Revelation. The moral ontology of the non-Mu'tazilah can be summed up in a sentence: "The true nature of the *ḥukm* is the dictum [from God]".[7] There is, for the non-Mu'tazilah therefore, no a priori link between being allowed or obliged to do something, and the determination that the thing is, from a transcendental point of view, good. "Do this!" has force for the anti-Mu'tazilah by reference to the actor and not the act. Nothing can be/need be known about the act itself.[8] Nothing links goodness and Permission or Obligation. The Mu'tazilah heard "Do this" and understood the specification of *this thing* as the point of the command; the anti-Mu'tazilah heard mainly the imperative voice.

Consequently, in this discussion the critics of the Mu'tazilah sought to avoid the thickets of ontology and sought to assert positively their own position. To some extent, however, particularly the modernists (*al-muta'akhkhirūn*), were drawn in to debate ontology, if only to point to obvious absurdities. It is to these tentative and dismissive ontological critiques that we now turn. Since the rebuttal is so occasional, however, we will have to jump from one critic to another to construct an overview of the attack on Mu'tazilī ethical theory. Most accounts allude to many more arguments than are amplified. We may take it that, with some exceptions noted, all of the critics would have subscribed to the arguments presented below.

The Relativity of Good

It is startling to see that by the middle of the fifth century Muslim scholars had formed a consensus that nothing is good for any reason other than that God has commanded it, and that His command is inscrutable in motivation and so, from any human perspective, arbitrary.

The locus classicus of this position is the famous statement of al-Ash'arī, "If He had esteemed [a falsehood] good, it would be good, and if He ordered [us] to it, there would be no gainsaying Him."[9] Al-Ghazālī similarly suggests (para. 63, 56–7) that God might have forbidden thanking Him, or that He might have prevented immorality rather than merely commanding us not to do it, and this is a theme that is picked up and echoed by later scholars. The plausibility of this perspective was strengthened by reflection upon, for instance, the acts of worship whose arbitrary nature was admitted even by the Mu'tazilah and their fellow travelers. Even one of the defining shibboleths of Muslim self-definition could not be assessed absolutely. "Forbidding (*taḥrīm*) is not an essential attribute of drinking [wine] for we deem it necessary to drink [wine] in necessity."[10]

In general, any willingness to entertain the possibility that in moral matters God might have commanded other than He did rests at bottom on an assumption of the utter relativity of the good and the detestable, the commanded and the forbidden.[11] To say that God might have commanded other than He did safeguards His sovereignty, but it requires that no act can have intrinsic moral status; otherwise how could the act be imagined as both good and bad? The critics' ontological position follows from this. Nothing is *absolutely* good.[12] The critics report a number of debates in which the issue is whether any act can be considered intrinsically good and thus always and everywhere good.

This question is discussed, among other places, in Fakhraddīn al-Rāzī's *Maḥṣūl*, the archetypal work of the modernist school.[13] As an example of the act that changes according to circumstances, he trots out the standard example of the lie to protect the Prophet.[14] In the dialog, his opponent asserts that the solution to the dilemma of the threatened Prophet is to use equivocal language so as to avoid lying. Using the language of jurisprudence, he asserts that "the assessment [good] obtains when the *ratio* (*'illah*) [in this case, the motivation to protect the Prophet] obtains," and the "assessment may be changed only because of a preventative exigency."[15] Thus, a lie remains detestable, but the circumstances demand equivocal language which here, at least, is good.

It would follow, Al-Rāzī replies, that if equivocal speech is unrestrictedly good, when there is some beneficial end behind it, then the dictum of God could never be taken in its straightforward sense (*ẓāhiruh*), unless one had proof that there was no good end that might motivate an equivocation in His speech. The lack of knowledge that this was so would not mean it was not so, since there might be a good end we could not discern. The result of his opponents' position, he says, is epistemological nihilism. It cannot be that equivocal speech is always and everywhere good.[16]

A more subtle, and characteristically formalist argument proves the same point:

> If one threatens another wrongfully and says, "I will kill you tomorrow," there is no doubt that when he does not do this, he has made the infor-

mational statement ["I will kill you"] a falsehood. Were falsehood [intrinsically] detestable, then [the failure to kill] would consequently bring about something detestable; that which brings about something detestable is [itself] detestable. It would follow that to shun [killing] would be detestable, and [killing him] would be good absolutely, but that is indisputably false.[17]

This criticism has the flavor of the language/logic paradoxes of which the legists grew increasingly fond, but its point is that once again a falsehood can be good and acting truthfully can be worse than acting untruthfully.[18]

Fakhraddīn al-Rāzī's is one of the two strands of anti-Mu'tazilism picked up and transmitted to al-Āmidī, Ibn al-Ḥājib, Qarāfī and others. In it they emphasize the separation of the name from the assessment.

> The word 'good' [among our colleagues] . . . is applied relationally and not in the most literal sense. . . . The application of the word 'good' to [something] . . . is not done by reference to its essence because of [the act's] different [status according to circumstances] and change-of-status in relation to the different interests, by contrast to the characterization of a substrate by "black" or "white."[19]

Knowing what an act is does not tell us how to assess it.

> What may be depended upon in this matter is to say, if a particular act were good or detestable of itself, then from the concept [of the act] we would [know] its detestability or goodness; but [goodness/detestability] are not themselves the same as the essence of the act; otherwise, one who knew the true nature of the act would know its goodness or detestability. But that is not so, as [is proved by] the possibility if knowing the true nature of the act while knowledge of its goodness or detestability awaits inquiry, such as the goodness of a harmful truth-telling, or the detestability of a useful falsehood.[20]

Another, less widespread line of criticism comes through Ibn Barhān to al-Ṭūfī.[21] This line seems better informed and less prejudiced than other groups of critics; they are no less partisan, however. At one point Ibn Barhān (and al-Ṭūfī from him) note that

> the Mu'tazilah do not mean by their saying that the '*aql* approves and detests that the '*aql* necessitates some things be good and some detestable; the '*aql* is a sort of immediate knowing, namely the knowing of what is necessary, possible, and impossible. Knowing does not necessitate the

> things known which are linked to it by an additional attribute. Rather, [the knowing] is linked [to the known] according to what is characteristic of it[22] . . . One approves some acts and detests some of them only because of their occurrence in some manner or state[23] because of which this attribute was good or detestable.[24]

Having seemingly referred to the *wajh* theory of the Basrans, Ibn Barhān drops it entirely, evidently not grasping that this was the pivot of Basran Mu'tazilī moral theory. Ibn Barhān's only real engagement with Mu'tazilī epistemology is to point out anomalies of consequence.

> If acts were divided into good and detestable because of attributes characteristic of them,[25] why is it one can conceive a difference between one [act of killing] and another? The Mu'tazilah differentiated between wrongful killing and statutory execution (*qaṣāṣ*) and judged the one good and the other detestable despite the two of them being equivalent as far as attributes are concerned. They may allege that the wrongful killing results in a heinous act and the execution leads to something salutary. Yet there is no meaning to heinous or salutary except that it results in the ordering of the world or leads to its corruption. That the world remain ordered in this particular way is not necessary, as far as the '*aql* can determine, according to our basic principles and yours, since it is good that the Maker most high annihilate it [at the end of time] . . . [26]

If there is any difference between wrongful killing and execution, it lies not, he says, in their nature but in their teleology. The Mu'tazilah had taken teleology and made it, with other circumstances, part of the act's ontology. For their critics, nothing ontological, circumstantial, or in any way mundane could be relevant to the assessment of the act. According to the method of al-Ṭūfī and his colleagues, the Obligatory nature of things Obligatory is known by Revelation; before the arrival of the *shar*' there is, basically (*aṣl*^{an}), no obligation.[27] Qāḍī Abdaljabbār's argument that the act's nature is known only by inquiry into the act as it exists was either not transmitted or not understood, and so we have no surviving refutation of the most sophisticated expression of the Mu'tazilī position.

Al-Ṭūfī was somewhat more engaged than most critics with ontological questions. He asserts that good is alleged to be a quality, but it is really an accident. Acts, for him, are accidents as well, and accidents cannot be added to accidents.[28] Al-Ṭūfī, as part of the line descended from al-Ghazālī, follows the latter's deft move from ontology to psychology. His opponent asks, how it is that, all things being equal, truth, or rescuing the threatened one, are preferred by all rational folk? Surely that is proof that these acts are intrinsically good. Al-Ṭūfī has a ready reply. No, he says, it is merely self-interest or human fellow-feeling that moves us to these acts, not a recognition of some quality that comprises them.[29] When the Mu'tazilah appealed to feelings and instinct to support their ontology, their critics effectively dismissed psychology as an unreliable guide and, in any case, one irrelevant to an ontological argument.

"Wine is forbidden" had been understood by the Mu'tazilah to be an elliptic statement by God that ran, "Wine is forbidden because it is itself detestable either because of some characteristic you can discern or for some reason only We know." For the non-Mu'tazilah, "Wine is forbidden" is not a description of the wine, it is a kind of contextual knowledge about the wine in relation to something else—the particular circumstances, the particular actor, and above all, a certain set of imperative statements about the consumption of wine whose origin, directly or indirectly, is transcendent. "Wine is forbidden" meant only 'do not drink wine or We will punish you for it." There can be no link, for the critics, between the value of an act and its being. The nature of an act is unaffected by statements about it, just as a thing is not affected by whether an observer knows it or not.

> If the *shar*' arrives [to declare] the goodness or detestability [of an act], His saying [do it or do not do it] does not entail an attribute for the act; nor has the act the goodness or detestability of which the *shar*' informs [us]. Nor, if [the act] is assessed thus, is it overlaid with an attribute, so that it would be, in its essence, characterized by it. This is just as knowing (*'ilm*) does not procure an attribute for a thing known, nor does it have a [particular] attribute in accordance with the *shar'ī* statement.
>
> The determinative command does not cause the [the act] to acquire an attribute, and [the act] does not acquire [from the *shar'ī* statement] a quality. From the statement ["this is good" for example], no attribute is acquired by the object to which the statement is attached, just as no attribute for the object to which the knowledge pertains arises from knowing it.[30]

As the *Baḥr* explains,

> This is like the one who knows that Zayd is sitting near to him. His knowing and his linking this [knowledge] with Zayd does not change a single one of Zayd's attributes, and nothing [new] has come to exist, as far as attributes are concerned, as a consequence of the linkage of knowing with Zayd.[31]

This is not a debate between two conflicting theories of moral ontology. It is, rather, analogous to logical positivists saying, "this is not a problem because it is non-sense." It is an attempt to end the discussion.

Ultimately, the most powerful criticism of the Mu'tazilī position was the consensus simply to ignore the entire apparatus so careful constructed by the later Basrans. It is remarkable how little space is given to refuting the ontological description of value. Ontology seemed so manifestly irrelevant to the non-Mu'tazilah in this context that a few simple sentences of dismissal were enough to take care of the issue.

By contrast, since the critics of the Mu'tazilah understood assessments to be statements ranking acts in terms of their consequences, they heard the Mu'tazilah arguments for the competence of the *'aql* to judge as a particular threat. To these arguments they responded at length.

Errors in Epistemology

Limitations on 'Aqlī Knowledge

> One needs the *'aql* before the *shar'* as a deputy (*nā'ib*) of the *shar'* to stipulate the preliminaries, such as the unicity [of God] and the possibility of the dispatch [of a prophet], and inquiring into the confirmatory miracle. This is like a king, who, when he takes a city, dispatches his deputy from his establishment to adorn it for his entry. He sets up celebrations for him and on his behalf he restrains the populace until the time the Sultan enters [the city]. At that time, the deputy is discharged and rule passes to [the Sultan]. Just so with the *'aql*. When it has established the preliminaries to prophecy and it comes about, [the *'aql*] is discharged and is commanded to follow what prophecy determines.[32]

The Mu'tazilah error most salient in the eyes of their critics was the misvaluation of the *'aql*. Their opponents dismissed ontology as of no consequence, but they spent large quantities of time and ink attacking the Mu'tazilīs from every angle on their approach to epistemology. Consequently, Western (and Muslim) students of this problem have tended to see the conflict as solely about the place of Reason vis à vis Revelation. (That this is incorrect, or at least incomplete, we hope we have shown above, and below we will discuss it further.) Now, however, we must discuss the critiques of Mu'tazilī epistemology, and the ways in which they were understood to have mistaken the deputy for the sultan.

Some of the Mu'tazilah's critics heard them asserting that the *'aql* was an indicant of the good or the detestable. To this they replied that the *'aql* cannot be an indicant (*dalīl*) of anything because the indicator pertains to what is indicated.[33] Indicants, it was generally agreed, were the means by which the unseen could be inferred from the seen.[34] Thus "one inferred [the thieves] by a thief's trace."[35]

> God arranged the normal course of things [such that] one obtains knowledge by inquiry and inference [literally, seeking indicants]) as He arranged the normal course of things [such that] one obtains taste as a consequence of tasting, and hearing as a consequence of listening. It is inconceivable to say that taste is obtained without tasting, or hearing without listening.[36]

Yet to be a valid indicant, there "must be something in the indicant that connects it to the thing sought; were it not so, the intellect would not move from it to the thing sought."[37] There was nothing, it was asserted, in the '*aql* that reliably moves us from the act or thing in question to its evaluation. Hence the '*aql* cannot be an indicant of the detestability of the lie, for instance.

In addition, the Mu'tazilah had asserted that because the moral knowledge of the '*aql* is necessary (*ḍarūrī*) knowledge, everyone reliably knows the good of thanking the benefactor and the detestability of the lie. To this it was replied that since the critics dispute that the '*aql* provides necessary knowledge, the detestability of the lie cannot be necessary knowledge since necessary knowledge is by definition indisputable.[38] Mu'tazilī attempts to provide proofs of the detestability of the lie contradict the notion that the detestability of the lie is necessary knowledge. Moreover, there may be reasons other than innate knowledge that account for a people, such as the Barāhimah, esteeming good what the *shar'* esteems good.[39] They may be influenced by *shar'ī* knowledge without our knowing it, for instance.

More generally, for the critics, this world is categorically separate from the next. Hence utility, which for al-Jaṣṣāṣ is so important, does not really indicate the act's transcendent valuation.[40] Al-Shīrāzī disregards utility, and cleverly argues that while it might seem that creation is intended to be of use, there are nonetheless difficulties with this position: both wine and pork might be considered useful according to the Mu'tazilah line of reasoning—but both are forbidden.[41] Or, al-Shīrāzī argues, the utility of an act might lie in shunning it rather than using it, once more instancing pork as an example.[42] Moreover, even if the significance of utility were conceded, it is not certain that "usefulness" establishes for whom the utility is intended.

> It is not self-evident that we are those [for whose use God has created things]. It is possible that He created it for us, and it is possible that He created it for a people other than us, providing it for them in another time, making for them a path. If [this] is possible, it is pointless to say He created them for use. And there remains no counter argument.[43]

Later opponents invoked purely formal arguments against what they understood to be Mu'tazilī epistemology, (which was for the most part only the Baghdādī perspective). Al-Ṭūfī, for example argued that goodness and detestability are either absent, in which case no assessment can be predicated upon them, or they must be either constitutive(*thubūtī*) or privative (*'adamī*). If privative, they cannot be the source of an assessment, and if constitutive they cannot be applied to non-existents, as when we say of a killing that it is detestable or of worship that it is good, before it has come into existence.[44] More elaborately:[45]

> The statement, "If I remain another hour I shall have spoken a falsehood" shows that it is impossible for a falsehood to be detestable per se (*li-dhātih*): If he does stay he has, as he said, spoken a falsehood, but in doing so, he has spoken truly.[46]
>
> If giving information falsely is detestable per se, then the statement "Zayd is in the house" when he is not, is false [and therefore detestable] because
> (a) of the phrase (*lafẓ*) itself, or
> (b) because of the absence [of Zayd] or
> (c) a combination of (a) and (b) or
> (d) something else.
>
> (a) Cannot be the case because the same statement is not detestable if Zayd is in the house.
>
> (b) would require that absence be the cause (*'illah*) for a constitutive (*thubūtī*) matter, as would (c). Both [b and c] are impossible because "not-ness" cannot effect a constitutive fact (*amr thubūtī*).
>
> If (d) were the case, the analysis would be repeated, which leads to infinite regress.[47]

Flaws in the 'Aql Itself

The critics' case against Mu'tazilī epistemology did not, however, rest upon what seem almost to be games. The matter was much more serious than that, since as they saw it, the *'aql* was an essential link in the chain of the Qur'ān's veridicy. It was the *'aql* that formulated the premises leading to the recognition of the Prophet's genuineness and the miraculousness of the Qur'ān. The *'aql* as independent knower could not be discarded as ethical ontology had been. Consequently the critique of Mu'tazilī epistemology had at its core two points. First, the *'aql* is simply not reliable—it esteems things Revelation tells us are bad; its judgments are deformed by self-interest. Second, whatever the *'aql* assesses has no necessary connection to transcendent assessments.

The *'aql* is not to be relied upon, first, because it is incapable of those tasks with which the Mu'tazilah charge it. It is, according to some, knowledge; according to others, it is the instrument of perception. Most critics, like the later Mu'tazilah, accept that it is certain basic knowledge.[48] This knowledge includes knowledge implanted by custom and habit. Thus, because of the *'aql*, says Abū

Ya'lá, if one were informed that the earth would split and an armed warrior would emerge to kill him, he would not flee.[49] The *'aql* is, most importantly, the ground for being made responsible (*taklīf*). Still, mere *'aql* is not sufficient grounds for being made responsible.[50] While legal culpability requires *'aql*, legal stipulations operate necessarily, regardless of competence.[51] Yet the *'aql* cannot be composed of all kinds of immediate (*ḍarūrī*) knowledge such as is obtained from the senses because that would imply that the blind and deaf are without *'aql*, which is not the case. Nor does the *'aql* include knowledge of the goodness of the good or the detestability of the detestable. This latter is a complex kind of knowledge, whereas the *'aql* comprises only the simplest sorts of knowledge, such as that one exists, that what exists is not also non-existent, that what moves is not at the same time standing still, and the like.

Some, indeed, according to Ibn Ḥazm, argued the futility of *'aqlī* proofs altogether, saying one can perceive and believe a thing and argue for it and be certain that it is truth; then something else appears to be the case. If *'aqlī* truths were veridical, how is it what they indicate appears to vary?[52]

Ibn Ḥazm, who despite his traditionist reputation has high regard for the *'aql*, disagrees. He says that true *'aqlī* knowledge is limited to what is known without intermediaries and irrespective of time.[53] Yet perhaps because of these characteristics, the *'aql* distinguishes only between attributes of existent things.[54] It cannot judge the ultimate reasons behind the assessments of the Creator.

> The true nature of the *'aql* is only that it distinguishes among things perceptible by sense or understanding or by knowledge of [the thing's] attributes which are characteristic of it, and nothing more. [These include] the necessity of the origination of the world; that the Creator is one, and does not cease to be; the validity of prophecy by one who establishes proofs of his prophethood. . . . As for the notion that the *'aql* requires pork or billygoat to be forbidden or permitted, and that the forenoon prayer is four [cycles] and the sunset prayer three [etc.] . . . either the *'aql* has no standing in these matters . . . or the *'aql* understands only based upon the commands of God.[55]

Indeed, the judgment of the *'aql* is often indeed at odds with what the critics take to be Revelationally informed knowledge. Ibn Ḥazm offers two rather pungent examples to show that the assessment of the *'aql* often diverges from *shar'ī* knowledge: He gives the example of a Christian monk living in his hermitage,

> who seeks God with all his mind (*qalb*), acknowledging God's unicity and calling nothing good but God's deeds, and nothing detestable but what He eschews. However, he lives on the islands of the Shāshīs (*jazā'ir al-shāshiyīn*) at the farthest[56] reaches of the world, where no

> mention whatsoever is heard of Muḥammad from any quarter save that it is followed by lies and odious attributes. He dies in this state, uncertain of [Muḥammad's] prophethood or considering it false. Is he not bound for all eternity in the fire?[57]

Ibn Ḥazm then makes a similar argument, in reverse. Here it is an odious Christian or Jew, a practitioner of every vice, who confounds reason. This vicious Person of the Book becomes suddenly convinced of the Prophethood of Muḥammad and the superiority of al-Islām. He so confesses and dies: "Is he not of the People of the Garden?" asks Ibn Ḥazm.[58] The *'aql* is unable to apprehend religio-moral assessments; it misleads, hence it can be of little value in the process of moral knowing. The examples of exceptions and improbables cited above not only established the non-essentialist view of goodness and detestability but also disconnected rational goods from moral goods.[59]

A more telling argument is al-Ghazālī's penetrating critique of the psychology of value-assessments. Since this argument is translated and discussed above, it is enough here to observe that the argument that self-interest compromises *'aqlī* assessments turns the Mu'tazilah's emphasis on the value of the purposeful act (*bi-l-gharaḍ*) as opposed to the pointless act (*'abath*) against them.[60] Purposeful acts may be better than pointless acts but they are not disinterested acts, and assessing goodness and badness is irremediably compromised by self-interest. When it is not naked self-interest in an obvious sense that compromises the *'aql*'s judgment, it is displaced self-interest, human sympathy, or conditioned response that disturbs the equilibrium necessary for the objective estimation of acts. Take away all of these compromising distractions and there is no reason to suppose the *'aql* will prefer truth to falsehood or rescuing one perishing, over against ignoring him.[61] It is only God, for whom all of our acts are equally insignificant, Who can rightly assign to acts praise and blame, and above all, punishment and reward.

Following al-Bāqillānī, al-Ghazālī admitted that the *'aql* does esteem some acts good and other detestable. These estimations are made on the basis of deeply ingrained aversions or attractions arising from self-interest or self-gratification. The point of dispute, however, is whether these carnal responses have anything to do, epistemologically, with the assessments brought by Revelation. If so, then before Revelation and after it, the *'aql* may be a trusty guide to the transcendent value of acts. Not surprisingly, this, says al-Ṭūfī, is the nub of the dispute.[62]

WHAT IS ASSESSED

Good and detestable in fact refer to three separate phenomenal categorizations. There are things attractive and unattractive to our animal nature, such as the sweet and the bitter. The words good and detestable are also used to refer to qualities of perfection and unrealized perfection or imperfection, as with knowledge and ignorance. We use the terms as well to refer to obedience and spurning obedience. But for humans, obedience has as a necessary condition a Revelational Designator.[63] There is no necessary connection between natural goods and moral goods.[64]

God rightly blames and punishes those who are disobedient, but how do God's sanctions connect to these rational senses of detestable? They do not, as Ibn Ḥazm points out:[65]

> We do not deny that the *sharī'ah* esteems only except what '*aql*s esteem, and finds detestable what ['*aql*s] find detestable; that is our very statement. What we deny is only that the '*aql* has standing (*rutbah*) in forbidding a thing or allowing it, in esteeming it or detesting it.[66]

The morally good and the morally detestable, as with transcendentally significant praise and blame, await Revelation. "Good and detestable follow being morally responsible. Whoever is not made-responsible—his acts are not characterized by either of these two [terms.][67] The fact is that God's dicta apply to actors, not acts, to humans, not things. This is a fundamental point, yet one so taken for granted that it seems to merit little discussion among the critics. The actor-oriented epistemology does seem more consistent with the kerygmatic tone of the Qur'ān, which does not so much construct a world of goods and detestables as it commands and exhorts humans to act in conformity with Revelation. Consequently the non-Mu'tazilīs and especially the Ḥanbalīs urged that assessments applied not to the thing but to the activity associated with it, not to the act, but the actor.

The Āl Taymiyyah preserve, in their section on the before revelation complex, a reference through Abū Ya'lá to a doctrine of Abū l-Ḥasan al-Tamīmī (a Permitter). "[All assessments]," he says, "are connected to the acts of actors, not the [thing itself (*al-maf'ūl fīh*)]. Things and bodies are not proscribed or permitted and are not obedient or disobedient."[68] The Taymiyyah dynasty saw this as a problem of interpretation. To say that juice was permitted and wine forbidden might be an acceptable, but metaphorical, usage.[69] They, however, say that if the "intelligible context" allows one to know the intention [when saying, 'juice is permitted'], the usage is not figurative."[70] Lost in all this is al-Tamīmī's original theological point:

> [The terms forbidden and permitted do not apply to things] because things in themselves (*al-a'yān*) are acts of God Most High; He created them. It is not permitted to displace the threat to His acts. [Hence] these [terms] are applied loosely or metaphorically. . . . [When one says juice is permissible] one means drinking juice is licit and Permitted.[71]

The "High" View of Revelation

The critics' goal was to disentangle humanity from the rest of creation and to disconnect the Muslim era from the rest of history. Surely the nature of wine remained the same before Revelation and after it, as did the act of drinking it. If the value of the act or thing resided in its nature, then the particularity of the post-Revelational era was compromised. It had to be that the actor's deed was the locus of value; not the a-temporal or generic act or thing.[72]

As we have seen, the line of criticism following al-Rāzī believed the essence of this discussion to be whether any act could be good or detestable absolutely—that is in all circumstances and conditions.[73] The historian of religion sees another question at the center of this dispute, namely, what is the nature and significance of Revelation and its bearer, the Prophet? What difference has the Muslim Revelation made? What differentiates those guided by the Muslim Revelation from those who are not?

> The Mu'tazilah say [the term] Permitted has no meaning other than the negation of harm for doing it, and that is established (*thābit*) before the arrival of *shar'* and continues after it, so that [Permitted] is not a *shar'ī* assessment.[74]

Thus, for al-Āmidī, not only is the uniqueness of the *shar'* denied by his opponents but a whole category of assessments is moved outside the *shar'ī* domain. In often emotional language the critics lambasted those who held what we have called a 'low' view of Revelation.

Al-Baghdādī seems to say that moral knowledge by the *'aql* arises from the equality of gracious endowments (*ni'am*) according to the Mu'tazilah. It would seem that for him equality of the *compotes mentis* amounts to a refutation of Prophecy.[75] More discerning critics correctly heard the Mu'tazilah dividing moral knowledge into three parts. That which the *'aql* knows certainly as good and evil—which Revelation would not (or could not, as critics more pejoratively heard) change. Then there were those things which might reasonably be supposed to be of one value but which Revelation described to have another, such as the value of pork. And finally, there were those things whose value reason and the *'aql* could in no way discern, such as the methods or times of ritual worship.[76] It was these latter two categories that were the provenance of Prophets and Messengers.

Yet as we have shown above, the impulse, from at least the late second Islamic century, was to aggrandize Revelation, to set its boundaries as widely and encompassingly as possible. The Mu'tazilah view of Revelation restricted its scope. "If the *'aql* makes Obligatory a particular assessment for specific acts, then it may not be that the *shar'* comes with what is contrary to that," they were understood to say.[77] While the Mu'tazilah saw the *'aql* as temporally and therefore conceptually prior to the *shar*‘, the critics understood the *shar*‘ to be supernatural and therefore hierarchically superior to the ‘*aql*. As al-Qāḍī Nu‘mān said (criticizing more than just the Mu‘tazilah),

> Prophets brought only that with which they were sent, and they said nothing of "essential nature" and they brought nothing of their [own] speculation or their own ‘*aql*s. . . . Creatures are incapable of arriving at the like of that which [the Prophets] brought.[78] For religious norms substantiate the ‘*aql* [rather than the other way around].[79]

The most straightforward way to read the sources is to see the critics exercised about the hierarchical relationship of the ‘*aql* to Revelation. The discomfort the Mu‘tazilah position produced in committed Ash‘arīs is clear in the shrill language used by al-Shahrastānī to describe the position of the two Jubbā’īs:

> They established an ‘*aqlī sharī‘ah* and relegated the Prophetic *sharī‘ah* to a few assessments: times of cultic acts (‘*ibādāt*) to which the ‘*aql* had no access or for which reflection provided guidance: [for them] it is by the determination of the ‘*aql* and [human] wisdom that the Judge must reward the obedient and punish the rebellious, save for punctuality and neglect which are known by Revelation *al-sam*‘.[80]

Fundamentally the Mu‘tazilah and their critics had two different theories of Revelation. As they saw it, the Mu‘tazilah believed the *shar*‘ came, and in the process stipulated and also confirmed the assessments of the ‘*aql*, "but as for us," says al-Ṭūfī, it is like its name: it initiates assessments.[81] The problem, he continues, is that, "they turn from the inerrant Word to follow blindly something that is notoriously imperfect, for the ‘*aql* suggests what is errant and draws one off the right course.[82]

Ultimately the question therefore is this: What is Revelation? As we have seen, for the Mu‘tazilah it is a form of knowledge, often described as something that discloses (*kāshif*) the nature of the act or the assessment appropriate to the act. On this view, Revelation is one source of knowledge among others. It is unique, and irreplaceable, but it is not categorically different from other kinds of knowledge such as that an elephant cannot pass through a needle's eye.

For the critics, however, Revelation was uniquely reliable and uniquely objective. It alone assessed acts from a perspective untainted by sympathy, self-interest, or passion. For the critics, Revelation was not knowledge but pure deontic force. As well as providing knowledge of moral values, it was the sole reason for the existence of any morality whatsoever. In al-Ṭūfī's view, "the *shar*‘ is for them confirmatory, for us it is foundational."[83] The whole of the non-Mu‘tazilī criticism can be seen as an attempt to put the *shar*‘ at the foundation of the Islamic legal-moral edifice, in contrast to the Mu'tazilah who, they believed, used the stipulations of Revelation as no more than one building block among many.

Summary

The critique of the Mu'tazilah, then, consisted of two parts. The first was a dismissal of the possibility that the assessment and its ontology—that is, that the name and its assessment were intrinsically linked. In this they proceeded by *reductio ad absurdum*. If goodness were part of the being of a thing, some things would be good absolutely, but none are. Knowledge of a thing is not knowledge of its moral quality. The second effort was to establish the hierarchy of Revelation and *'aql*— to determine which was Sultan and which the deputy, in al-Ṭūfī's simile.

Nothing in the act or the *'aql* guides us to knowledge of the act's value. The *'aql* is not reliable, particularly if the *shar'* is taken to be truth, since the *'aql* and the *shar'* are often at odds in their assessments—of virtuous monks, for example. The reason for the *'aql*'s unreliability lies first in the limits of what it knows—these are only the most immediate, primitive things. Second, the *'aql* is shaped by its environment in a way that impeaches it as an assessor: habit, conditioning, the biography of the person, self-interest, sympathy, a desire for gratification, all influence the assessments of the *'aql*.

That leaves one only with Revelation, the sole means to know the utterly otherly-nature of moral stipulations. The decisive event in Muslim history is thus placed in a unique position and it is safeguarded from any kind of relegation. Ethically, moral knowledge is grounded in certain, objective, and disinterested norms. The identity of law and ethics is perfected and mundane ethics are made transcendent.

The triumph of the critics' position was not inevitable, but throughout the fourth and fifth Islamic centuries they managed both to sap and to destroy the Mu'tazilah's positions and make their own impregnable. The critics' position was a noteworthy intellectual achievement and endured for nearly a millennium. In many ways it endures today.

Part V

Conclusions

The goal of this study has been to present the *religious* concerns of those who participated in the before revelation debate. Their debate was about Islam, not merely about doctrine, and the position of Muslims—even within the same school—changed with time. Mu'tazilīs argued with non-Mu'tazilīs, but also with each other; Ḥanbalīs were Permitters, Proscribers, and No Assessors. Yet it is clear that the before revelation complex was 'something to think with;' it was never itself the point of the argument. Instead, this debate was a way to reflect upon ontological, epistemological, and *heilsgeschichte* problems that increasingly sophisticated Muslims faced as they tried to understand what it meant to be Muslim. It is only when historians step back from mere doxography and view Muslim legal and theological texts as part of religious history that the task of correlating school positions and methods of argumentation with the historical milieu can begin.

That correlation might be the task of another book. Several important tendencies can be adumbrated here, however. As section three suggests, one of the most important historical and social transformations in Islamic history is the shift from Muslim Arabs as a religious and ethnic minority to Muslims as a majority comprised of various ethnic groups. This means that a scholar writing in the late fifth century in the central lands of Islam, in contrast to his second century equivalent, was not conscious of himself as an Arab and saw Islam, unreflectively, as a given, not a variable in the cultural and religious landscape. These changed circumstances are reflected in religious positions entertained by religious scholars.

For instance, proselytizing missionary religions in a dominant political position will surely find commonalities with those they rule whom they wish also to convert. The stable, assured, and unified 'Abbasid state was complemented by a religious ideology arguing that all humankind shares a kind of moral common sense, the '*aql*, which has always enabled humans to know the good from the detestable. In the process of trying to account for this universal knowledge, scholars sought to locate the acts' values in the act itself and the valuation of it in the *'aql*. Both the acts' ontology and the apparatus of moral perception were shared, in this view, by Muslims and non-Muslims alike. Muslim Revelation, consequently, was understood as a supplementary form of knowledge, one that confirmed the judgment of the *'aql* and added the details of cultus and practice to enhance the moral practices of the "anonymous Muslims" who lived morally if not yet Islamically. In identifying moral knowledge and human intellectual apparatus, the Permitters did no more than echo the message of the Qur'ān, itself at its beginning a product of a minoritarian missionary environment. The Qur'ānic message time and again appeals to impartial knowledge that confirms the Qur'ānic summons. Nature, the *'aql*, the cosmos and their patterns—all are appealed to say that the message of the Qur'ān is reasonable.

When those scholars who advocated these positions are placed in context, and cease to be hypostasized 'rationalists' but historically conditioned pietists, it is plain that their milieu is one in which Muslims rule, but as a minority. Our argument has been that Mu'tazilism represents an archaic form of Muslim thought carrying forward earlier ideas formed in a missionary, that is to say a minoritarian context. Mu'tazilism is begun in the mid C.E. 700s/A.H. 150s, and at least one scholar has argued that many doctrinal elements, including the 'five principles,' are articulated even this early, and are subsequently passed on as part of the Mu'tazilī heritage.[1] This is, according to the best study we have, considerably prior to the mass conversions to Islam in Iran and Iraq, and still further before those converted masses make themselves felt as Muslims.[2]

As nearly as can be determined, the conversion process does not take off until the third century, and subsequently, scholars no longer argue from their confident but minoritarian context. At this point Islam itself became the standard, and the congruence of reason and religion, which had once served to justify religion, now, at best, justified reason.

The fourth and fifth Islamic centuries, we argued, see a shift of the religious paradigm. Surely it is no coincidence that there is also a dramatic shift in the circumstances of cultural production at the same time. Now Muslims became the majority, but Arabs and their indigenous norms were just one set of ethnic values among many. At same the time, the world in which they found themselves was less stable, less confident, as kings and emirs fragmented the polity, and rival versions of Islam acquired cultural and military patronage. In another important change the scholars who wrote these texts through the fifth and sixth centuries wrote self-consciously as members of an academy, and lived and taught on stipends that insulated them to some extent from *hoi polloi* and turmoil.[3] As these scholars regarded the first four centuries of Islam, they viewed themselves as different from non-Muslims about whom they knew less and less, and so they viewed the Muslim Revelation as an event categorically different from any other; consequently the information and the commands it brought were of a sort different from anything before or after. They saw Revelation and the society it produced through a rosy rearview mirror, and believed the unity and coherence Revelation had produced was now at risk from human caprice and ambition. Their Islam is both imperious and insecure—it needs no further confirmation nor does it tolerate extra-Revelational authority. Their God is a Persian shah, not an Arab king. His laws are not negotiated but decreed. If, as al-Ṭūfī says, the *'aql* is to be thought of as a deputy sent before the king's arrival, he is become a lowly seneschal, not a powerful ally. Revelation in the sixth century is seen as a self-sufficient source of authority because the legists of the previous two centuries had worked so successfully to extend its scope and methodology that it stands before the sixth century Muslim as a marmoreal edifice—seamless, of towering authority, and coextensive with life itself. It is the success of Islam and Islamicate civilization that correlated with and conditioned the position that Islam's Revelation is unique in kind and content and disconnected from what came before, and also unlike any knowledge that can come afterwards.

Scholars have done a disservice to Islamic studies by presenting the rationalists and traditionists as competing teams vying for the Baghdad cup solely because they were on different teams. The first mistake is to see these teams as fully formed from the beginning, and figures like al-Shāshī as drafted and signed to play for the rationalists though later traded to the traditionists. Rather, Muslim religious scholars sought conscientiously to solve problems, and the largest problem for Muslims was, surely, what significance Revelation had for Muslims. As individual Muslims, and groups of Muslims, sought to understand this and other ancillary obscurities, they fell gradually into two perspectives, one optimistic, one pessimistic. One trusted the world, and trusted innate human ability to assess acts, the other did not. Yet the boundaries between these two tendencies were permeable, we have argued, and it is a shift in the circumstances of scholarly life, not a defeat, that led to the Mu'tazilah's demise.[4] In some respects even the pessimists trusted human capacity to know, e.g. that this person was indeed a Messenger sent by a God who was of the sort to send Messengers. In some respects the optimists believed that humans could not be trusted to act on their knowledge, and so required "Warners" to prod them to inquire and to act. The Permitter position, thought to characterize the Mu'tazilah, lived on in modified form among the Ḥanafīs, who were, it must not be forgotten, always the largest, and almost always the most missionary of the legal schools.

The most important finding in each chapter of this study, and cumulatively, is that Islamic intellectual history cannot be retrojected from the pieties and orthodoxies of the "classical" period—the fifth and sixth centuries of Islam. Like other traditions, Islam's orthodoxies developed gradually, even falteringly, as pious scholars tried and discarded ideas and methods, in what we assume to have been a sincere search for truth. This means that while later Ash'arīs and Ḥanbalīs saw a Mu'tazilī under every bed, we do not; and while later tradition concealed the rich diversity of Islam's early centuries, we should not.

The question of the "assessment of acts before Revelation" is one of many questions that were debated; only because the question was so important for both theology and law are our sources richer and more complex than might be the case with other topics. We believe that the plurality of voices and approaches on this question accurately reflects the general state of Islamic thought in the second, third, fourth, and even fifth Islamic centuries. Indeed, it should not be forgotten that on this question Ḥanafīs are still arguing in the A.H. twelfth and thirteenth/C.E. eighteenth and nineteenth centuries.

The first section of the book demonstrates this plurality, showing that members of each of the legal schools can be found who held each of the possible positions on the Before Revelation question. There are Ḥanbalī, Shāfiʻī, and Muʻtazilī Proscribers, Shāfiʻī, Ḥanbalī and Ḥanafī Permitters, and Shāfiʻī, Ḥanbalī and Ḥanafī No Assessors. Indeed the evidence shows that beginning with Ibn Surayj, at least two generations of Shāfiʻīs held Permitted as the school position. Yet it makes no sense to describe these scholars—in many ways the founding fathers of Shāfiʻism and sometimes of Ashʻarism—as Muʻtazilīs.[5]

In the second section we examined each of the three positions in detail and tried to understand what Islamic motives moved adherents to hold the Proscribed, Permitted, and No Assessor positions. Proscribed turned out to be the result of a pious scrupulousness (*warʻ*) that was entirely consonant with the ascetic skepticism of both the Baghdādī Muʻtazilīs and the Ḥanbalīs such as Abū Yaʻlá. The weakness of the Proscribed position was its trust of some natural knowledge (namely that the world ought to be mistrusted), but not another piece of natural knowledge (that it seems harmless, even beneficial to make use of useful things).

The Permitters, by contrast, were optimists and *sharʻī* expansionists. They trusted their own moral intuitions and trusted that these were congruent with the reasonable dictates of Revelation. By this means the scope of the *sharʻ* was expanded to include many things of which it did not directly speak; the Permitters also, as it were, extended Revelation backwards in time, to the period before Revelation itself. We suggested that the Permitted position and indeed any position that asserts an agreement between their particular religious summons and human faculties is useful in a minoritarian or missionary situation; it is less appealing to those who already belong, who are, in this case, already Muslims. A natural law position is attractive in plurality; it is subversive of hegemony.[6] A dominant group will wish to emphasize the events and symbols that distinguish them from their religious inferiors and will emphasize the discontinuity between the time before, and that after, Revelation.

The No Assessors did just that. Evolving from an agnostic position that said simply "we can't know how to assess acts before/without Revelation," the No Assessors came to affirm that without Revelation there cannot be any meaningful moral assessment. They said that assessments indeed are the address of Revelation to an act. If there is no Revelation, the act has not been addressed.

Al-Ghazālī and his ilk mistrusted the world as much as the Proscribers, and attributed all intuited moral impulses to Pavlovian conditioning or mere self-interest. They affirmed, however, the uniqueness of Islamic symbols and their indispensability for true moral life.

As a specific instance of moral assessment, Islamic scholars debated whether thanking the benefactor is indeed, as the Permitters asserted, an example of purely *'aqlī* assessment with which the *shar'* concurs, or whether it was a purely human convention grounded in self-interest and nothing more. We showed that the unmooring of Revelational dictates from the knowledge of the *'aql* was paralleled by a detachment of religious norms from social norms. God was no longer the super-patron of human clients but a capricious Other Who might equally justifiably have demanded ingratitude and inattention as gratitude and devotion. We closed by pointing out that, as is often the case, this theological anti-foundationism found absolutely no expression at the level of Islamic praxis, where the concept of Thanking the Benefactor remained among Islam's most potent symbols.

Our third section studied some of the more metaphysical issues that informed this debate at the background level. The limitations of Revelation were the most important of the questions that gave rise to the before revelation debate. We showed how, on the question of *nabīdh*-drinking, one side used techniques that came to be Islamically acceptable—such as extending *shar'ī* rulings by including the entire semantic scope of the word or word root in their assessment. The *nabīdh*-drinkers also used techniques that later scholars rejected, such as the appeal to the practice of other communities and other Revelations. Finally we suggested that it was inevitable that ontology become part of this discussion, given the belief in the identity of the name and its assessment affirmed by at least one early Shāfi'ī.

In the most technical part of this study we examined the intramural debate between Baghdādī and Basran Mu'tazilīs over the circumstantial quality of assessments. While the Baghdādīs tried to defend the rigorist position that "a lie is detestable and so is Proscribed," the Basrans developed a situational ontology that withheld assessment of an act until the time and circumstances of its actual occurrence.

The Basrans forged an ontological theory that made the assessment dependent on the evanescent aspect (*wajh*) that arose at the coming-into-existence of the act. They then constructed a psychological epistemology that grounded the recognition of that aspect in pietist fear and speculativist inquiry. On this account Revelation is another source of knowledge—like the knowledge that comprises the *'aql*. Revelation was privileged in content, but not in kind.

This minimization of Revelation was surely the goad that moved the critics of the Mu'tazilah to part ways with them. While they pointed out some ontological difficulties with Basran theory, for the most part the critics simply ignored ontology and concentrated on epistemology. They argued again and again the unreliability of the '*aql* and its frequent deviance from the knowledge provided by Revelation. It is not that they denied any value to the '*aql*, it is only that they wished it to be handmaid to the *shar*' rather than vice versa.

To close, we would like to try to provide an alternative to the map of Islamic intellectual history that we inherit jointly from Muslim doxographers and nineteenth and twentieth century Orientalists. The hope here is to "let the mind play freely around a subject in which there has been much endeavor and little attempt at perspective."[7]

As we see it, the faultline that divided Muslims was in a sense a temporal one. On the one side was a minoritarian, kerygmatic faith whose warning was to pay attention to what was already known but now acknowledged: that there was a single God Who because of the largess He has bestowed has a claim against humankind's behavior. What He claimed was devotion and moral conduct along the lines spelled out by Revelation.

On the other side of the faultline is a triumphalist, majoritarian Islam whose members live in a world dominated by professing Muslims. For them the most salient event in history was the Muhammadian Revelation. Yet for them there remain manifest imperfections and insecurity in the Muslim order which ceaselessly demonstrate the gap between immanent realities and transcendent ideals.

The Mu'tazilah, then, should be seen less as crypto-philosophers than as archaic pietists trying to use new language to express old values. This view of the Mu'tazilah is perfectly in accord with the picture of its origins so persuasively drawn by Sarah Stroumsa.[8] She depicts the founders of the Mu'tazilah as ascetics who withdrew from worldly pleasures and politics into devotion and missionary activity. The rigorist aspect of this movement was preserved by the Baghdādī Mu'tazilah, but the Basrans held the optimistic view of missionaries. Trusting Providence and themselves, the Basrans believed that things generally displayed their moral quality to those who regarded them attentively. The world was not a realm of deceit but of disclosure. This aspect of their thought we can, following Peters, call 'phenomenalist.'[9] After consideration, humans know the moral value of eating fruit or telling a lie because these phenomena disclose their nature to an observer. The motivation to inquire into the nature of these acts comes, in kerygmatic fashion, from fear, anxiety, and distress at the possibility of danger. For this reason, using the term 'rationalist' to describe their thought misleads. For us, 'rationalist' evokes eighteenth-century notions of sturdy, self-sufficient minds deducing truth in the face of obscurantist religious dogma. For the Mu'tazilah, the point of being a rationalist was to be open to all the forms of God's guidance, not just the positivist data of written Revelation. The '*aql* was not the human faculty in opposition to religious knowledge. Rather, it was one of several points in the epistemic chain where God entered in.[10]

We tend to suppose that the heirs of the Mu'tazilah are the scholastic moderns, like Fakhraddīn al-Rāzī or al-Taftāzānī with their elaborate theological terminology and apparatus, most of it plainly Greek-derived, and most of it dry and academic in style and content. There is a sense, however, in which the heirs of the Mu'tazilah are the Sufis whose missionary and pietist origins they share—not so much the Qushayrīs and Muḥammad al-Ghazālīs but Aḥmad al-Ghazālī, Ibn 'Arabī, Qunnavī and Suhrawardī al-Maqtūl with their mystically plural epistemology of private revelation, movements of the heart, dueling impulses, passion, fears and griefs. It is not merely that many of the most prominent figures in Mu'tazilī history were personally ascetic, but that one goal of asceticism is to become available to interior promptings. In this respect the Mu'tazilah must be understood to be psychologists, epistemologically.

Structurally the Mu'tazilah had to have a high anthropology because of their psychologism; they had a positive view of the world because of its teleology, predictability and reliability. The cost of this perspective, however, was a minimizing of the differences between the transcendent and imminent realms, since these conform to the same rules and each can be understood through the other. Another cost is the minimal view of Revelation and the Revelation event, since at most it provided knowledge humankind did not otherwise have; for the most part Revelation simply confirmed what could already be intuited.

The epistemological opposites of the Mu'tazilah were the Ash'arīs, and Ash'arī-derived theologians of later Ḥanbalism and Bukhāran Ḥanafism. The Ash'arīs, as is well known, were radical occasionalists believing that the world was utterly contingent, and as likely to vanish into atomic diffusion as to continue in its present form.[11] Likewise the human psyche was like the proverbial bag of wet cats—forever pushing in different directions; it was unreliable and untenable as a source of moral knowledge. The sole trustworthy and objective standard against which the world and the psyche could be measured was something from outside the contingent world—namely a Revelation preserved in language that was itself objective and stable because imposed from without.[12] Given these assumptions, Revelation must categorically alter morality and epistemology (though it has no effect on ontology—hence ontology can have no effect on moral assessment) and before Revelation *must* be different from after Revelation. Before or without Revelation *there can be no* moral knowledge.

What we see, then, is not two parties—one party Greek, the other Semitic—timelessly confronting each other over 'rationalism,' but a faultline in history, after which the Mu'tazilah become dated and irrelevant. As missionaries they have nothing to say to majoritarian Muslims; as optimists they have little to say to inhabitants of a realized Muslim society that, like all societies, retains its imperfections.

Islamic orthodoxies, like all orthodoxies, changed, but not in a schematic way. Rather, individual scholars turned now this way, now that as one argument or another captured the attention of the epistochracy. As a result of this study we have come to believe this: If the 'rationalists' lost out, it was because Islam, as a whole, succeeded. If the Mu'tazilīs disappeared, their psychologistic epistemology was carried forward in Sufi thought for another 700 years. If the boundaries of Muslim moral thought came to be drawn rigidly, it is because figures like Ibn Surayj drew them so broadly. If morality without Revelation came to be inconceivable, it was only because Islamic morality after Revelation was so successful.

Notes

Chapter 1: Introduction

1. I choose the word Revelation to approximate the scope of words like *shar*ʿ and *sam*ʿ as they are used in this context. It is of course the normative, praxic aspect of Revelation that legists discussed. Revelation was manifested through the Qur'ān and ḥadīth which expressed the sunnah of the Prophet. To signify translation of the legal technical terms *mubāḥ, maḥẓūr, wājib,* and *lā ḥukm lahu,* I capitalize these words and their derivatives: Permitted, Proscribed, Obligatory, No Assessment, Proscription, Obligation etc.

2. I use assessment as the usual translation for *ḥukm.* Other possible translations might be judgment, prediction, or opinion. In many cases, using these nouns or their verbs creates interference in English or too narrowly shapes the English-reader's understanding. Asssessment seems the best compromise for this complex word. For the only extensive discussion of *ḥukm,* see L. Gauthier, "La Racine [*ḥ-k-m*]." See also Anawati and Gardet, *Introduction,* 257–258: "N'est-il pas caractéristique d'ailleurs que ce même mot *ḥukm* désigne à la fois cet état juridique et l'acte du jugement en tant que deuxième opération de l'esprit? . . ." For further discussion of the semantic scope of the term, see Lane s.v. "*ḥ-k-m*" and *EI*2 "*ḥukm*" [no discussion of technical usages]; and Anawati and Gardet, *Introduction,* 381–382.

3. Al-Qarāfī, *Al-Iḥkām fī tamyīz,* 26–28.

4. Reinhart, "Islamic Law. . . ." p. 192; Zysow, "The Economy of Certainty," Chapter Five.

5. Al-Khaṭīb al-Baghdādī, *Kitāb al-faqīh wa-l-mutafaqqih,* 217.

6. Wehr, 1060.

7. For this usage see for instance the chapter heading, *Abū l-Ḥusayn al-Baṣrī, al-Muʿtamad* 2:573: "The permissibility of an act of worship being-in-effect [based upon] a unique report (*jawāz wurūd al-taʿabbud bi-akhbār al-āḥād*)."

8. I translate *qabīḥ* as detestable here and elsewhere since I believe the word's overtones are aesthetic rather than moral (as with the word evil). See Frank, *Beings* glossary "*q-b-ḥ*" and al-Kalwadhānī, *Tamhīd,* 4:298.

9. Both "Indifferent" and "Permitted" can translate the Arabic word *mubāḥ*. The difference between these two words is significant since one term implies a Permitter and the other simply refers to acts outside of the system of moral evaluation. Although in general I would say the Mu'tazilah thought of *mubāḥ* as meaning something close to Indifferent, for simplicity and consistency I have generally used the term Permitted, regardless of who is speaking. *Caveat lector.*

10. There is a fourth position; namely, that there is not enough information to determine whether acts have moral status before Revelation, or that acts *may* have such status, but what the assessment of an act might be cannot be known until after Revelation. Thus the knowledge of the act's assessment is In Suspension (*'alá l-waqf*). We will not be extensively discussing the *waqf* position here, as it seems rather insignificant. In addition to the brief mention in the al-Ghazālī translation (para. 103), the reader may consult *Baḥr* 18b–19a, and see below.

11. These two terms are used particularly by the Mu'tazilah. *Sam'* seems to refer to the temporal event of Revelation to the community, comprised of both the book and the sunnah (*Mughnī* 14:151). It seems not to be used of any other than the Muslim Revelation. Another term is *sharī'ah* which means, first, a specific stipulation of Revelation, i.e., pilgrimage or fasting, where it is often used in the plural. By extension it is beginning to be used to refer to the stipulation brought by Messengers. By the time of Abū l-Ḥusayn al-Baṣrī the term *shar'*, meaning the content of Revelation together with its stipulatory power, is current in Mu'tazilī circles. Hence "before Revelation" is a translation of *qabla majī' al-sam'* or *qabla wurūd al-sam'* in Mut'tazilah or Mu'tazilah-influenced sources. Non-Mu'tazilī sources tend to use *shar'* nearly exclusively.

12. That it is a question in *uṣūl al-fiqh* and not in *kalām* is suggested by the fact that a lengthy *kalām* text composed in the late three hundreds has no mention of this set of problems, but an *uṣūl al-fiqh* text, composed before the 370s (the *Fuṣūl* of al-Jaṣṣāṣ) deals with it at length. (See Gimaret, "Un document majeur pour l'histoire du kalām," 207–217 where Gimaret summarizes the sixty-six chapter, 330-page document; the text is by the Ash'arī master Ibn Fūrak (d. 406/1015).) See also Ṣadralsharī'ah, *al-Tawḍīh* and the commentary by al-Taftāzānī, *al-Talwīḥ* 1:330 where both the Ḥanafī and the Shāfi'ī agree that "the question of good and detestable is one of the most basic problems in principles of jurisprudence." (*al-ḥasan wa-l-qubḥ min ummahāt masā'il uṣul al-fiqh*).

Chapter 2: Development and Doxography

1. Plato, *Euthyphro,* 5,7,11. I am grateful to Walter Sinnot-Armstrong who first called this to my attention.

2. Although George Makdisi often reduces rationalism and traditionism to monolithic forces battling each other for the soul of Islam, the epigraph for this chapter might well be from his work. "We [Islamicists] set about looking for the characteristics of each movement based on the attitudes and views of a number of its representatives. The results are dubious at best, for they tend to violate the individuality of Muslim scholars who, like all thinkers, refuse to be reduced to a common denominator." Makdisi, "Hanbalite Islam," 240.

3. A remnant of the concern with acts performed before conversion or "before Islam" is found in the *hadīth* collections, e.g., Muslim, *Ṣaḥīḥ: Kitāb al-īmān,* chapters 54–56.

4. al-Zanjānī, *Takhrīj,* p. 369. In context, the issue is whether norms mentioned in the Qur'ān as practiced by other Scriptuary peoples apply to Muslims. Could one have vowed to sacrifice one's child, for instance? The Ḥanafīs say one could have, on the example of Ibrāhīm with his son. It is clear that use of other scriptures was in principle possible for most Ḥanafīs. For example, Izmīrī, *Mirāt al-uṣul* 2:247; see also ibid. 1:82. This position is also attributed to 'Umar b. al-Khaṭṭāb, cited in Juynboll *Muslim Tradition,* p. 26, from Sachau's edition of Ibn Sa'd III/I/243.

5. *Baḥr,* 16b:34; attributed to Murjī'ah by Aḥmad b. Ḥanbal in Abū Ya'lá, *Al-'Uddah*, 183A. See also *Uṣūl* of "al-Shāshī," 32.

6. Particularly for the two hundreds, a reliable attribution ought to include quotations from the author's texts.

7. *Al-Baḥr,* 18b. On 'Īsá see *GAS* 1:434; Ibn Abī l-Wafā', *Al-Jawāhir al-mudī'ah,* 1:401; *ṬU,* 1:139.

8. See al-Sarakhsī, *Uṣūl,* 2:20–21.

9. Al-Shāfi'ī, *Risālah,* section 71; cited in Hourani "Two Theories," p. 274; *Baḥr,* 20b:4.

10. Aḥmad ibn Ḥanbal, *Masāl'il Aḥmad, Riwāyat Isḥāq al-Naysabūrī*, p. 45 no. 257. " 'Uff Uff,' said Aḥmad. 'Is this the question of a Muslim?' And he grew angry."

11. On palm trees: Āl Taymiyyah, *Al-Musawwadah,* 460, and Abū Ya'lá, *Al-'Uddah*, 186a; on *salab,* ibid., 478.

12. The *Musawwadah* was written over three generations by Majdaddīn (653/1255), Shihābaddīn (682/1283), Taqiyaddīn (728/1326)—father, son, grandson—all named Ibn Taymiyyah. They are referred to henceforth as the Taymiyyah family (Āl Taymiyyah).

13. Goldziher, *The Ẓāhirīs,* chapters 3 and 4.

14. The Proscribed position is attributed to the Ẓāhirī/Ḥanbalī Abū Ṭayyib al-Kallāf; see charts below.

15. *EI2* 1:127ff.

16. Corrected from *fikr* in the text.

17. On which, see below p. 156f.

18. Al-Shahrastānī, *Milal,* 1:65 (margin).

19. *Al-Milal,* 1:90–91 (p. 106, Badrān edition). On Abū Ma'an Thumāmah b. Ashras al-Numayrī see *GAS,* 1:615; Ibn Nadīm, *Fihrist,* 207; Ibn Nadim/Dodge, *Fihrist,* 1:396; 'Abdalqāhir al-Baghdādī, *Al-Farq bayn al-firaq,* p. 182, no. 101; Nader, *Les Mu'tazilites* p. 40 (and see index); al-Shahrastānī (on margins of Ibn Ḥazm's *Fiṣl*), 1:89ff.

I use the word *'aql* without translation. The word is usually translated as intellect, rationality, or reason, but these words are uncertain enough in their English meaning, and, as we shall see, the very meaning of *'aql* is contested in this discussion. It can mean something like rationality, but often enough it means something like common sense, or mind. To keep the semantic scope of the word intact I retain the Arabic and use whatever English translation is appropriate to the context.

20. See 'Abdalqādir al-Baghdādī, *Al-Farq,* no. 101, especially pp. 182–183 where he is alleged to have held that God does not compel all to know Him, and that for those who do not, there is no prohibition of *kufr,* as there is not for other animals. Similarly, those who do not know God are exempt from Heaven or Hell, or indeed from an Afterlife altogether; instead at death they become mere dust (Shahrastānī, *Milal,* 1:90).

21. Al-Nāshī', *Kitāb al-awsat,* Section 121, p. 103 in van Ess, *Frühe Mu'tazilitische Häresiographie.*

22. See the discussion below al-Jaṣṣāṣ's *Aḥkām al-Qur'ān* on the obligations on the newly Islamized.

23. *Al-Baḥr,* 16b; Abū Ya'lá, *Al-'Uddah,* 186a. See below Chapter 4 on al-Qāḍī 'Abdaljabbār, and Chapter 3 on Abū l-Ḥusayn al-Baṣrī.

24. My first recognition of this point I owe to conversation with Aron Zysow in 1978. This point is mentioned also in Makdisi, "Juridical Theology," p. 13 and n. 4.

25. Al-Qaffāl al-Shāshī, *Maḥāsin al-sharī'ah.*

26. M. Bernand, "Ḥanafite *uṣūl al-fiqh.*"

27. Ibn Surayj, student of Abū l-Qāsim al-Anmāṭī, al-Subkī, *Tabaqāt,* 3:23 (henceforth, only "Subkī"); "energy" Ibn Khallikān, *Wafāyāt al-a'yān,* 3:241; for an overview of the early history of Shāfi'ism, see Madelung, *Religious Trends,* 26–28; See also Halm, *Ausbreitung.*

28. Al-Anmāṭī's teachers: Ibn Khallikān, *Wafāyāt,* 3:241. Two lines of Shāfi'ism: Subkī, 2:93 where al-Shāfi'ī says al-Muzanī could best the devil in debate; ibid., 134 where al-Qaffāl says that Rabī' was somewhat dim; both biographies accord to Rabī' the role of transmitting al-Shāfi'ī's books, and in Subkī's biography of Rabī' he is said to be the more literally accurate in transmission.

29. "Excelled." See the story in 3:302 of al-Subkī.

30. Ibn Surayj: (died *Jumādá al-Ulá* 306/Oct.–Nov. 918): *EI*1, 2:446; *EI*2, 3:949; *ṬU,* 1:165; Ziriklī, 1:178; Kaḥḥālah, 2:31; *GAS,* 1:495.

31. On his literary production see Abu Isḥāq al-Shīrāzī, *Ṭabaqāt,* 109; Subkī, No. 85, 3:23; al-'Abbādī, *Ṭabaqāt; ṬU,* 1:166.

32. For example, from *Wafāyāt,* 1:66: Once in debate against the literalist Ibn Dā'ūd, he said: "You hold the literal sense of words (*anta taqūl bi-ẓāhir*). So: one who does a *mithqāl* of a grain of bad, He sees it; but what of one who does half a *mithqāl*?" (a reference to Qur'ān 99:7–8).

Muḥammad [Ibn Dā'ūd] was quiet a long time.
"Will you not answer?" said Ibn Surayj.
"You have made me choke up" (lit: swallow my spit).
"I have made you choke on the Tigris (swallow the Tigris)."

33. Subkī, 3:22.

34. Subkī No. 85; 3:22.

35. Ibn 'Imād, *Shadharat al-dhahab,* 2:247; Abu Isḥāq al-Shīrāzī, *Ṭabaqāt,* 109.

36. Subkī No. 85, 3:21.

37. Ibn Hidayatallāh, *Ṭabaqāt,* 42; Abu Isḥāq al-Shīrāzī, *Ṭabaqāt,* 109.

38. Subkī No. 85, 3:26; another version, in *Ta'rīkh Baghdād*, No. 2044, 4:289: where a "*shaykh min ahl al-'ilm*" praises him thus.

39. *Baḥr,* 16b:21.

40. *Lam azal fī islāḥ mā afsadu* [ed. corrects to *afsadtuhu*]. *Ṭa'rīkh Baghdād* No. 2044, 4:289–290.

41. Subkī No. 85, 3:25.

42. Ibn Surayj was himself known for a series of Bach-like inventions, one might almost say, upon the theme of the divorce pronouncement, that is, on the nature of the performative utterance. He ruled that if one said "O Adulteress-if-God-wills, you are divorced," that person is a false-accuser of adultery and she is not divorced, since "adulteress" amounts to an accusation and the exception ("if God wills") does not [truly] apply to the noun. He also said that the phrase, "O Adulteress, if God wills you are divorced," is still not valid because "adulteress" is an [alleged] report of an act that has taken place and so the qualification cannot affect it afterwards. It is also he who posed the so-called Surayjian Question, in which a man says, "If I repudiate you, consider yourself to have been already repudiated by me three times," and then he repudiates her. Is she divorced? (Al-'Abbādī, *Ṭabaqāt,* 62–63). There is a kind of infinite regress here that only someone enamored of speculation and methodology could love. It is interesting to note that some 200 years later al-Ghazālī was still wrestling with this question. (Bouyges, *Chronologie,* p. 21).

43. *Baḥr,* 20a:14–16.

44. *Baḥr,* 18b:18, from Ibn al-Sam'ānī's *Qawāti'*; see also *Baḥr,* 16b.

45. On Abū 'Alī b. Khayrān, see Subkī, 3:271 (incomplete). He is linked with the "embarrassing" Shāfi'īs in Subkī's biography of al-Qaffāl (on whom, see below), 3:202. For Abū Sa'īd al-Ḥasan b. Aḥmad al-Iṣṭakhrī, see Subkī, 3:230. Also mentioned in Subkī's biography of al-Qaffāl to have held Mu'tazilī opinions (3:202; see below).

46. On this question, see Goldziher, *Zāhirīs,* 67f.

47. On this opinion, see *TU,* 1:178f; "only person to teach," ibid.

48. Ibn al-Nadīm, *Al-Fihrist,* 267.

49. One must mention Abū l-'Abbās al-Qalānisī, said by al-Zarkashī (*al-Baḥr* 18a) to have held the Permitted position. If this is true, it is important, for it shows a fundamental disagreement that would help account for the splint between the proto-Ash'arīs and al-Ash'arī himself, who almost certainly held and perhaps originated the No Assessment position (see below, this chapter). On him see Ibn 'Asākir *Tabyīn,* 398 and Watt, *Formative Period,* 287f. His death date is unknown; he is thought to be roughly contemporary with al-Ash'arī who died in 324/935.

50. Ibn al-Qāṣṣ was something of an innovator in *uṣūl,* holding that the *uṣūl* are seven: the three usual ones (Qur'ān, sunnah, and *ijmā'*) plus *al-lughah, al-'ibrah, al-ḥiss,* and *al-'aql.* Ibn al-Sam'ānī, *al-Qawāṭi',* 239. He was a student of ibn Surayj (Subkī, 3:59).

51. *TU,* 178.

52. On al-Ṣayrafī: *TU,* 1:180; *GAS,* 1:609; Kaḥḥālah, 15:220.

53. The estimation of him is from al-Qaffāl al-Shāshī: Ibn 'Imād, *Shadharat al-dhahab,* 2:320; his book, *Wafāyāt,* 4:199.

54. *Baḥr,* 16b–19a.

55. See translation below.

56. *Wafāyāt,* 3:286: "The Mu'tazilah had held their heads high until God caused al-Ash'arī to appear. Then he drove them through sesame funnels."

57. Al-Qaffāl al-Shāshī, Abū Bakr Muḥammad b. Ismā'īl: Abū Isḥāq al-Shīrāzī, *Ṭabaqāt,* 112, says he died 336/947–8. I am convinced that the later dating for him is correct: Dhū al-Ḥijjah 365/31 July 976 (Ibn 'Asākir, *Tabyīn,* 182), alternatively 291–370/904–972. Al-Ṣafadī, *Al-Wāfī,* 4:113, seems best informed when he says "Abū Isḥāq al-Shīrāzī said that he studied with Ibn Surayj. He did not have contact with him because he traveled from al-Shāsh in 309 and Ibn Surayj died in 306." See also *GAS,* 1:497; *TU,* 1:201–202; Kaḥḥālah, 1:308, and sources cited there.

58. From Transoxania he traveled to Khurasān, Iraq, (where he studied ḥadīth with Ibn Jarīr al-Ṭabarī), the Ḥijāz, Syria and then to the frontier outposts on the Byzantine border (*thughūr*), and finally back to Transoxania. Ibn Khallikān, *Wafāyāt* no. 575:4:200–201.

59. Ibn 'Asākir, *Tabyīn,* 182–183 for his works. For the *Maḥāsin*, I have used the Yale Landberg, 614, and Aḥmad, III 3398.

60. "*Al-Jadal al-ḥasan*" Ibn 'Asākir, *Tabyīn*, 182–183 ibid.

61. Ibid.

62. Ibn 'Imād, *Shadharat al-dhahab,* 51.

63. *Baḥr*, 16b:35.

64. *Baḥr*, 16b after 17; interestingly, though, he deviates from the Mu'tazilah position arguing that to thank the benefactor is known by inference, not by the *'aql*. (*al-Baḥr,* 17b after 29).

65. *Baḥr,* 18a, near top.

66. *Baḥr,* 18a after 13, although, according to al-Zarkashī, al-Tartūshī says in the *'Umad*, "at first this was their principle but then they returned from it to the right."

67. *Baḥr,* 16b:8–11.

68. Subkī is clearly confusing al-Qaffāl al-Kabīr with his son.

69. Subkī, *Ṭabaqāt,* 3:201–203. He goes on to say, "In the commentary on the *Risālah,* Shaykh Abū Muḥammad al-Juwaynī [says] that our colleagues forgave al-Qaffāl for having deemed Thanking the Benefactor Obligatory, inasmuch as he was not trained (*mandūb*) in *kalām* and its principles. I say that this is not acceptable to me for the reasons I have [already] related. Later in his book, Abū Muḥammad mentions that al-Qaffāl studied the science of *kalām* from al-Ash'arī, and that al-Ash'arī read *fiqh* with him. . . . But this story likewise indicates his knowledge of *kalām,* of which there is no doubt."

70. *Al-Baḥr,* 16b.

71. *Al-Baḥr,* 18b.

72. Al-Subkī, *Ṭabaqāt,* 3:202.

73. Al-Subkī, *Ṭabaqāt,* 3:202.

74. *Al-Baḥr,* 16b; also No Assessment: Abū Ya'lá, *Al-'Uddah*, 186b; *al-Baḥr,* 18a; al-Shīrāzī, *Al-Tabṣirah*, 532.

75. Ibn al-Sam'ānī, *Qawāṭi' al-adillah*, 239; *al-Baḥr*, 17b.

76. Abū Ya'lá, *Al-'Uddah,* 186; al-Shīrāzī, *Al-Tabṣirah*, 532; Fakhraddīn al-Rāzī, *Maḥṣūl,* 1/1:209.

77. *Al-Baḥr,* 18b:18.

78. Āl Taymiyyah, *Al-Musawwadah,* 473 from Ibn Barhān.

79. *Baḥr,* 16b; Subkī, *Ṭabaqāt,* 3:12–13 and 533.

80. *Al-Baḥr,* 16b.

81. *Al-Baḥr,* 17b; 18a.

82. *Al-Baḥr,* 18b:27.

83. Makdisi, "Hanbalite Islam."

84. On whom see Ibn Abī Ya'lá, *Ṭabaqāt al-ḥanābilah* (Fiqī ed.) 2: no. 616; Kaḥḥālah, 5:244; *Ta'rīkh Baghdād*, 10:461; al-Ziriklī, 4:16, Ibn al-Jawzī, *Al-Muntaẓam,* 7:110.

85. See al-Kalwadhānī, *Tamhīd,* 4:269ff.

86. On him see ibn al-Jawzī, *Muntaẓam,* 9:190–193; *GAL SI*, 687; Kaḥḥālah, 8:188; Ibn Abī Ya'lá, *Ṭabaqāt al-ḥanābilah,* 2:171–177.

87. See Goldziher, *The Ẓāhirīs,* 40–41, where usury of any but the six items mentioned is Permitted by Ẓāhirī legal thought. See above p.12.

88. We know that he believed indicants in a post-Revelational world to differ radically from those before (Ash'arī, *Maqālāt,* 557); he also believed that a *ḥadīth* ought to be ignored if it conflicted with the Qur'ān, sunnah, or proofs of the '*aql* (*ḥujjat al-'aql*). (al-Ka'bī, *Qubūl,* 16a). He assigned to the '*aql* a larger role in the validation of methodological principles (such as the acceptability of unique *hadīth*) than was believed usual. *Qubūl al-akhbār,* 16ff; and see Juynboll, *Muslim Tradition,* pp. 165–167, 169–176, and 193–196.

89. Van Ess, *Une lecture . . . du Mu'tazilisme*, 23–29.

90. For a discussion of his metaphysics, see below p. 33.

91. See Subkī, *Ṭabaqāt,* 3:295, al-Baghdādī, *Ta'rīkh Baghdād*, 8:371 No. 4686, *GAS,* I:495. Note that the ms. listed there as *Waṣf al-īman* is a rather undistinguished Hanbalī-type creed, un-datable on its content. Whether it is his or not, the school tradition was willing to father onto him this pietist, non-speculative creed.

92. Kaḥḥālah, 3:270f; Nawawī, *Tahdhīb,* 2:214, No. 327; al-Shīrāzī, *Ṭabaqāt,* 92; al-Ziriklī, 1:201.

93. See Subkī, 4:329, no. 384.

94. Ibn Farḥūn, *Al-Dībāj,* 255; *Ta'rīkh Baghdād* 5:462, no. 3004; *Fihrist,* 253; Ṣafadī, *Wāfī,* 3:308; Qāḍī 'Īyāḍ *Al-Tartīb,* 3:466–473; Makhlūf, *Shajarat al-nūr,* 91, No. 204.

95. For al-Ṣayrafī, see Qāḍī 'Iyāḍ, *Al-Tartīb,* 3:473; there is a reference to his suggesting the appointing of one Abū Bakr al-Rāzī, a Hanafī, to a qāḍīship (ibid. 470). He and al-Jaṣṣāṣ were almost exact contemporaries.

96. Ibn al-Farrā', *Ṭabaqāt al-hanābilah,* 2:171, No. 638; *GAS*, I:515; Makdisi, *Ibn 'Aqīl*, 227ff: introduction to the printed edition of *al-'Uddah*, 21–25.

97. Makdisi, *Ibn 'Aqīl*, 227.

98. Makdisi, *Ibn 'Aqīl*, 229.

99. Ibn Abī Ya'lá, *Ṭabaqāt al-ḥanabilah,* 2:171–174.

100. "Organisateur," Makdisi, *Ibn 'Aqīl*, 232; see ibid., 232ff. for an account of Abū Ya'lá; Ibn Abī Ya'lá, *Ṭabaqāt al-ḥanabilah,* 2:193ff: *GAL*, 1:398; SI, 686.

101. His *Kāfī fī uṣūl al-fiqh* has not been published, but most of *Al-'Uddah* in *uṣūl al-fiqh* and *Al-Mu'tamad* in the discipline of *uṣūl al-dīn* have been published, as has his *Aḥkām al-sulṭāniyyah.*

102. "Al-Jaṣṣāṣ," Makdisi, *Ibn 'Aqīl*, 235; "Shāfi'ism," ibid., 236.

103. Haddad, introduction to Abū Ya'lá, *Al-Mu'tamad*, 17–18.

104. On him, see Ibn Rajab, *Dhayl ṭabaqāt al-ḥanābilah* (Fiqī ed.), 1:106; Makdisi, *Ibn 'Aqīl*, 248.

105. Abū Ya'lá, *al-'Uddah*, 20; Abū Ya'lá, *Al-'Uddah*, 186a; Āl Taymiyyah, *Al-Musawwadah,* 478.

106. Abū Ya'lá, *Al-'Uddah*; Āl Taymiyyah, *Al-Musawwadah,* 460; 479 (same thing).

107. *Al-Baḥr,* 18b:19.

108. Āl Taymiyyah, *Al-Musawwadah,* 473; al-Mu'ayyid bi-llāh, *Al-Shāmil,* 12b; Ibn Taymiyyah, *Minhāj al-sunnah,* 316.

109. Ibn Qudāmah, *Rawḍah,* 22; Abū Ya'lá, *Al-'Uddah*, 186a; introduction to same, 20–21.

110. Ibn Qudāmah, *Rawḍah,* 22; Abū Ya'lá, *Al-'Uddah*, 186b.

111. Āl Taymiyyah, *Al-Musawwadah,* 481.

112. Āl Taymiyyah, *Al-Musawwadah,* 473; al-Mu'ayyid bi-llāh, *Al-Shāmil,* 12b; Ibn Qudāmah, *Al-Rawḍah,* 22; Abū Ya'lá, *Al-'Uddah*, 409.

113. *Al-Baḥr,* 16b.

114. Ibn Taymiyyah, *Minhāj al-Sunnah,* 318.

115. Gimaret, *La doctrine d'al-Ash'arī*, 544–545.

116. For the question of al-Ash'arī's *madhhab* affiliation, see Gimaret, *La doctrine d'al-Ash'arī,* 517–519.

117. See al-Shīrāzī, *Ṭabaqāt,* 121; Ibn Khallikān *Al-Wafāyāt,* 4:211, no. 583.

118. See Qāḍī 'Īyāḍ, *Al-Tartīb,* 3:585–602.

119. Qāḍī 'Īyāḍ, *Al-Tartīb,* 3:586; "most knowledgeable," ibid., 587.

120. Gimaret, "Un document majeur pour l'histoire du kalām," 191.

121. See Makdisi, *Ibn 'Aqīl*, 352–366; Ibn 'Asākir, *Tabyīn*, 308; *EI* 2, 5:527.

122. In addition to the biographical examples above, see Gimaret, "Un document majeur pour l'histoire du kalām," 189, n.32, and especially p. 191.

123. Though Makdisi and Ormsby have rightly cautioned against the notion that these doxia were stable or static: in *kalām/uṣūl al-dīn* (theology) and *uṣūl al-fiqh* (principles of jurisprudence) ideas and methods continued to evolve well into the fifteenth century, at least. (Makdisi, "Ash'arī and the Ash'arites," passim; Ormsby, *Theodicy*, passim). We use the term orthodoxy only for normative *ideas*, which were seldom of

praxic consequence. As many have observed, orthopraxy was for Muslims of more significance, referring as it does to normative praxis, and to the kinds of statements that one could make in public, to the non-expert and the laity.

PART II: INTRODUCTION

1. Discussed below in Chapter 9.

CHAPTER 3: Acts Are Proscribed

1. *Al-Baḥr,* 18b: [From Abu Isḥāq al-Isfarā'īnī]: "The Mu'tazilah of Baghdad [hold that these acts are Proscribed], and from among our colleagues, Abū 'Abdallāh al-Zubayrī subscribed [to this position]. Also Abū 'Alī ibn Abī Hurayrah, and ['Īsá] ibn Abān al-Ṭabarī held this and Abū l-Ḥusayn ibn al-Qaṭṭān . . . and some of the Ḥanafīs. [Salīm al-Rāzī] also said 'except they specify breathing and moving about from place to place and they say these are Permitted.' It is reported [too] of Mālikīs, as is understood from the approach (*madhhab*) of 'Abdalmālik in *Al-Mawāzinah* [Perhaps of Abū Qāsim al-Āmidī? See *Wafāyāt,* 4:15]. He was asked about [having] children [before Revelation?]—is it licit? and he said, 'No, God had not declared it licit.' The author of the *Maṣādir* said 'The affirmers of Proscription differ. Some say, that which the body cannot exist without, or life cannot be complete without, is Permitted. What is other than these is Proscribed. Others hold everything to be equally Proscribed.' "

2. See Watt, *Formative Period,* 221–224, but he looks mainly at the Baghdādī's earlier rather than the later period. The best discussion of the Baghdādī school and the doctrines of al-Ka'bī is scattered throughout McDermott, *The Theology of al-Shaikh al-Mufīd.*

3. "Categorical differences." See Gimaret, *Acte humain,* 324–326; On al-Ka'bī, see i.a. *EI*2, "Al-Balkhī"; *GAS,* 622–623; al-Ṣafadī, *Al-Wāfī,* 17:25–27 (no. 27); Ibn al-Murtaḍá, *Ṭabaqāt al-mu'tazilah,* 88–89; Balkhī et. al., *Faḍl al-i'tizāl,* 297–298. See also W. Madelung, "Imamism and Mu'tazilite theology," in *Religious Schools and Sects,* p. 24.

4. See below pp. 144–145.

5. Abū l-Ḥusayn al-Baṣrī, *Al-Mu'tamad,* 869:8–10; see also 870:10–14.

6. Pietists collected stories of proverbial scrupulousness and recited them to each other. "So-and-so recollected the scrupulous acts of so-and-so" (*dhakara war'a fulān*). See the *Kitāb al-war'* attributed to Aḥmad ibn Ḥanbal, passim.

7. Ibn Ḥanbal, *War',* 29–30.

8. For example, Ibn Ḥanbal, *al-War',* 28.

9. The *wajh* is the subject of much of Chapter 9, below. For al-Ka'bī's use of *wajh* in this way, see Abū l-Ḥusayn al-Baṣrī, *Al-Mu'tamad,* 870:2–6; 872:17 to 873:2.

10. For his Basran opponents, the *wajh* of its ambiguity reveals its ontological goodness.

11. Abū l-Ḥusayn al-Baṣrī, *Al-Mu'tamad*, 873:1.

12. Abū l-Ḥusayn al-Baṣrī, *Al-Mu'tamad*, 873:5–10.

13. Makdisi, "Hanbalite Islam," e.g., p. 239: "Rationalism and traditionism carried on their theological battles *within each of the legal schools* [original italics]. The Hanbalite school was alone in being at the same time both a legal and theological school." But also, "[T]he Hanbalite movement cannot, any more than the Ash'arite movement be considered to form a single monolithic phenomenon." ibid., p. 242.

14. Biography and doxography of the Proscribers is discussed above in Chapter One, beginning page 22.

15. The position of Abū Ya'lá himself is not completely clear. Later sources attribute the Proscribed position to him (Ibn Qudāma, *Al-Rawḍah,* 22, Āl-Taymiyyah, *Al-Musawwidah,* 481, al-Kalwadhānī, *Al-Tamhīd*, 4:270). On Abū Ya'lá, see *Ṭabaqāt al-hanābilah* of his son, Ibn Abī Ya'lá, 2:193ff. The case is complicated both by his extensive quotation from his teacher al-Tamīmī who held the Permitted position, and his unambiguous denial of a role for the *'aql* in approval or condemnation (*al-taḥsīn wa-l-taqbīḥ*), in his major theological work, *Al-Mu'tamad*, (p. 289). Since our sources believe him to have held the Proscribed position, we assume here that this somewhat oblique presentation represents his views. I am grateful to Frank Vogel who provided a copy of this important work in manuscript. I now find that this work has been edited, but the edited version ends just before the section with which we are concerned. All unreferenced folio numbers are to the Cairo manuscript of *Al-'Uddah* identified in the bibliography.

16. 183a. "From Aḥmad: Knowledge of God most high is in the mind (*qalb*) and it can excel [another's] and increase.

17. *Baqiya [Aḥmad] 'alá aṣli l-ḥaẓr*, 186a.

18. "The *'aql* is not to be separated from a *shar'* because if alone, without a *shar'*, neither utilizing nor refraining [from use] would be acceptable, due to the likelihood that both are wrong (*mafsadah*)" (186a–b).

19. 187b. Though al-Ghazālī uses a similar argument (para. 99), the force of the argument is different here because of the different context. For al-Ghazālī the point of this alternative explanation is simply to demonstrate the incapacity of the *'aql* to come to knowledge that accords with *shar'ī* assessments.

20. Bottom 187a to top 187b; for another Ḥanbalī (Permitter) version of this argument, see al-Kalwadhānī, *Al-Tamhīd,* 285f.—he does not believe that *'aql*, separated from the *shar'*, leads to this dilemma.

21. Also used on page 188a.

22. It is noteworthy that Abū Ya'lá reports that some would Proscribe eating, etc., even in need because of the harm one does to God's property. Top 188a.

23. 187b.

24. 188b. "Aḥmad said, "Praise God who in each time of no messengers caused people of knowledge to remain." (*Al-ḥamdu li-llāhi l-ladhī ja'ala fī kulli zamāni fatratan mina l-rusul baqiyyan min ahli l-'ilm.*) See also Abū Ya'lá, *Al-Mu'tamad*, 154.

25. 188a; top 188b.

CHAPTER 4: The Permitted Position

1. For example, Qur'an 24:61, 43:3; see G. Hourani, "Ethical Presuppositions." The root √*'-q-l* appears some 49 times, usually asking the hearer to reflect upon some phenomenon just described, thereby to understand God's role in it.

2. See below Chapter 3 on Thanking the Benefactor. The root √*n-'m* appears 139 times in the Qur'ān, e.g., 31:31: {Have you not seen the ships go upon the sea as God's benefaction?}, 16:14: {Eat of the lawful good provision and the benefaction of God.} "usefulness" (root √*n-f-'*) appears 80 times, often as a proof of God's might and generosity.

3. See, for instance, *Baḥr,* 16a and 16b, Ibn Qudāmah, *Rawḍah,* 22, Āl-Taymiyyah, *Al-Musawwadah,* 473; al-Ghazālī, *Mankhūl,* 8. It is unfortunate that not a single Shāfi'ī Permitted text has been transmitted in whole. The Shāfi'ī revisionism of the fifth and later centuries seems to have been quite thorough in its suppression of sources from its earlier pluralist period.

4. See below, chapter 9 note 1.

5. Which we shall regard as another Mu'tazilī witness. See Madelung, "Imamism and Mu'tazilī theology," 25–27. On Sharīf al-Murtaḍá, see *GAL* I: 404, *GAL: SI,* 704; Makdisi, *Ibn 'Aqīl*, 283.

6. On whom see *GAS,* I:627, *EI2 Supplement,* 1:25–26 and sources cited there. Abū l-Ḥusayn wrote two critiques of works by al-Sharīf al-Murtaḍá.

7. Madelung's strictures in "Imāmism and Mu'tazilite Theology" on the presumptive Mu'tazilism of Shī'īs are well-taken (and apply equally well to various Ḥanafī and Shāfi'ī figures who held what at first sight appear to be Mu'tazilī positions). Earlier Imāmī positions can be sketched from Shaykh al-Mufīd's *Sharḥ 'aqā'id al-ṣudūq*, 69, where he says that Abū Ja'far ibn Babuya held that all things are [presumptively] unrestricted (*muṭlaqah*) while Shaykh al-Mufīd himself says that the '*aql* recoils from some things which are Proscribed and the rest are neither Permitted nor Proscribed save by Revelation (*al-sam'*). Thereafter, things about which Revelation is silent, are unrestricted.

8. See below, Chapter 4.

9. Abū l-Ḥusayn al-Baṣrī, *Al-Mu'tamad*, bottom 868, top 869.

10. The *wajh* is discussed at length below, Chapter 9.

11. Abū l-Ḥusayn al-Baṣrī, *Al-Mu'tamad*, 879.

12. Other translations of *ḍarūrī* might include necessary knowledge, immediate knowledge, and indubitable knowledge. See Peters, *Created Speech,* 53–55. No single English term captures the notion that this knowledge is unreflective, irresistible, and above all, reliable.

13. *Lahu ṣifatu l-mubāḥ.*

14. Sharīf al-Murtaḍá, *Al-Dharī'ah*, 810–811.

15. Sharīf al-Murtaḍá, *Al-Dharī'ah*, 811–812.

16. Sharīf al-Murtaḍá, *Al-Dharī'ah*, 812.

17. Sharīf al-Murtaḍá, *Al-Dharī'ah*, 814.

18. Sharīf al-Murtaḍá, *Al-Dharī'ah*, 821–822.

19. See below p. 45 on al-Jaṣṣāṣ. Excepted are of course Madelung, in his various articles on Ḥanafism, and Frank, "Reason and Revealed Law." See p. 125, n. 2.

20. See below, Chapter 4.

21. See Madelung, "Spread of Maturidism," 118; "Early Sunni Doctrine," 233–238; *Religious Trends,* 13–20; 30–33.

22. For al-Jaṣṣāṣ see *GAS* I:444–445:23, Ziriklī, 2:7–8; Kaḥḥālah, 1:171, and, for example, *Ta'rīkh Baghdād*, 4:314–315.

23. *Ta'rīkh Baghdād*, 4:314–315; al-Tamīmī, *Ṭabaqāt al-saniyyah,* 1:479.

24. Edited Kilisli Rifat, Istanbul, 1335–1338. Also, Cairo, 1347.

25. *Fihrist,* p. 261.

26. Ibn Abī al-Wafā', *Ṭabaqāt al-saniyyah,* 480.

27. Ed. Farḥāt Ziyādah.

28. *TU,* 1:204.

29. Both *Great* and *Lesser.* See *TU,* 1:204.

30. On which see Saeedullah, "Life and Works."

31. *TU,* 1:204.

32. Compare in particular al-Karkhī's *Tā'sīs al-naẓar;* see *GAS* I:444:22.1 Note also N. Shehaby, "*'Illa and Qiyās,*" who advances this point. For another understanding of the significance of his *uṣūl* work, see M. Bernand, "Ḥanafite *uṣūl al-fiqh."* I am grateful to Mme. Bernand, and to the editor of the Islamics sections of *JAOS,* Jeanette Wakin, who let me see an advance copy of this article.

33. Introduction to the printed edition of the '*Uddah*, 1:41–42.

34. See above, Chapter 1, p. 24.

35. Marie Bernand, "Hanafite *uṣūl al-fiqh* through a manuscript of al-Jaṣṣāṣ"; Shehaby, "The influence of Stoic logic on al-Jaṣṣāṣ's legal theory"; Saeedullah, "Life and Works of Abū Bakr al-Rāzī al-Jaṣṣāṣ."

36. As does Madelung, "The Spread of Maturidism," 112, using as his source, Ibn al-Murtaḍá.

37. Shehaby, "The Influence of Stoic Logic," 66; this by way of an attempt to explain what Jaṣṣāṣ means by the term "divine writing" (ibid. supra).

38. *Qāla bi-l-'adl*, Ibn al-Murtaḍá, *Ṭabaqāt al-mu'tazilah*, 118. See also (al-Jushamī) *Faḍl al-i'tizāl*, 130–131.

39. Ibn al-Murtaḍá, *Ṭabaqāt al-mu'tazilah*, 129.

40. See Makdisi, *Rise,* 134, where Ibn Surayj is said to have regularly debated Ibn Dā'ūd al-Ẓāhirī. Quoting from Ibn Khallikān, 1:48–51 and 3:390–392; Ibn Abī l-Wafā', *Jawāhir al-muḍīah,* 2:419–420. Madelung, "The Spread of Maturidism . . . ," 111, calls Abū l-Ḥasan al-Karkhī a Mu'tazilī but once again, his source is Ibn al-Murtaḍá, *Ṭabaqāt al-mu'tazilah.*

41. *TU,* 1:195.

42. Compare *Faḍl al-i'tizāl*, p. 391. For an analogous appropriation, note al-Subkī's transformation of all Shāfi'īs into Ash'arīs. See Makdisi, "Ash'arī and the Ash'arites," 62–64.

43. Massignon, *Essai,* pp. 264, 266. This point may also be inferred from the wide variety of Ḥanafī schools cited by Madelung in "The Spread of Maturidism," 112–114. See also Watt, *Formative Period,* 164–165 for the ways in which one could come to be labeled "Mu'tazilite."

44. See Ibn al-Jawzī, *Al-Muntaẓam*, 7:105–106, essentially from al-Khaṭīb al-Baghdādī, *Ta'rīkh Baghdād*, 4:134. Al-Jaṣṣāṣ also persuaded Abū Ya'lá's father, a student of his and a Ḥanafī, not to take a judgeship. Makdisi, *Ibn 'Aqīl*, 233, n. 1.

45. See his biography of al-Jaṣṣāṣ in *Al-Muntaẓam,* 7:105–106.

46. Numbers in parentheses refer to paragraphs in the translated text.

47. His term is *ma'ná*; in later technical terminology, *'illah.*

48. It is noteworthy that al-Jaṣṣāṣ spends more of his time attacking the Proscribed position than in attacking the No Assessment position that eventually won the argument. This suggests that it was the former that was the dominant alternative to al-Jaṣṣāṣ's position in the Baghdad of the middle three hundreds where he wrote and debated, with, among others, many Ḥanbalīs. (See above p. 46.)

49. One wonders if this was because it was largely developed outside of Baghdad.

50. On *wajh,* see below Chapter 9.

51. See below. Chapter 9.

52. Al-Jaṣṣāṣ does say that detestable things may be Proscribed because they are "detestable," but I do not take this to refer to ontology (4,8b).

53. Ibn Qudāmah, *Al-Rawḍah,* 16.

54. For example, Qur'ān, 25:45–50; 16:3–16; 30:8–9, 17–27, and of course, passim. For al-Ghazālī's repudiation, see *Mustaṣfá* translation below, paragraph 99.

55. This might explain al-Jaṣṣāṣ's preference for the term *sam'*, an audited event and moment in human history, to *shar'*, rearranging, going into for the first time, beginning, initiating, etc.

56. It is easy to see how, in exploring the implications of arguments such as that of al-Jaṣṣāṣ, the Mu'tazilah moved toward an explanation of moral quality grounded in being, rather than in Revelational knowledge, since being is continuous between the world before the Qur'ān and the world after it.

57. *EI 2*, 6:847; see also Madelung's "Spread of Maturidism."

58. See Anṣārī, *Sharḥ musallam al-thubūt,* p. 25 for "moderns," and p. 47 and elsewhere for Iraqīs.

59. Note, however, that 'Alā'addīn al-Samarqandī's *Mizān* takes a No Assessor position, which would make it closer to the Bukhārans' position.

60. The commentary on *Musallam al-thubūt* (called *Fawātiḥ al-raḥmūt*) is by Barḥral'ulūm 'Abdal'alī Muḥammad al-'Ayyāsh (listed on the title page as Muḥammad Niẓẓāmaddīn al-Anṣārī) (d. 1235/1819), who, throughout the relevant section of the work on which he is commenting, seems to be backing away from the already somewhat Bukhāran position of the author of the *Musallam,* Muḥibballāh al-Bihārī (d. 1119/1707). See *GAL,* II:421 and S II:623–624, *TU,* 3:122. For earlier sources, compare 'Alā'addīn al-Bukhārī (d. 730/1330) author of *Kashf al-asrār* to Fakhralislām al-Bazdawī (a Samarqandī) (d. 482/1079) author of *Kanz al-wuṣūl* on which the *Kashf* is a commentary.

61. A good example of a modernist defending Bukhāran positions is the commentary on *Musallam al-thubūt.*

62. Al-Zanjānī, *Takhrīj,* 38. These two terms play on the roots √*h-k-m* which has to do with assessing (as for instance, *ḥukm:* assessment) and √*'a-b-d* which in the form used means also enslaving and is related to *'ibādah,* an act of bondsmanship which is also the term for the Islamic cultus—worship (*ṣalāh*) and pilgrimage (*ḥajj*) are both an *'ibādah.*

63. Al-Zanjānī, *Ṭakhrīj,* 40. Note that this seems to be a particularly Iraqi Ḥanafī view, though I believe it influenced the position of the Samarqandīs and the Bukhārans as well.

64. Al-Zanjānī, *Takhrīj,* 40.

65. Al-Zanjānī, *Takhrīj,* 41.

66. Ṣadralsharī'ah, *Al-Tawḍīh,* 1:365–366.

67. Al-'Ayyāsh, commentary on *Musallam al-thubūt,* 4:29.

68. Al-Biḥārī and al-'Ayyāsh, *Sharḥ musallam al-thubūt,* 4:28.

69. Al-Biḥārī and al-'Ayyāsh, *Sharḥ musallam al-thubūt,* 4:28; on the importance of experience and "attention" as a divine endowment, see al-Bazdawī, *Kanz al-wusūl,* 4:333–334.

70. Ṣadralshari'ah, *Al-Tawḍīh,* 1:365.

71. Al-Biḥārī and al-'Ayyāsh, *Sharḥ musallam al-thubūt,* 4:25, where *mu'tarif* "thing that makes known" is used to define the *'aql*; Ṣadralsharī'ah, *Al-Tawḍīḥ,* 1:365, where the term instrument (*ālah*) is used.

72. The term is usually translated herein as ratio for a judgment, but in logical parlance, *'illah* is the ultimate cause, while *sabab* translates proximate cause. See Reinhart, "Islamic Law."

73. Al-Bazdawī, *Kanz al-wuṣūl,* 4:229–230.

74. Al-Bazdawī, *Kanz al-wuṣūl,* 4:231: *anna l-'aqla mu'tabirun li-ithbāti l-ahliyyah.* On competence or capacity, see Brunschvig, "Théorie générale de la capacité."

75. Ṣadralsharī'ah, *Al-Tawḍīḥ,* 1:373–374.

76. For these terms and concepts, see Section 4.

77. There is surely some connection between the assertion of teleology, and the acceptance of legal discretion (*istiḥsān*) as a ground for preferring one possible assessment to another.

78. Ṣadralsharī'ah, *Al-Tawḍīḥ,* 1:375–378.

79. Reading *yuthīb* instead of the text's *yuthbit.*

80. Ṣadralsharī'ah, *Al-Tawḍīḥ* 1:332, 334, and 362; al-Anṣārī, *Sharḥ musallam al-thubūt,* 4:33–40.

81. On al-Ash'arī's doctrine of the acquisition of acts and their consequences, the best discussion currently appears to be Gimaret, *La doctrine d'al-Ash'ari,* 369–399; on the subjectivity of divine actions, see ibid., 441–447.

82. See *Mustaṣfá* translation, para. 63; noted in Ṣadralsharī'ah, *Al-Tawḍīḥ,* 1:367; al-Bihārī and al-'Ayyāsh, *Sharḥ musallam al-thubūt,* 4:25.

83. See Ibn Humām, *Al-Taḥrīr,* 218–219; al-Anṣārī, *Sharḥ al-taḥrīr,* 2:138ff.

84. Sharīf al-Murtaḍá, *Al-Dharī'ah,* 809. For a discussion of the connection between Refraining and No Assessment, see the next chapter.

85. See above p. 22.

86. Al-Kalwadhānī, *Al-Tamhīd,* 4:274.

87. Al-Kalwadhānī, *Al-Tamhīd,* 4:274, 283.

88. Qur'ān, 17:15.

89. Al-Kalwadhānī, *Al-Tamhīd,* 4:284.

90. Al-Kalwadhānī, *Al-Tamhīd,* 4:285–286.

91. Al-Kalwadhānī, *Al-Tamhīd,* 4:275.

92. Al-Kalwadhānī, *Al-Tamhīd,* 4:284.

93. Al-Kalwadhānī, *Al-Tamhīd,* 4:283.

94. Al-Kalwadhānī, *Al-Tamhīd,* 4:282.

95. Al-Kalwadhānī, *Al-Tamhīd,* 4:284.

96. Al-Kalwadhānī, *Al-Tamhīd,* 4:275, 277, 280.

97. Al-Kalwadhānī, *Al-Tamhīd,* 4:280, 274.

98. Al-Kalwadhānī, *Al-Tamhīd,* 4:277.

99. Al-Kalwadhānī, *Al-Tamhīd,* 4:277. He does not deny the difference between the time before and after Revelation or between the set of acts required and forbidden; these two eras differ only in the information available in them, not in kind. See, i.a., al-Kalwadhānī, *Al-Tamhīd,* 4:294.

100. Al-Kalwadhānī, *Al-Tamhīd,* 4:286–287.

101. Al-Kalwadhānī, *Al-Tamhīd,* 4:290: "Objection: If a *mujtahid* faces two mutually contradictory indicants in some event, he is Obliged to Refrain until [the matter] is clarified to him. Reply: Yes, although he may not say " 'God's assessment in this is to Refrain.' "

102. Al-Kalwadhānī, *Al-Tamhīd,* 4:287–288; also 293–294.

103. Al-Kalwadhānī, *Al-Tamhīd,* 4:294–296; see also 4:301: "this indicates that [these assessments such as that thanking the benefactor is Obligatory] are not established by Revelation (*al-sam'*), but are established only by the *'aql* which does not change and may not be abrogated nor reversed. . . . "

104. This is a precis of a less systematic argument found in al-Kalwadhānī, *Al-Tamhīd,* 4:296–297; the question of whether one can also simply refuse to hear Revelation is discussed al-Kalwadhānī, *Al-Tamhīd,* 4:298–299.

105. Al-Kalwadhānī, *Al-Tamhīd,* 4:298, "*fī bidāyat al-'uqūl.*"

106. The aesthetic component of moral thought is clear here: literally, praise for the beautiful, blame for the ugly (*al ḥamd 'alá l-jamīl wa-l-dhamm 'alá l-qabīḥ*) al-Kalwadhānī, *al-Tamhīd,* 4:298.

107. Al-Kalwadhānī, *Al-Tamhīd,* 4:298–299, *ahl al-adyān, al-dahriyyah, ahl al-tabā'i'.*

108. Al-Kalwadhānī, *Al-Tamhīd,* 4:303.

109. See Jaṣṣāṣ, translation, Section 8b.

Chapter 5: "No Assessment"

1. As Makdisi reminds us, however, not all Shafi'īs were Ash'arīs. See Makdisi "Ash'arī and the Ash'arites and, Chaumont, "Encore au sujet de l'ash'arisme d'Abū Isḥâq ash-Shîrâzî."

2. The earliest surviving text of something like this persuasion seems to be the work of al-Khaṭīb quoted above in Chapter 1, p. 5.

3. *Risālah,* section 71; cited in Hourani "Two Theories," p. 274.

4. See below p. 121.

5. Al-Ash'arī, *Luma'*, section 170. See also pages 98–99 where he argues that "the good is what He ordered them to do or commended them for doing and permitted to them."

6. The phrase "in suspension" or "people of Refraining" (*ahl al-waqf*) recurs often in earlier discussion of this position. It may be that this position was identical with a pietist disinclination to discuss theology, mentioned by Ibn Abī Ya'lá [*Ṭabaqāt al-ḥanābilah,* 2:176.] "I know of a party of our colleagues who, on questions both derivative and primary, proceeded according to suspension of judgment (*waqf*) and it is that one not give a *fatwá* concerning a thing save if there had been one previously; if not, silence on [the matter] was obligatory . . . ."

7. Al-Khaṭīb al-Baghdādī, *Kitāb al-faqīh,* 217.

8. *Ḥukmuhu mawqūfan 'alá wurūd al-shar'*, p. 218.

9. Al-Khaṭīb al-Baghdādī, *Kitāb al-faqīh,* 218–9; for responses to these arguments, see al-Kalwadhānī's discussion, above p. 57.

10. Al-Kalwadhānī, *Al-Tamhīd,* 4:287–88.

11. Al-Kalwadhānī, *Al-Tamhīd,* 4:288–9; 302.

12. Al-Kalwadhānī, *Al-Tamhīd,* 4:303–4.

13. Al-Sharīf al-Mutaḍá, *al-Dharī'ah*, 809.

14. For his importance to Ash'arism, see Gimaret, "Un document majeur," 191–2; for his citation in this argument, see al-Juwaynī, *al-Burhān*, 1:89–91, 107.

15. See al-Juwaynī, *al-Burhān,*1:95, 100, 102.

16. The term *khiṭāb* refers to a statement *addressed to someone*. It does not refer to statements or speech in the abstract. See Lane, s.v. *kh-t-b*.

17. Ibn Ḥazm, *Iḥkām,* 1:54.

18. On Dā'ūd's denial of the *'aql*, see *Uṣūl al-Jaṣṣāṣ ms. 229 folio* 237b:2–4. For Ibn Ḥazm's high valuation of the *'aql*, see *Iḥkām*, 1:62 and following.

19. Ibn Ḥazm, *Iḥkām:* 1:54.

20. Ibn Ḥazm, *Iḥkām,* 1:55.

21. Quotes this paragraph from Ibn Ḥazm, *Al-Iḥkām,* 1:56.

22. Ibn Ḥazm, *Al-Iḥkām,* 1:59.

23. Ibn Ḥazm, *Al-Iḥkām,* 1:63.

24. His major discussion of acts before Revelation is toward the end of his *Kitāb al-luma'*, where it would be expected in a Mu'tazilī work (pp. 68–70). That is, it comes after the discussion of Qur'ān and hadīth, in the chapter on juristic analogy, and immediately after the section on other somewhat marginal or suspect forms of knowledge, e.g., juristic preference. For Abū Isḥāq, the question of acts before Revelation is of concern—to judge from its location in his book—because it might be considered a legitimate form of knowledge. This might be a further indication that, as Chaumont speculates, Abū Isḥāq was not an Ash'arī in *uṣūl.* See above p. 202 note 1.

25. Al-Shīrāzī, *Al-luma'*, 69.

26. See the *Mustaṣfá* translation below, paragraph 39ff.

27. I am unable to resolve the problem of "sincerity" posed by the tendentious pictures later Ash'arīs presented of their opponents, particularly in their emphasis on (putative) Mu'tazilī beliefs that the *'aql* is a determiner (*ḥākim*). They distort the position of their opponents, and seem on the whole, not to understand the circumstance (*wajh*) position of the Basrans. Is it that they did not understand or that they distorted? Al-Ghazālī in particular seems willing to trade glibness for depth. Something of this distortion has been observed by the editor of Fakhraddīn al-Rāzī's *Al-Maḥṣūl*; see 1:1:185 penultimate paragraph. But see below in Chapter 10 where it is clear that Āmidī and others were familiar with this argument.

28. Called by al-Subkī "the riddle of the *ummah*" (cited in *EI* 2 2:605); Subkī, *Ṭabaqāt,* 5:192.

29. Al-Juwaynī seems particularly to have been impressed with al-Bāquillānī's *Tamhīd* of which he wrote an epitome, and many of the new arguments in the *Burhān* are attributed to al-Bāqillānī. For a discussion of al-Juwaynī's ethics as discussed in his *theological* works, see G. Hourani, *Reason and Tradition,* 129–130.

30. Al-Juwaynī, *Al-Burhān,* 1:87–88.

31. See Hourani, *Reason and Tradition,* 129–130 for the explanation of the insulting "they are ignorant like your ignorance" in *Al-Burhān,* 1:94.

32. Al-Juwaynī, *Al-Burhān,* 1:93.

33. Al-Juwaynī, *Al-Burhān,* 1:94.

34. *Rāji'ani ilá al-amr wa-l-nahy;* al-Juwaynī, *Al-Burhān,* 1:86–87.

35. Al-Juwaynī, *Al-Burhān,* 1:86.

36. Al-Juwaynī, *Al-Burhān,* 1:90. That is, the Ash'ariyyah understand non-Muslim infants to be eternally punished; and the causing of pain to animals by hunting or slaughtering them to be acceptable, since in their view both these positions are affirmed in Revelation. On infants, see Wensinck, *Muslim Creed,* 81, 262, 267.

37. Al-Juwaynī, *Al-Burhān,* 1:90.

38. Al-Burhān, 100.

39. Al-Burhān, 100.

40. Al-Juwaynī, *Al-Burhān,* 1:95–96.

41. Literally: "and for this cause a benefit which the '*aql* does not excuse our neglecting does not pass us by."

42. Following the variant in note 6 in the text.

43. Al-Ghazālī, *Al-Mankhūl,* 20.

44. Epistemology was clearly a matter of personal urgency in al-Ghazālī's formative period. See his *Freedom and Fulfillment* (*al-Munqidh*), 63–67 and notes. The personal concern in epistemology is also reflected in the refinement and elaboration of his ideas shown in his next-to-last work, the *Mustaṣfá.*

45. Numbers in parentheses refer to paragraph numbers in our translation of the *Mustaṣfá.* It will be clear that I am influenced here as elsewhere by G. Hourani's reading of al-Ghazālī's ethics, particularly by the article "Ghazālī on the Ethics of Action," less so by its reformulation in the superb *Reason and Tradition in Islamic Ethics.* Hourani's interests lay in synthesizing Islamic ethical thought in terms intelligible to Western ethicists. I am, to the contrary, interested in demonstrating the Islamic quality of these arguments, particularly their close dependence upon the premises and concerns of Islamic jurisprudence.

46. This distinction is explored at length in the chapter "Thanking the Benefactor," below.

47. This is in fact the Ash'arī enterprise: to take the *jamā'ī-sunnī* (as Hodgson styles them) slogans and expand and repackage them in the language of the more reflective and analytical scholastics.

Al-Jassas Translation

1. This translation was originally made from Dār al-Kutub manuscript 229 *uṣūl al-fiqh,* folio 212a and 29 *uṣūl al-fiqh,* folio 2b. Since then, the work has been (obscurely

and incompletely) published by the Ministry of Waqfs in Kuwait. I am very grateful to my lamented colleague Dr. Marie Bernand who procured a copy of volumes two and three of *al-Fuṣūl* and allowed me to borrow them for copying. Alas, the fate of volume 4, which would have had, among other things, the section on *ijtihād,* is unclear.

In translating, I have tried to preserve the somewhat terse form of the original. Passages in brackets are provided by the translator, so as to help make the prose, nonetheless, comprehensible. Arabic words are supplied where the terms are significant for our argument. Paragraph numbers are the translator's. The dialectic sequence "*in qāla . . . qīla lahu . . . :* ("if it is said . . . it is said to him") and equivalents are replaced with the more idiomatic "Objection . . . Reply. . . ."

2. *Wurūd,* in 229.

3. *Aḥkām.* It should be noted that al-Jaṣṣāṣ is not making a direct claim about the ontology of the act, but is discussing the assessment made of an act, or the category to which it belongs.

4. Or charged: *mukallafīn.* See Wehr, *Dictionary,* 837; Dozy, *Supplément,* 2:491–493. This term refers to those who, by virtue of their mental competence, are expected to observe the moral obligations imposed by God. It is significant that for al-Jaṣṣāṣ "being-charged" is possible in the absence of Revelation.

5. Or "indifferent." It should be noted that for al-Jaṣṣāṣ and for the Mu'tazilah, something *mubāḥ* was something with no moral consequences. The term implies the absence of information. For the non-Mu'tazilah, the term means that God has "Permitted" something in a positive sense.

6. For a discussion of deserving (*istiḥqāq*), see below p. 153f.

7. *Intifā'*: benefiting from, making use of; also usufruct.

8. *Dalla l-'aql 'alá qubḥihi aw 'alá wujūbihi.*

9. Ingratitude (*kufr*), oppression (*ẓulm*), falsehood (*kadhib*); affirming God's unicity (*al-tawḥīd*), thanking the benefactor (*shukr al-mun'im*)

10. "*Dhū hāl.*" Thus in 229. Ms. 29 reads unmistakably *dhū jawāz,* as does the printed edition.

11. Literally: "according to what is connected to it in doing it, of usefulness for the responsible party, and harm" (following ms. 29).

12. Ms. 229: *maṣlaḥah*; ms. 29 *maṣāliḥ.* For the significance of this root see R. Brunschvig, "Mu'tazilisme et Optimum (*al-aṣlaḥ*)."

13. It is a given that God cannot act pointlessly.

14. *'Alá ayyi wajh ya'tī lahum dhālika minhā.* For a discussion of the concept of "*wajh,*" see below p. 148f.

15. *Ḍarb min al-intifā'.* That is, by creating the world such that the process of inference is a kind of benefiting by creation, God has established that the usage of the useful things of creation is legitimate.

16. 29, *wurūd al-sam*ʻ; 229, *wurūd al-shar*ʻ.

17. Reading *lamā.*

18. A key passage. Jaṣṣāṣ argues first, that we do accept ourselves, the heavens, the earth, as positive proof of something. The absence of indicants ought therefore to be an indicant also. The absence of an indicant as to the assessment of an act or thing could suggest either that something was/is forbidden (no indicant that that thing is Permitted) or that it was/is Permitted (no indicant that it is forbidden). Revelation has confirmed that the things of the earth are Permitted and His signs are not repealed or overturned by Revelation, so we know that the absence of an indicant that something is forbidden indicates that it was/is Permitted.

19. 229: "explained."

20. Somewhat convoluted—literally: "And what is of this sort, it is not permissible that God most high deprive it of the establishment of a sign of the necessity of avoiding it, if it were Proscribed."

21. This is a very important passage. It shows that the issue is: what assessment may be attributed to an act after Revelation when there was no explicit treatment of it in the texts of revelation?

22. I am following ms 29. Ms. 229 and the printed text read *an yubīḥahu lī mālikuhu wa-māliku l-a*ʻ*wāḍi kulluhumā*. The ms. 29 reading makes more sense here.

23. What is between double virgules has dropped out of the printed text. It is present in both manuscripts, however.

24. Only in 229.

25. "And transgressions" not in 229.

26. Editors of the texts cite al-Darāquṭnī and al-Suyūṭī in *al-Jāmi*ʻ *al-Kabīr*, 1/170.

27. Editors cite al-Bukhārī, 9/117; Muslim, 4/1831.

28. That is, "commanded for you in the Book."

29. Al-Khaṭīb al-Tabrīzī, *Miskhāt,* tr. Robson, p. 895.

30. Editors cite Abū Dā'ūd, 3/354; Tirmidhī, 4/220; Ibn Mājah, 2/117.

Ghazali Translation

1. Based upon a reprint of the Būlāq edition. Page numbers of the printed text are indicated in square brackets.

2. In al-Ghazālī's organizational scheme this amounts to the first major section after the preliminary material (*muqaddimāt*).

3. The passage translated here concerns only the first *fann*, namely "the real nature of the assessment."

4. *Lā yuḥassin, wa-lā yuqabbiḥ.*

5. These are the three controversies discussed below.

6. *Ḍarūrī* and its derivatives will be translated according to circumstance as "immediately," "necessarily," "undeniably." The idea underlying the term is that some kinds of knowledge *force themselves upon the mind* (root meaning of *ḍ-r-r*).

7. Literally, acts of bondsmanship (*'ibādāt*).

8. *Bi-mā fīhā min al-luṭf al-māni' min al-faḥshā'.*

9. Reading *yasubbūn*[a].

10. Qur'ān, 16:12.

11. From *Musnad*, Aḥmad b. Ḥanbal; see Wensinck, *Concordance*, 3:387.

12. As with the Jaṣṣāṣ translation above, the Arabic "if he says . . . then we say . . . " is represented here by the catch-words "Objection" and "Reply."

13. Literally, "because of its essence" *li-dhātih.*

14. Plural of *compos* kindly furnished by Charles Stinson.

15. *Min ghayri iḍāfati ḥālin dūna ḥāl.* That is, in any and all circumstances a person recognizes the detestability of a lie.

16. *Bi-mā lā ya'qul.*

17. Literally: "on the condition," *bi-sharṭ.*

18. This may be a reference to a Mu'tazilī doctrine of metempsychosis, as is made explicit in the *Mankhūl*, 10: "God's causing pain to beasts is well known, while for you it is necessarily detestable if he is not able to compensate them. We dispute with you on just this [supposedly indubitable] knowledge, with the conviction that there is no compensation, and that the doctrine of metempsychosis is invalid." For a discussion of Mu'tazilī theories of compensation for pain, see McDermott, *Theology of Shaikh al-Mufīd*, 181ff. On compensation to animals, see *ibid.*, 186.

19. This is an anthropomorphist argument. See pseudo–'Abdaljabbār, *al-Muḥīt*, 1:234 (Cairo).

20. Al-Ka'bī said that plurally-transmitted (*mutawātir*) information is known through inquiry. Most scholars held that knowledge was immediate, undeniable, necessary (*ḍarūrī*). Zysow traces this doctrine to Bishr b. al-Mu'tamir (d. 210/825), a founder of the Baghdādī Mu'tazilah. Zysow, *Economy*, 21–22.

21. The point being that one might expect difference about which faculty perceives the knowledge. This disagreement does not disprove the assertion that the knowl-

edge itself is acquired immediately. What proves the Mu'tazilī argument remains the lack of disagreement among reasonable people about the content itself of the moral knowledge.

22. Carl Ernst reminds me that God cannot have objectives, because that would imply a lack on His part that He seeks to remedy; it would also constitute an accident, of which God is free. See Wensinck, *Creed*, 72, 273.

23. Al-Ghazālī's use of the word *wahm* is problematic throughout. The term itself has two senses, reflected, for instance, in al-Jurjānī's definitions (*Ta'rīfāt*, 276). It first seems to be a faculty that "perceives particular concepts (*ma'ānī*) connected to things perceived through the senses, such as the courage of Zayd or his generosity." In this sense, the *wahm* seems to be the bridge between the *'aql* and corporeal faculties. But the *wahm* is also a deceiver as Jurjānī notes next. For al-Ghazālī, the word carries both senses also. Jabre, *Lexique*, " . . . C'est là pure *illusion* sans indice aucun, qui la fonde (citing Iḥyā' 2:82 *Hādha wahm mujarrad lā adillat*[a] *'alayh*[i])). It is also however "la faculté estimative" the evaluative faculty. It seems to me that "fancy"—especially in the senses 1, 2, and 4 in the *Oxford English Dictionary sub verbo* "fancy" (n.)—captures the sense of *wahm* fairly well.

24. A euphemism for one bitten by a snake. Lane, 4:1416a.

25. Reading *li-annahu 'ammadahu bi-asbābi l-ni'am, fa-la'allahu* [*llāhu*] *khalaqahu* [*al-insāna*] *li-yataraffaha wa-li-yatamatta'*.

26. Reference here is to the natural capacities necessary to validate and commit oneself to the message of the Messenger. The Mu'tazilah typically argue that Revelation is compelling because of a prior and innate obligation to inquire into the nature of the world. Once the mind knows the existence of God, the possibility of messengerhood, of the good of thanking benefactors and the detestability of ingratitude (for example), then when a man comes with a book that conforms to this prior knowledge, Revelation is accepted and its content become compulsory. This Revelation is considered a kind of *knowledge* whose validity is established by inquiry (*naẓar*).

The Ash'arīs, on the contrary, argue that it is the miraculous quality of Revelation that *compels* assent and brings one to Islam. Revelation is therefore a *command,* not knowledge. See 'Abdalqāhir b.Ṭāhir al-Baghdādī, *Uṣūl al-Din,* 5, 154, 170.

27. Or "coming into force," *wurūd.*

28. Following Wolfhart Heinrich's suggestion: *al-hawāmm al-mu'dhiyah. sub verbo* $\sqrt{}$*h-w-m* in: Fagnon, *Additions,:* "Hāmat al-yawm: qui est près de mourir"; *sub verbo* $\sqrt{}$*h-m-m,* Wehr, *Dictionary:* "vermin, pest, reptile, (plural of *hāmmah*)."

29. The point here seems to be that the Warners are inseparable from the knowledge the Prophet brings. That, as it were, the conscience is formed by Revelation and is not independent.

30. This "perhaps" is ingenuous. The matter is exactly as he says. See the translation of al-Jaṣṣāṣ, section A, paragraphs 4, and 8c.

31. That is, apples can not exist apart from their characteristic taste.

PART THREE: THANKING THE BENEFACTOR

1. See Watt, *Formative Period,* for instance, 249.

2. For a list of such virtues, see *Mughnī,* 6/1, pp. 35–37.

3. These must have taken place in the late two hundreds or early three hundreds. See below, Appendix.

4. *Uṣūl al-Jaṣṣāṣ,* ms. Dār al-Kutub, Cairo, *uṣūl al-fiqh,* 26 3a. I think it is significant, though not precisely relevant to the present discussion, that *kufr,* which I am translating as ingratitude, serves as the conceptual opposite of both *īmān* (faith) and *shukr al-mun'im*, thanking the benefactor.

5. *The Spiritual Background of Early Islam.*

6. See Dozy, *Supplément,* 2:649: " . . . munificence, libéralité, générosité."

7. Which, when it serves as the opposite of *īmān,* "faith," is misleadingly translated by Bravmann is "unbelief." *Spiritual Background,* 201, n.2.

8. Bravmann, *Spiritual Background,* 207. The link between a supererogatory act and thanksgiving can be seen in later *uṣūl al-fiqh* literature (e.g., Sharīf al-Murtaḍá, *al-Dharī'ah*, 564).

9. Zayd had freed al-Ḥuṭay'ah as a *ni'mah.* Bravmann (201, note 2) cites *al-Aghānī,* 16:57, but he does not specify which edition. I used the Cairo 1389/1970 edition, 17:266. Sometime later, when Ḥuṭay'ah's tribe was once more at war with Zayd's tribe, Ḥuṭay'ah was asked to compose scurrilous poetry (*hijā'*) on Zayd and his tribe; the above was his reply. The account continues "They said, 'We shall give you a hundred she-camels.' [Ḥuṭay'ah] said 'By God, not if you made them a thousand, would I do that.' "

10. Al-Jarīr, *Kitāb al-Naqā'iḍ Jarīr wa-l-Farazdaq* (henceforth *Naqā'iḍ*), 740:7.

11. Bravmann, *Spiritual Background,* 200. *Naqā'iḍ,* 671–672, especially 672:11.

12. Bravmann, *Spiritual Background,* 202, note 2.

13. *Naqā'iḍ*, 1063:10–11; "*raḍiyā,*" a concept linked with *ni'mah,* as we shall see below. Bravmann has collected other usages interesting for us (including the cutting of the forelock to symbolize God's having spared one's life, so that by that acknowledgment God will grant (further) benefactions (p. 203, n. 1). The reader is referred to the entire article especially p. 209, for a discussion of this and other matters.

14. Al-Iṣfahānī, *al-Aghānī,* 17:266:4ff.

15. The root √*sh-k-r,* "to thank," appears 75 times in the *Qurān.* It appears six times in the same *āyah* (verse) with √*n-'-m*, and six with the opposite. √*k-f-r.* In many more cases, however, √*sh-k-r* appears in contexts with *n-'m* in preceding or succeeding verses. √*n-'m* appears 144 times and seems to be an important concept. Some of the more interesting instances of their usage are 14:28–29; 29:7; 16:14; 54:25.

16. Arberry, upon whose translation I base my own, is more accurate with "change His favor." (I:203). But see Pickthall, "changeth the grace," 175.

17. Al-Ṭabarī, *al-Jāmi' al-Bayyān*, 6:140.

18. It seems very likely that this letter dates from an early period. It seems probable to me, however, that the text Ritter presents includes interpolations from a generation or more later. Parts of this text appear to be the earliest surviving theological text in Islam. See van Ess, *Anfänge Muslimischer Theologie,* pp. 27–33; *EI*2 s.n. "Ḥasan al-Baṣrī"; Michael Cook, *Early Muslim Dogma,* pp. 117–123; Wansbrough, *Qur'ānic Studies*, pp. 160–63.

19. Ritter's edition, 69.

20. Is quit of you: *ghaniyyun 'ankum.*

21. This is the root $\sqrt{}$*sh-k-r,* usually translated "give thanks."

22. Ritter, 69.

23. I am indebted to Everett Rowson who first called my attention to this passage in Mottahedeh, *Loyalty and Leadership* (pp. 72–82, 168–70, and index), as well as to the *Encyclopedia of Islam* (2nd edition) article "Hiba," which see for a general discussion of gifts and gift-giving [the most helpful part being Rosenthal's introduction]. On gifts to the military see *EI* 2 also, article "In'am." Carl Ernst points out the relevance of Durkheim's *The Gift* which discusses at length the obligations created by gift-giving.

24. *Al-Burhān,* 1:94ff.

25. A certain theologization can be shown to have taken place earlier than this of course. In the *Kitāb al-'Ālim wa-Muta'allim* of pseudo-Abū Ḥanīfah 33 we find "The student said: . . . Inform me about ingratitude to the benefactor (*kufr al-mun'im*): what is it? [The Teacher] said: 'Ingratitude to the benefactor is for a man to deny that the benefaction is from God. If he denies a single benefaction, he is alleging that it is not from God, and he is a rejector of God (*kāfir bi-llāh*), because who rejects God rejects the benefaction. . . . For God says {They know the benefaction of God then they deny it. (16:83)} He says that the ingrates (*kufār*) know that the night is night and the day is the day, they know health and wealth and all that is changeable—comfort and ease—that it is a benefaction, although they attribute it to their objects-of-worship (*ma'būdihim*) whom they worship and they do not attribute it to God from whom the benefaction [comes]."

It seems to me that this text, from the late one hundreds or first half of the two hundreds, differs from al-Ḥasan's considerably. Here the issue is acknowledgment of the metaphysical source of the benefaction, but there is no obedience implied in the argument, and there is no evidence of the "social-contract" notion present in al-Ḥasan's argument. See Madelung. "Early Murji'a." p. 37, and Schacht, "An early Murci'ite treatise," pp. 99–100.

26. Watt's term. See *Muhammad at Mecca,* 24–25.

27. This is of course in part due to the definition of *wājib* used by the early Ash'arīs, i.e., an obligatory action is that for the neglect of which there is punishment.

If there is no knowledge of punishment, or no punishment in fact, then nothing can be said to be obligatory.

28. *al-Mankhūl,* pp. 14–15.

29. *al-Mankhūl,* p. 16.

30. Following the reading in note 2.

31. *Mankhūl,* p. 17.

32. Al-Ghazālī, *al-Mustaṣfá,* 1:61:6ff; see translation above, paragraph 66.

33. G. Hourani's phrase. See *Islamic Rationalism,* Chapter 3 and index.

34. Al-Shahrastānī, *Nihāyat al-Iqdām,* 415: "Thanks," 412.

35. See al-Bājī *Kitāb al-Ḥudūd, sub verbo.* *'aql*; this shift is apparent in the work of al-Qāḍī 'Abdaljabbār. See *al-Mughnī,* 14 (*al-aṣlaḥ*) 166–167, where he says that thanking is first, of the *qalb,* and second by declaration (*qawl*) or something that can stand in place of it. For the link of *shukr* with *'ibādah,* see ibid., 179.

36. See 165–168: "*Bāb mā jā'a fī l-shukr.*"

37. Al-Kharā'iṭī, *Faḍīlat al-Shukr,* 23.

38. Al-Kharā'iṭī, *Faḍīlat al-Shukr,* 33; on "praise," see passim.

39. Al-Kharā'iṭī, *Faḍīlat al-Shukr,* 41.

40. See al-Samarqandī's *Tanbīḥ,* pp. 165–168.

41. See Volume 4, Book 2, section 2.

42. *Iḥyā,* 4:80.

43. Ibid. Including, for {God is much-thanking and patient (64:17)}, "[Thanks] is one of the Lordly characteristics."

44. *Iḥyā',* 4:81.

45. *Iḥya',* 4:60.

46. Ibid.

47. *Baḥr,* 18A:8ff.

48. See 18A:4: The last referent is "and Ustādh Abū Isḥāq [al-Isfarā'īnī] transmitted it in the gloss on the *Kitāb al-Tartīb* . . . saying and al-Ṣayrafī belonged to this school of thought."

49. *Wa-yadiqq 'alayhi fi hādhā l-faṣl.*

50. Text not clear: I read *lam yanja' minhu.* Wolfhart Heinrichs suggests this might mean "to have a wholesome effect," and may reflect the influence of *waqa'a minhu,* "to make an impression in someone.

51. I am assuming a fourth form for *sh-n-'* the sentence does not make sense otherwise.

52. The point of this remark is not clear to me.

53. The manuscript has something like *b-ḥ-ḥ.* W. Heinrichs suggests IV *l-ḥ-ḥ.*

54. Thus there would be no possibility that God would punish for impertinence?

55. Subkī, 3:186–187.

56. *Bi-qarīnat al-shar' wa-l-sam' bih.*

Part IV: Introduction

1. Meron, "The Development of Legal Thought," 95–98.

Chapter 7: Conceptual Sources of the Problem

1. On the fivefold categorization of acts, Obligatory, Recommended, Permitted, Discouraged, Proscribed, see Reinhart, "Islamic Law as Islamic Ethics," 195–196.

2. Al-Qarāfī, *Tanqīḥ,* p. 68: *al-ibāḥah la tandarij;* p. 70: *al-mubāḥ laysa min al-shar'.*

3. *Al-Baḥr,* 32b:21. First sentence in the section on *mubāḥ.* Al-Zarkashī divides this first category into two: the first where Revelation explicitly says doing and not doing are equally acceptable, the second where Revelation declares something to be not-forbidden, and there is no evidence that the act is encouraged, either. This later category bridges the explicit permission of the first, and true Revelational Silence. For this discussion, see *al-Baḥr,* 32b–33a.

4. *Al-Baḥr,* 32b.

5. *Fa-hiya anna l-af'āla minhā mā lā ḥukma lahu ka-l-mubāḥāt.* Abū l-Ḥusayn al-Baṣrī, *al-Mu'tamad,* 1:370:7; unrestricted: Abū l-Ḥusayn al-Baṣrī, *al-Mu'tamad,* 1:370:13; revelational silence means good: Abū l-Ḥusayn al-Baṣrī, *al-Mu'tamad,* 1:366:12; for the Permitter Ḥanbalī, al-Kalwadhānī, "Permitted is a good thing the doing of which is not preferred to its neglect; the Proscribed is the detestable." *al-Tamhīd,* 4:289.

6. Ibn Qudāmah, *al-Rawḍah,* 21; al-Jaṣṣāṣ, *al-Fuṣūl,* translation paragraph (2).

7. Abū l-Ḥusayn al-Baṣrī, *al-Mu'tamad,* 1:364.

8. Abū l-Ḥusayn al-Baṣrī, *al-Mu'tamad,* p. 78.

9. *Al-Baḥr,* 32b:21. First sentence in the section on *mubāḥ.*

10. Al-Qarāfī, *Tanqīḥ,* pp. 70–71. *Baḥr,* 34a (though he may be paraphrasing al-Qarāfī here).

11. Al-Jaṣṣāṣ, translation para. 2; see also Ibn Qudāmah, *al-Rawḍah,* 21.

12. *Al-Baḥr,* 33b.

13. "The *mubāḥ* is not of the *shar'*." al-Qarāfī, *Tanqīḥ,* p. 70.

14. Al-Ghazālī, *al-Musṭaṣfá,* 1:74.

15. On subjectivist epistemology, see below p. 155ff.

16. Abū l-Ḥusayn al-Baṣrī, *al-Mu'tamad* 370:7: *fa-hiya anna l-af'āla minhā mā lā ḥukma lahu ka-l-mubāḥāt.*

17. Abū l-Ḥusayn al-Baṣrī, *Mu'tamad,* p. 78. On deserving (*istiḥqāq*), see below p 153f.

18. Abū l-Ḥusayn al-Baṣrī, *Mu'tamad,* 1:364; 1:366:12–13.

19. Al-Sharīf al-Murtaḍá had previously explained that the *mubāḥ* "correlates" (*'allaqa*) the knowledge of its harmlessness with the situation of the act. "*Wa-l-ta'līq huwa an yu'lama al-mukallafu aw yudalla 'alá dhālika min ḥālih.*" *al-Dharī'ah,* 805.

20. Al-Sharīf al-Murtaḍá, *Dharī'ah,* 805.

21. Perhaps the maximal expression of this position was that of the Baghdādī Mu'tazilī (and Proscriber) al-Ka'bī. He argued that, because we are Obliged to avoid the Proscribed, anything not Proscribed is in fact Obligatory, including the Permitted. Though this position was rejected by later scholars, it can best be understood as a kind of pious hyperbole that wishes to let no act lie outside of Revelation's boundaries. This position may have been more widely held than just by al-Ka'bī. Al-Qarāfī seems to suggest it was held by some Shāfi'īs as well; clearly some scholars continued to accept aspects of his argument, including al-Zarkashī and al-Āmidī; see al-Qarāfī, *Tanqīḥ,* 71; *al-Baḥr,* 34a–b. See also al-Baghdādī, *Uṣūl al-dīn,* p. 200.

22. Al-Ghazālī, *al-Mustaṣfá,* 1:75.

23. *Al-Baḥr,* 34b:11.

24. This of course was the Ẓāhirī solution. See Goldziher, *The Ẓāhirīs,* pp. 40–45.

25. *Baḥr,* 20a:14–16; discussed above p. 17.

26. Hourani: "Ethical Presuppositions. . . ."

27. "Permitted is what has no punishment when done or not done. And this is the case (*thābit*) before the *shar'* and after it." Al-Taftazānī commentary on *Sharḥ Mukhtaṣar al-Muntahá,* 2:6:9–10. Also: "The point (*fā'idah*) of the disagreement [about the status of acts before the *shar'*] is that those who make things Forbidden or Permitted [in the absence of Revelational knowledge], [in order to] achieve the continuity-of-effect of the original [state of things] (*istiṣḥāb ḥāl al-aṣl*)." Ibn Qudāmah. *Rawḍat al-Nāẓir,* p. 22; see also 79 where *istiṣḥāb* is explicitly linked with *dalīl al-'aql.*

28. See below in this chapter for a discussion of the licitness of *nabīdh.*

29. "The point of these controversies is that whoever forbids a thing or permits it, and then is asked for his evidence, would say 'I sought an indicant of the *shar'*, but

did not find one; so I remained with the assessment of the *'aql* in forbidding or permitting it.'" Al-Khaṭīb al-Baghdādī, *al-Faqīh,* 219.

30. On the two beverages see *EI* 2 *sub verbo* "*khamr,*" "*mashrūbāt,*" and "*nabīdh.*"

31. Ibn Qutaybah, *Kitāb al-Ashribah,* p. 53.

32. *EI* 2 "*khamr;* on this issue and the defense of *nabīdh* see also al-Jāḥiẓ, *The Life and Works of Jāḥiẓ,* pp. 52–55.

33. A principle that assumes the licitness of the world, with prohibition constituting the anomalous condition. Ibn Qutaybah, *al-Ashribah,* p. 53.

34. "*Nabīdh* is provided as a foretaste of the *khamr* of Paradise." *EI* 2, "*khamr.*"

35. Ibn Qutaybah, *al-Ashribah,* p. 57. The nature of the world then is a sort of sign of the intentions of the Creator, and is to be scrutinized as source of knowledge.

36. Ibn Qutaybah, *al-Ashribah,* pp. 53–54.

37. Note that, contrary to our expectation, the more literal the interpretation, the more restricted the scope of Revelation. This means that the more libertarian one's inclination, the more literal, or restricted, the interpretative method. On this general hermeneutic tendency and its consequence, see Goldziher, *Ẓahirīs,* 40ff.

38. Literally "changes" as bread does when leavened. See Lane, 2:808a.

39. Ibn Qutaybah, *al-Ashribah,* p. 58.

40. Reading *khamr* instead of *khamīr,* which does not make sense.

41. Ibn Qutaybah, *al-Ashribah,* p. 58.

42. Professor Heinrichs calls my attention to the possibility that this may be somehow a confusion with the night of the Last Supper. Could it be that, in some Muslim understanding, this was the night Jesus was taken up to heaven, and Judas was substituted for him? I am unable to document this reference.

43. Ibn Qutaybah, *al-Ashribah,* pp. 57–58.

44. See the accounts in Ṭabarī, *History,* volumes 1, 2, 4, and Kisā'ī, *Tales.*

45. Genesis, 9:21.

46. Genesis, 20:31–36.

47. For example, Matthew 26:26; there is no association in the canonical Christian works linking Jesus to wine *after* the resurrection.

48. Ibn Qutaybah, *Kitāb al-Ashribah,* 94; 23. The voweling for *faraq* from 109f. where he defines it as 16 *raṭls,* as opposed to the common understanding of 120 *raṭls* which is properly a *farq.*

49. Ibn Qutaybah, *Kitāb al-Ashribah,* 99–100.

50. For al-Shāfi'ī's position see *Umm,* 6:131; for that of his pupil, al-Muzanī, see *al-Mukhtaṣir,* 5:174f.

51. Though how it is intoxication rather than, say, its color, that effectively extends the meaning of the prohibition remains to be worked out in later theory. See discussion of *tarjīḥ al-'illah,* for example, in al-Qarāfī, *Tanqīḥ,* 418ff.

52. That is, as the opposite of *khāṣṣ,* "in a restricted sense, or with the command restricted in scope"; reading: *fa-mā lazimahu ismuhu lazimahu ḥukmuhu 'alá l-'umūm wa-l-ḥatm.* Al-Muzanī, *Kitāb al-Amr,* p. 153, lines 4–5 of the text after the *basmalah.*

53. No specification of circumstance: {Rise to prayer; pay the poor-tax. . . . (2:110)}; restricted circumstance: {God [has ordained] upon humankind pilgrimage to the House [for those] who are able. . . .} (Qur'ān: 3:97)

54. {We have caused to grow . . . edible fruits . . . to enjoy.} (80:27–31)

55. By "categorically" I refer here to the fact that a given act "Z-1" by virtue of belonging to the category "Z," belongs also to the category "good" (for instance) to which all "Z" acts are supposed to belong. Thanking the Benefactor is good; therefore some particular instance of thanking the benefactor, by virtue of being thanking the Benefactor, is good.

Later scholars did differentiate between the name and the thing. For the Ash'arī grammarians the name was connected only to the noetic concept of the thing, and for Mu'tazilī grammarians the name was connected to the thing only by the naming process (*tasmiyah*). But for earlier scholars the thing itself and its *ḥukm* were clearly connected in a way that led analysts of what constituted the thing to reflect upon those assessments that could be predicated of it, and the relationship between the thing and its assessment. Versteegh, *Greek Elements,* pp. 156–158.

Chapter 8: Abu l-Hudhayl and the Early Muʿtazilah

1. Gräf, in his "Zur Klassifizierung. . . ." p. 394, has pointed out that the Qur'ān generally judges things, not acts. It is wine that is forbidden, not "drinking wine." The distinction may seem unimportant, but the uncertainty of whether it is the thing or act that is assessed explains the fact that Mu'tazilīs judged the act, while some non-Mu'tazilīs judged the actor: see Abū Ya'lá, *al-'Uddah,* 191a ff. and al-Shahrastānī, *Nihāyah,* 370–371.

2. See below Chapter 9, note 1.

3. This account is heavily influenced by Frank's account of Abū l-Hudhayl's thought in *Metaphysics of Created Being.* See also *EI* 2 *sub verbo* "Abū l-Hudhayl."

4. Al-Ash'arī, *Maqālāt,* 569.

5. Al-Shahrastānī, *Milal,* 74.

6. Al-Ash'arī, *Maqālāt,* 480.

7. For *ḥiss* as "knowing," see *EI2 sub verbo ḥiss*. Otherwise, "sense perception" might be a good translation.

8. Al-Ash'arī, *Maqālāt,* 480.

9. See R. Brunschvig, "Théorie générale," 40–41. See also Schacht *Introduction,* 120–125 and *EI* 2 *sub verbo* "Bāligh."

10. Al-Ash'arī, *Maqālāt,* 480.

11. Al-Ash'arī, *Maqālāt,* 482.

12. *Fi l-ḥāli l-thāniyati min ḥāli ma'rifatihi bi-nafsihi.* This is evidently the stage of "inquiry and thought" (*naẓar wa-l-fikr*). 'Abdalqādir al-Baghdādī *Farq,* 130.

13. This assertion is connected to the problem of the punishment of the infant/child (*ṭifl*). See Wensinck, *Muslim Creed,* 43.

14. 'Abdalqādir al-Baghdādī, *Farq,* 129–130. This view was held, with variations, also by Bishr b. al-Mu'tamir, ibid., 130.

15. 'Abdalqāhir b. Ṭāhir al-Baghdādī understands from positions such as these that his opponents, such as Abū l-Hudhayl, are saying the human being is made-responsible (*mukallaf*) independently of Revelation. See *Uṣūl al-Dīn,* 207ff. See also, translation of al-Jaṣṣāṣ above, paragraph 30–32.

16. Al-Baghdādī, *Farq,* 125–126.

17. See Frank, *Metaphysics,* 13–16, 43. See also 'Abdalqāhir al-Baghdādī, *Farq,* 130 where "motion" inheres in all of the atoms of the moving thing, not just in some of them.

18. "Atoms" can translate both *juz'* and *jawhar.* See Frank, *Metaphysics, jawhar,* in index; and Peters, *Created Word,* 119–121.

19. Note that "act" is not by nature different from a "thing." Both are beings. For the early Mu'tazilah, a good act is a good thing generating effect. The act is initiated by the individual, but its effect is generated—perhaps by God. Al-Ash'arī, *Maqālāt,* 402–403; Frank, *Metaphysics,* 29.

20. See references cited above p. 194 n.3. The best discussion of his ontological theory is in various places in McDermott, *Theology of Mufīd,* particularly his Chapter 8.

21. McDermott, *Shaikh al-Mufīd,* 192ff.

22. *Bi-mā huwa 'alayhi tilka al-dhāt fī nafsihā wa-jinsihā*. Abū Rashīd, *Masā'il,* 357, top.

23. Abū Rashīd, *Masā'il,* 356 penultimate.

24. Juynboll, *Muslim Tradition,* citing 165–167.

25. Al-Ka'bī, *Qubūl al-Akhbār,* 16a.

26. Above, translation of al-Ghazālī, para. 25b.

27. Abū Rashīd, *Masā'il,* page 355, question 139. This seems to mean that things are detestable of themselves and may not become good. But if the act is good, detestability may subsequently arise within it.

28. Abū Rashīd, *Masā'il,* 355:15ff.

29. Because futile. Futile acts (*'abath*) are by definition detestable to the Mu'tazilah. See 133ff; Peters, *Created Speech,* 402.

30. Abū Rashīd, *Masā'il,* 354 to top of 355.

31. "If [an act] is detestable by its nature, knowledge of its detestability would have to be a consequence of knowing what the act is, per se, as itself and as a genus. . . . The detestable thing, were it detestable per se would also have to be detestable though non-existent. . . . [Further], it would be necessary that all detestable acts be like each other because they share an attribute (*ṣifah*) from among their essential attributes (*ṣifāt l-dhāt*). It would also be impossible that there be two similar acts, one of them good and the other detestable." Abū Rashīd, *Masā'il,* 357:1–2;4;7–8.

32. For this example, see *Mughnī,* 6/1:64; on riding beasts, which causes them pain, and causing pain in the furtherance of education, see 5:491.

Chapter 9. The Basrans

1. This section is part of the larger argument about the significance of the "Before Revelation Complex" of ideas. It is not a complete overview of Mu'tazilī ontology and epistemology, nor does it discuss differences among the Basrans. Of most use to us here has been the exhaustive and very clear work of Peters, *God's Created Word,* a *vade mecum* that no student of 'Abdaljabbār can do without. In some ways, the work of Richard Frank (*Beings and their Attributes*) is the opposite of Peters'; its initial obscurity is more apparent than real, particularly if read with the texts to which he refers. His meticulous sensitivity to language makes reading his work practically like reading the original—a two-edged compliment. He is the most useful and most reliable guide to the way 'Abdaljabbār and other Mu'tazilah actually thought about the world. George Hourani's brilliant, imaginative, and pellucid, *Islamic Rationalism* belongs to the family of philosophical discourse that appreciates and appropriates the thought of a figure and recasts it into more precise or more contemporary language. A western ethicist, almost certainly uninterested in theories of acts' ontologies, yet wishing to understand Mu'tazilah thought, will appreciate Mu'tazilism much more easily through Hourani; the works of Peters and Frank are too much embedded in the tradition to be readily comprehended. There is a cost to this lucidity however, and that is an imprecision in the representation of exactly how the Mu'tazilah carved up the world, as for instance, when Hourani procrusteanly makes *ground* the equivalent of *ma'ná, 'illah,* and *wajh* (p. 29;63). Marie Bernand's *Le Problème de la connaissance d'après le Muġnī du cadi 'Abd al-Ǧabbār* has the virtue of being somewhat less embedded in the texts than Peters and Frank, yet more faithful to 'Abdaljabbār's style than Hourani. Bernand also more clearly presents the subjectivist quality of Basran epistemology.

2. The traditionists raison d'être may indeed have been the critique of speculativist tendencies, but it would appear from the small portion of 'Abdaljabbār's works (and those of Abū Rashīd and Abū l-Ḥusayn as well), devoted to refuting traditionist positions, that traditionists were not taken seriously as opponents, at least not in the fourth and early fifth century from which our Mu'tazilah sources come. (Contra Peters, *Created Word,* 20).

It should be pointed out that to study the Basran Mu'tazilah is not to chronicle a lost cause: It is not that the Mu'tazilah were defeated. Nor is it merely that Māturīdīs and others adopted some of their positions on this question and others. Makdisi's point that Ash'arism is more akin to Mu'tazilah thought than it is to Ḥanbalism must be taken seriously here (Ash'arī and the Ash'arites," II:37). In an important sense the Mu'tazilah won, in that *uṣūl ad-dīn* continued as a legitimate, though devalued enterprise, one engaged in, finally even by arch-Ḥanābilah. Moreover, the techniques and terminology of al-Ījī say, or Fakhraddīn al-Rāzī, are kin to the Mu'tazilah in all but the positions they defend. For a clear discussion of Mu'tazilī influence on other schools' positions, see Madelung, "Maturīdism and the Turks."

3. Peters, *Created Word,* 404.

4. See Frank, "Bodies and Atoms," n. 19 in *Islamic Theology and Philosophy.*

5. Frank, *Metaphysics,* 38–40; 46, 47.

6. Peters, *Created Word,* 149–58; Bernand, 77. Peters, Bernand, Hourani, and Frank all discuss these concepts at length and all differ in their accounts from each other—Hourani differing most of all. The account of Peters seems clearest and most precisely to express the nuance of the texts, though Frank's discussion is essential. See *Beings,* Chapter 6.

7. Peters, *Created Word,* 157.

8. Peters, *Created Word,* 158.

9. Peters, *Created Word,* 151ff.

10. Peters, *Created Word,* 155.

11. For all of this see Frank, "*Ma'ná,*" and Peters, *Created Word,* 156ff. See also Bernand, *Problème,* 77, especially n. 267.

12. The clearest discussion of the conceptual need for the *wajh* is *Mughnī,* 6/1:57–60.

13. For example, 'Abdaljabbār, *Muḥīṭ,* 1:236:24.

14. That something is detestable only by virtue of the occurrence of a *wajh* of detestability is clear from, inter alia, 'Abdaljabbār, *al-Muḥīṭ bi-l-taklīf,* 236.

15. Abū Rashīd, *Masā'il,* 356:6.

16. Abū Rashīd, *Masā'il,* 356:1.

17. Abū Rashīd, *Masā'il,* 17–20, quoting his fellow-Baṣran and Mu'tazilī, Abū 'Abdallāh al-Ḥusayn b. 'Ali al-Baṣrī, (d. 369/980). See Ibn al-Murtaḍá, *Ṭabaqāt al-Mu'tazilah,* pp. 105–107. 'Abdaljabbār (teacher of Abū Rashīd) is known to have read his works. (ibid., 107.) See *EI* 2 supplement.

18. Wehr, *Dictionary,* 1052–1053; Dozy, *Supplément,* has technical meanings derived from *wajh,* 2:793–794.

19. Sometimes it means nothing more than "the way the act is done." See *Mughnī,* 8:348:4.

20. *Mughnī,* 8:350.

21. "As for [the notion] that we judged any *act* as bad or good [rather than the manner of its occurrence, (*wajh*)],—no indeed!" [Pseudo] 'Abdaljabbār, *Sharḥ al-uṣūl al-khamsah* (henceforth *Sharḥ*) 564:19; see also 566:12. The *wajh* is also said to "compel an attribute"; Abū Rashīd, *Masā'il,* 355. The legal sense of the word implies temporal novelty. See for example Abū Ya'lá, *al-Mu'tamad,* 106. *Wajh istiḥqāq al-dhamm wa-l-madḥ 'alá l-af'āl wurūd al-shar' bi-dhālik:* the occasion of deserving blame and praise for acts is the arrival of Revelation with [such blame and praise].

22. *Mughnī,* 6/1:52–53; 77ff; 'Abdaljabbār, *al-Muḥīt,* 1:236. And not all acts have *wajhs* of value. The acts of one asleep or unconscious have no *wajhs* and hence no assessments additional to their existence (*al-Muḥīt,* 1:21); but goodness and detestability are independent of intention, at least for 'Abdaljabbār. Hence even the act of someone unconscious can be oppression (*ẓulm*). *Mughnī,* 8:271:9f.

23. 'Abdaljabbār, *al-Muḥīṭ* 1:236:20.

24. *Mughnī,* 8:101.

25. *Mughnī,* 13:319:8.

26. 'Abdaljabbār, *al-Muḥīṭ,* 1:235: *yu'aththir al-wajh fī qubḥih.*

27. *Mughnī,* 8:105:7–8: "Every act must be conceivable as coming to be in a certain manner (*'alá wajh*); and then be assessed as [for instance] 'good'; what is contrary to this [hypothetical] particular manner of existence (*wajh*), then, is assessed as 'detestable.' " *Sharḥ,* 565:18.

28. See *Mughnī,* 8:101ff.

29. Literally, "non-existent," *ma'dūm.*

30. Abū Rashīd, *Masā'il,* 357:5–6; *Mughnī,* 8:103.

31. For this discussion see *Mughnī,* 6/1:68:3–19.

32. *Mughnī,* 6/1:52–53.

33. Extrapolated by Peters, *Created Word,* 269 from *Mughnī,* 182–184.

34. *Mughnī,* 8:349.

35. *Mughnī,* 8:350:6–7.

36. That the *wajh* is not perduring I take also from Abū Rashīd, *Masā'il,* p. 291:20–21. More importantly, *wujūh* are constantly said to occur, come into being (√*w-q-*'), or "the act *occurs* in some aspect (*wajh*) from among the aspects (*wujūh*) of detestableness," for instance (e.g. Abū Rashīd, *Masā'il,* 287:4). It is ontologically as real as the act itself. Frank, *Metaphysics,* 132 and note 45, quoting *Mughnī,* 6/1:52ff.

37. See Peters, *Created Speech,* 42–44 for this distinction.

38. On the theory of inquiry (*naẓar*) and psychic tranquillity (*sukān al-nafs*) see Peters, *Created Word,* 47–55; Bernand, *Problème,* 291–300.

39. *Mughnī,* 8:104:16ff.

40. Misunderstanding by Islamicists of the nature of the *'aql* was surely caused or at least conditioned by the powerful symbolism of such words as "reason" and "intellect" in the eighteenth and subsequent centuries—both in the West and Islamdom. Part of the misunderstanding is due also to the imbalance of our sources. Whether from misapprehension or willful distortion, the Ash'arī heresiographers were not much more accomplished than modern students at grasping the nature of Mu'tazilī theories of the *'aql,* (a point noted by W. C. Smith in "The Concept of *Sharī'ah*"; see especially 98–99). This is not to deny the applicability of the term rationalist to the Mu'tazilah, since they do stress "the power of a priori reason to grasp substantial truths about the world." (*Encyclopedia of Philosophy,* 7:69). It is only to deny that the term tells us very much about them, or why they were opposed by, for instance, the Shāfi'īs and Ḥanbalīs.

41. Muḥammad b. 'Abdalwahhāb al-Jubbā'ī; biography in Peters, *Created Word,* 18.

42. I choose this translation rather than "knowledge" though the word *'ilm* conveys both the sense of a verbal noun, and something substantial, something equivalent to "the known" (*al-ma'lūm*). "Knowledge" in English has something of both these senses of the word. In what follows, however, it is the responsive and dynamic quality of the *'aql* that is emphasized, even though these responses are, in a sense, unchanging.

43. Lane, 2113a.

44. al-Ash'arī, *Maqālāt,* 480-481.

45. *Mughnī,* 11:375:17f. *al-'aqlu huwa 'ibāratun 'an jumlatin mina l-'ulūmi al-makhṣūṣati* [corrected from text *makhṣūṣah* without the definite article to conform to 11:376:1]. See Peters, *Created Word,* 82, and ibid., n. 239. See also *al-Baḥr,* 15b:32.

46. *Mughnī,* 11:378:2–3.

47. *Mughnī,* 11:377:1.

48. Bernand, *Problème,* 317.

49. *Mughnī,* 11:378:15ff.; 379:1–2; nor was it corporeal (*jism*); see *Mughnī,* 11:378:4–5. Peters suggests "intuition" as the equivalent of the *'aql.* (*Created Speech,*

82–83). Intuition suggests an activity; it better translates *badāh* and its cognates. *Badāhah,* is the activity of the *'aql,* and it is perhaps the synonym of "knowing immediately" (*'ilm ḍarūrī*). (See al-Baghdādī *Uṣūl al-Dīn,* 8), as in "*al-'ilm bi-badīhat al-'aql*" (al-Mu'ayyad *al-Shāmil,* 12b; 19b; al-Baghdādī, *Farq,* 129; Ibn Ḥazm, *Iḥkām,* 1:65). Perhaps the meaning of *'aql* would be captured by "instinct." ("The innate aspect of behavior that is unlearned, complex and normally adaptive. . . . An innate aptitude"; it also has the appropriate sense of "instigating, urging on," (on which see below). *American Heritage Dictionary,* 680. For a Ḥanbalī definition of *'aql,* see Abū Ya'lá, *al-Mu'tamad,* 101ff; the notion that the *'aql* is an instrument (*ālah*) seems to have been a characteristically Māturīdī position. See Ṣadralshar'ah *Tawḍīḥ* 1:266f (bottom).

50. Frank, *Metaphysics,* 75–76; on "correspondence" see Frank, *Beings,* 14.

51. See, for instance, Frank, *Beings,* index, p. 194.

52. *Sharḥ,* 90–91.

53. *Encyclopedia of Philosophy,* 7:83. For the usual nineteenth century sense of the term, see for instance Adam Ferguson: "[Reason" means the] powers of discernment or his intellectual faculties which under the appellation of *reason* . . . refer to the objects around him either as they are subjects of mere knowledge or as they are subjects of approbation or censure." ("An Essay on the History of Civil Society" in Peter Gay, *The Enlightenment; A Comprehensive Anthology,* 557).

54. "God must create [this knowledge] in him." *Mughnī,* 11:372:1–2.

55. See Reese, *Dictionary of Philosophy and Religion,* p. 98: "A translation of Cicero of *koinai ennoiai* used by Stoics: all men have a common set of basic ideas which are the starting point of knowledge, of good and evil and of God's existence."

56. So, for al-Sarakhsī the *'aql* is the ability to understand the speech (*khiṭāb*) addressed to one. al-Sarakhsī, *Uṣūl,* 2:341.

57. *Mughnī,* 11:379: 12–13.

58. *Mughnī,* 11:383:6–7.

59. *Mughnī,* 11:383:19–20.

60. *Mughnī,* 11:384:1.

61. *Mughnī,* 11:385:2–3.

62. The account that follows is summary. For longer discussions, Hourani, *Islamic Rationalism,* chapter 2 and passim; *Reason and Tradition,* Chapters 5 and 7.

63. *Mughnī,* 11:384:12.

64. A very Mu'tazilī list of virtues and vices is found in Abū Ya'lá's *'Uddah,* transmitted from Abū l-Ḥasan al-Tamīmī, f. 190b.

65. *Mughnī,* 6/1:21:16. *al-'ilmu bi-qubḥih ka-l-far'i 'alá al-'ilm bi-annahu ẓulmun wa-l-'ilmu bi-dhālika far'un 'alá al-'ilmi bi-wujūdih.*

66. *Mughnī,* 11:384.

67. *Mughnī,* 11:384:13–16.

68. To the argument that it is sentiment, not knowledge, that inclines one to esteem acts good or detestable, al-Rāzī's opponent says, "one who writes an emotive *qasīdah* insulting angels and prophets—if he writes it in a fine hand, recites it in a superb and moving voice, one's nature (*tab*') inclines toward it while the '*aql* recoils from it." al-Rāzī, *al-Maḥṣūl,* 1/1:169.

69. *Mughnī,* 6/1:7.

70. *Mughnī,* 13:344.

71. *Mughnī,* 13:344:5–6; for the general question of deserving blame, see *Mughnī,* 14:181ff.

72. *Mughnī,* 13:344:4–5,7–8.

73. Concerning this problem, Hourani writes: " 'Deserves' seems to mean 'has as a fitting sequel'; thus the relation of 'desert' is one of fittingness or appropriateness between two successive events [the doing and the suffering of blame or punishment]. But what does 'fitting' mean? It is very difficult to explain it without making use of words which are admittedly terms of value, such as 'right' 'ought to be' or (in ethical contexts) 'just.' " (*Rationalism,* 45). He notes that 'Abdaljabbār is aware of this problem, and has his interlocutor say: "But your saying of pain that it is good [to administer it] because of its being deserved, is self-contradictory, because the meaning of [saying] that it is deserved is that it is 'good to do it'; when you say [the inflicting of punishment] is good because of this factor (*wajh*) it is as if you are saying, 'it is good because it is good'; this is self-contradictory." *Mughnī,* 13:346:1–3. Hourani says further: "What is it that would be useful as an explanation that would provide a valid cause for [blame's] being good?" *Mughnī,* 13:346:7. As I shall show below, both Hourani and the supposed opponent err in supposing that *istiḥqāq* is a valuative term, rather than a term referring to a phenomenal link among "detestable acts" "condemning" and "punishment."

74. *Min ḥaqqi l-dhamm an yakūna muqābilan li-l-qubḥ*. Hourani has for this passage "It is established by reason that *it is characteristic* of blame to be corresponding to detestability. . . ." which might otherwise be unexceptional, but in this particular case, as we shall see below, to translate it so prevents us from grasping the implications of 'Abdaljabbār's response.

75. *Mughnī,* 13:346:8–9, 10–13.

76. *Mughnī,* 13:344:6–7.

77. *American Heritage Dictionary,* 357, *sub verbo* "deserve": "To be worthy of; to merit. . . ."

78. *Mughnī,* 13:345:16–18.

79. *Inna l-jawhara yastahiqqu hādhihi ṣ-ṣifata* . . . noted in Frank, *Beings,* 56, n. 12. He also uses the term in this sense of God, in *al-Muḥīṭ,* 1:21: "Do you not see that the aim of demonstrating unicity is to distinguish Him by attributes of whose possession

there is no second with Him?" (*bi-ṣifāt lā thānī lahu fī isthqāqihā*). See also *Sharḥ,* 182: "The mode of His possessing (*istiḥqāqih*) the attributes."

80. In his glossary, *istiḥqāq* is "appropriately or necessarily to be such as to have. . . ." Frank, *Beings,* 189. Compare Lane, 2:607: "He demanded it as his right."

81. See Peters, *Created Word,* 57–61; Bernand, *Le Problème,* 201–217; 284.

82. *Mughnī,* 12:386.

83. Peters, *Created Word,* 61.

84. Of the standard sources, only Bernand gives fear and its adjunct, the "warner," their due. *Le Problème,* 180–199.

85. "The manner in which reflection is laid upon the reflector in both religious life (*dīn*) and worldly affairs (*al-dunyā*) does not differ, and it is that there be produced in him fear." *Mughnī,* 12:352.

86. *Mughnī,* 11:343: "It is necessary to acquire these knowings [of detestables, goods, and obligations] because if they are not obtained, the one made-responsible does not acquire the fear of not inquiring; and the beginning of being made-responsible is connected with it."

87. Lane, in fact, says *khawf* (fear) and *ẓann* (supposition) are used synonymously. *Lexicon,* 2:823.

88. "For the self," *Mughnī,* 12:389:8; "void," *naqs al-ẓann,* see *Mughnī,* 12:386:7.

89. ʻAbdaljabbār, *al-Muḥīṭ,* 26–7; *Mughnī,* 12:390:13, 12:386:10.

90. "One does not fear by any means other than a sign—information or something else." *Mughnī,* 12:386:10.

91. The only full discussion of the *khāṭir* other than Bernand's (*Problème,* 181ff.) seems to be in H. Wolfson, *The Philosophy of the Kalām,* pp. 624–644, which is a later revision of his article in *Studies in Mysticism and Religion Presented to Gershom Scholem,* pp. 366–379. I owe this reference to Wolfhart Heinrichs. The concept is mentioned in passing in Frank, *Metaphysics,* p. 32, note 32, and pp. 31 and 33, and Massignon, *The Passion of al-Ḥallāj,* (see vol. 4, Index; *sub verbo khāṭir*) where it is translated "movements of the heart." Aside from Muʻtazilī theology, the only other place that this doctrine consistently appears, so far as I can find, is in the description of the interior life by "mystics" (see for instance *Abd al-Raziq's Sufi Dictionary* (ed. Sprenger), p. 19:59. (See also references in the Wolfson article mentioned above to the descriptions of the Warners in al-Muḥāsibī and al-Ghazālī's *Iḥyā'*) as well as a few highly homiletic *ḥadīth* (e.g., Muslim, *Ṣalāh,* 19; *Īmān,* 312). Peters *Created Speech,* 63–64; Awn, *Satan's Tragedy,* 66–69; al-Qushayrī, *al-Risālah,* 1:242–3.

92. Abū Manṣūr al-Baghdādī, *Uṣūl al-Dīn,* 26:5ff.

93. *Mughnī,* 12:397:18.

94. *Mughnī,* 12:388:6.

95. *Mughnī,* 12:388:9–11; al-Ash'arī seems to have retained the Basran Mu'tazilī interest in the *khāṭir.* See "Risālah ilá ahl al-Thaghr," 86.

96. *Mughnī,* 12:386:6.

97. See Bernand, *Le problème,* 181–188 for Mu'tazilī views other than those of the Basrans.

98. *Mughnī,* 12:412; Qur'ān, 114.

99. See *Mughnī,* 12:388:10–15; 395:12–15.

100. *Mughnī,* 12:393.

101. *Mughnī,* 12:395:12 ff.; on this debate see Bernand, *Le Problème,* 188–195.

102. "Speech," *Mughnī,* 12:401; 12:411; language precondition, 12:391–392.

103. *Mughnī,* 12:397.

104. *Mughnī,* 12:398:15–16.

105. *Mughnī,* 15:109.

106. *Mughnī,* 5:109:18–19.

107. *Mughnī,* 15:111.

108. *Mughnī,* 15:43:4.

109. *Mughnī,* 16:81:17.

110. *Mughnī,* 6/1:53:17–19.

111. *Mughnī,* 6/1:64:13.

112. *Mughnī,* 13:280:14–15.

113. See *Mughnī,* 5:109.

114. *Mughnī,* 6/1:64.

115. 'Abdaljabbār, *Muḥīṭ,* 235.

116. *Mughnī,* 6/1;64.

117. *Mughnī,* 5:110; this seems aimed partly at the "Rawāndiyyah." See *Kitāb al-Radd 'alá l'bid'ah* of Abū Muṭī' al-Nasafī, 92.

Chapter 10. Critique of the Mu'tazilah

1. Al-Ṭūfī, *Sharḥ al-Rawḍah,* 1:403.

2. Madelung, "Spread of Maturidism," n. 26.

3. It may be objected that "non-Mu'tazilah" is too broad a category usefully to refer to Māturīdīs, Ash'arīs, Ḥanbalīs and others. Among those who discussed the question, however, there is a shared set of criticisms which is invoked regardless of school. No useful purpose is served here in differentiating among the various legal and theological schools.

4. References in al-Qarāfī, 88; introduction to *al-'Uddah* of Abū Ya'lá, p. 43.

5. An exception was Dā'ūd al-Ẓāhirī. See al-Jaṣṣāṣ, *al-Fuṣūl,* 3:369, and below, the position cited (and criticized) by Ibn Ḥazm.

6. See inter alia al-Bazdawī, *Uṣūl al-Dīn,* 11ff.

7. *Al-Baḥr,* 14a:31: *ḥaqīqat al-ḥukm al-khiṭāb.*

8. Abū Ya'lá, *'Uddah,* 191a; *Fatḥ al-Ghaffār,* 1:12:23–24.

9. Al-Ash'arī, *al-Luma',* sec. 170. For another example, see al-Baghdādī, *Uṣūl al-Dīn,* 24–25. This "theistic subjectivism" is much discussed in various works of G. Hourani, e.g. *Islamic Rationalism;* see index, *sub verbo* "subjectivism."

10. Al-Juwaynī, *Burhān,* 1:86. This sentence is part of the discussion already underway on whether an interdiction or command applies to the act or the actor.

11. Many factors enter into this discussion, such as whether God is obligated to do what is most beneficial to man (*al-aṣlaḥ*) [See Brunschvig, "Mu'tazilisme et Optimum," and Ormsby, *Theodicy,* 217ff.], whether God creates acts that are *qabīḥ* [Watt, *Formative Period,* 238 ff.], and to discuss all these issues is beyond the scope of even a larger book than this one.

12. Al-Ṭūfī, *Dar',* 19a says this is an attempt (by the modernists) to epitomize the nub of the question. He disagrees that this is the central point of dispute. See al-Baghdādī, *Uṣūl al-Dīn,* 131.

13. His discussion follows 1/1:177ff. in *al-Maḥṣūl.*

14. Probably first used in argument by al-Bāqillānī; see al-Juwaynī, *al-Burhān,* 1:90.

15. See discussion above of al-Muzanī's assertion that the name and the assessment go together. p. 136.

16. Al-Rāzī, *al-Maḥṣūl,* 1/1:178–179.

17. Rāzī, *Maḥṣūl,* 1/1:177–178.

18. See above p. 189 n.42 on the *dawrah Surayjiyyah.*

19. Al-Āmidī, *Iḥkām,* 1:113–114.

20. Al-Āmidī, 1:119. For "rigidity," see also *Sharḥ al-Muntahá,* 202 margin, and Juwaynī's *Burhān,* 90.

21. Ibn Barhān unites three different non-Mu'tazilī speculative traditions, since he studied with Ibn 'Aqīl, the Ḥanbalī theologian, al-Ghazālī, and al-Kiyā al-Ḥarāsī who was less philosophically oriented than his schoolmate al-Ghazālī.

22. *'Alá mā huwa 'alayhi.*

23. *Li-wuqū'ihi 'alá wajhin.*

24. Ibn Barhān, *al-Wuṣūl,* 1:58; al-Kiyā al-Ḥarāsī seems similarly to have caught the drift of the Basran position when he says, "Among [the Mu'tazilah], attributes are divided into attributes of the thing itself (*ṣifāt al-nafs*) and attributes proceeding from attributes of the thing itself (*ṣifāt tābi'atu li-ṣifāt al-nafs*). [Kiyā al-Ḥarāsī, *Uṣūl al-Dīn,* 200b:16f.].

25. *Li-ṣifāt hiya 'alayhā.*

26. Ibn Barhān, *al-Wuṣūl,* 1:61–62.

27. Al-Ṭūfī, *Dar',* 68b.

28. Al-Ṭūfī, *Dar',* 70a. This may be because accidents must inhere to a body and accidents lack the spatial dimension. (Frank, *Beings,* 39). Al-Ījī likewise says accidents cannot be added to accidents (al-Ījī, *al-Mawāqif,* 100–101). One supposes that, while for 'Abdaljabbār an act is a thing (Peters, *Created Being,* 116) for al-Ṭūfī inasmuch as an act is movement, which is an attribute of a thing, one cannot add another attribute to it (al-Ījī, *al-Mawāqif,* 167f.). That this is weak is as much as acknowledged when al-Ṭūfī says that some attributes such as "lightness" of a color arise by means of the another accident, such as the color "black." Good certainly seems more categorically distinct from movement than "light" seems from "black." He also briefly takes up Abū Rashīd's argument that no act can be assessed in its absence. Al-Ṭūfī, *Dar'*, 71b.

29. Al-Ṭūfī, *Dar',* 72a.

30. *Nihāyah,* 370. See also Juwaynī, *Burhān,* 87.

31. *Baḥr,* 14a:21.

32. Al-Ṭūfī, *Dar',* 70b.

33. Al-Kiyā al-Ḥarāsī, *Uṣūl al-Dīn,* 199b.

34. Al-Bājī, *al-Ḥudūd,* 38; al-Jurjānī, *al-Ta'rīfāt,* 109; Ibn Humām, *al-Taḥrīr,* 25.

35. Al-Bājī, *al-Ḥudūd, 38.*

36. Abū Ya'lá, al-*'Uddah,* ms. 183A:11.

37. Al-Izmīrī, *Mir'āt,* 1:80.

38. Al-Ghazālī translation paragraphs 27f. This argument appears first to have been advanced by al-Bāqillānī (al-Juwaynī, *al-Burhān,* 1:89–90).

39. Al-Ghazālī translation paragraph 30ff.

40. Al-Ṭūfī, *Dar*', 69b. He hears the Mu'tazilah saying "If an act includes an unmitigated benefit or a benefit that is preferable, this suggests to the '*aql* that God—glory be to him!—demands it."

41. Al-Shīrāzī, *Wuṣūl,* paragraph 429c.

42. Al-Shīrāzī, *Wuṣūl,* 429f and g.

43. Al-Shīrāzī, *Wuṣul,* 429d.

44. See also al-Qarāfī, as quoted in *Baḥr,* 17a:17ff. "The essential attribute is what follows the thing itself into existence and non-existence (*fī l-ithbāt wa-l-'adam*); this would necessitate the establishment of the good and the detestable primordially, and that would necessitate the deserving of blame for what has not taken place; and this is absurd."

45. What follows is a synopsis.

46. The act of remaining another hour is both *good* because it verifies the sentence and *detestable* because it contradicts the illocutionary force of the sentence. Which of the two attributes then is the essential one, and how is it that the act carries a second and contradictory (essential) attribute?

47. Al-Āmidī, *Iḥkām,* p. 120. Note that he dismisses this argument as unsatisfactory.

48. "The '*aql* is incapable of [establishing (*ithbāt*) an assessment]," says Ibn Qudāmah (*Rawḍah,* 79). Knowledge, see for instance Ibn Fūrak (quoted in Abū Ya'lá, *al-'Uddah,* 1:85): "It is knowledge by which one is prevented from doing the detestable." Instrument of perception: "It is not an indicant that obliges or prevents anything; by it there is only perception of matters, or it is an instrument of cognizance." *Al-Baḥr,* 16a:30, quoting Ibn al-Sam'ānī. The printed edition is slightly different; see Ibn al-Sam'ānī, *Qawāṭi'*, 239. Knowledges: Abū Ya'lá, *al-'Uddah,* quoting al-Tamīmī (d. 371), pp. 83–89, especially 84.

49. *Al-'Uddah,* 1:84.

50. "There is no being made-responsible through the '*aql*" says al-Qādī Nu'mān, *Ikhtilāf 'uṣūl al-madhāhib,* 149.

51. *Al-Baḥr,* 15a:27.

52. Ibn Ḥazm, *al-Iḥkām,* 1:14.

53. Ibn Ḥazm, *al-Iḥkām,* 1:16.

54. Ibn Ḥazm, *al-Iḥkām,* 1:27. The position is found already in al-Ash'arī, *Risālah al-Thaghr,* 3:102.

55. Ibn Ḥazm, *al-Iḥkām,* 1:28–29.

56. Wolfhart Heinrichs informs me that in Zuhrī's *Geography,* 295, he describes a certain Jazīrat al-Sakākīn, which is proverbial for being the end of civilization.

57. Ibn Ḥazm, *Iḥkām,* 55–56.

58. Ibn Ḥazm, *Iḥkām,* 56.

59. See for instance the commentary on the *Muntahá,* 198, bottom.

60. For the emphasis on the intentional act, see for instance Sayyid al-Murtaḍá, *al-Dharī'ah,* 814.

61. Al-Ṭūfī, *Dar*', 72a.

62. Al-Ṭūfī, *Dar*', 69b.

63. This common argument (after al-Juwaynī's time, at least) can be found frequently. See for example al-Āmidī, 1:113 or *Sharḥ Mukhtaṣar al-Muntahá,* 1:331, top.

64. Al-Taftazānī, *al-Talwīḥ 'alá l-Tawḍīḥ,* 198, bottom.

65. Ibn Qayyim al-Jawziyyah, *I'lām* 2:111; al-Sarakhsī, *Uṣūl,* 1:60; al-Juwaynī, *al-Burhān,* 1:91.

66. Ibn Ḥazm, *Iḥkām,* 1:57:11.

67. *al-Baḥr,* 20b:27. Note that al-Zarkashī says nothing about the value of *acts;* it is the characterization of persons that is at stake.

68. Āl Taymiyyah, *al-Musawwadah,* 481.

69. Āl Taymiyyah, *al-Musawwadah,* 481.

70. Āl Taymiyyah, *al-Musawwadah,* 93: "intelligible context," *qarīnah 'aqliyyah.*

71. Abū Ya'lá, *al-'Uddah,* 191a:10–20.

72. See Ibn Ḥājib, et al., *Sharḥ Mukhtaṣar al-Muntahá* where Permitted is asserted to be only a post-Revelational assessment.

73. Al-Ṭūfī, *Dar*', 72a.

74. *Ihkām,* 1:176. See also Ibn Ḥājib, et al., *Sharḥ al-Muntahá,* 2:6:8.

75. Al-Baghdādī, *Uṣūl al-Dīn,* 152.

76. Al-Ṭūfī, *Dar*', 69b.

77. Al-Shīrāzī, *al-Tabṣirah,* 533.

78. Al-Qāḍī Nu'mān, *Ikhtilāf uṣūl al-madhāhib,* 141–142.

79. Al-Qāḍī Nu'mān, *Ikhtilāf uṣūl al-madhāhib,* 149.

80. Al-Shahrastānī, *Milal* (Badrān), 120.

81. Al-Ṭūfī, *Dar*', 70b.

82. Al-Ṭūfī, *Dar*', 70b.

83. Al-Ṭūfī, *Dar*', 71a.

Chapter 11: Conclusion

1. See Daiber, "Anfänge muslimischer theologie," 386–391; cf Stroumsa, "Beginnings of the Mu'tazilah."

2. See Bulliet, *Conversion:* Iran becomes majority Muslim between A.H. 144–261; Iraq A.H. 174–364, and Spain, Syria, and Egypt much later. See p. 82 and passim.

3. On the lateness of the development of Ḥanbalism, see Hodgson, *Venture,* 1:392. See also Laoust, *Les Schismes,* 125, 155, for biographies that show the transition from *ḥadīth*-folk to Ḥanbalīs. For the lateness of Ash'arism, see Gimaret, "Une document majeur," especially 192–193.

4. I think particularly of the Mu'tazilah's inability to find positions in the new *madrasah*s and to find patronage after the decline of the Buyids.

5. This is equally true for a Ḥanafī such as al-Jaṣṣāṣ, as we showed in chapter 4.

6. Unless it is identified unilaterally with the norms of one particular group.

7. Matthew Arnold quoted in Frye, *Anatomy of Criticism,* p. 3.

8. Sarah Stroumsa, "The Beginnings of the Mu'tazilah, Reconsidered."

9. Peters, *God's Created Speech,* 404–405.

10. As Peters noted, *God's Created Speech,* 92.

11. Anawati and Gardet, *Introduction,* 62–64.

12. See B. Weiss, "Medieval Muslim Discussions of the Origin of Language," for the debate on the givenness of language.

Bibliography

European Language Sources

American Heritage Dictionary. Boston: American Heritage Publishing Co. and Houghton Mifflin, 1971.

Encyclopaedia of Islam; A Dictionary of the Geography, Ethnography and Biography of the Muhammadan Peoples, Prepared by a Number of Leading Orientalists (1st ed.). Leiden: E. J. Brill, 1913–36. Abbreviated *EI*1.

Encyclopedia of Islam. Second edition. Leiden: E. J. Brill, 1954–.

Encyclopedia of Philosophy. New York: Macmillan Publishing Co., 1967.

Oxford English Dictionary; Micrographic Edition. Oxford: Oxford University Press, 1971.

Anawati, Georges et Louis Gardet. *Introduction à la théologie musulmane: essai de théologie comparée*. Second edition. Paris: Librarie Philosophique J. Vrin, 1970 [1948].

Arberry, A. J. *The Koran Interpreted.* trans. of *the Qur'ān*; tr. Arthur Arberry. New York: Macmillan Co., 1969.

Awn, Peter. *Satan's Tragedy and Redemption: Iblis in Sufi Pyschology.* Studies in the History of Religions; 44. Leiden: E. J. Brill, 1983.

Bernand, Marie. "Hanafite Uṣūl al-Fiqh Through a Manuscript of al-Ǧaṣṣāṣ." *Journal of the American Oriental Society* 105/4 (1985): pp. 623–635.

Bernand, Marie. *Le Problème de la connaissance d'après le Muġnī du cadi* 'Abd al-Ǧabbār. Alger: Société Nationale d'Edition et de Diffusion, 1982.

Bouyges, Maurice. *Essai de chronologie des œuvres de al-Ghazali (Algazel).* Recherches publiées sous la direction de L'Institut de Lettres Orientales de Beyrouth, Tome XIV, Beirut: Imprimerie Catholique, 1959.

Bravmann, M. M. *The Spiritual Background of Early Islam; Studies in Ancient Arab Concepts*. Leiden: E. J. Brill, 1972.

Brockelmann, Carl. *Geschichte der arabischen Litteratur*. Leiden: E. J. Brill, [1898–1902] 1937–1943; 1943–1949. Abbreviated *GAL*.

Brunschvig. "Théorie générale de la capacité chez les Hanafites médiévaux." In *Études d'Islamologie*, vol. 2. Paris: Éditions G.-P. Maissonneuve et Larose, 1976, pp. 37–52.

Brunschvig, R. "Mu'tazilisme et Optimum (*al-aṣlaḥ*)." *Studia Islamica* 39 (1974): pp. 5–23.

Bulliet, Richard W. *Conversion to Islam in the Medieval Period; An Essay in Quantitative History*. Cambridge, MA: Harvard University Press, 1979.

Chaumont, Éric. "Encore au sujet de l'Ash'arisme d'Abû Isḥâq Ash-Shîrāzî." *Studia Islamica* 74 (1991): pp. 167–177.

Cook, Michael. *Early Muslim Dogma; A Source-Critical Study*. Cambridge U.K.: Cambridge University Press, 1971.

Daiber, Hans. "Anfänge muslimischer Theologie im Lichte eines neuen Textes von Wāṣil ibn 'Atā'." In *Islão e Arabismo na Península Ibérica; actos do XI congresso da união europeia de arabistas e islamólogos . . . 1982*, ed. Adel Sidarus. Évora: Universidade de Évora, 1986. pp. 383–391.

Dozy, R. *Supplément aux dictionnaires arabes*. Beirut [Leyde (sic)]: Librarie du Liban [E. J. Brill], 1968 [1881].

Ess, Josef van. *Anfänge Muslimischer Theologie*. Beirut: Franz Steiner, 1977.

Ess, Josef van. *Frühe Mu'tazilitische Häresiographie; zwei Werke des Nāši' al-akbar (gest. 293 h.) herausgegeben und eingeleitet*. Beirut: Steiner (in Kommission), 1977.

Ess, Josef van. *Une lecture à rebours de l'histoire du Mu'tazilisme*. Paris: Librarie orientaliste Paul Geuthner, 1984. (Extrait des tomes 46/2 to 40 47/1 (1978–1979) *Revue des études islamiques*).

Fagnan, E. *Additions aux dictionnaires arabes*. Beirut: Librarie du Liban, n.d. [1923].

Frank, R.M. "*al-Ma'ná*: Some reflections on the technical meanings of the term in the kalām and its use in the physics of Mu'ammar." *Journal of the American Oriental Society* 87 (1967): pp. 248–259.

Frank, Richard M. "Bodies and Atoms: The Ash'arite Analysis." In *Islamic Theology and Philosophy: Studies in Honor of George F. Hourani*. Michael E. Marmura, ed. Albany: State University of New York Press, 1984. pp 39–53.

Frank, Richard M. *The Metaphysics of Created Being According to Abū l-Hudhayl al-'Allāf; A Philosophical Study of the Earliest Kalām*. Leuven: Drukkerij Orientaliste, 1966.

Frank, Richard M. "Reason and Revealed Law: A Sample of Parallels and Divergence." In *Kalām and Falsafa, Recherches d'Islamologie; Recueil d'articles offert à Georges C. Anawati et Louis Gardet par leurs collègues et amis*, Bibliothèque Philosophique de Louvain no. 26. Louvain: Peeters, [1977]. pp. 123–138.

Frye, Northrop. *Anatomy of Criticism; Four Essays*. Princeton: Princeton University Press, 1957.

Gauthier, E. T. Léon. "La racine arabe [ḥ-k-m] et ses dérivés." In *Homenaje à D[on] Francisco Codera en su jubilación del profesorado; estudios de erudición oriental con una introducción de D. Eduardo Saavedra*, Zaragoza: M. Escar, tipògrafo, 1904. pp. 435–454.

Gay, Peter. *The Enlightenment; A Comprehensive Anthology*. New York: Simon and Schuster, [1973].

Gimaret, Daniel. *La Doctrine dal-Ash'arī*. Paris: Cerf, 1990.

Gimaret, Daniel. *Théories de l'acte humain en théologie musulmane*. Paris: Librarie Philosophique J. Vrin, 1980.

Gimaret, Daniel. "Un document majeur pour l'histoire du kalām: Le *Muğarrad Maqālāt al-Aš'arī* d'Ibn Fūrak." *Arabica* 32/2 (1985): pp. 185–218.

Goldziher, Ignaz. *The Ẓahirīs: Their Doctrine and Their History; A Contribution to the History of Islamic Theology*. Wolfgang Behn, tr. Trans. of *Die Ẓâhiriten; ihr Lehrsystem und ihre Geschichte* . . . Leiden [Leipzig]: E. J. Brill, [1884] 1971.

Gräf, Erwin. "Zur Klassifizierung der menschliche Handlungen nach Ṭūsī, dem Šaiḫ al-Ṭā'ifa (gest. 460), und seinen Lehrern." In *xix Deutscher Orientalistentag 1975 in Freiburg im Breisgau*. Wolfgang Voigt, ed. Wiesbaden: Franz Steiner Verlag, 1977. pp. 388–422.

Halm, Heinz. *Die Ausbreitung der šafi'itischen Rechtsschule von den Anfängen bis zum 8./14. Jahrhundert.* Beihefte zum Tübinger Atlas des Vorderen Orients. Reihe B, Geisteswissenschaften; Nr. 4, Wiesbaden: L. Reichert, 1974.

Hartmann, A. "Codocologie comme source biographique." In *Les manuscrits du Moyen-Orient : essais de codicologie et de paléographie;* Istanbul: n. p., 1989.

Hartmann, Agelika. "Islamisches Predigtwesen im Mittelalter: Ibn al-Ǧawzî und sein 'Buch der Schlußreden'." *Saeculum* 38 (1987): pp. 336–366.

Hartmann, Angelika. "La Predication islamique au Moyen Age: Ibn al-Ǧawzī et ses sermons (fin du 6e/12e siècle)." *Quaderni di studi arabi* 5–6 (1987–88): pp. 337–346.

Hartmann, A. "Les ambivalences d'un semonnaire ḥanbalite." *Annales Islamologiques* 22 (1986): pp. 51–115.

Hartmann, Angelika. *an-Nāṣir li-Dīn Allah: (1180–1225): Politik, Religion, Kultur in der späten 'Abbasidenzeit.* Studien zur Sprache, Geschichte und Kultur des islam- ischen Orients, n. F. Bd. 8, Berlin: de Gruyter, 1975.

Hodgson, Marshall G.S. *The Venture of Islam: Conscience and History in a World Civilization*. Chicago: University of Chicago Press, 1974.

Hourani, George. "Ghazālī on the Ethics of Action." *Journal of the American Oriental Society* 96/1 (1976): pp. 69–88.

Hourani, George. *Islamic Rationalism; The Ethics of 'Abdaljabbār.* Oxford: Clarendon Press, 1971.

Hourani, George. *Reason and Tradition in Islamic Ethics.* Cambridge, U.K.: Cambridge University Press, 1985.

Hourani, George F. "Ethical Presuppositions of the Qur'an." *Muslim World.* 70 (1980): pp. 1–28.

Hourani, George F. "The Rationalist Ethics of 'Abd al-Jabbār." In *Islamic Philosophy and the Classical Tradition; Essays Presented by his Friends and Pupils to Richard Walzer on his Seventieth Birthday.* Hourani Stern and Brown, eds. Columbia, SC: University of South Carolina Press, 1973. pp 105–115.

Hourani, George F. "Two Theories of Value in Medieval Islam." *Muslim World* 50/3 (1960): pp. 269–278.

Jabre, Farid. *Essai sur le lexique de Ghazali; Contribution á l'étude de la terminologie de Ghazali dans ses principaux ouvrages à l'exception du Tahāfut.* Beirut: l'University Libanaise, 1970.

Juynboll, G. H. A. *Muslim tradition: studies in chronology, provenance, and authorship of early hadith.* Cambridge and New York: Cambridge University Press, 1983.

Lane, Edward William. *An Arabic English Lexicon . . .* [Edinburgh] Beirut: [Williams and Norgate] Librarie du Liban, [1863–1893] 1968.

Laoust, Henri. *Les Schismes dans l'Islam.* Paris: Payot, 1965.

Leder, Stefan. *Ibn al-Ǧauzī und seine Kompilation wider die Leidenschaft: der Traditionalist in gelehrter Überlieferung und originarer Lehre.* Beiruter Texte und Studien; Bd. 32, Wiesbaden/Beirut: Steiner/Orient-Institut der Deutschen Morgenlandischen Gesellschaft, 1984.

Madelung, Wilfred. "The Early Murji'a in Khurāsān and Transoxania and the Spread of Ḥanafism." In *Religious Schools and Sects in Medieval Islam*, London: Variourum Reprints, [1982] 1985. Article III. (Originally in *Der Islam* 59, pp. 32–39.).

Madelung, Wilferd. "Early Sunnī Doctrine Concerning Faith as Reflected in the *Kitāb al-īmān* of Abū 'Ubaid al-Qāsim b. Sallām." *Studia Islamica* 32 (1970): pp. 233–254. Also article I in *Religious Schools and Sects in Medieval Islam.*

Madelung, W. "Imāmism and Mutazilite Theology." In *Religious Schools and Sects in Medieval Islam*, London: Variorum Reprints, 1985 [1979]. Article VII [Originally published in *Le Shî'ism imâmate*, T. Fahd, ed. Paris: Presses Universitaires de France, 1979. pp. 120–139.]

Madelung, W. *Religious Schools and Sects in Medieval Islam.* London: Variorum Reprints, 1985.

Madelung, Wilfred. *Religious Trends in Early Islam*. Columbia Lectures on Iranian Studies no. 4. Ehsan Yarshater, ed. New York: Bibliotheca Persica, 1988.

Madelung, W. "The Spread of Māturīdism and the Turks." In *Actas IV Congressio de Estudo Arabes e Islamicos: Coimbra Lisboa 1 a 8 Setembro 1968*, Leiden: E. J. Brill, 1971. pp 109–168. Also article II in *Religious Schools and Sects in Early Islam*.

Makdisi, George. "Ash'arī and the Ash'arites in Islamic Religious History." *Studia Islamica* 17, 18 (1962, 1963): pp. 37–80, 19–39.

Makdisi, George. "Hanbalite Islam." In *Studies on Islam*, Merlin L. Swartz, ed. New York: Oxford University Press, [1974] 1980. pp. 216–274. [Orignally published as "L'Islam Hanbalisant" in *Revue des études islamiques* (42) 1974, pp. 211–44; (43) 1975, pp. 45–76.].

Makdisi, George. *Ibn 'Aqīl et la résurgence de l'Islam traditionaliste au XIe Siècle* (*Ve siècle de l'Hégire*). Damas: Institut Français de Damas, 1963.

Makdisi, George. "The Juridical Theology of Shāfi'ī; Origins and Significance of 'Uṣūl al-Fiqh'." *Studia Islamica* 59 (1984): pp. 5–47.

Makdisi, George. *The Rise of Colleges; Institutions of Learning in Islam and the West.* Edinburgh: The University Press, 1981.

Massignon, Louis. *Essai sur les origines du lexique technique de la mystique musulmane*. 2nd ed., Paris: Librarie Philosophique J. Vrin, 1954.

Massignon, Louis. *The Passion of al-Ḥallāj; Mystic and Martyr of Islam*. Herbert Mason, ed. and tr. Princeton, NJ: Princeton University Press; Bollingen Series XCVII, 1982.

Mauss, Marcel. *The Gift; Forms and Functions of Exchange in Archaic Societies*. Ian Cunnison, tr. Glencoe, IL: Free Press, 1954.

McDermott, Martin J. *The Theology of al-Shaikh al-Mufīd (d. 413/1022).* Recherches publiées sous la direction de l'institut de lettres orientales de Beyrouth; Persian Studies series no.9, Beirut: Dar el-Machreq, 1978.

Meron, Ya'akov. "The Development of Legal thought in Hanafi Texts." *Studia Islamica* 30 (1969): pp. 73–118.

Mottahedeh, Roy. *Loyalty and Leadership in Early Islamic Society*. Princeton, NJ: Princeton University Press, 1980.

Nader, Albert N. *Le Système philosophique des Mu'tazilah (primiers penseurs de l'Islam).* Recherches de l'institut de lettres orientales de Beyrouth, tome III), Beirut: Éditions les lettres orientales, 1956.

Ormsby, Eric L. *Theodicy in Islamic Thought : The Dispute over al-Ghazali's "Best of All Possible Worlds"*. Princeton, NJ: Princeton University Press, 1984.

Peters, J. R. T. M. *God's Created Speech: a study in the speculative theology of the Mu'tazilī Qāḍī al-Quḍāt Abū l-Ḥasan 'Abd al-Jabbār ibn Aḥmad al-Hamadānī.* Leiden: E. J. Brill, 1976.

Pickthall, Muhammad M. *The Meaning of the Glorious Qur'an; Text and Explanatory Translation.* Muslim World League, 1977.

Plato, *Euthyphro.* Indianapolis and New York: Bobbs-Merrill Library of the Liberal Arts, 1956.

Reese, William L. *Dictionary of Philosophy and Religion; Eastern and Western Thought.* Atlantic Highlands, NJ: Humanitis Press, 1980.

Reinhart, A. Kevin. "Islamic Law as Islamic Ethics." *Journal of Religious Ethics* 11/2 (1983): pp. 186–203.

Rosenthal, Franz. *Knowledge Triumphant; The Concept of Knowledge in Medieval Islam.* Leiden: E. J. Brill, 1970.

Saeedullah, (sic) Qazi. "Life and Works of Abū Bakr al-Rāzī al-Jaṣṣāṣ and Principles of Muslim Jurisprudence (Chapters on Qiyās and Ijtihād) of Abu Bakr Ahmad bin Ali al-Razi al-Jaṣṣāṣ al-Ḥanafī." *Islamic Studies* 16/2 (1977): pp. 131–141.

Schacht, Joseph. "An Early Murci'ite Treatise: The Kitāb al-'Ālim wal-Muta'allim." *Oriens* 17 (1964): pp. 96–117.

Schacht, Joseph. *An Introduction to Islamic Law.* Oxford: Clarendon Press, 1964.

Schimmel, Annemarie. *Mystical Dimensions of Islam.* Chapel Hill: University of North Carolina Press, 1975.

Sezgin, Fuat. *Geschichte des arabischen Schrifttums.* Vol. 1 [Qur'ānwissenschaften; hadīt̲, geschichte, fiqh, dokmatik, mystik, bis ca. 430 h.]. Leiden: E. J. Brill, 1967. Abbreviated *GAS.*

Shehaby, Nabil. " 'Illa and Qiyās in Early Islamic Legal Theory." *Journal of the American Oriental Society* 102/1 (1982): pp. 27–46.

Shehaby, Nabil. "The influence of Stoic logic on al-Jaṣṣāṣ's legal theory." In *The Cultural Context of Medieval Learning: Proceedings of the First International Colloquium on Philosophy, Science, and Theology in the Middle Ages—September 1973.* John Emery Murdoch and Edith Dudley Sylla, eds. Dodrecht, Holland, Boston: D. Reidel, 1975. pp. 60–85.

Smith, W. C. "The Concept of Sharī'ah among some Mutakallimūn." In *On Understanding Islam; Selected Studies.* The Hague: Mouton, 1981. pp 88–109. [originally in Arabic and *Islamic Studies in Honor of Hamilton A. R. Gibb.* George Makdisi, ed. E. J. Brill, 1965: pp. 581–602].

Stroumsa, S. "The Barāhima in Early Kalām." *Jerusalem Studies in Arabic and Islam* 6 (1985): pp. 229–241.

Stroumsa, Sarah. "The Beginnings of the Mu'tazilah, Reconsidered." *Jerusalem Studies in Arabic and Islam* 13 (1990): pp. 265–293.

Tritton, A. S. "Theory of Knowledge in Early Muslim Theology." In *Woolner Commemoration Volume*. M. Shafi, ed. Lahore: Mehar Chand Lachman Das, 1940. pp. 253–256.

Vajda, Georges. "La connaissance naturelle de Dieu selon al-Ǧaḥiẓ critiquée par les Mu'tazilites." *Studia Islamica* 24 (1966): pp. 19–33.

Versteegh, C. H. M. *Greek Elements in Arabic Linguistic Thinking*. Leiden: E. J. Brill, 1977.

Wansbrough, John. *Quranic Studies: Sources and Methods of Scriptural Interpretation*. Oxford: Oxford University Press, 1977.

Watt, W[illiam] Montgomery. *The Formative Period of Islamic Thought*. Edinburgh: The University Press, 1973.

Watt, W. Montgomery. *Muhammad at Mecca*. Oxford: Clarendon Press, 1953.

Wehr, Hans. *A Dictionary of Modern Written Arabic*. Ithaca, NY: Cornell University Press, 1960.

Weiss, Bernard. "Language and Tradition in Medieval Islam: The Question of *al-Ṭarīq" Ilá Ma'rifat al-Lugha."* *Der Islam* 61/1 (1984): pp. 91–99.

Weiss, B. "Medieval Muslim Discussions of the Origin of Language." *Zeitschrift der Deutschen Morgenländischen Gesellschaft* 124/1 (1974): pp. 33–41.

Weiss, B. "A Theory of the Parts of Speech in Arabic (Noun, Verb, and Particle); A Study in *'ilm al-waḍ'*." *Arabica* 23/1 (1976): pp. 23–36.

Wensinck, A. J. *The Muslim Creed: Its Genesis and Historical Development*. London: Frank Cass & Co., 1965 [1932].

Wensinck, A.J. et al. *Concordance et indices de la tradition musulmane*. Leiden: E. J. Brill, 1969.

Wolfson, Harry. *Philosophy of the Kalām*. Cambridge, MA: Harvard University Press, 1976.

Zysow, Aron. "The Economy of Certainty; An Introduction to the Typology of Islamic Legal Theory." Unpublished dissertation. Cambridge, MA: Harvard University, 1984.

Arabic Language Sources

al-'Abbādī, Abū 'Āṣim b. Aḥmad (d. 458/1066). *Kitāb ṭabaqāt al-shāfi'iyyah; Das Klassenbuch der gelehrten Šāfi'iten des Abū 'Āṣim.* Miteinleitung und Kommentar herausgegeben von Gösta Vitestam. Leiden: E. J. Brill, 1964.

'Abdaljabbār, al-Qāḍī Abū l-Ḥasan [al-Asadābādī] (d. 415/1024). *Al-Mughnī fī abwāb al-tawḥīd wa-l-'adl.* Edited by Ibrāhīm Madkūr; Aḥmad Fu'ād al-Ahwānī. Cairo:

Mu'assat al-miṣriyyah al-'āmmah li-l-ta'līf wa-l-anbā' wa-l-nashr, 1960–1968. Abbreviated: *Mughnī*.

[pseudo] Al-Qāḍī Abdaljabbār; actually by Mānkdīm Sheshdīv, Aḥmad b. Abī Hāshim (d. 425/1034 (M.Sh.)). *Sharḥ al-uṣūl al-khamsah*. Edited by 'Abdalkarīm 'Uthmān. Cairo: Maktabat Wahbah, 1384/1965. Abbreviated *Sharḥ*.

[pseudo] 'Abdaljabbār, [actually Ibn Mattawayh, Abū Muḥammad al-Ḥasan b. Aḥmad] (before 550/1155 (IM)). *Al-Majmū'al-muḥīṭ bi-l-taklīf*. Edited by 'Umar al-Sayyid 'Azmī. Cairo: Mu'assasat al-Miṣriyyah al-'Āmmah li-ta'līf wa-l-anbā' wa-l-nashr, 1965.

[pseudo] Abū Ḥanīfah, al-Nu'mān b. Thābit (d. 150/767). *al-'Ālim wa-muta'allim; ru'āyat Abī Muqātil 'an Abī Ḥanīfah*. Edited by Muḥammad Zāhid al-Kawtharī. pp. 60. Cairo: Maṭba'at al-Anwar, n.d. The author is Abū Muqātil Ḥafs al-Samarqandi (208/823). See *GAS* 1:418; Madelung, in *Religious Trends* (p. 18–19).

Abū Ya'lá, Muḥammad b. al-Ḥusayn al-Farrā' al-Ḥanbalī (d. 458/1066). *Al-'Uddah fī uṣūl al-fiqh*. Edited by Aḥmad b. 'Alī Sayr al-Mubāralī. Beirut: Mu'assasat al-Risālah, 1400/1980.

Abū Ya'lá, Muḥammad b. al-Ḥusayn al-Farrā' al-Ḥanbalī (d. 458/1066). *Al-'Uddah fī uṣūl al-fiqh*. Ms. Cairo: Dār al-Kutub, *Uṣūl al-fiqh* 76.

Abū Ya'lá, Muḥammad b. al-Ḥusayn b. al-Farrā' al-Ḥanbalī (d. 458/1066). *Kitāb al-mu'tamad fī uṣūl al-dīn*. Edited by Wadī' Zaydān Ḥaddād. Beirut: Dār al-Mashraq, 1974.

Aḥmad b. Ḥanbal (d. 241/855). *Kitāb al-wara'*. n.c.: n.p., n.d.

Aḥmad ibn Ḥanbal (d. 241/855). *Masā'il—riwāyat Isḥāq al-Naysabūrī*. Edited by Zuhayr al-Shāwīsh. Beirut: al-Maktab al-Islāmī, 1400 a.h.

Āl-Taymiyyah, Majdaddīn (653/1255), Shihābaddīn (682/1283), Taqiyaddīn (728/1326) (653/1254). *Al-Musawwadah*. Edited by Muḥammad Muḥīaddīn 'Abdalḥamīd. Beirut: Dār al-Kitāb al-'Arabī, n.d. Gathered and redacted by Aḥmad b. Muḥammad al-Ghannī al-Ḥarānī al-Ḥanbalī (745/1344).

Al-Āmidī, Abū l-Ḥasan 'Alī b. Abī 'Alī (d. 631/1232–3). *Al-Iḥkām fī uṣūl al-aḥkām*. 1300/1980; Beirut: Dār al-Kutub al-'Ilmiyyah,

Amīr Bādshāh, Muḥammad Amīn al-Ḥusaynī al-Khurasānī al-Bukhārī al-Ḥanafī (d. 987/1579). *Tayasīr al-taḥrīr sharḥ 'alá al-taḥrīr* (of Ibn Hummām (d. 861/1355)). Cairo: Muṣṭafá al-Bābī al-Ḥalabī, 1350 a.h.

Al-Anṣārī, Niẓāmaddīn Muḥammad (d. 1235/1819). *Sharḥ Musallam al-thubūt [Commentary on the work of al-Bihārī, Muḥibballāh b. al-Shukūr (d. 1119/1707).* Bulāq: n.p., 1322. On margins of al-Ghazālī's *Musṭaṣfá*. Author of commentary identical with Baḥral'ulum 'Abdal'alī ibn Muḥammad whose death may also have been 1225/1810. See *GAL* II, 421; SII 624; *JASB* NS II (1911) p. 694.

Al-Ash'arī, Abū l-Ḥasan 'Alī b. Ismā'īl (d. 324/936). *Risālah ilá ahl al-thaghr bi-bāb al-abwāb*. In *Dār al-Funūn Ilâhiyet Fakültesi Mecmuasi* 8; Istanbul: Shahrzādeh Pashá Awqāf Maṭba'ası, 1928.

Al-Ash'arī, Abū l-Ḥasan Ismā'īl (d. 324/936). *Kitāb al-Luma' in the theology of al-Ash'arī: the Arabic texts of al-Ash'arī's Kitāb al-Luma' and Risālat Istiḥsān al-khawḍ fī 'ilm al-kalām*. Edited by Richard J. McCarthy. Beirut: Impr. catholique, 1953. "With briefly annotated translations, and appendices containing material pertinent to the study of al-Ash'arī."

Al-Ash'arī, Abū l-Ḥasan 'Alī b. Ismā'īl (d. 324/936). *Maqālāt al-Islāmiyyīn wa-ikhtilāf al-muṣallīn*. Edited by Helmut Ritter. pp. 690. Wiesbaden: Franz Steiner, 1980 [1929–30]. Bibliotheca Islamica, band I.

Al-Baghdādī, 'Abdalqādir ibn Ṭāhir (d. 429/1037). *Al-farq bayn al-firaq*. Edited by Muḥammad Muḥiyaddīn 'Abdalḥamīd. Beirut: Dār al-ma'rifah, n.d. Abbreviated "*Farq*."

Al-Baghdādī, Abū Manṣūr 'Abdalqāhir b. Ṭāhir (d. 429/1037). *Uṣūl al-dīn*. Istanbul: n.p., 1928.

Al-Bājī, Abū l-Walīd Sulaymān b. Khalf (d. 474/1081). *Kitāb al-ḥudūd fī l-uṣūl*. Edited by Nazīh Ḥimmār. Beirut & Damascus: Mu'assasat al-Zu'bī, 1392/1973.

Abū Qāsim al-Balkhī, et. al. (d. 319/931). *Faḍl al-I'tizāl wa-ṭabaqāt al-mu'tazilah*. Edited by Fu'ād Sayyid. Tunis: al-Dār al-tūnisiyyah li-l-nashr, n.d. "Chapter mentioning the Mu'tazilah" of Abū Qāsim al-Balkhī (d. 319/931), from his *Maqālāt al-islāmiyyin*; Qāḍī Abdaljabbār's (d. 415/1024) *Faḍl al-I'tizāl wa-ṭabaqāt al-mu'tazilah;* and "the 11th and 12 generation" from the *Kitāb sharḥ al-'uyūn* of al-Ḥākim al-Jushamī (d. 494/1101).

Al-Baṣrī, Abū l-Ḥusayn Muḥammad b. Aḥmad b. al- Ṭayyib (d. 436/1044). *Al-mu'tamad*. Edited by Muḥammad Ḥamīdallāh. Damascus: al-Ma'had al-'ilmī al-Faransī li-l-dirāsāt al-'arabiyyah bi-dimashq, 1384/1964.

Al-Ḥasan al-Baṣrī (d. 110/728). *Al-risālah fī l-qadar*. Edited by Helmut Ritter. In *Der Islam*; pp. 1–83. 1933. [Published as "Studien zur Geschichte der islamischen Frömmigkeit (I): Ḥasan al-Baṣrī".]

Al-Bazdawī, Muḥammad ibn Muḥammad Ṣadralislām Abū l-Yassar (d. 493/1100). *Kitāb ma'rifat ḥujjaj al-sharī'ah*. Edited by Marie Bernand. Forthcoming

Bazdawī, Abū l-Ḥusayn 'Alī b. Muḥammad Fakhralislām (d. 489/1089). *Kanz al-uṣūl*. Beirut [Istanbul]: Dār al-Kitāb al-'Arabī, 1393/1974 [1307]. Printed with al-Bukhārī's commentary *Kashf al-asrār*.

Bazdawī, Muḥammad ibn Muḥammad Ṣadralislām Abū l-Yassar (d. 493/1100). *Uṣūl al-dīn*. Edited by Hans Peter Linss. Cairo: Dār Iḥyā' al-Kutub al-'Arabiyyah, 1963.

Al-Bukhāri, 'Abdalazīz b. Aḥmad 'Alā'addīn (d. 730/1328). *Kashf al-Asrār 'an uṣūl Fakhralislām al-Bazdawī*. Beirut [Istanbul]: Dār al-Kitāb al-'Arabī, 1393/1974 [1307].

Al-Bukhārī, Abū 'Abdallāh Muḥammad b. Ismā'īl (d. 256/870). *Ṣaḥīḥ al-Bukhārī.* Cairo: Dār al-Sha'b, n.d.

Al-Dabūsī, Abū Zayd 'Ubaydallāh b. 'Umar (d. 430/1039). *Ta'sīs al-naẓar fī ikhtilāf al-a'immah.* Cairo: Zakiyyā 'Alī Yūsuf [reprint], n.d. printed together with Karkhī's *Risālah.*

Al-Ghazālī, Abū Ḥāmid (d. 505/1111). *Freedom and Fulfillment; An Annotated Translation of al-Ghazālī's Munqidh min al-ḍalāl.* Tr. Richard J. McCarthy; trans. of *Al-Munqidh min al-ḍalāl.* Boston: Twayne Publishers, 1980.

Al-Ghazālī, Abū Ḥāmid Muḥammad (d. 505/1111). *Al-Mankhūl min ta'līqat al-uṣūl.* Edited by Muḥammad Ḥasan Hītū. Beirut: Dār al-Fikr, 1390/1970.

Al-Ghazālī, Abū Ḥāmid Muḥammad (d. 505/1111). *Al-Mustaṣfá min 'ilm al-uṣūl.* Beirut: Maktabat al-Muthaná/Dār Iḥyā' al-Turāth al-'Arabī, n.d.

Al-Ḥakīm al-Samarqandī, Abū l-Qāsim (d. 342/953). *Al-Sawād al-a'ẓam fī l-kalām.* n.c.: n.p., n.d.

Ibn Abī al-Wafā', 'Abdalqādir ibn Muḥammad al-Qurayshī (d. 775/1373). *Al-Jawāhir al-muḍī'ah fī ṭabaqāt al-ḥanafiyyah.* Haydarabad: Dā'irat al-Ma'ārif al-'Uthmaniyyah, 1332/1914.

Ibn Abī Dunyā (d. 281/894). *Kitāb al-shukr.* Cairo: Maṭba'at al-Manār, 1349 a.h.

Ibn Abī Ya'lá, Abū l-Ḥusayn Muḥammad ibn Muḥammad ibn al-Farrā' (d. 526/1133). *Ṭabaqāt al-ḥanābilah.* Edited by Muḥammad Ḥamid al-Fiqī. Cairo: Maṭba'at al-Sunnah al-Muḥammadiyyah, 1371/1952.

Ibn 'Asākir, Abū l-Qāsim 'Alī b. Muḥammad (d. 571/1176). *Tabyīn kadhib al-muftarī fīmā nusiba ilá Abī l-Ḥasan al-Ash'arī.* Damascus: al-Qudsī, 1347/1928.

Ibn Barhān, Abū l-Fatḥ Aḥmad b. 'Alī al-Baghdādī (d. 518/1124). *Al-Wuṣūl ilá l-uṣūl.* Edited by 'Abdalḥamīd Abū Zayd. Riyad: Maktabat al-Ma'ārif, 1403/1983.

Ibn Farḥūn, Ibrahīm b. 'Alī b. Muḥammad al-Ya'murī (d. 779/1397). *Al-Dībāj al-dhahab fī ma'rifat 'ayān 'ulamā' al-madhhab.* Cairo: Maṭba'at al-Mu'āhid, 1351/1932. With Tumbuktī's *Nayl al-ibtihāj* on the margin.

Ibn al-Ḥājib, Abū 'Āmr 'Uthmān bin 'Umar, [together with, al-Ījī (d. 756/1355), al-Taftazānī (d. 791/1389), al-Jurjānī (d. 816/1413), and al-Harawī (d. 646/1248)]. *Shurūḥ sharḥ mukhtaṣar al-muntahá.* Edited by Sha'bān Muḥammad Ismā'īl. Cairo: Maktabat al-Kuliyyāt al-Azhariyyah, 1973/1393.

Ibn Ḥazm, Abū Muḥammad 'Alī b. Aḥmad (d. 456/1064). *Al-Fiṣl fī l-millal wa-ahwā' wa-niḥal.* Cairo: Maktabat al-Khānjī, n.d. With Shahrastānī's *Millal* on the margins.

Ibn Ḥazm, Abū Muḥammad 'Alī b. Aḥmad (d. 456/1064). *Al-Iḥkām fī uṣūl al-aḥkām.* Edited by Iḥsān 'Abbās. Beirut: Dār al-Āfāq al-Jadīdah, 1400/1980.

Ibn Hidayatallāh, Abū Bakr al-Ḥusaynī (d. 1014/1605). *Ṭabaqāt al-shāfiʻiyyah*. Edited by ʻAbbās al-ʻAzzawī. Baghdad: n.p., 1356/1937. (I consulted also, but did not cite, an edition by ʻĀdil Nuwayiḍ, Beirut: Dār al-Āfāq al-Jadīdāh, 1971.)

Ibn Humāmaddīn al-Iskandarī, Muḥammad b. ʻAbdalwāḥid al-Ḥanafī (d. 861/1457). *Al-Taḥrīr fī uṣūl al-fiqh; al-jāmiʻ bayn iṣṭalāhay al-ḥanafiyyah wa-l-shāfiʻiyyah*. Cairo: Muṣṭafá al-Bābī al-Ḥalabī, 1351.

Ibn ʻImād, Abū l-Falāḥ ʻAbdalḥayy b. Aḥmad (d. 1089/1622). *Shadharāt al-dhahab fī akhbār man dhahab*. Cairo: Maṭbaʻat al-Qudsī, 1350/1931.

Ibn al-Jawzī, Abū l-Faraj ʻAbdalraḥmān b. ʻAlī (d. 597/1200). *Al-Muntaẓam fī ta'rikh al-mulūk wa-l-umam*. Haydarabad: Dā'irat al-maʻārif al-ʻuthmāniyyah, 1357.

Ibn Khallikān, Abū l-ʻAbbās Aḥmad b. Muḥammad al-Barmakī al-Irbilī (d. 681/1282). *Wafayāt al-aʻyān wa-anbā' abnā' al-zamān*. Edited by Iḥsān ʻAbbas. Beirut: Dār al-Thaqāfah, 1972.

Ibn al-Murtaḍá, Aḥmad ibn Yaḥyá (d. 840/1437). *Kitāb ṭabaqāt al-muʻtazilah; Die Klassen der Muʻtaziliten* . . . Edited by S. Diwald-Wilzer. Wiesbaden: Franz Steiner, 1961.

Ibn Nujaym, Zaynaddīn ibn Ibrāhīm (d. 970/1561–2). *Fatḥ al-ghaffār bi-sharḥ al-manār al-maʻrūf bi-mishkāt al-anwār fī uṣūl al-manār*. Cairo: Muṣṭafá al-Bābī al-Ḥalabī, 1355/1936.

Ibn Qayyim al-Jawziyyah, Abū ʻAbdallāh. Muḥammad b. Abī Bakr al-Ḥanbalī (d. 751/1350). *Iʻlām al-muwaqqiʻīn ʻan Rabb al-ʻālimīn*. Edited by Taha Abdalra'ūf Saʻīd. Dār al-Jalīl, 1973/

Ibn Qudāmah, ʻAbdallāh b. Aḥmad al-Maqdisī (620/1223). *Rawḍat al-nāẓir wa-jannat al-munāẓir*. Cairo: al-Maṭbaʻah al-Salafiyyah, 1378/ .

Ibn Rajab, Abū l-Faraj ʻAbalraḥmān b. Aḥmad al-Salīmī al-Baghdādī (d. 795/1393). *Dhayl ʻalá ṭabaqāt al-ḥanābilah*. Edited by M. Ḥāmid al-Fiqī. Cairo: al-Sunnah al-Muḥammadiyyah, 1372/1953.

Ibn al-Samʻānī, Abū Muẓaffar Manṣūr b. Muḥammad al-Tamīmī (d. 489/1096). *Qawāṭiʻ al-adillah fī l-uṣūl*. Edited by Hītū. In *Majallat maʻhad al-Makhṭūṭāt* (Kuwait); pp. 209–288.

Ibn Taymiyah, Taqiyaddīn Aḥmad (d. 728/1328). *Kitāb minhāj al-sunnah al-nabawiyah fi naqd kalām al-shīʻah wa-al-qadariyah*. Edited by Muḥammad Sālim. Cairo: Dār al-ʻUrūbah, 1962.

Al-Ījī, ʻAbdalraḥmān bin Aḥmad ʻAḍudaddīn (d. 756/1355). *Al-Mawāqif fī ʻilm al-kalām*. Beirut: ʻĀlim al-Kitāb, n.d.

Al-Iṣfahānī, Abū l-Faraj ʻAlī b. al-Ḥusayn (d. 356/967). *Kitāb al-Aghānī*. Cairo: Hay'ah al-ʻĀmmah li-l-Ta'līf wa-l-Nashr, 1389/1970.

Al-Izmīrī, Sulaymān, a.k.a. Muḥammad b. Walī b. Rasūl al-Qashharī (d. 1160/1747). *Mir'āt al-uṣūl fī sharḥ mirqāt al-wuṣūl (of Mullah Khusraw (d. 885/1480)).* [Istanbul?]: Shārikat Ṣahāfiy-ye 'Uthmānih-ye Mudīr-i al-Ḥajj Aḥmad Khulūṣı, 1309.

Al-Jāḥiẓ (d. 255/868–9). *The Life and Works of Jāḥiẓ.* tr. Charles Pellat [into English by D.M. Hawke]. Berkeley and Los Angeles: University of California Press, 1969.

Jarīr, ibn 'Aṭiyyah and Farazdaq (Tammām ibn Ghālib) (d. 110/728–9). *Kitāb al-naqā'iḍ jarīr wa-l-farazdaq.* Edited by A. A. Bevan (recension of Abū 'Ubaydah). E. J. Brill: 1905–12.

Al-Jaṣṣāṣ, Abū Bakr Aḥmad b. 'Alī al-Rāzī (d. 370/980). *Uṣūl al-Jaṣṣāṣ [al-fuṣūl].* Ms. Cairo: Dār al-Kutub, Uṣūl al-fiqh 26. 165 ff.

Al-Jaṣṣāṣ, Abū Bakr Aḥmad b. 'Alī al-Rāzī (d. 370/980). *Uṣūl al-Jaṣṣāṣ [al-fuṣūl].* Ms. Cairo: Dār al-Kutub, Uṣūl al-fiqh 229. 331 ff.

Al-Jaṣṣāṣ, Abū Bakr Aḥmad ibn 'Alī al-Rāzī (d. 370/980). *al-Fuṣūl fī al-uṣūl.* Edited by 'Ajīl Jāsin al-Nashmī. Kuwait City: Wizārat al-Awqāf wa-shu'ūn al-Islāmiyyah; al-Turāth al-Islāmī, 14., vols. 1 & 2: 1405/1985; vol 3: 1408/1988. [Incomplete.]

Al-Jaṣṣāṣ, Abū Bakr Aḥmad ibn 'Alī al-Rāzī (370/980). *Aḥkām al-qur'ān.* Beirut [Istanbul]: n.p., [1335–1338].

Al-Jaṣṣāṣ, Abū Bakr Aḥmad ibn 'Alī al-Rāzī (370/980). *Sharḥ adab al-qāḍī al-Khaṣṣaf.* Edited by Farḥāt Ziyādah. Cairo: American University Press, 1978.

Al-Jurjānī, 'Alī b. Muḥammad (d. 816/1413). *Kitāb al-ta'rīfāt.* Lipsiae: [Guilielmi Vogelii, Filii] Beirut, Librairie du Liban, [1845] 1969.

Al-Juwaynī, Imām al-Ḥaramayn Abū Ma'ālī 'Abdalmalik (d. 478/1085). *Al-burhān fī uṣūl al-fiqh.* Edited by 'Abdal'aẓīm al-Dīb. Cairo: Dār al-Anṣār: 1400.

Al-Ka'bī, Abū l-Qāsim al-Balkhī (d. 319/931). *Qubūl al-akhbār wa-ma'rifat al-rijāl.* Ms. Cairo: Dār al-Kutub, muṣṭalaḥ al-ḥadīth. 111 ff.

Kaḥḥālah, 'Umar Riḍā. *Mu'jim al-mu'allifīn.* Beirut: Dār al-Turāth al-'Arabī, 1376/1958. Abbreviated: *Kaḥḥālah.*

Al-Kalwadhānī, Maḥfūẓ b. Aḥmad Abū l-Khaṭṭāb al-Ḥanbalī (d. 510/1117). *Al-Tamhīd fī uṣūl al-fiqh.* Edited by Muḥammad b. 'Alī Ibrāhīm. Jiddah: Dār al-Madanī, 1406/1985. Min al-turāth al-islāmī, Jāmi'at Umm al-Qurrah.

Kashānī, 'Abdalrazzāq b. Abī l-Faḍā'il Aḥmad (d. 730/1330). *Iṣṭilāḥāt al-ṣūfiyyah.* Edited by A. Sprenger. Calcutta: 1845. published as "Abdurrazzaq's Dictionary of the Technical Terms of the Sufies."

Al-Kharā'iṭī, Abū Bakr Muḥammad b. Ja'far (d. 327/938). *Kitāb fadīlat al-shukr li-llāh 'alá ni'matih wa mā yajibu min al-shukr li-l-mun'am 'alayh.* Edited by Muḥammad Muṭī' al-Ḥāfiẓ. Damascus: Dār al-Fikr, 1402/1982.

Al-Khaṭīb al-Baghdādī, Abū Bakr Aḥmad b. 'Alī (d. 463/1069–70). *Kitāb al-faqīh wa-l-mutafaqqih*. Edited by Ismā'īl al-Anṣārī. [Cairo]: n.p., n.d.

Al-Khaṭīb al–Baghdādī (d. 463/1069–70). *Ta'rīkh Baghdād*. Beirut: Dār al-Kitāb al-'Arabī, n.d. Abbreviated: *Tā'rīkh Baghdād*.

Al-Kisā'ī, Muḥammad b. 'Abdallāh (before d. 596/1200). *Tales of the Prophets of al-Kisa'i*. Trans. of *Qiṣṣaṣ al-anbiyā'*; tr. W. M. Thackston Jr., Boston: Twane Publishers, 1978.

Al-Kiyā al-Harāsī, Abū l-Ḥasan 'Alī b. Muḥammad (d. 504/1110). *Uṣūl al-dīn*. Ms. Cairo: Dār al-Kutub, 'ilm al-kalām 290.

Al-Makhlūf, Muḥammad. *Shajarat al-nūr al-zakiyya fī ṭabaqāt al-mālikiyya*. [Cairo] Beirut: Dār al-Fikr, [1349–1350/1930–1931].

Al-Marāghī, 'Abdallāh Muṣṭafá. *Al-fatḥ al-mubīn fī ṭabaqāt al-uṣūliyīn*. Beirut: Muḥammad Amīn Ramaj, 1394/1974. Abbreviated *TU*.

Al-Māturīdī, Abū Manṣūr Muḥammad b. Muḥammad (d. 333/944). *Kitāb al-tawḥīd*. Edited by Fathalla Kholeif. pp. 411+xliii. Beirut: Dar el-Machreq, 1970.

Al-Mu'ayyid bi-llāh, Yāḥyá ibn Hamzah ibn 'Alī, al-Imām (d. 743/1342–3). *Al-Shāmil li-ḥaqā'iq al-adillah wa-uṣūl al-masā'il al-dīniyyah*. Ms. Cairo: Dār al-Kutub, 29053b. 285 ff. Vol. 2 only. (Originally Ms. Ṣan'ā': Gharbiyyah Kalām 88; see Ḥibshī *Maṣādir* 567.)

Shaykh al-Mufīd, Muḥammad ibn Nu'mān (d. 413/1022). *Sharḥ 'aqā'id al-ṣudūq aw taṣḥīḥ al-i'tiqād*. Edited by al-Sayyid Hibbataddīn al-Shahrastānī/'Abbāqalī Wajdī. Tabriz: n.p., 1371.

Al-Munjid fī al-lughah. 20th ed., Beirut: Dār al-Mashraq, 1969.

Muslim, Abū l-Ḥusayn Muslim b. al-Ḥajjāj al-Qushayrī al-Naysābūrī (d. 261/873). *Ṣaḥīh Muslim*. Edited by Muḥammad Fu'ād 'Abdalbāqī. Cairo: Īsá al-Bābī al-Ḥalabī, 1374/1955.

Al-Muzanī, Abū Ibrāhīm Ismā'īl ibn Yāḥyá (d. 264/877). *Kitāb al-amr wa-l-nahy*. Edited by R. Brunschvig. In *Bulletin des Études Orientales*; pp. 145–196, 1945–46.

Al-Muzanī, Abū Ibrāhīm Ismā'īl b. Yaḥyá (d. 264/877). *Al-Mukhtaṣir [fī l-fiqh]*. Cairo: Kitāb al-Sha'b, 1388 [1321]. On Margins of al-Shāfi'ī's *Kitāb al-umm*.

Al-Nadīm, Abū l-Faraj Muḥammad b. Abī Ya'qūb Isḥāq (d. 380/990). *Al-Fihrist*. Edited by Riṣā Tajaddud. n.c.: n.p., 1391/1971.

Al-Nadīm, Abū l-Faraj Muḥammad b. Abī Ya'qūb Isḥāq (380/990) *The Fihrist of al-Nadīm; A Tenth-Century Survey of Muslim Culture*. Trans. of *Al-Fihrist*; tr. Bayard Dodge. New York & London: Columbia University Press, 1970.

Al-Nasafī, Makḥūl ibn al-Faḍl Abū Muṭī' (d. 318/930). *Kitāb al-radd 'alá l-bid'ah*. Edited by Marie Bernand. In *Annales Islamologiques:* 1980.

Al-Nashī' al-Akbar, Muḥammad ibn 'Abdallāh (d. 293/905–6). *Kitāb al-awsaṭ*. Edited by Joseph van Ess. Beirut: Franz Steiner, 1971. Also under van Ess as *Frühe Mu'tazilitische Häresiographie.*

Al-Nawawī, Abū Zakariyā Muḥīaddīn Yaḥyá ibn Sharaf (d. 676/1278). *Tahdhīb al-asmā' wa-l-lughāt.* Beirut: Dār al-Kutub al-'Ilmiyyah, n.d.

Al-Qāḍī al-Nu'mān, ibn Muḥammad (d. 351/962). *Ikhtilāf uṣūl al-madhāhib.* Edited by Muṣṭafá Ghālib. pp. 227. Beirut: Dār al-Andalus, 1393/1973.

Al-Qaffāl al-Shāshī, Abū Bakr Muḥammad b. 'Alī (d. 365/975). *Maḥāsin al-sharī'ah.* Ms. New Haven: Yale Landberg, 614.

Al-Qaffāl al-Shāshī, Abū Bakr Muḥammad b. 'Alī (d. 365/975). *Maḥāsin al-sharī'ah.* Ms. Istanbul: Ahmed III, 3198. 199 ff.

Al-Qaffāl al-Shāshī, Abū Bakr Muḥammad b. 'Alī (d. 365/975). *Uṣūl.* [India]: n.d.

Al-Qarāfī, Abū l-'Abbās Aḥmad b. Idrīs (d. 684/1285). *Al-Iḥkām fī tamyīz al-fatāwá 'an al-aḥkām wa-taṣarrufāt al-qāḍī wa-l-imām.* Edited by Abdalfattāḥ Abū Ghiddah. Aleppo: Maktabat al-Matbu'āt al-Islāmiyyah, 1387/1967.

Al-Qarāfī, Abū l-'Abbās Aḥmad b. Idrīs (d. 684/1285). *Sharḥ tanqīh al-fuṣūl fī ikhtiṣār al-maḥsūl fī al-uṣūl.* Edited by Tāhā 'Abdalra'ūf Sa'īd. Cairo: Maktabat al-Kuliyyāt al-Azhariyyah, 1393/1973.

Al-Qushayrī, Abū l-Qāsim 'Abdalkarīm ibn Hawāzin (d. 464/1072). *Al-Risālah al-Qushayriyyah.* Edited by 'Abdalḥalīm Maḥmūd. Cairo: Dār al-Kutub al-Ḥadīthah, 1966.

Qāḍī 'Īyāḍ, Abū Faḍl 'Īyāḍ ibn Mūsá al-Yaḥṣūbī (d. 544/1149). *Tartīb al-madārik wa-taqrīb al-masālik li-ma'rifat a'lām madhhab Mālik.* Edited by Aḥmad Bakīr Maḥmūd. Beirut: Dār Maktabat al-Ḥayāh, 1967.

Al-Razī, Fakhraddīn (d. 606/1209). *al-Maḥṣūl fī uṣūl al-fiqh.* Edited by Tāhā Jābir Fayyāḍ al-'Alwānī. n.c.: Jāmi'at al-imām Muḥammad ibn Su'ud al-Islāmiyyah, 1401/1981.

Ṣadralsharī'ah al-thānī, 'Ubaydallāh ibn Mas'ūd al-Maḥbūbī al-Bukhārī al-Ḥanafī (d. 747/1346). *Al-Tawḍīḥ 'alá tanqīḥ al-uṣul.* Cairo: Muḥammad 'Alī Ṣubayḥ, n.d. Printed together with al-Taftāzānī's commentary, *al-Talwīḥ 'alá al-tawḍīḥ.*

Al-Ṣafadī, Khalīl ibn Aybak (d. 764/1363). *al-Wāfī bi-l-wafayāt.* Edited by various. Istanbul & Wiesbaden: Steiner/Bibliotheca Islamica, 1931–.

Al-Samarqandī, Abū Layth Naṣr b. Muḥammad (d. 373/983). *Tanbīh al-ghāfilīn bi-aḥdāth sayyid al-anbiyā' wa-l-mursalīn, (together with) Bustān al-'ārifīn.* Beirut: Dār al-Kitāb al-'Arabī, 1399/1979.

Al-Samarqandī, 'Alā'addīn Manṣūr b. Muḥammad b. Aḥmad (d. 553/1158). *Mīzān al-wuṣūl fī natā'ij al-'uqūl.* Ms. Cairo: Dār al-Kutub al-Miṣriyyah, uṣūl al-fiqh 778. 275 ff.

Al-Sarakhsī, Abū Bakr Muḥammad b. Aḥmad (d. 490/1097). *Uṣūl*. Edited by Abū l-Wafā' al-Afghānī. Cairo: Dār al-Kitāb al-'Arabi, 1372.

Al-Shāfi'ī, Muḥammad b. Idrīs (d. 204/820). *Al-Risālah*. Edited by Aḥmad Muḥammad Shākir. Cairo: Maktabat Dār al-Turāth, 1979/1399.

Al-Shāfi'ī, Muḥammad b. Idrīs (d. 204/820). *Kitāb al-umm*. Cairo: Kitāb al-Sha'b, 1388 [1321]. Contains various other treatises of al-Shāfi'ī, his *Musnad* and the *Mukhtaṣar* of al-Muzanī; equivalent to the Bulāq edition.

Al-Shahrastānī, Abū l-Fatḥ Muḥammad b. 'Abdalkarīm (d. 547/1153). *Nihāyat al-iqdām*. Edited by A. Guillaume. Oxford: Oxford University Press, 1939.

Al-Shahrastānī, Abū l-Fatḥ Muḥammad b. 'Abdalkarīm (d. 547/1153). *Kitāb al-milal wa-al-niḥal*. Cairo: Maṭba'at al-Khānjī, n.d. On margins of Ibn Ḥazm's *Fiṣl*.

Al-Shahrastānī, Abū l-Fatḥ Muḥammad b. 'Abdalkarīm (d. 547/1153). *Kitāb al-milal wa-al-niḥal*. Edited by Muḥammad ibn Fatḥallāh Badrān. Cairo: Maṭba'at al-Azhar, [1951–55]. Noted as "Badran edition."

Sayyid [Sharīf] al-Murtaḍá, 'Ālamalhudá (d. 436/1044–5). *Al-Dharī'ah ilá uṣūl al-sharī'ah*. Edited by Abū l-Qāsim al-Kurji. Tehran: Chāpkhāneh-e Dāneshgāh, 1346–48.

Al-Shīrāzī, Abū Isḥāq Ibrāhīm b. 'Alī (d. 476/1083). *Al-Luma' fī uṣūl al-fiqh*. Cairo: Muṣṭafá al-Bābī al-Ḥalabī wa-awlāduh, 1377/1957.

Al-Shīrāzī, Abū Isḥāq Ibrāhīm (d. 476/1083). *La profession de foi d'Abu Ishaq al-Sirazi*. Cairo: Institut francais d'archeologie orientale, 1987. Supplément aux *Annales islamologiques*, cahier no. 11.

Al-Shīrāzī, Abū Isḥāq Ibrāhīm b. 'Alī (d. 476/1083). *Sharḥ al-luma'*. Edited by 'Abdalmajīd Turkī. Beirut: Dār al-Gharb al-Islāmī, 1408/1988.

Al-Shīrāzī, Abū Isḥāq Ibrāhīm b. 'Alī (d. 476/1083). *Ṭabaqāt al-fuqahā'*. Edited by Iḥsān 'Abbās. Dār al-Ma'rifah: 1970.

Al-Shīrāzī, Abū Isḥāq Ibrāhīm b. 'Alī (d. 476/1083). *Al-Tabṣirah fī uṣūl al-fiqh*. Edited by Muḥammad Ḥasan Hītū. Damascus: Dār al-Fikr, 1400/1980.

Al-Shīrāzī, Abū Isḥāq Ibrāhīm b. 'Alī (d. 476/1083). *Al-Wuṣūl ilá masā'il al-uṣūl*. Edited by 'Abdalmajīd Turkī. Algiers: Al-Sharikah al-Waṭaniyyah li-l-nashr wa-l-tawzī', 1399/1979.

Al-Subkī, 'Abdalwahhāb b.'Alī Tājaddīn (d. 771/1330). *Al-ṭabaqāt al-shāfi'iyyah al-kubrá*. Edited by Maḥmūd Muḥammad al-Ṭanāhī and 'Abdalfattāḥ Muḥammad al-Ḥulw. Cairo: 'Īsá al-Bābī al-Ḥalabī, Abbreviated: Subkī, 1964/1383.

Al-Ṭabarī, Abū Ja'far Muḥammad b. Jarīr (d. 310/923). *The History of al-Ṭabarī: General Introduction and From the Creation to the Flood*. Trans. of *Ta'rīkh al-rusul wa-l-mulūk;* tr. Franz Rosenthal. Albany: State University of New York Press, 1989. Volume 1.

Al-Ṭabarī, Abū Ja'far Muḥammad b. Jarīr (d. 310/923). *The History of al-Ṭabarī: Prophets and Patriarchs*. Trans. of *Ta'rīkh al-rusul wa-l-mulūk;* tr. William M. Brinner. Albany: State University of New York Press, 1987. Volume 2.

Al-Ṭabarī, Abū Ja'far Muḥammad b. Jarīr (d. 310/923). *The History of al-Ṭabarī: The Children of Israel*. Trans. of *Ta'rīkh al-rusul wa-l-mulūk;* tr. William M. Brinner. Albany: State University of New York Press, 1991. Volume 3.

Al-Ṭabarī, Abū Ja'far Muḥammad b. Jarīr (d. 310/923). *Jāmi' al-bayān 'an tā'wīl al-Qur'ān*. Cairo: Muṣṭafá al-Bābī al-Ḥalabī wa-awlāduh, 1388/1968. Referred to as "*Tafsīr al-Ṭabarī*.

Al-Taftazānī, Sa'daddīn Mas'ūd ibn 'Umar al-Shāfi'ī (d. 791/1388). *Al-Talwīh 'alá al-Tawḍīḥ li-matn al-tanqīḥ*. Cairo: Muḥammad 'Alī Ṣubayḥ, n.d. Printed on the upper portion, together with Ṣadralsharī'ah's *Tawḍīḥ sharḥ al-tanqīh*. The *matn* is by Sadradlsharī'ah also.

Al-Taftāzānī, Sa'daddīn Mas'ūd b. 'Umar (d. 792/1388). *Al-Talwīh 'ala l-tawḍīḥ*, Cairo: Ṣubayhḥ, n.d. See Ṣadr al-Sharī'ah.

Tamīmī al-Dārī, Taqīaddīn 'Abdalqādir (d. 1010/1601). *Al-Tabaqāt al-saniyyah fī tarājim al-ḥanafiyyah*. Edited by 'Abdalfattāḥ Muḥammad Hulw. Cairo: al-Majlis al-a'lá li-shu'ūn al-islāmiyyah, 1970.

Al-Khaṭīb al-Tibrīzī, Muḥammad b. 'Abdallāh (fl. 737/1337). *Miskhāt al-Maṣābīḥ*. tr. James Robson. Lahore: Sh. Muhammad Ashraf, 1963–65.

Al- Ṭūfī, Abū Rabī' Sulayman b. 'Abdalqawwī al-Ḥanbalī (d. 712/1312). *Sharḥ Mukhtaṣar al-rawḍah*. Edited by 'Abdallāh al-Turkī. Beirut: Mu'assat al-Risālah, 1408/1987.

Al-Ṭūfī, Abū Rabī' Sulaymān b. 'Abdalqawī Najmaddīn (d. 716/1316). *Dar' al-qabīh bi-l-taḥsīn wa-l-taqbīḥ*. Ms. Istanbul: Şehid Ali, 2315. 64b–147b ff.

Al-Zānjānī, Abū Manāqib Shihābaddīn Maḥmūd ibn Aḥmad (d. 656/1258). *Takhrīj al-furū' 'alá l-uṣul*. Edited by Muḥammad Adīb Ṣāliḥ. Beirut: Mu'assat al-Risālah, 1398/1978.

Al-Zarkashī, Abū 'Abdallāh Muḥammad (d. 794/1392). *Al-Baḥr al-muḥīṭ*. Ms. Paris: Ms. Bibliotheque Nationale, Arabe 811. Abbreviated: *Baḥr*.

Al-Ziriklī, Khayraddīn. *Al-A'lām, qāmūs tarājim li-ashhar al-rijāl wa-l-nisā' min al-'arab wa-l-musta'ribīn wa-l-mustashriqīn*. 4th ed., Beirut: Dār al-'Ilm li-l-milayīn, 1986. Abbreviated: *Ziriklī*.

[pseudo] Al-Zubayrī, Abū 'Abdallāh al-Zubayr b. Aḥmad (c 317/929). *Waṣf al-Īmān wa-sharā'i'ih*. Ms. Munich: Bayerische Staatsbibliothek, Cod. Arab 893. 53–163ff. This is very unlikely to be the work of al-Zubayri. It is a standard *ḥadīth*-party type creed.

INDEX

When alphabetizing Arabic words and names, the definite article (al-) is disregarded, and proper names are listed under each person's cognomen. All books are alphabetized under "K" (for Kitāb)

'abath, 43, 64, 80, 97, 171, 217; *'abathan*, 59, 88
Abbasid state, 177
'Abdaljabbār, 46, 71, 139, 146, 149, 151–154, 157–161, 165, 217, 222, 226; 'Abdaljabbār's works, 218
'Abdalmālik, 194
al-Abharī, Abū Bakr Muḥammad, 23, 27
Abū 'Alī b. Khayrān, 18, 20, 189
Abū Ḥanīfah, 11, 12, 19, 44, 53, 54
Abū Hurayrah, 86
Abū l-Hudhayl, 13, 138, 143, 146, 160, 216; moral epistemology of, 139–141; his moral ontology, 141–142
Abū Ya'lá, 24, 31, 37, 170, 172, 180, 195; as Proscriber, 34–36
Adam, 66
'adl, 107
Aḥmad b. Ḥanbal, 12, 14,24, 27, 32, 34, 36, 37, 63, 194
Ahwaz, 45
Āl Taymiyyah, 12, 172; explanation of term, 187
al-Āmidī, 75, 164, 173, 203, 213
'Āmir ibn Sa'd, 86
'Āmir, 109, 113
'Amr b. 'Amr, 109
'Amr, 89
al-Anmāṭī, 15, 17
'aql, 13, 17–22, 29, 32–41, 43, 44, 46, 47, 51–60, 62–71, 73, 74, 76, 79–82, 85, 87, 88, 90, 94, 97, 99, 100–103, 108, 114–116, 125, 132, 135, 139, 140, 143, 151–161, 164, 165, 167–171, 173–75, 177, 179, 181, 182, 188, 191, 192, 195, 196, 200, 201, 203, 204, 208, 214, 220–222, 227; as God's participation in epistemology, 151; as knowledge, 139; as means of knowing, 139; as process of knowing, 139; Basran Mu'tazilī theory of, 151–153; limitations of, 66; limits on, 33, 69; limits to, 71, 74; link to moral obligation, 140; non-Mu'tazilī view of, 167–171; place in legal responsibility, 140; unreliability of, 169–171; Western use of in Islamic studies, 220; Ḥanafī doctrine of, 55; *'aql*: English equivalents of, 188, 220–221; *al-'uqūl*, 69, 172, 174; *'aql* as instrument (*ālah*), 52, 152, 200, 221
'aqlī, 19, 43, 48, 53, 70; *'aqlī* assessment, 55, 181; *'aqlī* assessments, 73, 171; *'aqlī* detestability, 53; *'aqlī* judgments, 66; *'aqlī* knowledge, 23, 41,

108, 116, 170; *'aqlī* proofs, 170; *'aqlī sharī'ah*, 174; *'aqlī wājib*, 19
Arab humanism, 115
al-Ash'arī, Abū l-Ḥasan, 18, 25, 27, 63, 108, 118, 119, 121, 122, 139, 140, 163, 190, 200, 202, 227; al-Ash'arī as No Assessor, 25
Ash'arīs, and Ash'arism, 20, 22, 27, 44, 46, 51, 53, 55, 56, 62, 63, 65, 67, 68, 73, 94, 102, 103, 114, 116, 145, 179, 180, 183, 198, 202–204, 208, 210 , 218, 229; No Assessor theory of, 67–75; and No Assessment, 25; early Ash'arīs, 210; Ash'arite movement, 195; goals in No Assessor argument, 68; link to No Assessor position, 65; sincerity of representation of opponents' positions, 203; Ash'arī enterprise, 204; Ash'arī grammarians, 215; Ash'arī heresiographers, 220; Ash'arī scholars, 120; Ash'arī theologians, 67; Ash'arī thought, 24; Ash'arī *uṣūl*, 67; Ash'arī *uṣūlīs*, 72; Ash'arī school, 67
al-aṣlāḥ, 225
Assessment, Arabic equivalent of, 185; identical with name, 136; of act not substances, 172; of act vs. assessment of substance, 166; tensions in, 4; an assessment is the dictum of shar', 72; assessment (ḥukm) is the dictum (khiṭāb) of God, 71; aḥkām, 19, 79; names and assessments: separation of, 164. *See also ḥukm*
al-'Ayyāsh, Baḥral'ulūm 'Abdal'alī Muḥammad, 44, 51, 199

Baghdad, 15, 18, 22, 23, 45, 63, 121, 143, 179, 198
al-Baghdādī, Abdalqāhir b Ṭāhir, 173, 216
al-Baghdādī, Al-Khaṭīb, 22, 64, 185
al-Bāqillānī, al-Qāḍī Abu Bakr, 16, 20, 24, 25, 65, 67, 68, 123, 171, 203, 226
Barāhimah, 156
al-Bardā'ī, 46
al-Baṣrī, Abū l-Ḥusayn, 31, 39, 40, 49, 130, 161, 185, 186, 194; as Permitter, 40–41
al-Bazdawī, Fakhralislām, 54, 199
Before Revelation: defined, 7–8
Before Revelation Complex: defined, 5–6, 7–8; Ibn Surayj as first user of, 17; possible responses defined, 6–7; purpose of debating, 5; structure of argument, 29
Bernand, M., 46, 139, 217, 218
al-Bihārī, Muḥibballāh, 199, his Permitter argument, 54
Bishr b. al-Mu'tamir, 207
boundaries, 127
Bravmann, M., 109
al-Bukhārī, 'Alā'addīn, 199
Būyids, 113

al-dahr, 89, 100
al-Daqqāq, al-Ḥasan ibn 'Alī, 23
ḍarūrī, 41, 68, 91, 168, 170, 207; meaning of, 196
Dā'ūd al-Ẓāhirī, 12, 14, 22, 63, 66, 225
Deserving (*istiḥqāq*): 222, Basran Mu'tazilī theory of, 153–155. *See also istiḥqāq*
detestable: Arabic equivalent of, 185
dhamm, 49, 130, 153
distortion by later Islamic perspectives, 10–11

Euthyphro, 10

fā'idah, 97, 116, 213
al-falak, 89
fear (*khawf*), 223; as motivation to moral action, 156
Ferguson, A., 221
fiqh, 14–16, 20, 23, 24, 45; *fiqh* sciences, 115
Frank, R., 40, 139, 217, 218

gharaḍ, 40, 43, 70, 88, 93, 115, 148. *See also* interest
al-Ghazālī, Muḥammad, 25, 34, 67, 68, 70–76, 115, 116–120, 138, 143, 148, 163, 165, 171, 181, 183, 186, 189, 195, 203, 204, 208, 226; psychologism of, 171; as No Assessor, 70–75; development of his No Assessor argument, 70–71; his influence on later Shāfi'ī *uṣūl* scholarship, 72; his psychologism, 70, 71, 73–74; his theory of interests, 73–74; his view of Thanking the benefactor, 115–117; on thanking God, 119
al-Ghazālī, Aḥmad, 183
God: as apart from humans, 120; as owner, 64; as owner of the world, 35, 57, 58, 68; *Ṣāḥib al-shar'*, 7; *al-Ṣāni'*, 19, 91
good: definition of, 72; Ghazālī's definition of, 73; the relativist view, 162–165

ḥadīth, 14, 18, 20, 22, 23, 27, 49, 65, 85, 86, 118–120, 143, 185, 187, 192; *ḥadīth*-transmitters, 23; *ḥadīths*, 119. *See also* traditionist
ḥajj, 88
al-Jushamī, al-Ḥakim, 46
Ḥanafīs, 39, 44, 46, 52–56, 61, 62, 75, 129, 133, 179, 187, 194; as Permitters, 43–56; doctrine of *'aql*, 55; relations to Mu'tazilah, 52–53; Samarqandīs and Iraqīs, 51–56; their relation to the Mu'tazilah, 56; school of Aḥmad, 33
Ḥanafism, 40, 44, 45, 51–53, 180, 186, 198; Bukhāran Ḥanafism, 51, 183, 199; Iraqi Ḥanafism view, 14, 51, 199; Samarqandī Ḥanafism, 51, 199; Ḥanafī Permitters, 52
Ḥanbalīs, 21, 22, 24, 31, 33, 34, 38, 44–46, 50, 51, 52, 54, 55, 57, 62, 65, 70, 75, 94, 172, 177, 179, 180, 198, 220; linked to Baghdādī Mu'tazilah, 24; links with Mu'tazilah, 34; Permitters, 21–22, 57–60; Proscribers, 24, 33–36
Ḥanbalism, 26, 33, 183, 218, 229; Ḥanbalī methodologians, 22; Ḥanbalī pietism, 37; Hanbalite school, 195
Ḥārith b. al-Abraṣ, 109
al-Ḥasan al-Baṣrī, 112, 113, 115, 117, 210; his understanding of Thanking the benefactor, 112–113
al-ḥaẓar, alá 101. *See also* Proscription, Proscribed
ḥiss, 139
Hourani's, G., 9, 12, 39, 62, 63, 139, 204, 217, 218, 222
ḥukm, 16, 65, 87, 98, 108, 131, 136, 147, 162, 185, 215; *ḥukm shar'ī*, 65; *ḥukms*, 149; *al-ḥukm khiṭāb al-shar'*, 70. *See also* Assessment
al-Ḥulwānī, Abū l-Fatḥ Muḥammad, 24
al-Ḥuṭay'ah, 109, 209

'ibādah, 199, 211; *'ibādāt*, 117, 174
al-ibāḥah, alá, 79, 101. *See also* Permitted
Ibn 'Abbās, 111
Ibn Abī Dunyā, 118, 119
Ibn Abī Hurayrah, 23, 31, 108, 121, 122, 194
Ibn Abī Ya'lá, 22, 202
Ibn 'Aqīl, 34, 226
Ibn 'Arabī, 183
Ibn 'Asākir, 20, 21
Ibn Barhān, 164, 165, 226
Ibn Dā'ūd al-Ẓāhirī, 15, 16, 19, 188
Ibn Fūrak, 186, 227
Ibn al-Ḥājib, 164
Ibn Ḥāmid al-Warrāq, 24, 27, 34, 70
Ibn Ḥazm, 66, 170, 171; his view of the *'aql*, 170–171
Ibn Humām, 53, 54
Ibn al-Jawzī, 22, 47
Ibn Mattawayh, 155
Ibn al-Murtaḍá, 46, 198
Ibn al-Qāṣṣ, 18; his doctrine of seven *uṣūl*, 190

Ibn al-Qaṭṭān, Abū l-Ḥusayn Aḥmad, 23, 121, 194
Ibn Qudāmah, 50, 75, 227
Ibn Qutaybah, 133, 135, 136
Ibn al-Rūmī, 95
Ibn al-Sam'ānī, 227
Ibn Surayj, 14–23, 27, 44, 46, 70, 180, 184, 189; ambivalent reception by later Shāfi'īs, 15–16; the "Surayjian Question," 189
al-idhn wa-l-ibāḥah min al-sam', 43
'illah, 35, 40, 55, 122, 147, 154, 169, 200; *'illahs*, 148
'ilm, 119, 150–152, 155, 166, 220; English equivalent of, 220; *'ilm iktisābī*, 152; *'ilm ḍarūrī*, 152; *'ulūm*, 151
Imāmī Shī'ī, 40; Imāmī positions, 196
immanent and transcendent (*shāhid/ghā'ib*), 72; difference between, 69, 71, 75, 120, 168; *al-ghā'ib*, 39, 69, 114, 120; *al-shāhid*, 39, 69, 114, 120
influence approach to study of Islamic intellectual history, 10
inquiry: as first duty of moral agent, 156. *See also naẓar*
al-inṣāf, 108, 153
interests: al-Ghazālī's theory of, 73–74. *See also* Ghazālī, *gharaḍ*
'Īsá ibn Abān al-Ṭabarī, 11, 194
al-Isfarā'īnī, Abū Isḥāq 16, 20, 65, 67, 114, 121, 123
al-Iṣṭakhrī, Abū Sa'īd al-Ḥasan b. Aḥmad, 18, 20, 189
istaḥaqqa, 155; *al-istiḥqāq*, 149, 153, 154, 222, 223. *See also* deserving
istiḥsān, 129, 200
istiṣḥab, 213
'Īyāḍ, Qāḍī, 25
al-Izmīrī, 187

Jaṣṣāṣ, Abū Bakr, 15, 23, 24, 35, 45–51, 54, 72, 79, 80, 85, 108, 109, 113–115, 129, 168, 186, 198, 199, 205, 206; alleged Mu'tazilism of, 46–47, 49; as Permitter, 47–51; his theory of Revelation, 51; importance of, 45–46
jawhar, 100, 147, 152, 216
jizyah 'an yad, 109
al-Jubbā'ī, Abū 'Alī, 13, 27, 46, 151, 152, 157
al-Jubbā'ī Abū Hāshim, 46, 157
al-Jurjānī, 208
al-Juwaynī, Abū Muḥammad, 122
al-Juwaynī, 25, 65, 67–71, 76, 114–116, 118, 120; as No Assessor, 67–70; position on Permitters, 68; view of Thanking the benefactor, 113–115
Juynboll G., 187

Ka'bī, Abū l-Qāsim al-Balkhī, 23, 31–33, 35, 36, 70, 91, 142, 145, 147, 149, 160, 194, 207, 213; his moral epistemology, 142–143; criticism of his moral epistemology, 143–144; his theory of Permitted acts, 213
kalām, 15–17, 20, 25, 63, 85, 186, 191; *kalām/uṣūl al-dīn*, 193
al-Kalwadhānī, Abū l-Khaṭṭāb, 22, 57–60, 64, 185, 201; as Permitter, 57–60
al-Karkhī, Abū l-Ḥasan, 45
khamr, 133–136, 214. *See also* wine, *nabīdh*
al-Kharā'iṭī, 118, 119
al-Khaṣṣāf, 45
al-Khaṭīb, Imām al-Ḍiyā', 15
al-khāṭir, 13, 29, 156, 157, 223, 224; *khāṭirayn*, 156, 157; *khāṭirān*, 100. *See also* Warners
khiṭab, 65, 87, 97, 203, 221
al-Khushanī, Abū Tha'labah, 85
K. (*Kitāb*) *al-Aghānī*, 109, 110
K. *Aḥkām al-Qur'ān*, 45
K. *al-'Ālim wa-Muta'allim*, 210
K. *al-Ashribah*, 133
K. *al-Baḥr al-Muḥīṭ*, 121, 166, 186
K. *al-Burhān fī uṣūl al-fiqh*, 67, 69, 114
K. *al-Dharī'ah*, 39, 41, 57

K. *Faḍīlat al-shukr li-llāh 'alá ni'matih wa-mā yajib min al-shukr li-l-mun'am 'alayh*, 118
K. *al-Faqīh wa-l-mutafaqqih*, 64, 185
K. *al-Fuṣūl*, 15, 44–47, 49, 108, 186
K. *al-Iḥkām fī tamyīz*, 185
K. *Iḥyā' 'ulūm al-dīn*, 119
K. *al-Irshād*, 20
K. *Ithbāt al-qiyās*, 16
K. *al-Luma'*, 63, 203
K. *Maḥāsin al-Sharī'ah*, 18
K. *al-Maḥṣūl*, 163, 203
K. *al-Mankhūl*, 70, 71, 75, 207
K. *al-Mawāzinah*, 194
K. *Mirāt al-Uṣūl*, 187
K. *al-Mīzān*, 54
K. *al-Mukhtaṣār*, 45
K. *al-Munqidh*, 204
K. *Musallam al-Thubūt*, 51, 53, 54
K. *al-Mustaṣfá*, 70, 71, 75, 116, 204
K. *al-Mu'tamad*, 24, 32, 39, 185, 194, 195
K. *al-Risālah*, 14, 18, 62, 122
K. *Sharḥ Musallam al-thubūt*, 44
K. *al-Shukr*, 118
K. *al-Takhrīj*, 52, 187
K. *Ta'līq fī uṣūl al-fiqh*, 16, 20
K. *al-Ta'līqah*, 123
K. *al-Talwīḥ*, 186
K. *al-Tamhīd*, 64, 185, 201
K. *Tanbīh al-Ghāfilīn*, 118, 119, 157, 158
K. *al-Taqrīb*, 16, 20, 123
K. *al-Tawḍīh*, 186
K. *al-'Uddah*, 24, 31, 34, 46, 195
K. *Tā'rīkh Baghdād*, 22
al-Kiyā al-Ḥarāsī, 226

legal schools, Central Islamic, 33
luṭf, 88

Madelung, W., 46, 51
madḥ, 49, 130, 153
madhhab, 11, 20, 21, 27, 44, 94; *madhhabs*, 9; link to specific before revelation complex disputed, 27; *madhhab* positions: variance in, 179–180; *madhhab*-allegiance, 46; *madhhab*-chauvinism, 45
majnūn, 151
Makdisi, G., 24, 62, 198, 186, 218
Mālikism, 23; Mālikī, 23; Mālikī Ash'arī, 24, 6; Mālikī *madhhab*, 25; Mālikīs, 75, 194
ma'ná, 55, 83, 84, 134, 143, 144, 147, 148; *ma'nás*, 148; *ma'ānī*, 134
al-Marwazī, Abū Isḥāq, 18, 23
al-Marwazī, al-Qāḍī Abū Ḥāmid, 15, 18
Massignon, L., 46
al-Māturīdī, 54; Māturīdīs, 218; Māturīdism, 51
maturity (*al-bulūgh*), 66, 140
Messenger, 179; role in Mu'tazilī epistemology, 208; Messengers: importance in Basran Mu'tazilī moral theory, 159
moral epistemology: problem of, 138
Moses, 159
Mottahedeh, R., 113
mubāḥ, 8, 40, 58, 79, 87, 128–131, 185, 186, 205, 212, 213; consequentialist understanding of, 129; defined, 8; deontologists understanding of, 131–132; Mu'tazilah definition of, 40; subjectivist understanding of, 129–131; English equivalents of, 186; definition of, 128–132. *See also* Permitted
Muḥammad, 159
mukallaf, 12, 47, 50, 129, 216; *mukallafīn*, 205
Muslim history: effect of on intellectual positions, 182; link of intellectual positions to, 178
Muslim intellectual history: view of, 182–184
Muslim majority: implications of for ideation, 117
al-mutafaqqihūn, 140
al-muta'akhkhirūn, 162
al-Muṭawwi'ī, Abū Ḥafṣ, 15

Mu'tazilah, Baghdādī, 23, 24, 31–34, 139, 146, 149, 143, 168, 180–182, 194; as center of Proscription movement, 31–33; linked to Ḥanbalīs, 24
Mu'tazilah, Basran, 23, 31, 46, 51, 144–148, 151, 153, 155–158, 160, 165, 167, 181, 182, 218; moral epistemology, 151–157; ontology theory of, 147–151; phenomenal moral theory, 147; Revelation, theory of, 157–160; their analysis of moral knowing, 144–145; theories of motivations to moral action, 155–157; theory of conditioning accidents, 147; theory of the *wajh*, 148–151; Basran moral system, 139; Basran moral theory, 160; Basran Mu'tazilī moral theory, 165; Jubbā'ī Mu'tazilah, 129
Mu'tazilah, 16, 20, 27, 31–34, 44, 52, 53, 55, 56, 71, 72, 88, 90, 92, 97, 101, 103, 107, 114, 116, 120, 122, 123, 125, 144, 151, 152, 155–157, 160–169, 173–175, 179, 181, 183, 186, 199, 205, 208, 217, 218; archaic nature of, 178; conservative nature of, 120, 182; critique of their epistemology, 167–172; critique of their ontology, 162; decline of, 161; other studies of Mu'tazilī metaphysics, 217; relations with non-Mu'tazilah described, 26–28; their conservatism, 107; Mu'tazilah view of Revelation, 173; Mu'tazilah as Permitters, 39–43; Mu'tazilah line of reasoning, 168; Mu'tazilah's critics, 167; Mu'tazilism of Shī'īs, 196; Mu'tazilī beliefs, 203; Mu'tazilī doctrine of metempsychosis, 207; Mu'tazilī epistemology, 165, 167, 168, 169; Mu'tazilī ethical theory, 162; Mu'tazilī grammarians, 215; Mu'tazilī heritage, 178; Mu'tazilī history, 183; Mu'tazilī moral epistemology, 153; Mu'tazilī ontology, 70; Mu'tazilī ontology and epistemology, 217; Mu'tazilī theories of the *'aql*, 220; Mu'tazilī theory of knowledge, 155; Mu'tazilī understanding of Revelation, 159; Mu'tazilīs, 26, 31, 33, 38, 40, 44, 51, 125, 143, 161, 177, 181, 184, 215; links with Ḥanbalīs, 34
al-Muṭī', 46
al-Muzanī, 15, 16, 136, 138, 142, 143; his theory of assessment, 136

nabīdh, 133–135, 181, 214; controversy over drinking of, 133. *See also* wine, *khamr*
Al-Nāshī' al-Akbar, 13
natural knowledge, 60, 62
naẓar, 91, 148, 155, 208, 220. *See also* inquiry
al-Nīsāpūrī, Abū Rashīd, 161, 226
Nishapur, 45
Niẓāmiyyah college, 71
No Assessment: evolution of, 25–26; No Assessment position: described, 62–76; No Assessment position: defined, 7; No Assessor: doctrine of Revelation, 62; No Assessor position: two prerequisites, 63; *lā ḥukma lahu*, 7, 67, 185
non-Mu'tazilah: view of Revelation, 173–175; non-Mu'tazilīs, 172
Nu'mān, al-Qāḍī 174

Obligatory: definition of, 72; *wājib*, 50, 79, 87, 97, 185, 210
ontology: problem of, 138

Permitted: definition of, 72; Permitted position: defined, 6–7, 38–39; described, 38–61; implications of, 60–61; objections to, 39; *al-ibāḥah*, 84; Permitters: critique of Refrainers(*waqf*), 59; Permitters: as conservatives, 38; critique of No Assessors, 58–60; critique of opponents, 56–60; No Assessor critique of, 67; Shāfi'īs, 17–21; theory of Revelation,

51; Ḥanbalīs, 21–22, 57–60. *See also mubāḥ*
Peters, J., 139, 182, 217, 218
principles of jurisprudence, 125; as domain of the before revelation complex, 186. *See also uṣūl*
Proscribers: Ḥanbalīs, 24, 33–36; Proscribed position: defined, 6; described, 31–37; evolution of, 22–24; possibility of corrupt act as reason for, 32; *al-ḥaẓr*, 79, 84; *maḥẓur*, 31, 79, 185

qabīḥ, 108, 185, 225; *qabīḥah*, 88; *qubḥ*, 143, 147
qabla majī' al-sam', 79; *qabla nuzūl al-farā'iḍ*, 13; *qabla wurūd i l-shar'*, 6
al-Qaffāl al-Shāshī al-Kabīr, Abū Bakr 18–23, 49, 122, 123, 179; as Permitter, 18–21; Mu'tazilism of, disputed, 19; on assessments, 19; problems of dating his life, 190
al-Qalānisī, Abū l-'Abbās, 190
qalb, 93, 170, 211
al-Qarāfī, 164,185, 213
Qays b. al-Muntafiq, 109
qiyās, 15, 19, 20, 24
Qur'ān, 57, 65, 110, 112, 117, 120, 136; as source of Permitter position, 38; Jaṣṣāṣ's theory of its significance as source of knowledge, 49; *shukr* in, 209; Qur'ānic locution, 136; Qur'ānic norm, 113; Qur'ānic usage, 112; Qur'ānic world, 117
al-Qushayrī, Abū l-Qāsim, 23, 183
al-Qushayrī, Abū Naṣr, 25

al-Rabī', 15
rationalism, 21; not distinguishing feature of Permitted position, 39; rationalist, 182, 220; rationalists, 27, 33, 52, 137, 179
al-Rāzī, 75, 163, 164, 173, 183
reason, 221; Reason versus Revelation, 161. *See also 'aql*
Refrainer (waqf) position: described, 63–65. *See also waqf*
Revelation: Arabic equivalents of, 185; Revelation: absence of, 34; Arabic terminology of, 186; as a source of Permission, 131; Basran Mu'tazilī theory of, 157–160; extension of, 135; Ibn Surayj's approach to, 16–17; information from non-Muslim, 134–135; limits of, 132; non-Mu'tazilī view of, 173–175; restricted scope of, 133; Revelational silence, 132; equivalent to Permission, 134

Ṣādralsharī'ah, 54, 186
al-*Ṣ*affār, Abū al-Ḥasan, 20
ṣalāh, 88, 117
al-salīm, 94
al-sam', 13, 19, 33, 35, 60, 79, 80, 88, 92, 108, 123, 140, 157, 159, 174, 185, 186, 196, 199; 201; *sam'ī mumkin*, 19. *See also* Revelation
al-Samarqandī, 51, 118, 119
al- Ṣāqaṭī, Abū 'Alī, 121
al-Sarakhsī, 12
satisfaction (*r-ḍ-y*) of the benefactor, 109; *riḍā'*, 113; *raḍiya*, 112, 209
al-Ṣayrafī, Abū Bakr Muḥammad b. 'Abdallāh, 18, 21, 23, 122, 123; as Permitter, 18
Shāfi'ī *madhhab*, 14–18, 20–27, 34, 38, 40, 44–46, 51, 52, 54, 62, 65, 67, 69, 70, 75,114, 129, 180, 181, 186, 188, 198, 220; Shāfi'ī No Assessors, 52; Permitters, 17–21; Shāfi'ī revisionism, 196; Shāfi'ī-Ash'arī, 118; Shāfi'īan *fiqh*, 19
Al-Shāfi'ī, 12, 14–18, 27, 31, 46, 62, 63, 122, 133, 136; his hermeneutic rule, 136
al-Shahrastānī, 118, 120, 174; his view of Thanking the benefactor, 117–118
al-shar', 33–37, 53, 55, 56, 58, 59, 62, 64–67, 75, 87, 89, 90, 96, 98, 99, 101, 102, 104, 120, 123, 128–131, 140, 158, 159, 165–168, 173–175, 181,

182, 185, 186, 195, 199, 213; No Assessors' doctrine of, 66–67; *shar'* and *'aql*, 33, 35, 58, 74, 108; *shar'ī*, 19, 21, 34, 158, 166, 173; *shar'ī* assessments, 52, 55, 195; *shar'ī* concepts, 52; *shar'ī* expansionists, 180; *shar'ī* knowledge, 168, 170; *shar'ī* rulings, 181; *shar'ī*-minded, 39; *sharā'i'*, 95, 157, 158; *sharī'ah*, 12, 172, 186; of Scriptuary peoples, 187. *See also* Revelation
al-Sharīf al-Murtaḍá, 39–42, 57, 65, 130; as Permitter, 41–43
al-Shaybānī, 12, 45
Shehaby, N., 46
al-Shīrāzī, Abū Isḥāq, 67, 70, 168
shukr, 108, 110, 111, 113, 114, 117, 119, 120, 211; *shukr al-mun'im*, 108, 113, 114–117, 209; defined, 8. *See also* Thanking the Benefactor
ṣifah, 144, 147, 217; *ṣifahs*, 148; *ṣifāt al-nafs*, 226; *ṣifāt tābi'atu li-ṣifāt al-nafs*, 226
Socrates, 10
Stroumsa, S, 182
al-Subkī, 20, 121–123
Sufi, 23; Sufis, 32, 183; as heirs of Mu'tazilī epistemology, 183
Sufyān al-Thawrī, 133
al-Suhrawardī al-Maqtūl, 183
al-Ṣu'lūkī, Abū Sahl, 20, 121
sunnah, 27, 135, 143, 159, 185, 186
Sunnī: *jamā'ī-sunnī*, 204

al-Ṭabarī, Abū 'Alī, 23
al-Ṭabarī, 121
al-Ṭaftazānī, 183, 186
al-Ṭaḥāwī, 45
al-taḥsīn wa-l-taqbīḥ, 49; *al-taqbīḥ wa-l-taḥsīn*, 8, 161; *taḥsīn al-'aql*, 101; defined, 8
taklīf, 82, 131, 170
al-Tamīmī, Abū l-Ḥasan, 22, 36, 57, 59, 172, 195
taqlīd, 91, 150
tarjīḥ al-'illah, 215
Thanking the Benefactor, 8, 59; al-Ghazālī's view, 115–117; al-Juwaynī's view, 113–115; al-Shahrastānī on, 117–118; al-Ḥasan al-Baṣrī's usage, 112–113; as pre-Islamic Arab social norm, 108–110; as religious duty, 118–120; defined, 8, 109, 110; obligation created by Revelation, 114; obligatory nature of, 116; Qur'ānic usage, 110–111
theistic subjectivism, 62, 75, 117
Thumāmah, 13
traditional(ist) Islam, 27; traditionalists, 27, 137; traditionism, 27; traditionists, 23, 179
Transoxania, 18, 20
Al-Ṭūfī, 161, 164, 165, 168, 171, 174, 175, 179, 226

'Ukāshah ibn Muḥṣan, 86
'Umar b. al-Khaṭṭāb, 187
uṣūl, 14, 20–22, 45, 65, 114, 190
uṣūl al-dīn, 24
uṣūl al-fiqh, 14, 16, 18, 20, 24, 26, 27, 31, 40, 45, 47, 51, 72, 114, 186, 193; development of, 14–15; *uṣūl al-fiqh* literature, 138, 209; *uṣūlī* scholarship, 72; *uṣūlīs*, 75. *See also* Principles of Jurisprudence

wajh, 32, 40, 41, 49, 144, 146, 148–150, 165, 181, 195, 203, 218–220, 222; Basran Mu'tazilah theory of, 148–151; *wajh* of detestability, 218; *wajhs*, 144, 148–150, 160; *wajhs* of value, 219; *'alá wajh al-naf'*, 43; *wujūh*, 81
al-wājib, 108, 130. *See also* Obligatory
wahm, 74, 92, 208
waqf, 57, 58, 104, 202; *waqf*-position, 64; *ahl al-waqf*, 63, 202; *aṣḥab al-waqf*, 102; *'alá l-waqf*, 64, 101, 186

war', 32, 180; link to Proscriber position, 37
warner: as motivation to moral action, 156–157; as source of moral knowledge, 156; other discussions of, 223; 100, 179. *See also khāṭir*
waswās, 157
wine, 68; *see also khamr, nabīdh*
Ẓāhirī, 46, 66; Ẓāhirīs, 12, 22
al-Zanjānī, 52, 187
ẓann, 155, 223
Al-Zarkashī, 16, 19, 121, 129, 212, 213
Zayd, 89, 110, 166, 209
al-Zubayrī, Abū 'Abdallāh, 23, 194
al-Zuhrī, 86
ẓulm, 90, 108, 148, 153, 219